D1301079

P
121
.L386
1984

85-0786/7279

DATE DUE

TEXAS WOMAN'S UNIVERSITY
LIBRARY
DENTON, TEXAS

DEMCO

Language Science

Editor in chief, Speech, Language, and Hearing Science Series
Raymond G. Daniloff, PhD

Language Science

Recent Advances

edited by

Rita C. Naremore, PhD

**Department of Speech &
Hearing Sciences
Indiana University**

 COLLEGE-HILL PRESS, San Diego, California

College-Hill Press
4284 41st Street
San Diego, California 92105

© 1984 by College-Hill Press, Inc.

All rights, including that of translation, reserved. No part of this publication may be reproduced, stored in a retrieval system, or transmitted in any form or by any means, electronic, mechanical, recording, or otherwise, without the prior written permission of the publisher.

Library of Congress Cataloging in Publication Data

Main entry under title:

Language science.

Bibliography: p.
Includes index.
1. Linguistics   2. Language and languages.
I. Naremore, Rita C.
P121.L386   1983   410   83-7728
ISBN 0-933014-97-X

Printed in the United States of America

P
121
.L386
1984

Publisher's Note

These volumes were developed under the supervision of a group of leading scientists charged with the responsibility of assessing the most critical book needs of the speech-language-hearing profession. In consultation with William H. Perkins and Raymond G. Daniloff, serving as editors in chief of the ensuing volumes on speech, language, and hearing disorders (Perkins) and speech, language, and hearing science (Daniloff), the publisher planned a series of nine mutually independent texts covering the entirety of state-of-the-art knowledge in these disciplines, with contributions by respected, productive, and current scholars known for their expertise as specialists in key areas.

Each contribution has been stringently refereed for content, pedagogy, and practical value for students and practitioners by the individual volume editors, Charles Berlin, Janis Costello, Raymond Daniloff, Audrey Holland, James Jerger, Rita Naremore, and their designated reviewers, in close consultation throughout with the editors in chief and the publisher. Users are thus assured that their needs for accurate, timely information, reflecting the highest standards of scholarship and professionalism, have been faithfully met.

On behalf of the speech-language-hearing profession, its researchers, teachers, practitioners, and students, present and future, the publisher thanks the more than 100 authors and editors who have given generously of their time and knowledge to produce this magnificent contribution to the literature.

85-0786

Language Science, edited by Rita C. Naremore, is one of nine state-of-the-art volumes comprising the College-Hill Press series covering the current body of knowledge in speech, language, and hearing.

Volume Titles:	Editors:
Speech Disorders in Children	Janis Costello
Speech Disorders in Adults	Janis Costello
Speech Science	Raymond Daniloff
Language Disorders in Children	Audrey Holland
Language Disorders in Adults	Audrey Holland
Language Science	Rita Naremore
Pediatric Audiology	James Jerger
Hearing Disorders in Adults	James Jerger
Hearing Science	Charles Berlin
Editor in chief, Speech, Language, and Hearing Disorders Series:	William H. Perkins
Editor in chief, Speech, Language, and Hearing Science Series:	Raymond G. Daniloff

Contents

Contributors

Elizabeth Bates, PhD
Department of Communication
Disorders
University of California, San Diego
San Diego, CA 92182

Hugh W. Buckingham, PhD
Interdepartmental Program
in Linguistics
Department of Speech
Louisiana State University
Baton Rouge, LA 70803

Helen Smith Cairns, PhD
Graduate Studies & Research
Queens College
Flushing, NY 11367

Daniel A. Dinnsen, PhD
Department of Linguistics
Indiana University at Bloomington
Bloomington, IN 47405

Judith F. Duchan, PhD
Department of Communication
Sciences & Disorders
State University of New York
at Buffalo
4226 Ridge Lea Road
Buffalo, NY 14226

Raymond D. Kent, PhD
Department of Communication
Disorders
University of Wisconsin—
Madison
1975 Willow Drive
Madison, WI 53706

Patricia B. Launer, PhD
Department of Communicative
Disorders
San Diego State University
San Diego, CA 98182

Sandra McNew, PhD
Department of Psychology
University of Colorado
Boulder, CO 80309

Marilyn Newhoff, PhD
Department of Speech &
Hearing Sciences
University of California, San Diego
San Diego, CA 98182

Richard G. Schwartz, PhD
Department of Audiology &
Speech Science
Purdue University
West LaFayette, IN 47907

Lynn S. Snyder, PhD
Department of Speech Pathology
& Audiology
University of Denver
Denver, CO 80208

Preface

The topics chosen for coverage under the title of this book could be a subject for almost endless debate. There are times, indeed, when "language science" appears to encompass a protean range of concerns. Arriving at a manageable scope involved asking two questions: Where are our biggest gaps—in information, in methodology, in theory? and where do we appear to be on the verge of breakthroughs, again, in information, in methodology, or in theory? Those topics which came up as answers to both questions became topics for this book. Whether discussing methodological problems, as Schwartz does in his treatment of one- and two-word utterances, or theoretical issues as McNew and Bates do in their consideration of pragmatic bases for syntax, the authors all touch on both gaps and breakthroughs in the literature.

A reader approaching these chapters from the perspective of recent training in the study of language may have no difficulty accepting either the range of topics being considered or the focus of individual chapters. Those whose primary training was obtained during some previous, perhaps theoretically doctrinaire, period may find some of the assumptions unfamiliar and many of the traditional landmarks missing. A brief history of how we got to where we are may prove useful.

The history of language research is a long one, filled with controversy. In part, the controversy in language research has mirrored that in language theory. As our ideas about what children learn when they learn language and how this learning occurs have shifted, our research techniques have shifted as well.

Behaviorist Approaches

For many years, language learning was viewed as a fairly simple process. It was believed that children learned to talk by imitating what they heard, and that parents or other adults shaped children's language by correcting their mistakes. This kind of description received scientific respectability in the work of B. F. Skinner and other behaviorists. These theorists hold that learning occurs when a child's behavior results in some behavior from the environment or some reaction within the child that is reinforcing.

One problem with this approach, of course, lies in what is to be regarded as reinforcement. It is difficult to find any clear explanation of what kinds of behavior by parents or others in the environment can be reinforcement for the child's learning of adult-like grammatical patterns. In addition, as a child's behavior cannot be reinforced until it has been emitted, the question of how the child ever comes to make grammatical sentences for parents to reinforce remains unanswered. In essence, this behaviorist approach suggests that the language learning child is a passive participant in the learning process, highly dependent on the actions of others in the environment for his or her learning. In addition, what is being learned (language) is viewed as largely irrelevant. That is, language learning is no different from learning to ride a bicycle or work a puzzle. The process remains the same.

Not surprisingly, the behaviorist approach to language has not provided us with much sophisticated language research. Since behaviorist learning theory emphasizes the process of learning rather than the product of that learning, language research resulting from it consists basically of asking "how much" rather than "what" the child has learned. Thus, a behaviorist approach to learning may cause us to count vocabulary items or sentence types but does not result in any analyses of the child's language output. This theoretical approach can often be found in reports of case studies demonstrating that a particular child can be taught to produce a particular language form under particular conditions of stimulus-response-reinforcement. Both as an explanation for language learning and as a research model, behaviorism quickly fell from grace in the late 1960s.

The Structural Revolution

It took a revolution in linguistic theory to rid us of behaviorist approaches to language learning and cause us to look at the child as an active participant in the learning process. Noam Chomsky's theory of transformational grammar shifted our focus from the process of language acquisition to the product of that learning. Chomsky argues that language is a rule governed system and that an infinite number of sentences can be accounted for by a finite set of grammatical rules. Integral to his theory is the idea that users of language "know" these grammatical rules and use them to interpret or construct sentences. This knowledge is referred to as "linguistic competence", and the child's task is to acquire this competence. In other words, the child learning language is not simply imitating sentences he or she hears, but rather is learning the rules which can be used to generate those sentences. The evidence in favor of rule induction and against imitation as an explanation of how the child learns language has mounted sufficiently to leave little doubt that the view of the child as an active hypothesis tester is the more reasonable one.

In addition to providing us with a different outlook on the process of language learning, Chomsky's theory has also caused us to take a new look at the child's output. Language researchers, looking with new eyes at the utterances of young children, are asking not "how many words does the child use?" but instead "what rule does the child know which would account for this utterance?". The realization that children's utterances are as systematic and rule governed as adult utterances has led to attempts to identify stages of language development, an approach now being extended to the study of phonology, as Dinnsen's chapter points out.

While the acquisition of rules for grammar and phonology is obviously a part of the child's language acquisition—it is not the only part, as recent acquisition theorists have pointed out. In particular, Lois Bloom's (1970) discovery that children may often use a single grammatical structure ("mommy sock") to represent quite different meanings ("This is mommy's sock" or "mommy put my sock on me") caused researchers to begin to look beyond linguistic forms to the meanings children express with these forms. Schwartz's chapter presents an excellent treatment of the issues arising from this approach to the study of one- and two-word utterances.

Semantics and the Cognition Hypothesis

The emphasis on meaning, or semantics, coincides with a return in cognitive psychology to the work of Jean Piaget. Language researchers ask what meanings the young child might be able to express in language, and Piagetian psychologists have provided a set of possible answers drawn from their research into children's early cognitive development. Generally stated, this approach to children's language acquisition leads to ideas such as that expressed by Bloom et al. (1975) that children learn grammar as a means to represent what they already know about events in the world. Numerous studies (Bowerman, 1976; Clark, 1973; Cromer, 1974) have been conducted attempting to show the relationships between the child's development of sensorimotor intelligence and the child's early language. Miller et al. (1980), in a study of language comprehension among children at sensorimotor stages V and VI point out that it is exceptionally difficult to find clear-cut causal relationships between cognitive level and comprehension of sentence meaning, and suggest instead that we retreat to a correlational version of the cognitive hypothesis. In other words, the research to date makes it possible to say only that certain cognitive levels and certain language behaviors seem to occur around the same time as children mature. It is also worth noting that research has been limited to children in the sensorimotor stage of development, and we know almost nothing about the relationship between later cognitive levels and later language development. These problems are addressed in Snyder's chapter in this volume.

Functionalist Theory

Although functionalist approaches to language acquisition theory are a recent development, the call for such approaches to children's language is not new. In 1970, Cazden wrote:

> Study of the acquisition of language has been based on the assumption that what had to be described and explained was the acquisition of a repertoire of responses (in the terminology of behaviorism) or the acquisition of a finite set of rules for constructing utterances (in the terminology of developmental psycholinguistics). On this assumption, the school language problems of lower class children can have two explanations: either they have acquired less language than middle class children, or they have acquired a different language. The less-language explanation has been given various names— *cultural deprivation, deficit hypothesis, vacuum ideology*—all with the connotation of a nonverbal child somehow emptier of language than his more-socially-fortunate age mates. The different-language explanation is forcefully argued by William Stewart and Joan Baratz. It states that all children acquire language but that many children—especially lower-class black children—acquire a dialect of English so different in structural (grammatical) features that communication in school, both oral and written, is seriously impaired by that fact alone. . . .Both the less-language and different-language views of child language are inadequate on two counts. First, they speak only of patterns of structural forms and ignore patterns of use in actual speech events. Second, they speak as if the child learns only one way to speak, which is reflected in the same fashion and to the same extent at all times. On both theoretical and practical grounds, we can no longer accept such limitations. (pp. 81, 83)

What Cazden is calling for is a functionalist view of language—a focus on how the child brings language to bear to meet the demands of the situations in which language is used.

The key to this approach is the notion that grammatical structure cannot be understood outside the context in which language is used. The functionalist approach to language holds that grammar is a secondary or derived system, related to the constraints of the communication task. As Bates (1979) expresses it, "the child's acquisition of grammar is guided, not by abstract categories, but by the pragmatic and semantic structure of communications interacting with the performance constraint of the speech channel" (p. 168). The child's task, if we take this view of language, becomes one of mapping a diverse set of semantic and pragmatic functions onto a finite set of grammatical forms. Children discover the structure of grammar through their experience with its use in a variety of communication contexts. A functionalist approach forces us to concentrate first on *what we can do with language*. We may then regard individual variation in language as different mappings of language form onto language actions. Chapters in this volume by Newhoff and Launer, McNew and Bates, and Duchan all address various issues arising from the adoption of a functionalist approach to language learning.

The Endpoints

While acquisition theorists and researchers have struggled to explain both what normal children are doing with language and how they do it, another group of theorists and researchers have been at work attempting to explain the endpoints: what adults do with language. Addressing such issues as "do language rules have psychological reality" and "how does the human brain function in regard to language," these researchers have been somewhat less buffeted by theoretical shifts than they have been by methodological advances. Cairns' chapter presents a compelling view of issues relating to language processing while Buckingham and Kent discuss the relations between brain and language.

A Word of Thanks

One researcher has pointed out that attempting to describe the state of the art in language research is rather like attempting to nail jello to a tree. There is a certain accuracy in this comparison, and every author whose chapter appears in this volume would readily agree. Nevertheless, these authors have completed an often frustrating and sometimes messy task with consummate skill. All of us who benefit from their dedication to the task owe them our thanks.

Rita C. Naremore
Editor

Richard G. Schwartz

Analysis of One- and Two-Word Utterances

Introduction

A wide variety of methodologies and conceptual frameworks have been employed in recent years in attempting to determine young children's linguistic knowledge, use, and understanding. The emergence of so many different approaches, particularly in the areas of semantics and pragmatics, justifies some serious consideration of the appropriateness and the accuracy with which they characterize children's one- and two-word utterances. Increasingly, investigators in the area of child language have raised critical questions concerning the analyses that have been employed. The purpose of this chapter is to summarize and evaluate the procedures used in analyzing one- and two-word utterances.

At the heart of the methodological and conceptual issues surrounding these procedures is the qualitative change that has occurred in child language research over the last several decades. From minimally descriptive listings of linguistic events and units, we have turned to the inference of the intents and the conceptual underpinnings of linguistic behavior. We seem to be well past the point of arguing whether there is more to a child's early linguistic behavior than what we are actually able to observe. Relying only on what we observe in a single unit or event, such as a one- or two-word utterance, may often cause us to miss important information. The following example provides a convincing argument.

© College-Hill Press, Inc. All rights, including that of translation, reserved. No part of this publication may be reproduced without the written permission of the publisher.

Child:	bʌk/bʌk	bug/bug	Child pointing to the door.
Adult:	Bug? Where's the bug?		Adult looking around the door.
Child:	bʌk/bʌk	bug/bug	Child pointing to the door.
Adult:	I don't see any bugs. Where are the bugs? There are no bugs there.		Adult looking around the door.
Child:	bʌk/bʌk (louder, almost screaming)	bug/bug	Child point to the door.
Adult:	Oh! You want the door closed so the bugs don't get in. (The child had been told repeatedly in the past that the door has to be kept closed so the bugs don't get in.)		Adult notices the door is slightly ajar.
Child:	koʊs/koʊs	close/close	Child nodding yes.

In this case it seems clear that any analysis of the child's initial utterance (bʌk/bʌk), independent of the rest of the conversation or the adult's knowledge of the child's experience, would be incomplete. To understand the knowledge, intent, and communicative abilities underlying this behavior we must go beyond the observable utterance and its immediate context. The central question we have been faced with, however, is how far we can go with such inferences. While the literature is replete with anecdotes permitting this type of inference, not all linguistic behaviors are amenable to informed inference. Even in seemingly clear cases, many pitfalls exist.

We are invariably at a disadvantage in drawing such inferences, because we operate from an adult perspective and knowledge base. It is certainly legitimate to argue it is this adult system that is the goal or endpoint of acquisition, and thus, the child's system can only vary so much within the envelope of the adult system. However, this does not guarantee that at a given point in development the child's conceptual and linguistic systems will be subsets of those adult systems. There may be both quantitative and qualitative differences in certain areas. This would not pose a problem if adults could accurately adopt the child's perspective. However, it seems unlikely that adults can recapture developmentally earlier states of knowledge in order to make inferences regarding the child's linguistic behavior. Consequently, any analysis may be subject to some bias resulting from the adult's knowledge and experience. This problem is related to a distinction between etic and emic approaches to language (Pike, 1967).

An etic approach involves the imposition of a preconceived set of categories or system upon some set of language data (e.g., categorizing words as nouns or verbs). Alternatively, an emic approach involves the derivation of categories or description based solely on the data. The notion of a purely emic approach may be somewhat idealistic, since it is difficult to leave behind one's own knowledge and experience. Consequently, we can only approach emic analysis as a goal along some continuum. Our methods of analysis of children's one- and two-word utterances need to be evaluated in terms of the extent to which these analyses are etically and emically based. While a certain degree of etic orientation is appropriate, since children are acquiring the adult system, for the reasons described above, it seems that methods should fall on the emic side of this continuum whenever possible.

This chapter will focus on various facets of this central issue and the questions of how much and what we can infer from children's observable linguistic behavior. These issues and questions are relevant to the entire period of one- and two-word utterances. However, for organizational purposes the discussion is sequenced along developmental lines. Some further specification of these issues should prove helpful in unifying the chapter.

Specific Issues

Two general research activities seem to generate most of the specific issues concerning the analysis of linguistic behavior during this period: inferring intentions or underlying knowledge and categorizing linguistic behaviors. Both are complex undertakings, subject to innumerable difficulties and potential errors.

For many years the influence of empiricism, at least in part, made researchers reluctant to undertake such tasks. Because of the apparent richness of children's linguistic behaviors, as demonstrated in the example provided earlier, failure to make such inferences and categorizations belies the complexity of early language. In spite of this, such endeavors cannot be undertaken lightly. Their results often have a significant impact upon subsequent research (e.g., the application of case grammars) and upon theory building (the little that goes on in the area of child language). It seems important for researchers engaged in such activities to demonstrate that a given inference or categorization actually represents an advantage in providing a better understanding of the behavior. Descriptive adequacy is an important consideration, but it is not necessarily sufficient. Finally, and perhaps most importantly, evidence of some degree of psychological reality for the child must be provided. Without this, not only are we left at a descriptive level, but the description provided may only represent the adult's view of the child's behavior. The child's actual knowledge, intent, and abilities may be substantially different from the description provided by our inferences and categorizations.

At the most basic level, researchers in the area of child language make inferences and categorizations of the intentionality/nonintentionality of given behaviors. The underlying assumption, of course, is that not all behaviors are intentional. For the purpose of this discussion, intentional behaviors are taken to be *actions* (i.e., those behaviors with an intended or planned goal) as opposed to *movements* (i.e., those behaviors with no intended goal). With adults, this distinction is usually a relatively easy one to make. The distinction is often marked linguistically in English, as well as in other languages (i.e., I *fell* into the pool. vs. I *jumped* or I *dived* into the pool.) Additionally, we can simply ask whether a given behavior was intended or not. In young children though, this determination may be far more difficult. Obviously, young children are poor informants. Limitations in production and comprehension vocabularies typically preclude the linguistic distinction between intentional and nonintentional behaviors. Finally, at certain points in development gestures and vocalizations which may later be *intended* are reflexive, vegetative, or simply random occurrences. Consequently, we must rely on other types of evidence in making this distinction between intentional and nonintentional behaviors.

Two possible sources of such evidence include the systematic repetition of a behavior or some indication of outcome expectancy. There are, however, some serious limitations inherent in these types of evidence. Repetition of a behavior alone does not insure its intentionality. Many behaviors that are repeated with a great deal of consistency may be reflexive (e.g., patella tendon- "knee-jerk" reflex) or vegetative (e.g., noises made while eating). Furthermore, other more complex behaviors (e.g., nonvegetative vocalizations, gestures, etc.) may be repeated, but with such a high degree of variability due to motor and representational (in terms of the representation of plans for motor action) immaturity, that separate instances may not be identifiable as repetitions of the same behavior.

There are also limitations in using indications of outcome expectancy as evidence for intentionality. For example, at a given point in development a child may respond to any novel object by performing his or her entire repertoire of actions on objects. Such a response may be essentially reflexive in nature. A child's pause time between such actions may be erroneously interpreted as evidence of expectancy. Alternatively, these actions may be intentional in nature with exploration serving as a child's motivation or goal. The results of these actions may prove to be very surprising or unexpected for the child. The child's response in such cases may be misinterpreted as a lack of expectancy. Thus, evidence of expectancy or lack of expectancy of outcome may lead to both overestimations and underestimations of the intentionality of early behaviors.

In spite of these limitations, systematic repetitions and expectancy may still be the most useful types of evidence for intentionality available. However, this evidence must be supplemented by other data. First, it seems important that researchers begin to specify the range of variability in children's early gestural and vocal behaviors across different instances and situations. It is likely that an ethologically oriented approach will be needed to demonstrate that different vocalizations or gestures are actually variants of a single behavior, and thus, are systematic repetitions. Controlled procedures may need to be added to naturalistic observations in order to demonstrate that certain behaviors recur with certain recurring situational conditions. There is also a critical need for evidence, independent of the child's vocal and gestural behavior, of the ability to plan and execute motor behavior. Beyond certain ages, researchers have simply assumed this ability to be present rather than providing supportive evidence.

Once some implicit or explicit decision has been made regarding the intentionality of a given behavior, researchers typically attempt to infer or categorize the specific nature of the behavior. Such inferences or categorizations predominantly concern the form, the apparent and underlying semantic content, and the communicative functions of these behaviors. There are as many, if not more, difficulties posed by these more specific inferences and categorizations. Certain categories naturally occur in the adult language being acquired (e.g., nouns and verbs), or in the structure of the world (e.g., instigators vs. recipients of actions), or are inherent in social interaction (e.g., requesting vs. asserting). While it is important to know how children's linguistic behaviors correspond to such categories based upon the judgments of adults, this does not represent an explication of children's behavior or development. There is no assurance that the child is aware of or behaves consistently with such categories. This is true even in cases where independent judges can agree on the categorizations or inferences regarding linguistic behaviors. As was mentioned earlier, this places us in a situation where we may attain descriptive adequacy, but not explanatory adequacy, in research findings and conclusions. Clearly, what is needed is some type of evidence, independent of reliable adult categorical judgments, for the existence of such categories or underlying knowledge in children. Furthermore, some additional caution must be exercised in the analysis and interpretation of children's language samples collected under so-called natural circumstances, since many aspects of children's underlying knowledge may be obscured by this method of data collection.

The remainder of this chapter will focus on recent research involving the analysis and interpretation of children's linguistic behaviors beginning with prelexical forms and proceeding developmentally to one- and two-word utterances. This research will be reviewed critically in terms of the issues raised above, and some suggestions that may serve to ameliorate the problems identified will be presented.

Prelexical Forms

Investigators have recognized for some time now that the transition from prelinguistic vocalizations to linguistic productions is gradual rather than abrupt. In fact, there appear to be transitional forms that bridge the apparent gap between babbling and true words. These forms generally differ from babbling in that they are isolable (i.e., bounded by pauses), appear to have a closer, more consistent relationship with some recurring condition or aspect of context, and are somewhat more consistent phonetically. They have been varyingly referred to as vocables (Ferguson, 1978a; Halliday, 1975; Leopold, 1947; Lewis, 1936), sensorimotor morphemes (Carter, 1975, 1979b), protowords (Kent, 1982a, 1982b; Menn, 1976) and phonetically consistent forms (Dore, Franklin, Miller, & Ramer, 1976). Although, there seem to be some differences in the specific definitions of these various terms, and consequently, the vocalizations to which they have been applied, they appear to refer to the same general phenomena. In general, such forms have been identified in children ranging from approximately 10 to 16 months. Thus they may precede and co-exist with true words.

Distinguishing Prelexical Forms From True Words

The dividing line between these prelexical forms and true words remains rather indistinct. However, it is clear that they differ along at least several important dimensions. Menn (1976) identified three such dimensions: (1) phonetic consistency, (2) semantic coherence, and (3) symbolic autonomy. Although prelexical forms appear to be less variable than babbling, they are still highly variable as compared with later appearing true words. The variability must be limited at least to the extent that vocalizations on various occasions are identifiable as instances of the same prelexical form. In other words, there is a shrinking phonetic envelope or set of boundaries in which a form may vary. Such boundaries may not exist for babbling patterns; they may first be established with production segmentation. As development proceeds, this envelope becomes smaller, but continues to exist. Variability in phonetic form continues to persist through the period of early word use and to a more limited degree through adulthood. Again, the dividing line here is not yet clear, but intuitively, there are increasing limitations in the extent of variability which occurs and which is acceptable at various points in development. For a vocalization to be categorized as a true word, it must bear some minimal resemblance to the general form of items in the adult lexicon, and may vary only within certain limitations (e.g., consonant substitutions that differ on various occasions, omission or inclusion of certain consonants or syllables, etc.).

There also appear to be qualitative differences between prelexical forms and true words in terms of their semantic coherence. Semantic coherence concerns the degree of relatedness of the apparent referents. In general, prelexical forms are described as less semantically coherent than words. Thus, it may be more difficult to identify those factors that are consistent across the situations in which a child produces a prelexical form. For instance, Menn reported the production of a form similar to the adult word *hello* in greeting situations, as well as in situations where there was no evidence that the child she was studying was in, or pretending to be in, a greeting situation. She was unable to identify any commonalities among these situations. Menn concluded that in some cases, Jacob may simply have been exhibiting some preference for producing that particular combination of sounds.

The criterion of semantic coherence for distinguishing prelexical forms and words is similar to the criteria proposed by Dore et al. (1976) for identifying referential utterances. The two criteria are:

(1) They must *indicate* in the sense that an act of indication serves to point to some thing or event, often singling it out in a larger field and so calling attention to it; and (2) their use must provide some differentiation among alternatives which results in the use of the same form for members of a given group and the use of different forms for different groups of entities. In other words, the term *A* refers if it is used consistently to indicate any member of the set (X, Y, Z) whose members have something identifiable in common, and is *not* used to indicate any member of the set (Q, R, S). To this may be added the more stringent criterion that a term *A* may be said to refer only if there is another term *B* which is used consistently to indicate a member of (Q, R, S) but is not used to indicate a member of (L, M, N) (p. 19).

Some of the prelexical forms identified by Dore et al. (1976), termed *indicating phonetically consistent forms,* meet the first of these criteria, but do not distinguish among referents as the second criterion requires. Such forms appear to be generally indicative or deictic in nature such as the adult word *that,* and are comparable to the vocalizations which occur as part of what Bates, Camaioni, and Volterra (1975) identified as protodeclaratives. For example, Dore et al., reported that one child studied produced a consonant-vowel form ([bæ] or [dæ]) when simply looking at a variety of objects, but not giving any indication of wanting or trying to obtain them. In other children, they reported that similar forms accompanied pointing at a variety of objects.

Another type of phonetically consistent form, termed *grouping expressions* (Dore et al., 1976), appears to more closely approach the criteria for referentiality. In these forms, there appears to be some interaction between the child's internal or affective state and attention to object properties. Children appear to use a given form in the presence of a limited set of objects when they are in a certain affective state (e.g., [ubiba] in the presence of a peg, a jack-in-a-box, a puppet, and a crayon with some indication of mild frustration, Dore et al., 1976). The basis for the object grouping is at least unclear to an adult. However, examination of the child's spontaneous speech revealed that, under conditions of apparent frustration with other objects, this form was not used.

As in the case of the phonetic consistency criterion, it is relatively easy in some cases to distinguish between prelexical forms and words. In other cases however, the dividing line becomes rather indistinct. Two specific problem areas can be identified. The first concerns some confusion between two equally important and interesting questions: (1) When do children begin using adult words as adults use them, differing only in the exact phonetic form and range of referents to which the words are applied? and (2) When do children begin to use vocalizations in the way that adults use words in terms of reference and semantic coherence? These will obviously yield very different answers. Furthermore, these questions will lead researchers to look at very different behaviors. The first limits an investigator to look only at those instances that at least resemble adult words in types of object properties that serve as the basis for groupings (a good deal of variance in phonetic form could be permitted). These groupings might be the prelexical forms of interest, and may be followed developmentally until they precisely conform to adult usage. The second question leads to fewer limitations in what is to be examined. It is intended to imply that children's groupings may be markedly different from adults' in terms of the properties of objects, situational factors, and affective states. Consequently, early on, one would not necessarily look for correspondence between the groupings of children and those of adults. The question chosen may, at least in part, determine where one draws the line between prelexical forms and words in terms of semantic coherence. In the first case, something may only be categorized as a word when there is some resemblance to adult groupings. In the second case, the requirement for categorization as a word may simply be evidence of a selective grouping.

The second problem area in the criterion of semantic coherence concerns the real and apparent semantic coherence of adult words. Some groupings represented by adult words are related as complexes (Vygotsky, 1962). In these instances, the objects or events referred to by the word do not all share common properties. Instead, each referent shares some property with perhaps only one other referent, and thus the relationship among referents is successive rather than simultaneous. For example, the adult usage of family names (e.g., *Smith*), and words such as *cut* (with scissors, with a knife, cards, a cut on a finger, a cut of beef etc.) appear to be complexes. Other adult words may be based upon some affective state and are used in relation to a variety of objects with no apparently shared properties (e.g., chocolate chip cookies make me *happy*, and so do good movies, books, music, friends, and the ending of winter). It is likely that many more instances of apparently incoherent adult words could be identified. Although some investigators have allowed for less than perfectly coherent instances in their category of true words (e.g., Menn, 1976), others have not. Failing to credit children with true words in instances where the semantic coherence is no worse than for some adult words raises some serious questions regarding the appropriateness of such categorizations.

The third dimension along which prelexical forms appear to differ concerns what Menn has referred to as symbolic autonomy. It should be noted that while aspects of symbolic autonomy are inextricably tied to the dimension of semantic coherence, other aspects are clearly independent. Menn described symbolic autonomy in terms of independence from a motor act or ritual, from a single intonation contour and from a single speech act context. The thrust of this criterion is similar to that suggested by Werner and Kaplan (1963) and Piaget (1962) in distinguishing between vocables or semi-verbal signs and words. The difference between these two types of behaviors is that the earlier forms involve a lack of distinction between subjective and objective or between the child and his or her environment. Part of Menn's criterion for symbolic autonomy also bears some relation to the notion of contextual flexibility (Snyder, Bates, & Bretherton, 1981). That issue is whether the child's vocalization is actually functioning as a symbol. To do so, it must serve as a signifier (i.e., something that stands for something else) that bears an arbitrary relationship to some signified object or event (that thing for which it stands). It must also be independent from the signifier (i.e., at least to the extent that it may be used in the absence of the signified object or event). Finally, it must be autonomous to the extent that there is some separation between the word and the child's actions, rituals, or states. Vocalizations that do not have these characteristics may simply be signals, such as the noises children make when pushing a toy car. In such cases, the vocalization may have the same status as other sensorimotor activities directed toward objects (e.g., pushing, banging, etc.).

As in the case of semantic coherence, there are some problems in clearly distinguishing between words and prelexical forms on the basis of symbolic autonomy. Sampling of children's behavior may be particularly problematic in determining whether a given form is symbolically autonomous. Simply because instances of use occur within a given context, with a given action, or as a single speech act, it is not certain that the form could not be used under varying conditions. A related problem concerns the way in which adults use certain words (e.g., *hello, thank you*). Given limited samples, it may appear that such words are not symbolically autonomous at all. While they are clearly more limited in this regard than other words (e.g., *ball*), we do know that they can be used in the context of other communicative functions (e.g., an adult telling a child "Say thank you.") Returning to children's word use, such demonstrations of symbolic autonomy for this type of word may represent unreasonable requirements in terms of the syntactic and pragmatic complexity involved. Thus in some cases the lack of evidence for symbolic autonomy may simply be the result of limitations in other linguistic abilities. As was mentioned earlier, the dimensions of semantic coherence and symbolic autonomy are not completely independent. It seems that as a child adds semantically coherent instances in which a given word or form is used, the likelihood that there will be evidence of symbolic autonomy increases.

There appear to be several factors that may cause investigators to underestimate symbolic autonomy, and to incorrectly categorize productions as prelexical forms rather than words. In certain instances, the distinction between these behaviors may be unclear. In other instances, evidence for the use of a form independent of the child's actions, independent of rituals, in the absence of referents, or across communicative situations, may serve unambiguously as a basis for categorizing it as a word.

It is possible that goal of drawing a clear dividing line between prelexical forms and words is unrealistic or perhaps even inappropriate. Rather than a true dichotomy, these behaviors may simply represent points on a continuum of lexical development (see Snyder et al., 1981). Most of the investigators who have examined prelexical forms have reported gradual development in the semantic coherence, symbolic autonomy, phonetic consistency and reference of these forms. In some cases, the growth across these areas is extremely uneven, complicating attempts at categorization. For instance, forms may be extremely stable phonetically and yet clearly lack symbolic autonomy. A detailed description of the nature of such forms and early words along the dimensions described may ultimately prove to be a more appropriate goal than dichotomizing such productions prior to the point they actually resemble specific adult words.

Methodological Issues

In further describing and explicating prelexical forms, a number of methodological issues warrant consideration. To date, the study of such forms has been limited predominantly to naturalistic observation either in the form of diary studies or longitudinally collected samples. It should be apparent that intensive observation over this period of development is necessary not only to specify the situations in which such forms are produced, but simply to identify them. The phonetic variability and the lack of semantic coherence characterizing such forms make identification difficult. Any type of periodic sampling may compound these problems, in that many instances of usage may be missed. This does not mean that only diary data are acceptable. Even this does not necessarily solve the problem. Procedures involving greater situational controls seem to be indicated.

Given the information we have thus far, it seems as though researchers need to form hypotheses regarding the conditions of use for given forms and present the child with controlled situations to test their hypotheses concerning the conditions for production. To arrive at such hypotheses, videotaped data that have been available in some longitudinal studies, but not diary studies, are necessary. An ethologically-oriented approach to the transcription of such data involving as complete as possible a record of objects, events, and affective states at the time of usage seems most appropriate. Such a general approach is far from foolproof. Attentional and motivational factors may influence children's productions in controlled situations. Even the most complete situational transcription may be limited in that it represents an adult perspective rather than the child's. In spite of these limitations, controlled situations and complete situational transcriptions would represent an improvement over some of the previous investigations. More recently Kent and Bauer (1982) have reported preliminary results of an investigation in progress concerning the transition from early vocalizations to words. One aspect of this investigation involves the use of standardized sampling situations as suggested above.

Another methodological weakness in studies of prelexical forms is the lack of developmental information gathered concerning the changes in such forms over time. Some of the investigations mentioned have provided such information (e.g., Bates et al., 1975; Carter, 1975, 1979b; Menn, 1976), but these tend to be the exceptions rather than the rule. During this period it is likely that prelexical forms undergo rapid change. It may be as important to understand the nature of these changes as it is to understand what such forms are like at a given point in time. One interesting approach to such a description was taken by Carter (1975, 1979b). Rather than simply following prelexical forms through their development, she back-traced a number of words to their prelexical precursors. While not all prelexical forms necessarily develop into words, such an approach provides information concerning the developmental history of words that might otherwise not be readily apparent.

A final methodological issue concerns the phonetic characteristics of these forms. In those few studies providing specific details concerning the phonetic characteristics of these productions (e.g., Dore et al., 1976; Menn, 1976), no reliability for transcription is reported. This is of particular concern when variability is a major characteristic. Furthermore, it is questionable whether perception-based judgments represent sufficiently accurate descriptions of these behaviors. Instrumental analyses such as those being conducted by Kent (1982) may provide us with more detailed and accurate information regarding the range of variability within a given form as well as across forms.

The current literature concerning prelexical forms seems to be replete with definitional, methodological, and theoretical difficulties affecting both categorization and inference. However, the importance of this period of development and its associated behaviors remains clear. An important step in understanding the nature and process of language acquisition is the decription and explication of the transition between apparently unsystematic vocalizations and the use of words as communicative linguistic symbols. It is hoped that work in this area will continue along some of the lines already established, as well as those suggested here. Perhaps with further research, at least some of the difficulties encountered thus far will be resolved.

Single-Word Utterances

Investigations of children's single-word utterances have focused almost exclusively on the period during which such utterances predominate. This period is generally defined as extending from approximately 12 to 18 months of age, when children also acquire a production lexicon of about 50 words (Nelson, 1973). The following discussion will focus on several aspects of this period: (1) the nature and determinants of lexical acquisition in production and comprehension, (2) the inferred concepts and categories underlying these words, and (3) the use of single-word utterances in terms of their inferred semantic and pragmatic intent. Although a large body of information concerning this period has been accumulated, a number of methodological issues remain unresolved and warrant discussion.

Composition of Early Lexicons

Of major interest to researchers in recent years has been the composition of early lexicons. In what has become a seminal study of children's word acquisition during this period, Nelson (1973) reported on the lexical composition of the first 50 words for 18 children. Based upon periodic observation and parental report, she found that nominals (words used like proper nouns) and general nominals (words used like common nouns) represented the largest category (65%). Other categories such as action words (13%), modifiers (9%), personal-social words (8%) and function words (4%) lagged far behind. A generally comparable distribution, except for action words which involved a more broadly defined category, was reported by Benedict (1979) for eight children. Clearly, the most striking aspect of these results is the preponderance of object words in early production lexicons. Benedict also found that while there were substantial temporal differences in the acquisition of a comprehension lexicon (i.e., 50 words acquired by an average age of 1;1) and some differences in distribution, a smaller, but still substantial gap between object and actions words remained.

These findings represent extremely important descriptive information. However, their explanatory value is seriously limited by a number of methodological problems. Foremost among these problems is the categorization employed. Many of the categorizations made are based upon surface form and may not accurately reflect the actual lexical distribution for the child. Benedict did make some further efforts in this regard, particularly in the action category (e.g., including words referring to social-action games and locative actions, etc.), but the problem is not wholly resolved. For instance, it is plausible that early in development an object word (i.e., general nominal) may refer to an entire situation involving an action on an object, as well as the object itself. Additionally, in some situations a child may produce an object word (e.g., *ball*) in requesting some specific action (e.g., *throw*). In such cases, it is not at all clear that this should be classified as an object word unless other evidence is obtained. Additionally, these investigations provide information regarding the types but not the tokens of words produced. Thus, it is not clear whether object words dominate children's lexical and comprehension behavior or simply their lexicons. Further investigations are needed to determine whether the proportions of types of words in children's early lexicons is comparable to the distributions of tokens they produce. Finally, the reliance in both of these investigations on parental diary data may have added additional information in some cases and some distortion in others. Benedict noted that mothers tended to under-report the number of action words understood. While she was able to correct for this to some degree through comprehension testing, it is possible that some instances were missed and that distortion in other categories remained undiscovered.

Even a more accurate description of the distribution of words within children's early lexicons would not serve to explain asymmetries among categories. So many factors may serve as determinants of distribution (frequency of occurence in input, frequency of opportunity for production or comprehension, various inherent differences between different word types, etc.) that explanations, such as those provided by Benedict for the object word-action gap, are highly speculative. Investigations involving controls for some of these variables may help to confirm or disconfirm some of these speculations.

One earlier study that represents an attempt to introduce some control in determining young children's lexical repertoires was reported by Goldin-Meadow, Seligman, and Gelman (1976). They tested the comprehension and production of a standard set of words cross-sectionally in a group of 2-year-old children. Three children were also followed longitudinally. Goldin-Meadow et al., found that overall, children comprehended more words than they produced and that there was a consistent gap between nouns and verbs (their terms) favoring nouns. Additionally, they noted that developmentally, children evidenced two apparently successive periods. During the receptive stage, children understood many more nouns than they produced and understood a number of verbs, but did not produce any. During the productive stage, children produced almost as many nouns as they comprehended and produced a number of verbs, but not as many as they comprehended. These data are extremely interesting in that they are based upon standardized production elicitation and comprehension procedures. However, there were some methodological problems and some limitations inherent in these procedures. First, the standardized stimuli involved 70 preselected nouns and 30 preselected verbs, which pilot work had indicated to be familiar to 2-year-olds. Thus there was an inherent bias in favor of nouns. Furthermore, given the potential for individual differences in early lexical acquisition, it is possible that many words produced and comprehended by the children were not tested. Finally, even with the addition of a more controlled procedure, this investigation still served more to describe differences in the production and comprehension of object and action words than it did to explicate these differences.

More recently, a somewhat different paradigm has been employed in examining children's acquisition of object and action words. The paradigm, which employs either nonsense words or unfamiliar words referring to unfamiliar objects (e.g., a hasp, a glide) or to unfamiliar actions (e.g., veer, dip), is based on Berko's (1958) use of nonsense words in testing morphological acquisition and Nelson and Bonvillian's (1973, 1978) demonstration that young children are able to acquire unfamiliar or contrived names for unfamiliar object referents. Across a number of investigations, this paradigm has been employed in examining children's acquisition of both object and action words of varying types. The advantage of such an approach is that input and exposure may be carefully controlled, since it is unlikely that the children will encounter the words or their referents outside of the experimental situation. Typically, the words have been presented to children a number of times in each of approximately 10 experimental sessions. Spontaneous and imitative productions are noted along with responses to production probes or pre- and posttests, as well as comprehension probes and pre- and posttests in some cases. To date children ranging in level of development from production vocabularies of five true words (Schwartz & Leonard, 1980; Schwartz & Leonard, 1982) to children with production vocabularies of between 20 and 75 words (Leonard, Schwartz, Morris, & Chapman, 1981; Leonard, Schwartz, Chapman, Rowan, Prelock, Terrell, Weiss, & Messick, 1982) have been employed as subjects. Additionally, across these investigations, object words with single referents and object words with multiple referents have been employed, as well as both transitive and intransitive actions differentiated by the presence vs. the absence of an object of the action.

These investigations have consistently revealed that object words are acquired in greater numbers than action words. The primary importance of these findings is not in the fact that they confirm previous observations, but rather in that they indicate that under conditions of equal frequency in input and exposure, the object word/action word gap remains in both comprehension and production. This supports previous speculation based upon diary accounts that object words dominate early lexicons (Gleitman, Gleitman, & Shipley, 1972; Huttenlocher, 1974; McNeill, 1970). These findings also point to the possibility that there are inherent differences in the production and comprehension of object and action words. In part, the gap may be due to the fact that children view objects as things to be named and actions as things to be done (Benedict, 1979). While this may explain why the gap is smaller in comprehension than in production, it does not explain why more object words are comprehended than action words. Another possibility is that the referents of object words tend to be perceptually more stable than the referents of action words, which are more transitory in nature. This might explain why older children (including older language-impaired children at the one-word stage) tend to have a smaller gap. If abilities to store or represent more transitory referents are actually a determinant of the gap between object and action words, some independent measures of these abilities are needed. Finally, there may be some inherent differences in the complexity of object and action words which account for the differences in their acquisition. Gentner (1978) has suggested that action words are more complex in that they refer to relations minimally between an actor and some movement (in more complex cases between an actor, some movement, and an object or a recipient), while object words may simply refer to a thing or set of things. In the research cited above, different types of action words have been used in different investigations (e.g., transitive action words involving an object—Schwartz & Leonard, 1980; intransitive action words without an object—Leonard, et al., in press). Similar gaps in the acquisition of object and action words appear to occur regardless of whether the action words employed are transitive or intransitive. However, to provide a clearer test of Gentner's suggestion that relational complexity of referents may be a determining factor, acquisition of intransitive and transitive action words should be directly compared. Benedict's data suggest that the opposite is true (more transitive than intransitive action words are acquired during this period). However, a more controlled comparison is needed and is currently in progress (Schwartz & Leonard, in progress).

While the advantages of nonsense word/unfamiliar word and unfamiliar referent paradigms have been extolled, some limitations should be noted. First, although exposures to the words and their referents have generally been fairly intensive (i.e., five times per session) the length of exposure has only been 10 sessions in most cases over periods ranging from 3 weeks to approximately 4 months. It is likely in some cases children's experience with real words extends over longer periods of time. Thus, while in some cases, the amount and period of exposure may be comparable to that for real words, in other cases it is not. The extent of acquisition may, therefore, be somewhat less for these experimental words than for real words in some instances. A second issue arising in some of these investigations concerns the definition of object words and action words. In one particular study (Schwartz & Leonard, 1980), it is possible that the adult categorizations of object and action words were not consistent with the children's views of the referents of these words. This investigation involved groups of four objects and groups of four actions which served as the referents for the words (e.g., *bobo*-baton, tire pressure gauge, pen light, curtain rod; *tete*-four different actions to spin objects). The investigator performed an action on each of the experimental objects presented, and each experimental action was performed on a familiar object. It is not absolutely clear that the children recognized object words as referring only to the experimental object or action words as referring only to the experimental action. While indirect evidence suggesting that children's referents corresponded to the referents assumed by the adult (e.g., lack of generalization across categories in instances where such generalization might have been likely, such as experimental objects that were spun and experimental actions involving spinning objects), it is possible that there were some differences. Subsequent studies involving this paradigm have been designed to minimize this possibility by either employing intransitive actions and objects presented in non-action contexts or by expanded posttesting to insure that words acquired refer to the intended objects or actions independent of their presentation contexts.

Even with these limitations, this paradigm has permitted investigations of children's lexical acquisition involving controls on variables such as input and exposure frequency which are simply not possible in observational procedures. It has also facilitated investigation of other potential determinants of lexical acquisition such as the phonological composition of words (Leonard, Schwartz, Morris, & Chapman, 1981; Leonard et al., 1982; Schwartz & Leonard, 1982), input frequency (Schwartz & Terrell, 1983), and action (Schwartz, 1980).

Thus far the discussion of the distribution of words within children's early lexicons has disregarded any individual differences which may exist. An important aspect of Nelson's (1973) findings was her division of subjects into two groups, termed referential and expressive. These children were distinguished primarily on the basis of the percentage of general nominals in their 50-word lexicons. General nominals represented more than 50% of the lexicons of referential children, and less than 50% of the lexicons of expressive children. Additionally, expressive children's lexicons included a greater percentage of personal-social words and specific nominal than referential children's lexicons. Nelson characterized these differences as differences in lexical style reflecting the children's differing views of language. Referential children were characterized as viewing the function of language to be naming objects. Alternatively, expressive children were characterized as viewing the function of language as a primarily social interaction. Nelson also noted other apparent differences between the groups such as the number of phrases produced during this period favoring the expressive group and the pace of word acquisition. Additionally, there were differences between the groups at ages 2 or 2½ years in terms of size of vocabularies with referential children exhibiting larger, more diverse lexicons. More recently, Nelson (1981) has characterized this as a continuum with some children falling at the extremes and others exhibiting characteristics of both styles.

Perhaps the greatest weakness in Nelson's description of these styles was her reliance on surface form categorizations rather than any formal examination of lexical use. Thus, it is conceivable that the differences among children simply lie in the specific types of words they acquire rather than in their actual views of language function and use. Strong support for differing styles or strategies of lexical acquisition and early language learning comes from a variety of sources.

Bloom (1973) also described individual differences among children. She characterized these differences in terms of the relative frequency of relational words or phrases (e.g., *all gone*) and substantive words (e.g., *ball*).

The children using more relational words produced pivot-open utterances, imitated more frequently, and used more pronouns early in development (Bloom, Lightbown, & Hood, 1975). The children who used more substantive words appeared to use more varied syntactic constructions, nouns more frequently than pronouns, and imitated less frequently. Brannigan (1977) and Peters (1980) also report instances of compressed sentences or gestalt language that appear to be more frequent in some children. Such productions appear to be comparable to the early phrases identified by Nelson. The use of *dummy* or *empty* forms (e.g., [widə], Bloom, 1973; [gɔkIŋ], Leonard, 1976) which are combined with words to form multi-word utterances, has been noted by a number of investigators (Brannigan, 1977; Peters, 1980; Ramer, 1976). Nelson (1981) suggested that such usage corresponds to the apparent emphasis upon sentence targets as opposed to single words exhibited by expressive children.

Certain nonlinguistic behaviors also appear to suggest that there are significant individual differences among children. Rosenblatt (1975) was able to differentiate among children who spent a greater proportion of play time engaged with objects and children who spent a greater proportion of play time engaged with people. Her description of these two groups of children appears to indicate that children who spent a greater amount of time in play engaged with objects acquired more object words than the other group of children. Thus, it appears that similarities are evident in children's styles of play and lexical production. Further evidence of this was provided by Wolf and Gardner (1979) who distinguished between two groups of children labeled patterners and dramatists. Patterners seem to focus their attention on objects and object properties in terms of both language and play and interact with other people primarily as means to ends (e.g., obtaining objects). When presented with a set of objects, patterners tend to sort them on the basis of physical properties. Dramatists seem to be more socially oriented in their language and their play. These children seem more likely to take a presented set of objects and create some type of social situation (e.g., setting a table and eating), playing with the objects symbolically.

Two more recent investigations have added further information to our understanding of these individual differences. Leonard et al. (1981) employed an unfamiliar word paradigm involving object and action words to determine if children identified as referential and children identified as expressive would differ in the number of object words acquired. As might be expected, the referential children acquired a greater number of object words than did the expressive children. Since the object and action words were presented an equal number of times, it appears that the proclivity of referential children to acquire object words is not due solely to some continuing bias in the input frequency of such words. A second investigation involving a nonsense word paradigm (Ross, Nelson, Wetstone, & Tanouye, in preparation, cited in Nelson, 1981) compared functions of language use in two extreme groups of nominal users and pronominal users. The groups differed significantly in the expected directions for the categories *name-refer* (favoring nominal users), *personal* (favoring pronominal users), and *interactive* (favoring pronominal users). The groups did not differ in their use of utterances categorized as *comment-describe*. Thus, although there was some inconsistency in nominal/pronominal usage and language functions employed, functions generally corresponded with inferred lexical style.

In spite of the information we currently have regarding these individual differences, a number of issues remain unresolved. For instance, although there is consistency across a number of behaviors (nominal/personal-social word usage, early phrases, extent of formulaic speech, play, and pronominal/nominal usage) in children at the extremes of these differences (Nelson, 1981; Weiss et al., in press), such consistency does not occur in many children, particularly those between the extremes (Nelson, 1981; Weiss et al., 1982). Additionally, evidence regarding the consistency of these differences over the course of development is rather mixed (see Nelson, 1981). In some cases it appears that later individual differences are consistent with earlier differences (e.g., R. Clark, 1974; Peters, 1980). In other cases, there appears to be evidence of developmental shifts in these differences (e.g., Bloom et al., 1975; Brannigan, 1977; Horgan, 1978). Finally, explanations of the origins and maintenance or shifts of such differences remain largely speculative (see Nelson, 1981). Although there is some evidence (Lieven, 1978) that these differences may have their origins in the nature of the input to the child, there appear to be instances in which mothers' styles differ from those of their children (Nelson, 1973). It is perhaps this specific issue which warrants substantial attention in future investigations of individual differences. Such research might provide important information concerning the extent to which individually different paths in acquisition are determined actively by the child or more passively in response to the nature of the input.

The importance of these individual differences lies not only in their existence and explication, but in their methodological implications for investigations of early word acquisition and language use. First, indications that some aspects of style may vary situationally (Peters, 1977) suggest that sampling language under limited conditions may lead to incomplete descriptions of language usage. The differences among children suggest that grouped data may result in some significant distortions of general patterns of acquisition (e.g., composition of the lexicon, early phrase, or pronominal

usage). This presents a rather strong argument for the use of within subject designs in experimental investigations of early language acquisition.
Such designs are not only stronger in that each subject may serve as his
or her own control, but they may in some ways facilitate the identification
of individual differences. Other, though less satisfactory, alternatives may
involve the use of matched pairs designs using those dimensions of individual differences of which we are aware, or more detailed subject descriptions than have been generally employed in the past. Finally, this body of
research has brought to our attention an apparently common phenomenon
for some children which has been previously ignored, the use of gestalt
or compressed speech (Peters, 1977; Brannigan, 1977). The fact that such
utterances occur poses substantial problems for our methods of analysis,
which are almost exclusively analytic in nature and are geared toward the
progression from one- to two-word to three-word utterances and beyond.
Not only does this have implications for lexical, semantic, and pragmatic
analyses, but also for phonological analyses, which are almost exclusively
word-based. As we examine this phenomenon further, we may have to
modify substantially our analytic methodologies as well as our overall views
of the nature of language acquisition.

Inferring Concepts and Categories

A major focus of research in the area of early lexical acquisition has
involved inferences concerning the categories and concepts which underlie
children's words during this period. Two investigators put forth theoretical
proposals during the early 1970s, which have since stimulated a great deal
of research in this area. E. Clark (1973, 1974, 1975) proposed a semantic
feature theory of lexical acquisition. According to Clark, children form
lexical concepts (i.e., use the same word to apply to various objects) and
extend these concepts primarily on the basis of shared perceptual attributes.
These attributes are those simple or additive combinations of primarily
static features that represent perceptual categories of information processing
(i.e., shape, size, texture, movement, and taste). Based on her examination
of diary data Clark noted that children extend and sometimes overextend
(i.e., apply a word to instances not included in the lexical concepts or
categories of adults) on the basis of the perceptual similarities of referents.
Clark proposed that children first acquire the meaning of a word by attaching
one or more perceptual features. The meaning of the word is equated with
those features. The occurrence of overextensions is thus assumed to be the
result of the fact that at the outset, children do not attach the full adult
complement of features to their words or employ this full set in applying
words to referents. It should be emphasized that Clark did not suggest that

children are unable to distinguish between instances of an apparently overextended concept. Instead, her position was that children simply do not at this stage realize the linguistic (i.e., lexical) consequences of these distinctions.

Clark's early focus upon children's apparent overextensions is not surprising, since such "errors" are so salient in children's lexical productions. However, other investigators noted that the lexical categories or concepts of children and adults may be related in other ways as well (Anglin, 1977; Reich, 1976). There may be overlaps, discontinuities or non-overlaps, underextensions, or equivalencies. Although these relationships may be more difficult to detect, they may also provide valuable information regarding the structure of children's lexical categories and concepts and their relationships to adult categories and concepts.

A number of investigators raised serious questions concerning various aspects of Clark's proposal (Anglin, 1977; Bowerman, 1978; Nelson, 1974; Reich, 1976). Perhaps most prominent among these objections was Nelson's criticism of the prominent role which Clark assigned to static perceptual features. Operating from a Piagetian perspective, Nelson maintained that children initially come to know objects, and form concepts through their actions and through the actions of others upon those objects. Her position was that the dynamic, functional, and relational properties of objects play a prominent role in concept formation and development. For some time these two differing viewpoints were viewed by child language researchers as diametrically opposed positions regarding the role of static perceptual features and dynamic functional or relational features in children's formation and development of concepts and categories.

Subsequent writings (Clark, 1975, 1978; Nelson, Rescorla, Gruendel, & Benedict, 1978) and both experimental (Schwartz & Leonard, 1980; Rosch et al., 1976) as well as observational research (Bowerman, 1978) taken together suggest that the issue is somewhat artificial. Both functional characteristics and perceptual characteristics play a role in the formation and extension of lexical concepts and categories. Furthermore, in more recent work there appears to be more general agreement regarding the occurrence and importance of underextension, as well as other relationships, between child and adult lexical categories.

An alternative to Clark's (1973, 1974, 1975, 1978) and Nelson's (Nelson, 1974; Nelson et al., 1978) positions which is consistent with both functional-feature-based and perceptual-feature-based views is represented by the proposals of Rosch and her colleagues (Rosch, 1975, 1977; Rosch, Mervis, Gray, Johnson, & Boyes-Braem, 1976; Mervis & Rosch, 1981). They have revived the family resemblance notion originally proposed by Wittgenstein (1953) in describing the structure of concepts. The proposal involves the notion of one or more most prototypical exemplars within a concept.

Such exemplars are in essence the "best" examples of a category by virtue of the features (both functional and perceptual) which they share with other, less prototypical members of that category. For instance, within the category of birds, a robin may be considered to be highly typical, but, because of its lack of feathers and failure to fly, a penguin might be viewed as a less typical category example. Rosch and her colleagues have also suggested that the lexicon of languages may be organized in terms of levels of generality with what is termed the *basic level* being at the center of the lexicon. Basic level categories are comprised of members that share at least some of the same functional and perceptual characteristics while being as general as possible. Additionally, within category similarity is at a maximum relative to similarity with other categories. The other levels, superordinate and subordinate, are more general and more specific, respectively. In some respects the definition seems vague, but can be clarified by example. For instance, in an adult lexicon, *furniture* represents a superordinate level, *chair* may represent a basic level, and *recliner* may represent a subordinate level.

At least for object categories and concepts, these proposals provide an interesting framework within which children's categories and concepts may be discussed and perhaps explained. Some preliminary observational evidence (Bowerman, 1978, 1980) suggests that the first referents of children's early words are most often good examples (i.e., highly prototypical members) of the adult categories to which they belong. In part this may be attributable to the child's familiarity with the particular referent due either to the mother's bias in naming and presenting objects (see Anglin, 1977) or to the structure of the world. Additionally, there is some evidence that children's early categories are basic level rather than superordinate or subordinate in nature (Anglin, 1977; Mervis & Rosch, 1981). Furthermore, it has been suggested that there may be substantial differences in the basic level categories of children and adults (Mervis, 1981, 1982). Mervis argued that children may attend to different attributes or assign different weights to attributes in forming such categories. She suggested three reasons to explain why this might occur. First, children may not be aware of certain attributes (e.g., a child may not be aware of the actual function of a round, ball-shaped candle). Second, children may be aware of certain attributes that adults recognize, but they may not be as salient for the child as they are for the adult. Finally, children may make errors in the attributes they identify with certain objects. Such errors may be based upon unusual idiosyncratic experiences (e.g., throwing round candles) or in some cases adult attempts at simplifications for the child (e.g., mothers may tell children that leopards "meow, " Mervis & Mervis, 1982).

In the context of these proposals Mervis and Canada (in press) present data from a longitudinal study of three children which provides evidence of overextensions corresponding to predicted child basic categories. They suggest that this argues against the conclusions of previous investigators (Chapman & Thompson, 1980; Fremgen & Fay, 1980; Thompson & Chapman, 1977). These earlier investigations indicated that the extent of overextension differed in comprehension and production. In one case fewer overextensions were found in comprehension than in production (Thomson & Chapman, 1977). However, Fremgen and Fay found no evidence of overextension in comprehension although production overextensions were evident. In spite of these differences in findings (discussed in greater detail below), the conclusion drawn in both of these investigations was that children's overextensions are in general the result of performance limitations in production due to retrieval. Thomson and Chapman add the possibility that in cases where overextension is evidenced in comprehension and production, the overextension can be attributed to the course of feature acquisition as was described by Clark or to parents' acceptance or lack of correction.

When the results of two more recent investigations are considered, the picture becomes even more confused. Although previous investigations had for the most part been designed to examine overextensions, as mentioned earlier, there is also evidence of underextensions (Anglin, 1977; Bloom, 1973; Nelson, Gruendel, Rescorla, & Benedict, 1978; Reich, 1976; Rescorla, 1976). Often evidence for overextensions or for underextensions has been used to support one of two opposing viewpoints suggesting that children's early concepts either are narrow or broad in nature. However, it is possible that both narrow and broad concepts or categories exist within a given child at a given point or points in development (see Nelson & Bonvillian, 1978). Kay and Anglin (1982) employed unfamiliar words which were then trained in order to determine the extent of overextension and underextension in both comprehension and production. They found evidence for both, although overextension occurred more frequently in comprehension and underextension occurred more frequently in production. These findings contradict previous indications that words are less overextended in comprehension than in production (Fremgen & Fay, 1980; Gruendel, 1977; Huttenlocher, 1974; Thomson & Chapman, 1977). Kay and Anglin argue that performance factors such as retrieval limitations do not adequately explain their findings.

While most investigators have characterized overextensions as reflecting either performance or competence limitations, Winner (1979) has suggested that some early word usage may be metaphorical or analogical in nature rather than literal. She proposed a set of criteria to differentiate literal from nonliteral usage, primarily based upon evidence that the child was either engaged in some form of symbolic play or that the child actually knew the word for the referent that was incorrectly named. In line with this proposal, Chapman and Leonard (1981) tested overextensions in comprehension and production for language impaired children ranging in age from 2;8 to 3;4 who were still in the one-word period of language usage. Instances in which the child evidenced either comprehension or production knowledge of the correct referent label on two trials were classified as analogy. Instances in which the child's responses were inconsistent either in production or comprehension were classifed as either competition between two incorrect terms or competition between the incorrect and correct terms. Finally, instances in which the child exhibited a consistent error in the label of the referent were viewed as overextensions. The largest percentage of responses were classified as overextensions.

Inappropriate word extensions have thus been varyingly characterized as competence limitations that are the result of narrower, broader, or simply different concepts and categories than those of adults; performance limitations that may be the result of factors such as retrieval difficulties; and expressions of metaphors or analogies. In a recent paper Kamhi (1982) suggested that overextensions may have multiple functions: (1) communication — the correct label is known to the child, (2) heuristic, or (3) hypothesis-testing when the correct label is not known. Underextensions, however, are simply characterized as representing incorrect hypotheses.

Taken as a whole, this body of literature presents both conflicting findings and interpretations. If it were not for the potential importance of these phenomena in describing the nature of early categories and concepts, it would be tempting to simply ignore the confusion. The bases for these differing results and interpretations, as well as some methodological issues which need to be considered in future investigations, warrant further discussion. First, it seems clear that investigations based on naturalistic observation, diary data, or informal and vaguely described probes provide inadequate and, in some cases perhaps, inaccurate descriptions of children's lexical categories and concepts (e.g., Clark, 1973; Rescorla, 1980). In such cases underextensions may be overlooked and the full range of extension (i.e., the things to which the words are applied) and intension (i.e., the features or characteristics which serve as the basis for category inclusion) may remain unspecified. Furthermore, it is difficult, if not impossible, to interpret the results of probes when the methodology and stimuli remain unspecified (e.g., Rescorla, 1980).

Experimentally controlled studies with well specified methodologies and stimuli are unfortunately not a panacea. As may be evident in the preceding review, such studies yield markedly conflicting results. As was mentioned, these differences may be at least partially attributed to methodological variations. In most cases investigations have been limited to examinations of overextensions. Consequently, with few exceptions (e.g., Kay & Anglin, 1982) underextensions have not been examined. If we are to understand the range and boundaries of children's lexical categories, all possible relationships between child and adult categories need to be examined. As Kay and Anglin noted, the range of methodologies employable in testing production are limited. Typically, a child can be asked "What's this?", "Is this a ——?", or "Is this a —— or a ——?" It is hard to imagine many other alternatives. Some variation can occur though in the objects which are included within such probes. For example, while Thomson and Chapman (1977) tested a variety of appropriate exemplars, possible overextended exemplars, and familiar unrelated objects, Fremgen and Fay (1980) seemed to only employ possible overextended exemplars and one appropriate exemplar for a given word. Such differences may have a significant impact upon the nature of children's responses. Furthermore, even with the detailed description of stimulus selection criteria provided by Thomson and Chapman, it is not clear that the stimuli chosen will tap the full range of extension of a given word in production. Since experimental investigations have the disadvantage of the extent of behavior sampling available, it seems that some compensation must be made in terms of repeated and extensive testing. Furthermore, the exclusive use of pictorial stimuli may represent a significant limitation. If indeed children's categories are based in part upon functional considerations, pictorial stimuli may exclude such factors. For instance, if a child has the opportunity to roll or throw a round piece of fruit, he may be more likely to name that object a ball, than if he only sees a picture of it. Finally, the fact that no study of lexical extension to date has taken phonological factors into account is a matter of some concern. The fact that homonymy may be a relatively common occurrence in the early speech of some children (Ingram, 1981; see also Priestly, 1980 for a critical review), casts some doubt upon a portion of those instances identified as overextensions in productions. For instance, a child may produce the words *car* and *truck* as [kʌ] because of phonological simplifications, not because the child includes cars and trucks in the same category. Because most transcriptions provided in previous investigations of lexical behavior are presented in orthographic form, it seems unlikely that this factor has been considered. Phonological analyses based upon transcription and phonetic analyses based upon instrumental analyses can and should be used in ensuring that instances of assumed overextension are not simply instances of homonymy.

The degree of variation in comprehension procedures seems even greater than the possible variation in production procedures. For example,

in Thomson and Chapman's data it appeared that overextensions occurred most frequently in those trials including a possibily overextended
exemplar and an unrelated exemplar. They also included trials involving
an appropriate exemplar and an unrelated exemplar. Far fewer instances
of overextensions seemed to occur on such trials. Fremgen and Fay invariably included an appropriate exemplar in their arrays and found no
evidence of overextension. Additionally, they criticized Thomson and
Chapman for their use of repeated items involving the same word. It may
well be the case that when children respond to items in which an adult-
appropriate exemplar is included by indicating the most prototypical or
representative exemplar. In many cases this may be the adult-appropriate
exemplar (Kuczaj, 1979). Consequently, overextensions are not observed
in such instances. Alternatively, when the best example in the array is an
exemplar which corresponds to the child-basic category it will be chosen.
Errors in these cases may be attributed to factors such as fatigue, social
conventions such as a desire to please an adult experimenter, or to true
overextension (Mervis & Canada, in press; Thomson & Chapman, 1977).
Some evidence may be brought to bear in eliminating the first two
possibilities: some control over the testing situation in terms of time of
day and length, evidence of change in responsiveness over the course of
the session, reliable refusal responses, alternate responses (e.g., going to
a toy box and choosing an exemplar not included in the array), asymmetries in overextensions (see Mervis & Canada, in press). As in the production testing procedures, some argument can be made here for the need
for more extensive testing across a broader range of exemplars to determine the range and boundaries of categories in comprehension. Finally,
there are differences among these investigations in the type of stimuli
employed ranging from photographs to line drawings or objects. The influence of such differences is undetermined.

Besides differences in the methodologies of these investigations some
similarities in findings have led to widely divergent conclusions. Although
Thomson and Chapman conclude that at least some overextensions are
the result of performance limitations (as do Fremgen and Fay), Mervis
and Canada as well as Kay and Anglin conclude that there are competence-
based overextensions. Although aspects of both arguments are convincing
and evidence may be marshalled to support them it is not clear that we
as yet have incontrovertible evidence to eliminate either possibility. In fact,
it may ultimately prove to be the case that both occur. Investigations involving converging methods of testing might be helpful in providing some
supportive or refutive evidence. Additionally, if in fact overgeneralizations
are due to performance factors, it seems critical that such factors be identified. Investigations are needed to determine what factors might be

manipulated to facilitate production. Such data might serve to demonstrate that there are such factors at work. Finally, phonological considerations have been ignored here. It has been demonstrated that phonological factors (similarity to words attempted and produced by a child) have a significant influence upon lexical production and acquisition (Schwartz & Leonard, 1982), but not upon comprehension (Leonard et al., in press). Phonological selectivity thus may represent an important performance factor in that children may comprehend words that are not produced because of their phonological characteristics.

Other views of lexical extension also warrant further investigative consideration. For instance, while Chapman and Leonard's inferences regarding analogical usage are extremely interesting, their data do not rule out the possibility that the intitial overextension was due to other factors either inherent in the situation or in the child's performance. Kamhi's proposals concerning the heuristic or hypothesis-testing functions of overextension require more experimental verification. It may be possible, using either nonsense words or unfamiliar word paradigms, to provide children with certain predetermined feedback to determine whether in fact children are able to make adjustments in their categories. This would provide at least indirect evidence that this behavior can serve a discovery or learning function for the child. It may also be possible to create situations in which the pressure to communicate is increased and the child has labels which can be overextended, but no appropriate label, to examine Kamhi's proposed communicative function.

As has been mentioned repeatedly, none of the investigations discussed has provided a complete description of the range and boundaries of children's early lexical categories and concepts. Clearly, such a description would represent a major undertaking. It seems that we need to consider some alternative paradigms. One potential source of such paradigms is the literature concerning the development of categories in infants (e.g., Cohen & Strauss, 1979; Ross, 1980). In this literature habituation-dishabituation paradigms have been employed in determining the range and boundaries of infants' categories. The assumption is that with repeated presentations of members from the same category infants will habituate and attention (e.g., gaze time) will decrease. When a stimulus which does not belong to that category is then presented, dishabituation occurs and thus attention increases. Although in the past such experiments have employed stimuli within a single modality (e.g., visual), it is conceivable that stimuli could be presented in two modalities (e.g., a word and a visual stimulus). For example, in this type of paradigm, the presentations would involve an unchanging auditory stimulus (e.g., *dog*) along with objects or pictures representing assumed category members until habituation is evident. The same auditory stimulus might then be presented along with a picture or object representing a hypothesized category member or nonmember (e.g., a cow). If dishabituation were then to occur, it might be concluded that this is not a member of the child's category of "dog. " However, if the child were to remain habituated, it would not be clear whether the response indicated category membership for the cow or whether the child was simply responding to the lack of change in the auditory stimulus. Consequently, an identical set of visual presentations might be employed without accompanying auditory presentations. If the child fails to dishabituate in response to the presentation of the cow under these conditions, the case for including it in the child's category of "dog" becomes substantially stronger. Before such a paradigm is applied, other procedural details may need to be considered. In spite of the number of trials which may be needed to map the boundaries of even a single category, this may prove to be an paradigm worth considering further.

A second alternative approach may be found in the paradigms employed in examining infants' speech perception (e.g., Kuhl, 1980). In this type of paradigm, the goal is to identify discrimination by conditioning the infant to turn his or her head in response to some target stimulus or stimuli, but not in response to others. It may be possible to adapt this type of paradigm to allow presentation of some type of visual stimuli (e.g., referents from an assumed category) along with an auditory stimulus (e.g., a word). Once some initial instances of a category coupled with a given word are established as eliciting a head turn response (or some other behavioral response) other referents might be introduced to determine whether the response generalizes or fails to generalize to such instances.

In general such paradigms may be more amenable to the task of determining the range and boundaries of children's lexical categories. However, it should be emphasized that these paradigms are not without limitations. Evidence of habituation-dishabituation or head turn response generalization or lack of generalization may be influenced by attentional, motivational and other factors. In spite of this, though, they may provide significant advantages in terms of control and the range of stimuli which might be presented. Combined with previously employed methodologies they may provide us with much stronger evidence regarding early lexical categories.

The preceding suggestions are exclusively concerned with comprehension. As was mentioned earlier, alternatives in production are far more limited. However, there is one avenue, parallel to the above proposals, which might be explored. Snyder (1978) presented repeated instances of an enactment (e.g., throwing a ball into a pail) to children and then changed one element of the act (e.g., throwing a doll into a pail). When children produced a word in this situation, in most cases it referred to the element which had changed (i.e., *doll*). Although this has been attributed to other factors, in a sense it is like the habituation-dishabituation paradigm. Further exploratory work needs to be done to determine the reliability of this response. However, if it does turn out to be a reliable response, it may be possible to use this procedure to discriminate objects (i.e., different members of a single category) which the child views as not involving a change and consequently does not name from those objects which are viewed as changing (i.e., members of a different category). Again, such data must be used and interpreted cautiously, but it has the potential of adding to the existing repertoire of production probes.

Regardless of the methods employed in future investigations, it seems clear that more specific information regarding children's responses and more stringent statistical procedures are needed. With the exception of Thomson and Chapman, few investigators provide specific details regarding response probabilities beyond those for individual arrays (e.g., 1 out of 4 or .25). In this regard, Oviatt's (1980) approach may serve as a model of sorts. She evaluated children's comprehension responses in terms of baseline measures of looking at or touching objects in the experimental situation, false positive responses, and responses to the appropriate exemplar. An alternative statistical model, conceptually similar to Oviatt's approach, is a signal detection approach. Signal detection theory (Green & Swets, 1966) compares the probability of a response to a signal (e.g., a word) as compared with the probability of a response to noise (e.g., an unrelated or nonsense word). To date only one reported investigation has employed such an approach in examining lexical comprehension (Thomas, Campos, D. Shucard, Ramsey, & J. Shucard, 1981). In this investigation, the age at which lexical comprehension emerged, 12 months, was later than had been previously assumed. Although some methodological limitations in the stimuli employed may have been responsible for this finding, this does not negate the strength of this approach.

One final methodological issue warrants discussion. In several of the investigations discussed, comprehension and production data were combined in making inferences regarding children's lexical extension. While this is intuitively tempting, it may lead to some serious problems. Asymmetries in production and comprehension have often been noted (e.g., Benedict, 1979). In part this may be due simply to the developmental precedence of comprehension. However, there is at least some evidence that at various points in development comprehension differs markedly from production not only in the nature and level of response, but also in the inferred basis for such responses (e.g., Chapman, 1978; Miller, Chapman, Branston, & Reichle, 1980). These investigators have suggested that the strategies or bases of such responses may differ markedly. Consequently, combining comprehension and production data without regard to these differences may introduce some distortion. It may be best to proceed as though these are two related but separate systems, at least early in development.

The discussion in this section has focused almost exclusively upon concepts and categories underlying object words. This largely reflects the emphasis of research appearing in the literature. In part this emphasis is justified by the frequency of such words in children's early lexicons. In part it is likely due to the fact that object words are inherently easier to investigate. With a few exceptions of diary data reports (Clark, 1978) and theoretical discussions (Gentner, 1978) little experimental attention has been paid to the categories and concepts underlying other types of early words. There is clearly a need for further investigations in this area.

Inferring Semantic Notions and Pragmatic Functions

The proposal that single-word utterances involve more than the use of a lexical item to refer to a member of a category is not a new idea. It has now been almost a century since it was first suggested that children's single-word utterances represent or imply sentences, propositions, or whole thoughts (see Dore, 1975; Greenfield & Smith, 1976; Stevenson, 1983, for complete reviews). More recently, such views have been theoretically updated and expanded upon. One view (e.g., McNeill, 1970) is that such utterances reflect innate, syntactic deep structure relationships between noun phrases and verb phrases. It is then suggested that the reason children do not produce more than a single word is because of some performance limitations. Additionally, it was assumed that comprehsion so far exeeds production that children are likely to have knowledge of syntactic structures and relations. Such notions have been criticized in some detail by Ingram (1971) and Bloom (1973). It is simply not clear that there is sufficient evidence to support the attribution of the syntactic knowledge described in such accounts.

The weakness of syntactically oriented holophrastic views led some investigators (e.g., Greenfield & Smith, 1976; Ingram, 1971) to put forth semantically oriented holophrastic views. Ingram employed a modified version of Fillmore's (1968) case grammar as a means of describing single-word utterances. It is generally forgotten that Fillmore's proposal, while radically different in its use of cases, was very much a syntactic grammar in its deep structure. Thus, to some extent, the same degree of complexity is being attributed to the knowledge base of single-word utterances. Ingram attempted to avoid this problem by suggesting that the child's word expresses a single constituent, while other constituents are expressed nonlinguistically (crying, gestures, etc.). Unfortunately, the evidence for the consistent use of such nonlinguistic features is lacking. Furthermore, it is unclear that children can be appropriately credited at this point in development with underlying knowledge of formal relationships between linguistic and nonlinguistic behaviors.

Of recent holophrastically oriented descriptions of single-word utterances, Greenfield and Smith's is perhaps the most divergent. In fact, they distinguished their approach from previous holophrase proposals by suggesting that the "combinatorial" meaning of these single words is not contained within the word, but instead results from a combination of the word with aspects of the nonlinguistic context. In and of itself this notion is not troubling. However, the evidence Greenfield and Smith provide for their categorizations is. First, they make some assumptions which may not be accurate. They assume children distinguish animate from inanimate entities. There are some indications that children's notions of animacy differ from those of adults (Piaget, 1929). They also assume that children's gestures relate directly to their vocalizations. Actions and gestures may not always be unambiguously related to vocal productions. For instance, Rodgon, Jankowski, and Alenskas (1977) found a number of instances in which they appeared to be unrelated. Additionally, Greenfield and Smith assume that phonetic resemblance to an adult word ensures at least some semantic resemblance. In many cases this may be true, but it is not a certainty. Finally, they assume that adult expansions can be used to infer semantic categories. While they recognize that alternative expansions are possible, they fail to explore the full range of expansions for any given situation. For example, in one case where one of the children says "break" as his mother breaks some eggs, the two expansions considered are *the eggs break* and *mommy breaks the eggs*. Other possibilities include *the eggs are broken* and *mommy breaks* (children do not necessarily know that *break* requires an object). Thus here as well as elsewhere expansions are far from unambiguous.

The categories are no less ambiguous. For instance, simply because the child utters *dada* in a situation when someone comes in and *mama* when his mother is given a book, is not sufficient justification for attributing two separate semantic categories to the child (agent and dative). Even the evidence of sequence of acquisition, use of a word across situations with the same semantic meaning, multiple word use for a given category, or productivity do not provide convincing evidence of the psychological reality of such categories.

It should be emphasized that these general and rather basic criticisms do not negate the importance of Greenfield and Smith's work. Their investigation has great value in the detailed description of the varied contexts of word usage by the two children studied. It provides an important starting point for descriptions of the semantic categories of children's single-word utterances. However, a critical piece of information is missing: whether children are aware of and somehow differentially code broader semantic categories such as agent and dative. Without such evidence we are left with adult inferences of the semantic notion of the child's utterance in relation to the adult perception of the context (regardless of how reliable such judgments are across adults).

One type of evidence for such semantic categories which has been suggested by at least two more cautious investigators (Brown, 1973; Leonard, 1976) concerns alternation in usage in recurring contexts. For example, if the child's mother throws a ball on two separate occasions and the child says "ball" one time and "mommy" the other time the child may be credited with separate categories of object and agent. However, other factors such as the preceding event may be responsible for such alternation. Furthermore the child may be simply naming different aspects of the situation without broader knowledge of categories such as agent or object.

The preceding discussion paints a rather bleak picture of the outlook for semantic notion coding of single-word utterances. As had been noted here and elsewhere (Bloom, 1973) the evidence for such inferences and categorizations is simply not present in children's corpora. However, it is not absolutely clear that we should abandon such endeavors at least in the interest of arguments for continuity in development and the question of when such broader semantic knowledge emerges. We have at least some preliminary evidence that children at this point in development comprehend relations among words (Sachs & Truswell, 1978). Additionally, there is an increasingly large body of literature using habituation paradigms involving visual stimuli in the form of films which to some extent indicate that children are sensitive to certain aspects of situations (e.g., changes in actors vs. recipients of actions); see Golinkoff (1981) for an extensive review. These represent two potentially fruitful paths for demonstrating some knowledge of situational relations and perhaps semantic notions. As was mentioned earlier, receptive or comprehension information alone may be inadequate. Consequently, some investigations of production under conditions involving control over the salience of certain aspects of the situation are needed. One final possible source of evidence may be employed. Braine and Wells (1978) have employed a conditioning procedure with older children in which they were trained to place a chip on elements of a picture corresponding to certain semantic categories. It is conceivable that such a procedure might be adapted for use with younger children.

Dore (1975) argued, quite convincingly in some cases, that categorizations based upon the function of such utterances are far less problematic than syntactically- or semantically-based categorizations. Certainly, in a general sense they are since they avoid the sentential type of inference of holophrastic approaches. However, many of the same problems arise. Unambiguous evidence for the existence of such categories, as they have been described, is not always available from children's corpora. For instance, Dore's description of primitive speech acts relies heavily upon intonation, citing Menyuk and Bernholz (1969) as the basis for assuming that intonation is used to consistently contrast function. This particular study was based upon a single child and only preliminary examination of the data without statistical analyses. Thus we do not have evidence that intonation is used contrastively. Either supportive or nonsupportive evidence would represent an important step forward. Even if supportive evidence is forthcoming, closer attention to suprasegmental aspects of children's utterances by means of reliable transcription or instrumental annalyses will be needed.

Two critiques of this functional approach have appeared recently (Francis, 1979; Wells, 1982). Francis suggests that formal criteria such as those specified by Searle (1969) are necessary to justify the inference of specific communicative intents. While the need for that degree of formality is not clear, evidence along such lines is needed. We need to identify evidence of differential encoding, awareness of differential intents and awareness of some of the underlying assumptions of specific communicative functions. Some such evidence is already available (e.g., Bates et al., 1975). However, it is seldom presented (e.g., Halliday, 1975). More specifically, Wells (1982), in reviewing a recent book by McShane (1980), points out that even what is assumed to be a very basic distinction between assertions and requests is not supported. In a case where a child is making what appears to be a request (*more* and later in the dialogue *store*), it is not demonstrated that the child is not simply making an assertion about where more of something might exist. Evidence for such distinctions may be readily available in the child's behavior, but it remains unspecified.

As in the case of semantic notions, the suggestion is not that we abandon such inferences and categorizations. Instead, it is argued that a concerted effort needs to be made to provide evidence for the validity of such endeavors.

Two-Word Utterances: Inferring
Semantic Relations and Pragmatic Functions

Almost all of the research concerning children's two-word utterances has focused on the inference and categorization of semantic relations (in terms of case grammars) and communicative functions. This approach has been termed interpretive analysis. In general, investigators (e.g., Brown, 1973; Bloom, 1970; Leonard, 1976 among others) appear to be more comfortable in ascribing semantic relations to children's utterances when two words are present. Besides some general assumptions regarding the child's underlying abilities at this point in development, researchers seem assured by the apparent existence of consistent word order, orders of acquisition, and frequency of productions in making these inferences and categorizations. However, in 1976 Howe argued that there were some serious problems in the evidence for such approaches. She argued that categories are not mutually exclusive; that the use of context is limited because children may be referring to different aspects of the situation than those assumed by the adult; that children are likely to be unable to make conceptual distinctions among these categories; that children may be lying, prevaricating, or fantasizing; there is little evidence for consistent word order and given utterances could be assigned to more than a single interpretation. While at least some of Howe's criticisms are rather extreme and likely to be incorrect, other points, echoed by others (e.g., Duchan & Lund, 1979; Rodgon, 1977), have some merit.

After a delay of 6 years, two responses to Howe's criticisms of interpretive analysis have appeared (Bloom, Capatides, & Tackeff, 1981; Golinkoff, 1981). In general these responses have included some recognition of the limitations of previous and current evidence for interpretive analysis along with some suggestions as to how we might proceed. Additionally, these responses address the alternatives offered by Howe.

It seems to be generally agreed that at least some of the initial evidence for semantic relations was extremely weak. Evidence of differential word order is problematic because of the inconsistencies (i.e., groping patterns) which appear to occur in children's speech (Braine, 1976). Orders of emergence demonstrating differential points of acquisition for different categories may be useful, but collapsing across studies there seem to be at least some relations which emerge simultaneously (see Leonard, 1976). Productivity criteria are only truly helpful in identifying distributional tendencies, not the psychological reality of these categories. One additional type of evidence for the reality of these categories is held over in this more recent exchange, reliability of experimenter coding (Bloom et al., 1981). Reliability appears to be quite high across judges within given studies and across investigations in the types of relations identified. Certainly, we would need to be concerned if such reliability or consistency were not in evidence. However, it only assures us that adults (specifically child language investigators) have a similar perspective in describing children's utterances.

Bloom et al. (1981) cite some indirect evidence for the appropriateness of these categorizations and inferences and against some of the assumptions made by Howe. For example, they note that successful adult-child communication would be impossible if adult and child-views of the world were truly disjoint sets. Their point is well-taken, but it does not guarantee that these views are isomorphic. Bloom et al. recognize that other types of evidence are needed. A review of available evidence is provided by Golinkoff (1981). She notes that currently there is evidence from production, in terms of stress, of differentiation among utterances assumed to encode different relations (Wieman, 1976). Although the reliability of coding was not assessed in this investigation, it is an avenue which warrants further exploration. She also cites evidence from comprehension (e.g., Golinkoff & Markessini, 1980) which suggests that children understand aspects of the possessive relation. More recently, Angiolillo and Goldin-Meadow (1982) have provided evidence which demonstrates that comprehension of agent-patient categories is dependent upon these categories rather than animacy distinctions. Finally, Golinkoff presents a review of nonlinguistic evidence for the existence of such concepts and categories. It must be clearly acknowledged that such evidence is generally preliminary and far from conclusive. However, it represents an important step for child language research in the validation of our descriptive methodologies.

As noted by Bloom et al. and Golinkoff, other methodologies need to be explored as well. Braine and Wells (1978) provided one such methodology in the training study mentioned earlier. Leonard (1975) provided another training methodology which may be employed to demonstrate lack of generalization across certain categories, given carefully chosen stimuli and probes. Finally, other production procedures remain to be explored.

In her response to some of these criticisms, Howe presented data which she interpreted as supportive of her alternative to interpretive analysis. Howe had suggested that only three concept categories be employed: action of concrete object, state of concrete object, and name of concrete object. It should be noted that this is not a solution, but rather an alternative system which must be validated as other, more detailed systems must be validated. Her investigation seemed to demonstrate at least for locative and benefactive versus agentive roles, children do not make such distinctions in comprehension at the time when they begin to produce word combinations. Instead, such distinctions in comprehension appear to be made only shortly before or concomitantly with the appearance of these roles in production marked by prepositional phrases (e.g., to ——, for ——) or possessive inflections (e.g., *baby's*). Thus Howe argued that children's early noun-noun utterances (e.g., "sweater chair" or "cake mommy") should be characterized as entity-entity rather than in terms of more specific roles. However, it is not clear that Howe has provided incontrovertible evidence of children's lack of conceptual understanding of these specific semantic roles. Her task appeared more specifically to assess the children's understanding of the relationship between word order and these semantic roles. Clearly, further research is needed to support or to refute Howe's proposals.

It seems that we need to reserve judgment concerning specific aspects of interpretive analysis. However, there is sufficient evidence to justify the general endeavor of such analyses. Howe (1981) noted that her initial intent was not a total attack upon such endeavors. Instead she had hoped to raise issues which she felt needed to be addressed. It appears that she accomplished her goal.

Conclusion

The amount of literature cited and discussed in this chapter attests to the accomplishments of developmental psycholinguists in describing children's one- and two-word utterances. For a number of years we have relied upon the fact that child language study is a relatively young area of investigation in accounting for our lack of theoretical frameworks and our emphasis upon descriptive rather than experimental research. It seems that we have reached or are about to reach an important turning point, in that before new descriptive analyses, inferences, and categorizations are introduced, we need to examine the validity of previous descriptions. Such a change would not only strengthen our positions regarding inference and categorization, but also might prove useful in the generation and refinement of theoretical frameworks. This chapter has been somewhat negative and critical in the picture of inference and categorization described. However, if it serves to stimulate thinking and consequently, research activity which will critically examine our descriptions of one- and two-word utterances, it will have served a useful function of its own.

Marilyn Newhoff
Patricia B. Launer

Input as Interaction: Shall We Dance?

Like the proverbial tango, it takes two collaborating individuals to participate in meaningful communication. Once the steps have been learned, the setting, tempo, or partners may change, but the routines are not forgotten. In the *verbal* tango, positions change, too; one is sometimes the leader, sometimes the follower, sometimes the speaker, and sometimes the listener. Every child must learn to join in the dance, acquiring the rules for semantics and syntax and the cultural conventions for the use of language. This knowledge is gained through interaction with the environment. Factors such as shared knowledge, status of the participants, cultural biases, extra-linguistic context, and linguistic information contribute to the nature of the interaction. Conversational appropriateness varies markedly from culture to culture and from context to context within a given culture. The learning process requires some fancy footwork on the part of the child.

For years, researchers have been intrigued by the ways in which children accomplish the language learning task. One promising line of investigation concerned the input provided to young children, the reasons for the specialized adjustments observed in language input, and the effects of these modifications on language acquisition. When the focus of input studies shifted to interaction, there were additional speculations on the influence of the *child* on the incoming language of the caretaker. Despite the large body of literature presently available, we are still uncertain about the nature or the extent of the effects of early interactions on the language learning of children. Fortunately, the story does not have to end here. For

© College-Hill Press, Inc. All rights, including that of translation, reserved. No part of this publication may be reproduced without the written permission of the publisher.

through the investigative undertakings in the area of input and interaction, we are now in a better position to delineate our research questions, refine our methodologies, and increase our understanding of how language acquisition is influenced by the environment. Tracing the course of these developments will be the focus of this chapter.

Dancing Without Music

Input Without Interaction

A review of child language acquisition research over the last two decades indicates a shifting emphasis from syntax to semantics to pragmatics. Each emphasis has resulted in theoretical stances regarding how language is acquired. While it initially appeared that each theoretical position had to stand alone, it now seems more likely that they are interactive; that is, the syntactic, semantic and pragmatic domains are not easily separable. Rather, each appears to influence, and be influenced by, the development of the others. Further, each position has been responsible for the current interest in studies of the language learning environment.

Chomsky's (1957, 1965) theoretical model, which emphasized the formal linguistic structures of language (i.e., syntax), was based on the major underlying assumption that children are biologically programmed to acquire language. Environmental influence, therefore, was relegated to a relatively minor role in the process. Other language learning, such as that represented in the pragmatic dimension, was not taken into account in Chomsky's theory. Therefore, children's acquisition of the knowledge required for a broader based "communicative competence" (Hymes, 1972) could not be addressed within the context of this model.

Some investigators reacted specifically to Chomsky's conclusion that children's structural learning was due to species-specific, innate language abilities. For example, Sinclair (1971) noted similarities between a child's sensorimotor knowledge and language learning. Underlying cognitive abilities thus were supported as explanations for linguistic attainments. Over the past decade, the role of cognition in language acquisition has been given somewhat different emphases as new knowledge has become available (Cromer, 1974, 1976; Schlesinger, 1977; Slobin, 1973).[1] What is important to the present discussion is the fact that, unlike Chomsky's position, current accounts of cognitive and linguistic parallels are viewed as interacting with environmental influences. Thus, it is the case that neither an innatist perspective nor cognition alone can account for language acquisition. The pragmatic functions served by children's earliest productions, as well as the utterances directed to them, must also be considered for the richest account of language learning. From these influences, a rationale for the study of language acquisition in context was born.

The earliest studies of the language learning environment were designed to describe input *to* children, rather than the interactive nature of conversations *with* children. Mothers were typically the input source, and investigators frequently served as the comparison conversational partner. From these earlier works, it became apparent that mothers make rather consistent modifications in their speech to young children. The description which emerged was of speech that was syntactically simple, highly repetitive and fluent, containing a large proportion of interrogatives and imperatives, as well as being delivered in a higher pitch with exaggerated intonation contours (Broen, 1972; Holzman, 1972, 1974; Moerk, 1974; Phillips, 1973; Sachs, Brown, & Salerno, 1976; Snow, 1972).[2] Further, these modifications occurred regardless of social class, maternal status, or the sex of the child (Snow, 1977). Although these studies represented an important beginning for speculation about the influence of the environment on language acquisition, some methodological issues became apparent. For instance, most of these investigations were cross-sectional in design; rarely were longitudinal data provided. Additionally, there was a paucity of information regarding populations other than middle class Americans. Finally, child initiations and responses were not included in the analyses, yielding a unidirectional description of speech to children. There were also variations in terminology; the simplified register that was described was variously referred to as baby talk, parental speech, motherese, nursery language, or simply as input. Later studies indicated that fathers, older siblings, and peers are also capable of providing a simplified register in their speech to young language learning children (Berko-Gleason, 1977; Marinkovich, Newhoff, & MacKenzie, 1980; Newhoff, Silverman, & Millet, 1980; Sachs & Devin, 1976; Shatz & Gelman, 1973). Taken together, however, the descriptions which emerged from these studies offered little insight into the effects of input on the language acquisition process. On the other hand, several researchers did speculate as to why modifications occurred at all in child-directed speech.

Why Modify?

One of the earliest speculations as to the impetus for specialized input to children concerned the notion that such modifications allow for children's exposure to an "ideal teaching language" (Snow, 1972). While input may serve a teaching function, mothers do not report teaching to be a conscious effort on their part. Rather, mothers claim that they modify to ensure communicative effectiveness with their children (Garnica,

1977). Some researchers have suggested that mothers may, in fact, perform a teaching function, but only in certain situations. For example, Moerk (1975) described eight such contexts, including book-reading tasks, descriptions of ongoing activities, providing corrective feedback, and answering questions. Others have argued that teaching occurs through interaction, but it is aimed at cognitive elements (i.e., enhancing world knowledge), rather than at providing language lessons (Cicourel, 1974; Corsaro, 1977).

Newport, Gleitman, and Gleitman (1977) took a strong position on input as a communicative rather than a didactic strategy. They contended that the special characteristics of language spoken to children arise for purposes of here-and-now communication with a limited and inattentive listener. In their view, input modifications cannot be attributed to a language instruction motive. Brown (1977) also suggested that modifications occur to ensure communication and to keep both adult and child conversationally focused. Others have proposed that the desire to communicate reciprocally with children may be the crucial factor in restricting the topics discussed by adults and in limiting the semantic and syntactic complexity of their input (Bateson, 1975; Snow, 1977).

Snow (1977) posited that the simplified register addressed to children occurs as a result of the desire to maintain dialogue. Caretakers will therefore accept the most minimal response as the infant's conversational turn, and will then continue their input. At times, caretakers assume both roles of the interaction; for instance, they may answer their own questions. It may be, then, that the desire for conversation motivates any modifications in speech addressed to a conversationally undeveloped partner. Even as children get older, and more stringent conversational rules are applied, caretakers appear to accept almost anything as an opening for a linguistic interchange.

Although the initial studies of input rarely controlled for the child's comprehension and/or cognitive level, some evidence indicated that mothers vary their mean length of utterance (MLU) in relation to the child's rate of comprehension development (Furrow, Nelson, & Benedict, 1979). It appears more likely that the nature of the speech adjustments addressed to children vary from context to context. The influence of the child's comprehension and responsiveness, the desire for a two-way interchange, and other factors seem to combine in various ways to produce observed modifications. Such a notion would support the conversational model proposed by Snow (1977). More recently, other interactional explanations for input modifications have been offered (Camaioni, 1979; Ochs, 1979a). For instance, Ochs (1979a) postulated that mothers' use of communication checks (e.g., repetitions or semantically related utterances) may ensure joint focus and shared knowledge.

An interesting perspective on speech modifications was taken by Hirsh-Pasek and Treiman (1982) in their investigation of *doggerel*—the speech directed by female masters to their dogs. The authors observed that *motherese* and *doggerel* were strikingly similar from a syntactic perspective, but different in that doggerel did not employ deixis. Deixis is addressed to children in a teaching fashion, to point out objects, to label them, and to introduce new words and concepts. It seems logical, therefore, that this functional difference would be found in comparisons of speech to children and pets. Such findings led Hirsh-Pasek and Treiman to suggest that motherese is not elicited in response either to the linguistic or the cognitive levels of children. Pets and children seem to share one common feature; that is, they are both socially responsive. Thus, in the view of these investigators, motherese is motivated by the socially responsive behavior of the conversational partner.

Finally, what adults know, or think they know, about their children's language may govern the types of modifications made. Berko-Gleason and Weintraub (1978) have suggested that mothers and fathers are quite adept at judging the linguistic capabilities of their children. Although far more information is needed to support such a contention, it is not surprising that such perceptions may influence the communicative style of speech addressed to children. Conversely, the communicative style of the child may have an influence on parents' input adjustments. We will return to this point in a later section.

What seems most important to the present discussion is that the proposed motivations for a simplified register do not help to elucidate the precise role of input in language acquisition. Several investigators did, however, attempt to define this relationship.

Input as a Facilitator of Language Acquisition

In an effort to determine the impact of input on language acquisition, several researchers related the frequency with which certain structures are used by caretakers to the emergence of these structures in the child's language system. For example, the frequency of WH-questions, as well as the order of their appearance in caretakers' speech, have been found to correlate with the order of emergence in children's language (Brown, Cazden, & Bellugi, 1969). Additionally, semantic categories which occur infrequently in child speech (Brown, 1973) also have been shown to occur infrequently in adult speech to children (Rondal, 1978). Finally, in developmental studies of sentential meanings and the auxiliary verb system (Wells, 1970; Wells & Woll, 1979), the order of emergence for the terms analyzed was more highly correlated with frequency of usage in adult speech to children than with syntactic or semantic complexity. Although such correlations have been reported, a cause-effect relationship between frequency of occurrence in input and resultant learning by the recipient remains to be demonstrated.

Child language scholars have speculated about the influence of input on the acquisition of particular language dimensions, but few have been successful in documenting this relationship empirically. Some studies have indicated that particular features of input to children may affect the *rate* of language learning, either positively or negatively.

Following the observation of Brown et al. (1969) that expansions occur frequently in parental speech to children, several investigators sought to relate a variety of expansion-like utterances to language learning. Nelson, Carskaddon, and Bonvillian (1973) reported that linguistic development can be accelerated by exposure to sentences that preserve the semantic intention of the child's immediately preceding utterance, while supplying additional syntactic information.

The *quality* of mothers' interactions with young children was implicated in a study by Nelson (1973). Her suggestion was that language could be delayed if the mother assumed an active role in directing her child's behavior (e.g., through the use of affirmative imperatives). On the other hand, when a mother responded to the child's ongoing verbal or nonverbal activity, whether positively or negatively (as with the use of a variety of expansion types), language learning could be accelerated.

Newport, Gleitman, and Gleitman (1975) also indicated that certain features of input language served a facilitative effect. The more frequently mothers in their study produced deictic utterances, the more quickly their children's vocabulary size and noun-phrase elaboration progressed. Also, the more frequently mothers produced auxiliary fronted yes-no questions, the more rapidly children acquired auxiliaries. Newport et al. (1977) suggested that deictic usage could be influential in vocabulary development, expansions could aid in syntactic development, and repetition of maternal utterances, allowing for rehearsal and comparison among input structures, might facilitate both vocabulary and syntactic development. Conversely, affirmative imperatives and poor intelligibility of mothers' speech were thought to delay the acquisition process.

Cross (1975) described the speech of mothers to linguistically accelerated children of two age groups (1:6 to 2:6 and 4:0 to 6:0). Semantically related responses, repetitions, and paraphrases occurred more often in speech directed to the younger age group. Mothers of the younger children appeared to direct their children's behavior less often. Further, following a child-initiated utterance, these mothers were most likely to respond with a semantic extension. In a subsequent study, Cross (1978) compared mothers' speech to normal and linguistically accelerated children. From these results, Cross surmised that an increase in language acquisition rate was most closely tied to the frequency of maternal utterances that were semantically in tune with the child's verbalizations and objects of attention.

Several researchers, therefore, have supported the contention that semantically related utterances may facilitate the rate of language acquisition. And it does seem likely that if children are to benefit from the input provided them, it will be at those times when there is a synchronous relationship among the child's attentional focus and cognitive organization of the world, his or her verbalization, and the adult's comment. It may be that certain input features correlate well with the speed at which children learn some aspects of language. Recognition of this, however, does not singularly support their *necessity* in the acquisition process. The limitations of such a view are addressed elsewhere (see McNew & Bates, this volume). Such studies have been quite important, however, in promoting an understanding of the child's language learning task. As Rice (1982) has suggested, when comparisons are made among the task, the environment, and what is learned by the child, inferences regarding intervening mental processes can be made. In the input literature, increasing emphasis has been placed on the influence of the child on the input he or she receives. The reciprocal nature of caretaker-child interaction, therefore, is given high priority in current research.

Getting into the Dance

The Child as Social Interactor

Until recently, the prelinguistic infant was given little credit for his or her ability to participate in social interactions. During the last decade, as professionals have concerned themselves with the period of early infancy, this assumption has been dramatically modified. Today, the newborn is viewed as interactive with the environment from birth. Moreover, this interactive capacity is thought to be biologically determined. Schaffer (1977), for instance, has suggested that the infant is preadapted to behave in certain ways. Infant behaviors serve to elicit responses which contribute to the child's earliest learning; therefore, learning is essentially social. Not only is the child thought to be preadapted to such behaviors, but parents and caretakers are mutually involved in the process. Thus, a form of "communication" (Thoman, 1981), manifested in the behavioral rhythms of caretakers and infants, begins at birth. This mutual adaptation, characteristic of caretaker and infant interaction, supports the "organismic hypothesis" espoused by Thoman. It is also considered to be prerequisite to both cognitive and language development. Growth in language or cognition is dependent on the current stage of development in the child, which in turn is dependent on previous environmental interactions (Wells, 1981). This view is currently reflected in many studies of the role of the environment in child language acquisition.

Bruner (1975) was among the first to suggest that regardless of one's perspective on language acquisition, the role or significance of the child's prespeech communication system must be given due consideration. His discussion included an emphasis on the regulation of joint attention and activity between mother and infant. Primary caretakers have since been viewed as responsible for establishing the reciprocal basis for communication. As Newson (1977) observed, the primary caretaker attends to infant gestures and vocalizations which may be potentially communicative, and begins to set up temporal patterns which serve to enhance reciprocity.

Such periodicity also has been observed in other caretaker-child behaviors. For example, Condon and Sander (1974) contended that infants participate in human language from the day they are born. Support for this contention was found in neonatal movements that were well synchronized with the "articulated structure" of adult speech. Brazelton (1976) described the cyclical patterns of interaction between an infant subject and his caretakers in terms of tuning-in, give and take, and moving toward and away. Brazelton judged these patterns to be basic to the development of infant-caretaker reciprocity.

Reciprocal gaze behavior was the emphasis of a study by Stern (1974). Following observation of mothers with their infants (3 to 4 months of age), Stern described maternal behavior as unlike that employed in speech with another adult. For instance, mothers gazed almost continuously at their infants, taking both conversational turns. Their gaze, facial and vocal behaviors served to elicit, and to hold, the infant's gaze. Mutual gaze sequences were terminated by the infants 94% of the time.

These behavioral observations led Stern to suggest that such interactions assist the infant in learning to regulate "interpersonal mutuality." The two-way exchange necessary for successful communication, therefore, seems to be rooted in early prelinguistic infant-caretaker interactions.

Bateson (1975), in observing one mother and her infant (49 to 105 days old), noted alternation of vocalization turns that seemed to be patterned on a conversational model. Similarly, alternating vocalization was found to occur in approximately 33% of mothers' interactions with their 3- to 4-month-old twins (Stern, Jaffe, Beebe, & Bennett, 1975).

Social, cognitive and language learning are an outgrowth of these patterns of reciprocal interaction, which seem to be particularly well suited for modeling conversation. From this perspective, the child can be viewed as an equal contributor to the infant-caretaker dyad and to the resultant input received.[3] Eventually, the child's contributions to the interaction develop into recognizable elements of the native language.

Input as Verbal Interaction

As children begin to talk, interactions with primary caretakers may continue to resemble the "conversations" of the prelinguistic period. As suggested by Wells (1981), the child's contribution must be interpreted by the adult in terms of the immediate context, the focus of joint attention, and the child's preceding communication. At the same time that the adult's contribution is "modified in timing, form and content to the child's receptive capacities...(it) must also provide the means whereby the child can enlarge his linguistic resources and, through them, his understanding of the content of the communication" (p. 108). Thus, conversational interaction, initially aimed at maintaining shared attention and activity, continues to be a necessary element in the child's social, cognitive, and language development. Here, we will concern ourselves primarily with language development in its social context, although as previously mentioned, it is difficult to separate these influences from the cognitive dimension.

According to Rice (1982), this sociolinguistic perspective presumes the following: (1) social context influences both the interpretation of language and rules for its use; (2) the discourse unit, rather than the sentence, is the more appropriate unit for analysis; (3) variation of language rules according to social features such as age, sex, and setting are to be expected; and (4) language functions are diverse, varying both culturally and developmentally.

Through interactions with adults, children are exposed to their culture's shared meanings for words. As Dore (1979) suggested, adults also provide examples of how intention is conveyed through choice of words in particular contexts. Such interactions help children to modify their communicative forms so that they approximate more closely the adult system. A number of researchers have investigated language learning through reciprocal interactions. Several observations will be discussed here.

Children and their primary caretakers participate in routinized forms of language use (Gleason & Weintraub, 1975). In some routines, language is relatively fixed, as is the case with politeness forms. Other routines are established between child and caretaker through specific activities. These routines involve various components of conversational form that may facilitate the child's language learning. Social games provide one example of such routines.

Ratner and Bruner (1978) analyzed child-caretaker participation in "appearance and disappearance" games. They observed little variation in the semantic domain, high redundancy, explicit positions for vocalization, and role reversals between child and caretaker. Similarly, language produced during play, even between peers, has been observed to be clear, predictable, and well contextualized in the here-and-now (Hatch, Peck, & Wagner-Gough, 1979).

Another type of routine, "book-reading," was investigated by Ninio and Bruner (1978). In this type of task, children participated in a dialogue wherein both participants' utterances were unvarying and familiar. Four utterance types were observed in the output of mothers in this study: request for attention (e.g., *Look*), What-questions (e.g., *What's that?*), labeling of the picture, and feedback (e.g., *yes*). When more than one utterance type was included in a conversational cycle, the typical order of appearance was *Look*, *What's that?*, followed by labeling of the picture.

Ninio and Bruner also described mothers' feedback to their children as it changed over time. The child's language abilities seemed particularly influential. For example, once a child began to use meaningful words, the mother corrected any error in labeling. In 80% of the cycles, mothers acknowledged correct labeling at least once. Ninio and Bruner found a preferential order in labeling behavior. Children most often provided a label when the cycle was self-initiated, less frequently in response to *What's that?* and *Look*, and least often when mothers provided the label themselves.

The primary caretaker's role in supporting and extending the child's behavior through routines has been termed "scaffolding" by Bruner and his colleagues (Bruner, 1978; Ninio & Bruner, 1978; Ratner & Bruner, 1978). Scaffolding occurs as the child and caretaker engage in a joint interaction with a common focus, within a narrow context. Routines are thus viewed as an ideal framework within which to learn language and language use.

Turn-taking obviously involves mutual exchange. Moreover, younger children must refine their turn-taking skills through developmental interaction (Ervin-Tripp, 1979). Lieven (1978a) has suggested that the amount, type and scope of mothers' turn-taking behavior may directly influence child language learning. In observing three mothers and their 17- to 19-month-old daughters, over a period of 7 to 12 months, Lieven found that at the earliest ages very little turn-taking occurred. As the children advanced in age, the amount of turn-taking varied among the dyads. In one dyad, both participants contributed often to the sharing of turns. In another, the child began to take more turns than the mother. And in the third, minimal increments in turn-taking were observed for either participant. Lieven's findings led to the suggestion that turn-taking patterns may enhance the child's capacity to use language in a coherent, organized fashion.

Children also learn to make their conversational turns contingent on preceding adult utterances. Bloom, Rocissano, and Hood (1976) studied this longitudinal development in four children from 21 to 36 months of age. Throughout this period, children's utterances most often were immediately preceded by an adult utterance (i.e., adjacent). With increasing age, children's utterances became increasingly contingent on the content of the preceding adult utterance. That is, children's ability to respond on topic (with or without the inclusion of new information) improved with age. Through interactions with primary caretakers, therefore, children became better able to use information from the adult to form their own contingent response.

Conversations with primary caretakers may also provide children with information that enables them to progress from here-and-now discussions. Sachs (1977a, 1979) analyzed data obtained from interactions of two parents and their child (17 to 36 months of age). These parents seemed to introduce topics unrelated to the immediate context in a systematic way: first in less abstract terms, as in discussion of an absent family member; and later with greater abstraction, as in reviewing the past day's events. By 36 months of age, the child participated actively in discussions of nonpresent objects and/or past events, although the child infrequently initiated these topics. Based on these observations, Sachs suggested that parents structure conversations to allow for effective child participation and to provide opportunities for the child to acquire new forms.

Scollon (1979) discussed the potential influence of interaction on the child's acquisition of syntax. From observations of a child during the single word period of development, Scollon described four types of *vertical constructions* which were produced prior to the use of *horizontal constructions*. The vertical constructions occurred during conversations with the experimenter whose input helped to provide the child with a display of the undeveloped horizontal construction. In one example cited by Scollon, the child is "reading" to him from a book of pictures. The following dialogue ensues:

> Child: cook.
>   say.
> Experimenter: What'd the cook say?
> Child: something. (p. 219).

Scollon proposed the notion that through such conversational exchanges, children sequentially (vertically) encode three units that can later be combined to produce a horizontal syntactic construction (in this case, *cook say something*).

Children's nonverbal behaviors may also affect the conversational exchange and the information received. Messer (1978), for instance, found that when children manipulated a toy, mothers were most likely to make reference to it. In addition, mothers' reference was most often associated with actions that might include joint attention to the toy. In this way, children receive information about objects when attention is focused on the objects.

Bohannon and Marquis (1977) studied the effects of children's comprehension on the linguistic complexity of utterances addressed to them. Adults were found to reduce the length of their utterances in successive steps when they addressed an imaginary child, a child who signaled comprehension, and a child who signaled lack of comprehension. These authors concluded that through comprehension feedback, children may affect the complexity of their linguistic environments.

Conversely, children's world knowledge may mask their lack of comprehension. Shatz (1978) looked at children's comprehension of their mothers' question-directives. Shatz found that children between the ages of 1;7 and 2;4 responded with action to requests for action, regardless of the complexity of the request (e.g., direct or indirect). Shatz cautioned that these findings should not be interpreted to indicate comprehension of indirect requests on the part of the young child. Rather, it seems more likely that children in this age range most often respond with action to any utterance addressed to them, regardless of the form the utterance takes.

This review of input studies focused on interactions with children who were judged to be developing normally. Other writings have been concerned with interactions between primary caretakers and children who are language disordered, hearing impaired or blind. In a few studies, the primary caretaker is blind or deaf and the child has the assumed potential for normal development. Each of these areas of investigation has provided additional insights into the reciprocal nature of child-caretaker interaction.

Several studies have compared the language behavior of mothers of normally developing children and mothers of language disordered children (Buium, Rynders, & Turnure, 1974; Lasky & Klopp, 1982; Newhoff, Silverman, & Millet, 1980; Siegel, Cunningham, & van der Spuy, 1979; Wulbert, Inglis, Kriegsmann, & Mills, 1975). Even when children in these studies have been matched for MLU, mothers of language disordered children generally have been observed to provide less facilitative linguistic environments. That is, mothers of language disordered children are more direct and controlling, they relate fewer responses to their children's immediately preceding utterance, and they respond less often to their children's focus of attention. Methodologies have varied considerably, however, with varying degrees of control for the child's comprehension and production levels. Although no known attempt has been made to observe or categorize maternal conversational styles in speech to language disordered children, it has generally been assumed that the child's reduced intelligibility and lack of conversational responsiveness, as well as a history of unrewarding interaction, contribute to observed differences. Recently, it has been demonstrated that language disordered children do not show mastery of many of the linguistic structures that appear in the productions of normal language learners of the same MLU (Johnston & Kamhi, 1980). Moreover, some language disordered children may be deficient in certain dimensions of conversational competence (see, for example, Fey & Leonard, 1983). Mothers, therefore, are required to participate in conversations with children whose language may be deviant in both syntactic and pragmatic domains. How these differences directly affect maternal language remains to be demonstrated.

Hearing mothers of deaf children have also been found to exhibit interactional styles less favorable to the development of language. Goss (1970) compared mothers' conversations with hearing children to interactions with severely to profoundly hearing impaired children. Results indicated that mothers of hearing children used more questions, solicited opinions more often, and tended to agree more frequently with their children. On the other hand, mothers of hearing impaired children showed more disagreement and "antagonism," and made suggestions more often than mothers of hearing children.

In a similar vein, Meadow, Schlesinger, and Holstein (1972) observed mothers of deaf children who were judged to be "high communicators" and "low communicators," and compared these observations to data on mothers of hearing children. From their results, Meadow et al. suggested that the parent-child interaction is adversely affected when the child is deaf and the mother is not. Additionally, interactions of mothers with deaf children judged to be low communicators seemed to be the most affected. In these dyads, mothers appeared to be more controlling, disapproving, didactic, and inflexible. The children in the dyads were described as less compliant and creative (cf. Greenberg, 1980). In a later study, Lee (1978) supported the observations of Meadow et al. Moreover, Lee found that, over time, the interactional style of mothers of high communicating deaf children became more like that of mothers of hearing children. Lee also suggested that this interactional style was a factor in promoting communication competence in these deaf children.

Fraiberg (1977), in her longitudinal study of 10 blind children, discussed the difficulty mothers have in maintaining a normal interactional style with these children. Responses which might be elicited by sighted children's signs of discrimination, preference, and valuation are limited due to the absence of mutual gaze. According to Fraiberg, it is at first difficult for primary caretakers to recognize the blind child's unique need for tactile intimacy or to acknowledge their own inadequacy in interpreting the child's "alien sign vocabulary."

When the caretaker is blind and the infant sighted, a disruption in prelinguistic interactional patterns might also be expected, but this does not appear to be the case. For instance, in one investigation, an infant (2 to 20 weeks of age) was videotaped during interactions with her blind mother (Brazelton, Tronick, Adamson, Als, & Wise, 1975). Observations indicated that the facial unresponsiveness of the mother initially interfered with early interaction. The infant searched the mother's face and, receiving no mutual gaze, averted her own. However, by the time the child reached 8 weeks of age, Brazelton et al. reported that a mutually satisfying interaction had developed through other modalities.

Thus far in this section we have concentrated on the child as a social interactor, beginning at birth and continuing into the earliest periods of language acquisition. We have discussed some proposed explanations of language development through interactions with primary caretakers. It is a recognized fact, however, that variation exists among children in the acquisition strategies they employ. And recent investigators have posited variations in the conversational styles of children and of their primary caretakers. It seems likely that the reciprocal nature of interaction, as well as the potential benefits to language learning, may be influenced by such variation.

It's Just a Matter of Style

Both intra- and inter-subject variation have been described in children's language learning styles. For instance, some children show a preference for the use of pronouns in their earliest multiword utterances, while others seem to prefer nouns (Bloom, Lightbown, & Hood, 1975). When Eve and Sarah were at comparable language stages, Brown et al. (1969) observed that Eve's speech contained a larger proportion of contentives. Sarah, on the other hand, had fewer errors in marking grammatical distinctions, such as number. Nelson (1973) noted that during early lexical development, some children demonstrate a preference for referential words, while others prefer personal-social lexemes. And Bloom (1970) discussed the different strategies Eric, Kathryn, and Gia applied to their language learning.

Children also appear to develop strategies for dealing with their inadequacies as conversational partners. Sacks (1974) observed that in an attempt to gain the attention of a reluctant adult, 3-year-old children use conversational openers, such as *You know what, Daddy?* French and Woll (1981) noted that such questions require a question response (e.g., *What?*), which serves to return the conversational floor to the child. Children may also initiate such an interaction with an utterance which constrains the adult to seek clarification. Once clarification is sought, it is once again the child's turn. Children who are capable of applying these strategies seem to have some knowledge of conversational rules.

Primary caretakers use different interactional styles in different contexts. For example, Blount and Kempton (1976) described three distinct parental strategies employed during interactions with children 8 to 22 months of age. An affective interactional strategy was used for the initiation of exchange, a didactic strategy served to focus the child on speech as an activity, and a semantic strategy attributed meaning to the child's utterances and to the activity.

Variation in parental requesting behavior was observed by Bridges, Sinha, and Walkerdine (1981). Caretakers used *presequences* to denote the conversational topic before the request was verbalized. At other times, caretakers made their request and then followed it with additional information to help identify the response expected from the child. Clues about the use, physical properties, or location of requested objects were also provided by caretakers. In each instance, according to Bridges et al., caretakers were applying strategies that would ensure comprehension and elicit interaction on the part of the child.

McDonald and Pien (1982) found that mothers' conversational behaviors tended to co-vary in two negatively related clusters. This variation seemed to be in response to two underlying interactional purposes: to elicit conversational participation from the child and to control or direct the physical behavior of the child. The former purpose was manifested in the use of low-constraint question types and brief conversational turns, while the latter purpose was reflected in the mothers' use of directives, attention devices, and monologues. The findings of McDonald and Pien did not, however, confirm hypotheses that mothers show stability across interactions in focusing on one or the other of these purposes.

Lieven (1978a) also noted substantial differences in the number of conversational turns taken by three mothers she observed. In another report, Lieven (1978b) described significant differences in two mother-child dyads followed over a 6-month period. One child's mother responded more frequently and used a greater number of expansions and extensions. Other features of simplification were not different. However, Lieven found major differences in the children's linguistic styles, in spite of their similar MLUs. One child was highly repetitive, frequently producing notice relations and utterances designed to obtain the mother's attention. The second child, whose mother was more responsive and informative, spoke more slowly and clearly about objects in her environment and used more utterances which referred to locative action or attribution. These variations serve to underscore the reciprocal nature of child-caretaker interactions.

Based on the initial work of McDonald and Pien (1982), Olsen-Fulero (1982) studied the style and stability of 11 mothers' speech to children in the age range of 2:5 to 3:0. Two experimental sessions were conducted 2 to 7 days apart. Mothers' conversational behaviors in the two sessions were compared on the basis of various categories of communicative intent. They were not found to vary significantly from one session to the next. Mothers could be differentiated, however, on the basis of style.

Two general categories of conversational influence were identified: mothers were influential through social interaction or through tutorial interaction. The socially interactive mothers were further categorized as directive, conversational, or intrusive. *Directive* mothers did not seem to focus on the verbal participation of the child. A large proportion of their input utterances (49%) either elicited or provided feedback for the physical actions of their children. These mothers provided directive prompts and attentional devices to ensure their child's attention; they spoke in monologues, with a low proportion of real and verbal-reflective questions.[4] Conversely, *conversational* mothers used a large proportion of real (48%) and verbal-reflective (45%) questions in order to pass conversational turns to their children. The content of the interactions did not seem to be a high priority for these mothers; rather, maintaining a conversation seemed most important. *Intrusive* mothers used a combination of the directive and conversational styles. Their speech was characterized by elicitation of conversational participation from their children and by linguistic devices to ensure compliance. These mothers were described by Olsen-Fulero as "nonstop talkers" whose total attention was focused on their children.

Tutorial mothers were generally *didactic* in their conversational style. These mothers talked little, rarely produced monologues, and in general avoided dominating the interaction. Only one third of their responses were questions and, of these, 73% were real or test questions. Therefore, didactic mothers implemented a conversational style which seemed to instruct their children and guide their thoughts. Neither elicitation of conversation nor direction of physical actions seemed important to these mothers. They appeared to be concerned with the content of the interaction, and in this sense, their conversations with their children resembled more closely adult-adult interchanges. The use of a large proportion of declaratives supported this notion.

Olsen-Fulero referred to one mother's speech style as "the exception." Her style seemed to incorporate a variety of characteristics of the other maternal conversation styles. She was like the didactic mothers in that she appeared unmotivated to elicit conversational participation or to direct physical activity. Her intensity and involvement in the interaction (i.e., amount of speech) were much like the intrusive mothers'. Although many declaratives and acknowledgments were utilized, there were few test or real questions. Unlike the input of didactic mothers, this mother's speech to her child would not be similar to the speech addressed to another adult. More information on the language levels and conversational styles of the children in this study would be helpful in speculations concerning reciprocity of interaction. Olsen-Fulero's study, and the resultant categorizations of style, however, represent important forward steps in further delineating variation among caretakers' communication styles.

Howe (1981) applied a rigorous methodology in her observations of 24 mother-child dyads videotaped 6 months apart (1:6 to 1:8 and 1:11 to 2:1). Interactions occurred in highly similar surroundings for all dyads and at both time periods. Howe applied a narrow definition of conversation: each participant in the dyad had to be addressing the other directly, with the dialogue centering around a request for information or a response to such a request. Howe omitted any nonconforming utterances, such as those used to direct behavior, and further stipulated that a request for information had to receive a response in order to be included in the data. In her analyses, Howe identified three maternal interaction styles. *Excursive* mothers initiated exchanges less frequently than other mothers and provided a moderate number of extended replies to their children's initiations. *Recursive* mothers, on the other hand, produced a high frequency of self-initiated utterances but provided few extended replies to their children's utterances. *Discursive* mothers initiated requests often and frequently replied to their children's productions in an extended fashion. Whether stability among these mothers would be found across other types of interaction sequences is unknown. Based on the work of Olsen-Fulero, however, it seems probable that it would be.

A review of recent research suggests that adult strategies for interaction with children vary both within and among primary caretakers. There is also variation in the conversational strategies of children, who are viewed as equal contributors to the nature of the interaction. Why such variations exist may never be adequately documented. The reasons are probably as diverse as those factors that contribute to diversity among personality types. However, it may be assumed that cultural beliefs and expectations will account for some of the language behavior observed. The relationship between societal expectations and language input/acquisition have been addressed in cross-cultural research.

Dancing to a Different Tune:
Cross-Cultural Studies

There have been three basic approaches to the investigation of the speech style adjustments which characterize input to young children across a variety of languages: (1) a descriptive approach, noting primarily affective and paralinguistic features, such as alteration in rate and intonation and the appearance of special "baby talk" words; (2) more detailed and systematic approaches, describing input modifications in linguistic terms; and (3) approaches which examine input within a larger context, in terms of cultural transmission and language socialization. Each approach fosters different hypotheses about the role and function of the speech modifications addressed to young children. For example, modifications may be made to attract and maintain children's attention; to convey affect; to direct children's attention to speech as an activity; to relate speech to the environment in meaningful, referential ways; to teach the lexicon, morphology, and syntax of the language; to facilitate appropriate, contextual language use; and/or to "enculturate" children so that they assume the expected attitudes, beliefs, and status roles within their cultural group or society. All three approaches continue to appear in the input literature, but the focus here will be on studies oriented toward linguistic and ethnographic description.

Studies of Input Structure

Some very early anthropological studies compared child-directed input to standard adult forms in languages such as Nootka (Sapir, 1929) and Comanche (Casagrande, 1948). Somewhat later, Ferguson (1964) summarized a description of "baby talk" in six languages (Syrian Arabic, Marathi, Comanche, Gilyak, Spanish, and American English). Ferguson found structural similarities in the modifications which appeared across languages and cultures. Subsequently, with a larger sample of languages, Ferguson (1977) noted that the processes of modification (e.g., simplification, reduction, and redundancy) are common to a variety of speech communities, and some linguistic features tend to occur regularly across societies. In fact, Bynon (1968), in studying a Berber tribe of Central Morocco, suggested that the existence of a special set of speech forms for talking to young children is so widespread, even across historically unrelated societies, that it may actually be a linguistic universal.

A variety of structural elements has been examined in cross-cultural studies. For example, Rūke-Draviṇa (1977) looked at Latvian input in terms of paralinguistic, phonological, morphological, lexical, and syntactic features. In comparing the Latvian data to input in Lithuanian, Polish, and Russian, Rūke-Draviņa found similar structural elements, but differences in phonetic inventory and semantic relations.

Blount and his colleagues (Blount & Kempton, 1976; Blount & Padgug, 1977) compared English and Spanish input in terms of 34 paralinguistic, prosodic, and interactional features. Although they found a high degree of similarity across parents and languages, they noted several discrepancies that were attributed to differences in cultural style of interaction. English-speaking parents seemed to rely more heavily on affective input, particularly in relation to paralinguistic features, whereas Spanish-speaking parents appeared to be more directly interaction-oriented, more frequently employing attention-getting devices, repetition and instruction. The initiation and maintenance of interaction were viewed as the focus of activity in both cultures, but the role or response of the child was not specified.

Some researchers postulated that the structure of input has a direct effect on child language acquisition. However, as in the English language literature (see previous discussion), the cross-cultural studies have yielded inconsistent results. For example, Klein (1974) noted that, in Dutch, children's productions mirrored the word order preferences of their mothers. On the other hand, Savić (1978) found that the order in which Serbo-Croatian-speaking adults asked their children different types of questions did not correspond to the order in which those questions appeared in the children's speech. The effect of structural input modifications on children's acquisition of the formal devices of their language has yet to be definitively determined.

One unique area of cross-linguistic investigation also crosses language modality, and it relates to a defined subculture of American society. Research in this area focuses on the acquisition of American Sign Language (ASL) as a first, native language by deaf children of deaf parents. In the studies conducted by Maestas y Moores (1980) and Launer (1982a, 1982b) ASL input modifications paralleled those described for spoken languages, particularly in terms of simplicity and redundancy. In addition, deaf parents, like their hearing counterparts, employed certain strategies aimed at communicative effectiveness in addressing an infant (e.g., positioning themselves to maximize attention; interspersing nonvocal affective acts with language acts; and using alternate or simultaneous sensory modalities). However, there were several features of ASL input which seemed to be modality-specific.

In sign language, the articulators are visible and manipulable, and this provides for certain input strategies that are unavailable in spoken language. For example, the following were observed in the aforementioned ASL input studies: signing on the body of the infant or placing the infant's hands on the parent's body to form signs; molding or physical guidance of the child's hands to form movement patterns and/or hand configurations; or using objects in the environment as part of the actual sign.

In spoken languages, for example English and Spanish, exaggerated intonation is often cited as a feature of input to young children. The sign language counterpart seems to be exaggerated size. Another common feature of input is the repetition of lexical items and whole utterances. This occurs in ASL, as in spoken language, but in ASL input there is also multiple repetition of the movement *within* a given sign.

A fundamental difference between ASL and spoken languages is the extent of transparency or iconicity, that is, the resemblance between a form and what it denotes. Iconicity pervades all levels of ASL (lexical, morphological, syntactic, discourse). In their input to young children, deaf parents might be expected to exploit this direct method of representing meaning through form but, in fact, Launer (1982a) found that this occurred in only 8% of all sign tokens addressed to two deaf children under 2 years of age.[5] Launer described the input and acquisition of one special set of nouns and verbs in ASL, pairs that are related in both meaning and form. She found that, in their input to children under 2 years of age, mothers obliterated the particular morphological features which distinguish nouns from verbs, thereby producing ungrammatical forms that were neither noun nor verb, nor were they possible forms in the adult language. The deaf children's early productions of related nouns and verbs were also devoid of the morphological markers. Somewhat later, the children began to distinguish nouns and verbs in "non-canonical" or idiosyncratic ways. In terms of this one derivational process, then, deaf parents did not seem to be concerned with providing an accurate morphological model in their early input. Perhaps they intuitively felt that the young children could not perceive or produce these fine movement distinctions, or in the interest of maintaining attention and conversational interaction, they merely presented the global shape or *essence* of signs, without regard to the particular morphological details.

Most studies of spoken language input avoid any mention of ungrammatical forms, or note that they rarely, if ever, occur (Blount & Padgug, 1977; Newport et al., 1977). However, one observation comparable to the ASL finding comes from Bynon (1977). In his investigation of Berber nursery words, deletion was the most frequent derivational process in the proposed formation of baby talk. When this process is applied, there may be "loss of all exponents of grammaticality so that the baby talk word is marked neither for gender nor for number nor for the opposition definite/indefinite; grammatical meaning is, in fact, totally eliminated" (p. 263).

Whether input is well-formed or ungrammatical, children do not necessarily replicate the forms addressed to them. What may be simple or salient to the adult may not be so to the child. In discussing the acquisition of ASL, Bellugi and Klima (1982) have suggested that, regardless of the modality of a language or its apparent directness of representation, or, we might add, the structural particulars of the input model, children seem to perform their own analysis of the discrete components of the system and to acquire language in a rapid, patterned, and "linguistically-driven" manner.

Launer's (1982a) findings are consistent with this view (cf. Meier, 1982). Additional supportive evidence comes from Ingham's (1978) study of the acquisition of Persian. Ingham observed that certain morphological structures produced by the child did not occur in adult speech. These forms were considered to be "linguistic creations" that resulted from the child's analysis of the adult language. In this type of data, child output does not match adult input.

Caretaker input to young children may include phonological, lexical, morphological, and/or syntactic adaptations. The underpinnings and the effects of these structural variations are not yet clear, but perhaps they should be viewed in relation to the cultural variations that may influence the organization and systematic use of verbal and nonverbal communication. As an example of this type of orientation, Jocić (1978) suggested that, in terms of the morphological and syntactic adaptations in child-directed Serbo-Croatian, the bases for the changes and differences were in the emotional relationship between child and adult. That is, the stronger the emotional tie, or the more the adult cares for the child, the more frequent are the grammatical adaptations in adult speech. In this view, input modifications are produced in relation to the child's interactive environment and the culture or society in which it exists. These are basic tenets of the ethnographic approach to the study of language.

Ethnographic Studies

Systematic cross-cultural research on socialization is a recent phenomenon in studies of child development. The early investigations did not include language as a product of socialization or as an integral part of the socialization process. Hymes (1961) was the first anthropologist to point out the paucity of research on language socialization. Hymes noted that the acquisition of communication skills is basically a social phenomenon that requires social interaction. Gumperz and Hymes (1964) labeled the research approach that developed from ethnography and sociolinguistics the "ethnography of communication." In this approach, emphasis is placed on interaction in the study of child language, with stress on the description of communicative competence, which is assumed to underlie language use.

The first group to look at language acquisition within the broader context of social and cultural learning was composed of linguists, psycholinguists, and anthropologists. The addition of anthropologists to the study of language development led to a focus on the cultural organization of inter-action and interactive environments. The Berkeley group, a cross-disciplinary assemblage of researchers, proposed guidelines for investigating grammatical development, language use in social context, and belief systems surrounding language socialization. These guidelines appeared as *The Field Manual for Cross-Cultural Study of the Acquisition of Communicative Competence* (Slobin, Ervin-Tripp, & Gumperz, 1967). However, once the field work was initiated, several of the basic assumptions of the group were called into question, as Brukman (1973) pointed out in summarizing the observations made in Kenya, India, and Samoa. First, mothers were not found to be the primary caretakers or providers of input in all cultures. In the Luo, Koya, and Samoan societies, primary socialization was distributed among a variety of kin and non-kin interactors. Second, it was not found, as had been anticipated, that caretakers were responsive to children's language errors. In these societies, there was virtually no attention to the correctness of children's linguistic structures; instead, it was the social appropriateness of children's speech that took precedence. Schieffelin (1979) observed that, despite the initial intentions of the Berkeley group, the three components of language acquisition (i.e., the grammatical rules, the use of language in context, and the cultural belief system) were nonetheless studied individually rather than holistically in the earlier investigations.

Geertz (1973) suggested that an ethnographic approach is a "thick description" that should include detailed observations from the viewpoint of the outside observer, as well as data on the significance of the events observed from the viewpoint of the participants. Therefore, in her ethnographic study of Papua, New Guinea and the Kaluli people, Geertz determined, by means of observation and adult interviews, the significant situations and interactions that recurred in the child's everyday life. This information was then used to select the most appropriate contexts and situations in which to collect interactional data. Geertz also ascertained the cultural belief systems relating to child development, childrearing practices, and language and sex role socialization. Similarly, Corsaro's (1979) ethnographic approach to childhood socialization (interactions of three English-speaking children with parents, peers, and the experimenter) was an attempt to generate theory from the data, not to verify a deductive theory. In his study of communicative functions, Corsaro remarked on the controlling nature of adult language. He proposed the notion that the features of adult interactional style are a reflection of the communicative demands placed on adults when interacting with young children who cannot yet completely fulfill the requirements of their conversational role. Corsaro observed that adults try to transform any particular interactive event into a learning experience of more general social significance from the adult's perspective.

Schieffelin and Eisenberg (in press) also noted that the beliefs held by adults in a society influence and pattern the types of interactions fostered with young children. Therefore, the social organization of any culture determines how children learn their roles in verbal interaction and the appropriate use of their native language. That is, language is acquired in the context of the culture. According to Schieffelin and Eisenberg, a variety of interrelated cultural and social factors contribute to the structure and function of child-adult conversations. In particular, there will be cross-cultural differences dependent upon the following factors: the identity and role of caretakers; societal ideas about how children learn to speak; the behaviors presumed to indicate child comprehension and the development of production skills; the age at which the child is thought to be a co-conversationalist; the amount of verbal interaction between children and adults; the appropriate topics of conversation between children and adults; who is considered to be responsible for initiating and maintaining conversation during interaction; the social role accorded to children in society; the rules for turn-taking and interruption; the repertoire of speech acts expected of children and caretakers; politeness conventions and the range of direct/indirect approaches; and the nonverbal aspects of communication. In the studies conducted from an ethnographic or sociolinguistic perspective, a number of these distinguishing features have been linked to observed cross-cultural differences in language input, acquisition, and interaction.

Societal Factors Related to Cross-Cultural Differences

Societies have been found to differ in terms of the person(s) who assumes the caretaking responsibility for the child. In middle-class America, the primary caretaker is usually the mother or another female adult. In other cultures, it may be the extended family, or older children, or peer groups. For instance, in the studies of Luo society (Blount, 1972, 1977) the mother is initially the primary caretaker, but by the time the infant reaches 10 to 12 months of age, the responsibility has been delegated to a nursemaid, a boy or girl age 5 to 12 years. By 18 to 20 months of age, the child is almost exclusively in the company and care of other children, with increasing social distance from adults. According to Blount (1977), this distance fosters the acquisition of deferential speech.

It has been suggested that older children do not interact with young children in the same way that adults do. For example, Blount (1972) noted that older Luo children were less likely to use baby talk features in their input to younger children and they were more demanding of actual words in child production as well, rejecting any baby talk. Moreover, older siblings refused to imitate the utterances of younger children and did not respond to their babbling.

Harkness (1977), in her studies of a Kipsigis community in Kenya, also found differences between mothers' and children's speech to babies. The mothers' input included a higher MLU, greater linguistic complexity, more question-asking behavior, and more continuous dialogue than in child-child interactions, which generally consisted of intermittent dialogue based on statements rather than questions. Harkness contended that there may be a variety of optimum styles of communication for different classes of speakers addressing young children. She noted that the higher rate of verbal interaction between adults and young children seems to lead to more rapid language acquisition, but the input of older children can also have a positive impact on the young child's language.

There may also be variations in acquisition relating to the number of people involved in the young child's everyday interaction. Dyadic communication, for example, demands different attention-getting and turn-taking patterns from group interactions where the child is not the primary focus (Schieffelin & Eisenberg, in press). It seems, then, that what children learn relates to the age and relationship of the primary caretaker. Another factor is the perceived role or status of the child in the society. This role definition can determine what the child is expected or permitted to say in certain interactions.

In America, children are generally accorded the status of conversational peers. Adults seem to consider it important to elicit speech from children and to foster socialization through production and interaction; this is also true of the Kaluli in Papua, New Guinea (Schieffelin, 1979). In other societies, such as Luo and Samoan (Blount, 1972) and rural Louisiana Blacks (Ward, 1971), there may be a hierarchical relationship between adult and child. The adult may assume a superordinate position in the interaction, serving as the initiator, and the child may be encouraged to be quiet and to speak only when spoken to. In the Luo and Samoan data (Blount, 1977), there was a large percentage of commands and questions, but none of the yes/no questions which elicit preference responses from children. In Black English input, there were more yes/no questions, and children were given choices which reinforced their roles as conversational equals

(Blount, 1972). Buium (1976) found similar variations in the question-asking behavior of Israeli and American parents. In Hebrew input, there was a greater proportion of WH-questions which seemed to place the burden of interaction on the child; in English, as in Blount's Black English data, there were more yes/no questions. Wooton (1974) found that in middle and working class American families, where the child was treated as a conversational equal, adults solicited information about the child's internal states. In Kipsigis, however, mothers seem to socialize their children through silence, with infrequent use of grammatical forms designed to elicit speech (Harkness & Super, 1977). In a western Samoan village, where young children have the lowest status, Ochs (1980) found that children are neither expected nor encouraged to initiate topics of conversation. Among rural Louisiana Blacks, there is greater value placed on child comprehension than production; caretakers frequently expand their own utterances rather than expanding the child's speech (Ward, 1971).

Fischer (1970) noted some fundamental differences between Japanese and American attitudes toward social position of the child. Although both are considered to be *child-centered* societies, there is more of a hierarchical adult-child status in Japan. Japanese caretakers do not discourage speech in children, but they talk less to their children than do American mothers, and the children talk later. Further, Japanese mothers emphasize nonverbal communication, and they tend to anticipate the child's needs before they are verbalized. Japanese mothers use more baby talk than Americans in their input. They also allow its use for longer periods in children, often well into the school years, thus permitting children to extend their child status.

Other cultural biases may contribute to the child's social status. For instance, in the Kenyan Kipsigis community, Harkness (1977) observed that the amount of attention devoted to young children was determined by birth order. Single children or last-born children were provided with more play, more talk, and more general interactions with adults; they also exhibited advanced linguistic development.

Thus, the status of children and their allocated social positions within a given society seem to affect the nature of adult-child interactions. It appears that cultural definitions of social position determine the form of speech addressed to young children and serve to regulate what is expected of children, as well as what the forms and functions of interaction should be.

There are also cultural differences in terms of beliefs about language acquisition. In Kaluli, for example, adults feel that children must be taught to speak, especially by the mother (Schieffelin, 1979). There is no special baby talk lexicon, but mothers involve infants in dialogues with themselves and others, speaking for the child in a high nasal voice register and moving the child as if he or she were conversing. Kaluli children are taught social, linguistic, and discourse routines by imitation.

As mentioned earlier, Gleason and Weintraub (1975) observed that middle class American mothers teach routines (e.g., *bye-bye*, *say thank you*). English-speaking children are often provided with direct (cultural) instruction in terms of labeling, discussing past events, and describing the pictures in storybooks. Luo caretakers also teach important lexical items, with particular focus on names and labels which the child repeats after the child-nursemaid (Blount, 1972).

On the other hand, in the Kipsigis community, it is believed that children learn to talk on their own, but they must be taught to understand requests and commands. These forms, in addition to prohibitions, appear most frequently in input to young children (Harkness & Super, 1977). Again, in terms of cultural beliefs, language input, acquisition, and use are a part of interactional relationships; language is viewed as a social skill, not just a verbal skill.

Blount (1977) suggested that the primary task of ethnographic research on language socialization is to identify the culturally-defined categories for assessing the child's interactional capacities and overall competence. Blount sees terminology as one source of evidence, noting, for example, the socialization categories in white America (infant, baby, toddler, child, preschooler) with additions from Black culture (lap baby). Each of these categories carries associated expectations for parental behavior and speech adjustments. Blount noted that a given society's view of children can also be determined by how it identifies and responds to particular developmental milestones, such as the appearance of the child's first words. In Luo, this development is accompanied by a considerable decrease in the number and frequency of baby talk features in parent input (Blount, 1972). Among the Kaluli, language is only considered to have begun if two specific lexical items appear (the words for *mother* and *breast*). Schieffelin (1979) interpreted this observation in terms of the social view of language taken by Kaluli, since it underscores the importance of learning particular words pertaining to the child's first social relationship. Schieffelin notes that "while Western researchers have often separated linguistic competence from social competence, these two phenomena are perceived and evaluated by the Kaluli as one thing" (p. 86).

It seems that in more societies than the Kaluli, social settings and relationships are not independent of language. In all cultures, children gain their linguistic knowledge through social interaction. The alterations in adult and child input to young children vary according to the child's level of development. Caretakers may be modifying their input on the basis of the child's linguistic capacity, but as Blount (1977) suggested, there must be more than that since caretakers generally seem to exhibit minimal interest in linguistic technicalities. It appears that caretakers primarily attend to the child's ability to communicate, assessing overall competence in relation to culturally-defined categories which are based on stages of overall development. These categories seem to be societally-specific. Therefore, in studying the contexts of language acquisition and the child's development of communicative competence, cultural factors should be considered. Cross-cultural research is extremely enlightening; it provides us with insights into the societal influence on language use and the acquisition of linguistic and interactional skills.

An Upbeat Ending

Although we have amassed a great deal of data, it is still largely unknown how the development of language is influenced by children's myriad social/verbal interactions. However, the paths taken to reach this goal continue to be a worthy concern for researchers in the area of child language acquisition.

We have attempted to demonstrate that, regardless of interactional styles of caretakers, or differences in language, or societal and cultural expectations, children do become proficient speakers of their native language. Rather inconsistent results have been obtained from studies dealing with the influence of input on syntactic and semantic acquisition. But children do seem to learn the rules of language *use* through conversation. In the future, researchers may be able to delineate the ways in which specialized input, at particular moments, within specific contexts, may directly contribute to acquisition in the semantic and syntactic domains. We question, however, the justification for such a separatist approach.

Like many researchers before us, we proceed from the assumption that it is through interaction with the environment that socialization, cognition, and language are developed. Moreover, learning in one area most likely influences further development in the others. Where language acquisition is concerned, syntax, semantics, and pragmatics are likewise mutually influential. A holistic approach to the study of language learning, therefore, seems most appropriate. Such study can be accomplished through continued observation of children involved in environmental interchanges; these observations should be made both within and across cultures.

Throughout the past decade, as increasing information has become available, research methodologies for the study of child-caretaker interaction have been refined. We are still in the process of change, however, learning and benefiting from previous investigations. In this light, some additional design possibilities are offered.

Recent research has provided a range of hypotheses about variation in children's language learning styles. Although variation must be determined by overt language behaviors, children do seem to show individual differences in comprehension as well as production. Few studies have attempted to control for such variations. Before formulating theories of the child's influence on input modifications, it would seem to be important to document the child's comprehension and production levels. Descriptions of the child's general conversational style would also be enlightening in this regard.

Differences in caretakers' interactional styles have been noted. Prior to any investigation, categorization of caretaker *and* child styles of interaction could provide insights into the reciprocal influences of the child on the caretaker and/or the caretaker on the child. In this vein, a laboratory experiment might prove valuable. For example, in a cross-sectional study, mothers exhibiting various interactional styles would converse with different children who represent a variety of language levels and conversational styles. This approach might assist in identifying stylistic matches and mismatches, and in delineating which partner influences the other in conversational exchanges.

Most studies have concerned dyadic interactions, but many conversations occur with three or more participants present. It is unclear how the presence of additional persons of varying linguistic abilities might color the interaction of child and caretaker. Research endeavors with this point in mind could offer additional information about interactional styles and adjustments.

Interactional partners should also be followed over time, in a variety of contexts. We are still unsure of the effects of different child language levels on the interactional patterns of caretakers. Most studies focused on very early input. We do not yet know what changes might occur in conversations with children whose metalinguistic abilities are evolving. Will children then benefit from more tutorial interactions?

Earlier studies compared mothers' speech to children with that addressed to another adult, whereas later studies made comparisons among various child-caretaker dyads. Perhaps a combination of these approaches would facilitate understanding of the influence of the child on the caretaker's language. That is, interactions of child-caretaker dyads should be compared with caretaker-adult dyads on the conversational dimensions currently under study (e.g., speech acts and their linguistic correlates). The difficulty with such an approach, however, rests with the nature of the task from which comparisons are made. Obviously, adults engage in quite different activities with young children than they do with other adults.

Additional evidence concerning role expectations in various contexts would be discerned if similar contexts and topics could be designed.

Cross-cultural studies should continue to provide a more complete description of varying approaches to language acquisition and interaction. Both the similarities and the differences among cultures contribute to our global understanding of the unique human capacity for language. Moreover, cross-cultural studies allow for a clearer description of the manner in which context, assumed role or status of the participants, and beliefs about language learning influence conversational use.

Finally, we need to clarify and standardize the terminology used across disciplines in referring to conversations with children. Current references do not specifically reflect the variety of conversational partners with whom the child is interacting, nor the particular age of the child. It might be more fitting to focus on the child rather than the caretaker. Perhaps terms such as *Infant-Adapted-Communication (IAC), Toddler-Adapted-Communication (TAC), Preschool-Adapted-Communication (PAC),* and *School-Adapted-Communication (SAC)* could be used for interactions with children from birth to 1 year, 1 to 2 years, 2 to 4 years, and beyond 4 years of age, respectively.

In this type of terminological approach, the emphasis is appropriately placed on the interaction, and on the language adjustments for particular communicative partners, i.e., language learning children. Early in life, children pick up on societal rhythms. At first, they may miss a few beats and step on some toes, but eventually they master the local folk dance—language interaction in its cultural context.

Notes

[1] For a fuller account of the hypotheses governing the relationship of language to cognition, *see* Cromer, 1981; Karmiloff-Smith, 1979; Rice, 1980; Snyder, this volume.

[2] For a review of these earlier works, and others, *see* Blount and Padgug, 1977; Chapman, 1981; Snow and Ferguson, 1977.

[3] An even stronger position is offered by Trevarthen (1974), who holds that infants as young as 2 months of age are responsible for the direction of *conversations* with adults.

[4] Real questions are those for which the speaker does not have an answer. Verbal-reflective questions repeat, reduce, or paraphrase the listener's prior utterance (e.g., He does? It is? He does, doesn't he?).

[5] Comparable elaborations of the image base, i.e., highlighting iconicity, occurred in the deaf children's signs with greater frequency than in input; in child production, this represented 15% of all sign tokens appearing in the data collected during the period from 1 to 2 years of age.

Sandra McNew
Elizabeth Bates

Pragmatic Bases for Language Acquisition

Introduction

The question of how pragmatics interacts with syntax and semantics, the question of whether it has a central role in informing or interacting with these other linguistic domains or whether it simply represents syntactic and semantic "leftovers," and the question of what it takes for a full accounting of language acquisition are all open questions. The relevant data are not all in, and sometimes even the sorts of empirical questions that could be used to resolve such controversies have not been clear. In this chapter we would like to examine several domains of research on language development that could bear on these issues.

One relevant body of literature is that on processing universals or primitives. Developmentally, this literature deals with evidence for the conceptual or categorical bases or hypotheses that a child might have, need, or generate in attempts to organize and make eventual grammatical sense of the language stream. Some theories emphasize innate syntactic primitives such as *subject* and *verb*. Others emphasize more semantic and pragmatic organizing notions such as *agent* and *topic*, and there are other possibilities. We shall examine the empirical evidence supporting each contrasting type of primitive and process.

Another body of literature has not generally dealt directly with the issue of what the *child* brings to linguistic interaction; it has focused instead on what the *adult* brings. Dealing with qualities of language input that

© College-Hill Press, Inc. All rights, including that of translation, reserved. No part of this publication may be reproduced without the written permission of the publisher.

are pragmatically different from those occurring in language to adults, this body of literature has attempted to provide descriptions of the general restrictions on the range of input language that, more or less, all language learners receive. Recognition of some pragmatic differences between adult-adult talk and adult-child talk or "motherese" has led naturally to questions of if and how differences might be useful for language learners. These questions have not usually been addressed directly and empirically, primarily because there are very few children who are confronted with language that is not substantially different from adult-adult language—even if the speech they receive does not reach the full heights of which motherese is capable. Because of this, many researchers have turned to what is in fact a logically different sort of question. They have not asked what would happen if there were *no* motherese available to children or what would happen if children were exposed to language outside the normal range provided for language learners by the species. Instead, they have asked about the effects of environmental *variability* within the already restricted range of syntax, semantics, and pragmatics that motherese represents, and they have asked whether those individual differences in the dynamics and tailoring of linguistic interaction might facilitate acquisition rate. A few researchers have looked at the relatively rare cases in which children have received essentially no motherese. We shall be examining the results of these varying inquiries, their universality and what they can and cannot imply for the roles of syntax, pragmatics and semantics in acquisition.

Consider first the rationale behind the kind of theoretical approach and research domain that focuses on what the child brings to the language acquisition task. For those predisposed toward Kierkegaardian leaps of faith, it may seem intuitively reasonable that a child who has one major referent (e.g., who says "ball" in a particular context) can go on to use maternal expansions (like "oh, the ball rolled away") or other environmental input to figure out how to put two major sentence constituents like "ball" and "roll" together. Similarly, it may seem a simple matter for a child who produces "ball roll" to use expansions or to search for relevant linguistic instances to develop finer details of grammatical usage. But how does a child know on what basis to generalize from grammatical expansions which are given in the context of particular words to all of their appropriate contexts of use? What kinds of conceptual leaps is the child capable of? In what way does he or she come to know that "the" goes with "shoes" and all other nouns as well as "ball" and that "ed" goes with "jump" and other verbs as well as "roll"? In other words, how and when and by what process does he or she know to treat "ball" and "shoes" as instances of the same general category? And how does he or she decide when a verb should agree with "ball" and "shoes" and when it should not?

Many researchers working specifically on such problems, whether from a functionalist or a formalist perspective, have felt that the linguistic environment per se could not give children the basis for treating some words as instances of a particular class. This is because in some ways, as Pinker (1979) suggests, the problem of language acquisition is part of the more general problem of induction. Any finite data set, including parental language, could be conceptualized or organized by a recipient in many different ways; environments themselves do not simply provide regularity for an organism to capture. This is an obvious principle for researchers working in an ethological tradition with nonhuman species; they generally spend much of their time trying to establish the boundaries or limits to learning as these differ among species, and they have been particularly interested in the ways in which biological priming or preparedness allow specific connections among stimuli. For instance, for different species of songbirds, quite different sorts of initial organizing cues (e.g., auditory, visual, or social) determine which songs they will attend to and learn. And even that directed attention has some specific properties. Swamp sparrows seem to initially key in on syllables within songs, but only later develop an appreciation of their temporal patterning (Marler, Zoloth, & Dooling, 1981). Laughing gull chicks also organize their early behavior preferentially around quite provisional stimuli: a red spot on a simple background the width of an adult gull's beak is the functional stimulus for attempting to take food, although it is only a small part of the stimulus complex represented by adult gull heads. Within a few weeks, chicks develop a much finer appreciation of many of the elements of their parents' heads, and all of these are then required to elicit feeding behavior (Hailman, 1967). In other words, young organisms clearly capture and use quite specific, limited and changing *realities* from a multi-dimensional *objective reality* that could allow for alternate interpretations and conceptualizations.

In raising the general problem of induction, Pinker (1979) is really voicing the same kinds of concerns about biological preparedness for interpreting linguistic stimuli; he asks the important question of why and how language learning does not lead to infinite wild goose chases and generalization in every conceivable direction but rather to languages that are learned and learnable. Thus, he asks how a child's processing (or a learning space) might be constrained so that the child's grammar eventually conforms to that of his or her native language. In fact, although many researchers presumed and hoped that it would, the fact that the linguistic environment seems relatively tailored to the child in some ways does not automatically do away with the general problem that many researchers are trying to address: the bases on which children develop and generalize linguistic hypotheses. This is because one needs to specify the ways in which children use and interpret the input they receive, and not simply to characterize the input—if one is to have a process model of language acquisition. The precise nature of the useful interface between the child and her environment certainly remains to be established. Thus, we would like to briefly detail and contrast the varying approaches and evidence for processing constraints in the child, indicating the questions that remain open or problematic from each theoretical perspective.

We will consider three approaches that focus on biological preparation of the child in some depth. Proponents of the first approach propose that the child has a basic set of innate organizing constructs or hypotheses of a very abstract and specifically grammatical nature.

Other researchers, working within generally more cognitive and functionalist frames also address the question of how the child might actively organize the information the environment provides (e.g., Bates & MacWhinney, 1982). In other words, the latter researchers tend to be equally interested in biological preparedness and the relative constraints implied by the language channel. However, they ask what the role of more *psychological* and functional processing constraints and motives for language structure might be: evolutionarily, historically, developmentally, or in normal adult use. For instance, they suggest that more psychologically specifiable categories than the grammatical "subject" (e.g., animacy/agency and givenness vs. newness of information) might provide the organismic motives for using and making sense out of grammar, either for adults or for children in the acquisition process.

Still other researchers, exemplified here by Maratsos and Chalkley (1980) have quite different notions of the emergent properties of grammar. They do not see syntactic categories or relations as innate, nor do their models lead to necessarily universal syntactic categories or relations, as in many formalist models. But while they feel that it is only over the acquisition process that formal, grammatical categories do attain psychological reality, they are not entirely sympathetic to functionalist models. Instead they suggest that attention to formal detail and co-occurrences are critical in the acquisition process.

A necessarily partial and selective examination of these alternative models for class equivalence may lead us to some appreciation of the theoretical gaps and empirical questions that remain in specifying what the child brings to the language acquisition task. Armed with that appreciation, we will then attempt to describe what the restricted structure of the environment could add if it were to work in tandem with child capacities conforming to any of these visions.

Formal Models of Language Learning: Grammatical Primitives

The most successful formal model of the process of language acquisition (Hamburger & Wexler, 1975; Wexler, Culicover, & Hamburger, 1975) presumes that the child has simultaneous access to a linguistic input string and its meaning. This simultaneous access has some rather interesting properties. A sentence meaning is presumed to be represented by a tree or mobile structure that has the same hierarchical breakdown of constituents as the grammatical base structure of the sentence. However, the initial grammatical constituents in the base structure are not yet ordered in any particular way, as they must be in a transformational grammar. In other words, children begin with an automatic correspondence between the particular meaning elements that form the semantic structure and grammatical primitives such as subject, verb, and so forth. Since children recognize elements that correspond, but do not know how to use them grammatically, they must first establish the rules ordering the deep structures that define the languages being learned. Then children must figure out how their languages transform these syntactic base strings into the surface structures of questions, imperatives, and the like. Using two principles (the *binary* and the *freezing*) that we need not detail here, it can be logically proven that, by simply enumerating sets of possible transformations, children can eventually discover all the transformations used in a particular language and reject all others. In addition, children are able to do so on the basis of relatively few exemplars.

Unfortunately, although logically powerful, this formal model does not guarantee acquisition in the normal span. It is also doubtful that enumeration of all possible transformations within the group of natural languages is plausible as a learning mechanism; in addition to its presupposition that all possible rules are in some way known and simply must be retrieved and tested against input, simple enumeration does not seem to guarantee any particular order of rule hypothesizing. In other words, it does not deal with the effects of psychological qualities (i.e., the "grabbiness" of particular forms in particular languages) nor with apparent effects of frequency, confusability, recency, and the like. Yet it appears that children acquire their initial grammatical morphemes in rather well specified orders (R. Brown, 1973), within a given language. In a random enumeration procedure without additional constraints it would seem that hypotheses should be tested in rather random orders. It is thus not at all clear that this acquisition model can guarantee acquisition within the normal time span nor that it can do so in a manner that conforms to the developmental data.

The enumeration procedure does have the formal advantage that it logically guarantees that a child will *eventually* converge on the properties of his or her language and that a child could learn any language equally well. Pinker (1979) asserts that these are two quite important aspects of a language acquisition model; any procedure must encompass both guarantees of *learnability* and *equipotentiality* of the learning mechanism, such that it will allow learning of any natural language that the child might confront.

Yet a possible problem for the equipotentiality condition comes from the fact that the abstract entities or initial organizing principles postulated by this model are not as universally specifiable as initially hoped. For instance, *subject* does not appear to be criterially definable even in fully-formed adult language, across all languages (Keenan, 1976). If we are to say that all children use the same innate version of this grammatical relation to acquire their respective languages, it would be useful to have a clear specification of its essential nature. The approaches of various ergative languages to subject phenomenon have seemed to be particularly problematical, with their tendencies to treat what we would call intransitive subject and transitive *object* as a single morphological category and to distinguish intransitive subject from transitive subject—thus implicating a particularly obvious grammatical role for agency (Comrie, 1978; Dixon, 1979; Plank, 1979). Further, Li and Thompson (1976) have examined the relationship between the formal category subject and the more pragmatic category *topic*. Topics are, of course, linguistic specifications of what people are talking about or what they make comments about. In some languages like English, topics usually correspond to the formal category of subject. Other languages seem to give equal structural prominence to both the formal and the pragmatic category, and some show a relative or even complete neglect of subjects and concentrate on topics. This cross-linguistic evidence brings into question the notion that subjects are universal. If they are not, and the organizing notion they represent is not specifiable, a good deal of the psychological force behind the suggestion that they form children's universal first organizing principles is lost.

A second point about this model is that it presumes that every language has one grammar, and that all speakers must converge on exactly that grammar. This convergence seems to be the essence of the learnability notion; there is one thing that must be learned. Yet work by Gleitman and Gleitman (1970) seems to suggest that not all speakers of English do converge on the same grammar. Speakers' interpretations of fragments of English suggest that they share some core aspects of grammar, but that there is a large area of semi-grammaticality around this core. Only some speakers of English (undoubtedly including the class of all linguists and psycho-linguists) seem to have mastered this grammatical penumbra. Similarly, Bates, McNew, MacWhinney, Devescovi, and Smith (1982) have found that in interpreting simple fragments of language like "the cup ate the pig," about two-thirds of English speakers seem to use grammatical strategies while one-third use semantic and other organizing notions. Despite the fact that there may be some statistical biases toward a particular grammar in the group as a whole and that linguists may be able to formally characterize the domain of all acceptable English sentences, many speakers of English may not accommodate them by giving all aspects of that formal grammar full psychological status. This raises the possibility that the concept of universal attainment on which learnability is based is somewhat strong, and that there are alternatives to the formal models that will buy a large measure of basic grammatical structure.

The model has other properties that could be questioned. For instance, one might ask whether children have full and simultaneous access to *all* aspects of the linguistic strings they hear and their meanings. Shatz' (1975) work on directives and questions would suggest that they do not. Even relatively linguistically sophisticated children, with a mean length of utterance (MLU) of 3.5, indicate rather imperfect understanding of some sentential elements that do not carry major referential meanings. Children with lower mean MLUs, averaging 2.3, are considerably more likely to respond nondifferentially to meanings that are created by those nonreferential elements, e.g., to differences between directives and informational questions. For instance, younger and linguistically less sophisticated children may not say "yes" or "no" to the information-requesting question, "can you talk on the telephone?" but may treat it as equivalent to the directive "talk on the telephone," even when the question occurs in clearly informational contexts built up by other questions such as "who talks on the telephone in your house?" That is, these children may not have at their disposal a full understanding of the meanings and demands of nonreferential elements like "can you?". The Wexler, Culicover, and Hamburger model (1975) does not really seem to allow such partial pairings of major sentential elements and their abstract counterparts; it requires the child to use complex sentences with two levels of embedding as the basis for his or her grammatical hypotheses. The child thus require sentences like "The man who married the woman who became the first supreme court president was head cheerleader" or "The cat who chased the bat that ate the fly lives in my house." Do the short sentences with which children are more typically faced really play little or no role in the generation of hypotheses about grammar?

In view of these properties, the model seems to fall somewhat short, because it requires as its basic *input* types or amounts of information that may not be available to the child early on. Furthermore, the proposed mechanisms may not be consistent with what is known about the *cognitive* or perceptual/mnemotic capacities or biases of the child.

The advantage of such a formal proof is that it makes very explicit its postulates, its procedures, and its outcomes. It suggests to us some of the parameters we must think about in describing any hypothetical acquisition process. We are free to challenge or substitute aspects of the model, but we should bear in mind that this is one of the few models of grammatical primitives (or any primitives) that has been made so explicit. Other models with equally clear and testable formulations should also be helpful to us in establishing what we want a model to do and how we should get it to do it. On the other hand, it is clear that the tendency to take syntactic primitives as self-evident, sufficient, or logical default primitives is a bit premature; we are far from having shown that they can do all of the job that they are intended to do.

We should note that other formalist models that attempt to characterize some innate linguistic apparatus of the child do exist (e.g., Bresnan, 1978; Chomsky, 1981). Chomsky, for instance, has an even more highly constrained model than that of Wexler et al. (1975). (In his model, innate knowledge about language is highly detailed, so a child learning language has only to consider a small set of structural possibilities that differ in relation to particular language-specific parameters.) While this and other proposals may be consistent with particular formal characterizations of adult grammar, none has tried to meet all of the kinds of tests to which formal models should be put. And thus all are still far from being able to explain or predict the full and natural course of language acquisition.

Functionalist Models of Language Learning: Semantic and Pragmatic Primitives

Proposals by Bates and MacWhinney (1982) and others (e.g., Givon, in press) suggest that initial organizing concepts in sentence-level grammars are generally more likely to be semantic and pragmatic (e.g., agent and action or givenness and newness) than syntactic. For instance, Bates and MacWhinney have suggested that the grammatical phenomena that we call *subjectivalization* is a function of competition and convergence among a number of discourse specific and general psychological motives. These include the semantic notion *agent*, a summary notion related probabilistically to factors such as humanness, animacy, activity, causality, and perspective. Agency seems to be a potent notion because it indexes the default or preferred perspective that a human being might take in designing a sentence as well as in other activities—one similar to his or her own. That is, because speakers are human, animate, active, and causally inclined they might be expected to speak from a generally agentive perspective. A concept such as agency might also be biologically salient and relevant because agents other than the self have the capacity to have considerable impact on the self. Other more idiosyncratic speaker characteristics may also influence the tendency to take a particular perspective in some cases, on a "closeness to ego" principle. Thus, while a cowboy might say "the cowboys and Indians," putting his own perspective first, an Indian might say "the Indians and cowboys," taking the opposite perspective.

The discourse notion of topic is somewhat different. It is what is being talked about. In the 1982 Bates and MacWhinney model, topic is not considered to be a motive itself, but rather an outcome of competition or convergence among motives. It is considered to be influenced by all the motives that determine what is talked about, including agency or perspective and saliency, as well as givenness. In other formulations, topic is treated as if it were equivalent to psychological "givenness." But this is not a difference which need concern us here. We should, however, note that when we are dealing with givenness, by whatever name, we are dealing with a condition that can be established either anaphorically in discourse, exophorically in context, or by inferential construction. We should also note that givenness or availability of information usually encoded by the topic is psychologically opposed by "new" information, usually encoded in a comment or predicate. For instance, suppose a speaker asks, "Where's John?". *John* becomes an anaphoric or linguistic given for the listener, who can simply add the comment or new information "in the kitchen." Similarly, if a child is playing with a truck, that truck is exophorically given. Thus, if the child says, "big," that new information can be referred back to the contextually given truck.

The question is whether formal devices or pieces of grammar correspond in some ways to variation in semantic and pragmatic motives such as those outlined, or whether they map directly onto syntactic categories or relations or yet other types of primitives.

Functionalists obviously hypothesize a critical role for semantics and pragmatics. What kind of preliminary evidence leads them to do so? Several kinds, which cover the ontogenetic span and many language families and suggest that concepts like subject can be broken down into more basic and atomistic elements. Some suggestive natural adult evidence on the fuzziness and lability of the subject notion across languages was presented earlier. Let us now consider the experimental adult evidence, and then turn to the child data, in both cases considering the question of what the subject of a sentence will be.

First, it has been experimentally demonstrated that some components of agency affect preferential subject choice. Clark and Begun (1971) find a preferred subject hierarchy with humans at the top, nonhuman animates next, followed by inanimate concrete objects and then abstract nouns. Flores d'Arcais (1975) also presents evidence for agency, and Osgood (1971) has shown that when people see a chain of actions they usually choose the first mover (i.e., the agent) as the sentence-initial element. These experimental results and hypotheses are related to a hierarchy for promotion to subject status (i.e., agent ▶ experiencer ▶ dative ▶ instrument ▶ patient ▶ location) that has been drawn from more naturalistic data in many languages by numerous authors (e.g., Fillmore, 1968; Givon, 1976; Kuno, 1976; and Zubin, 1979). Both indicate that there is substance to the notion that agents are psychologically the most robust and acceptable subjects.

There is also both naturalistic and experimental evidence from adults that a full accounting of variation in grammatical usage also requires the incorporation of pragmatic or discourse notions like givenness and its interactions with agency. As early as 1958, Carroll first used anaphoric or discourse-induced topic manipulations to induce systematic changes in subjectivalization and consequent changes in grammatical form of responses. Several situations were staged before classes of high school students. In one a professor manipulated some blocks. In that situation, asking the students to "describe (in writing) what the professor did" led to a high incidence of active constructions with the professor as subject (e.g., "the professor moved the blocks around"). Decreasing use of "the professor" as subject and a corresponding increase in passives occurred with other instructions: "describe what happened," "describe what was done to the blocks," and "describe what happened to the blocks," in that order. Effectively, setting up a bias toward the blocks as a discourse topic changed the subsequent linguistic status of that acted-upon element. It tended to promote it to the subject role in a sentence at the expense of the usual agentive subject (thus giving it all the attendant privileges of verb agreement, and the like), and induced the passive voice (e.g., to "describe what happened to the blocks," the student was likely to reply "the blocks were pushed around by the professor").

But these topic manipulations also seemed to interact with possibilities for agentive assignment. In a second staged situation the professor asked a student to erase the blackboard. The student refused, and the professor then asked him to report to the principal. The results for this scene were similar to the first, except that there was also a small proportion of active sentences with the student as subject, especially in the latter three conditions. This could reflect the fact that in this situation the acted-upon student has some of the attributes of an actor (his refusal), as well as of an acted-upon entity. Thus the student can be assigned a subject role in which weights from both the discourse-established topic and some degree of action-established agency may converge enough to sometimes override the tendency toward the passive. Indeed, in additions to weightings the student may have had on humanness, animacy, and some degree of causality, he may have had an additional advantage in a competition for subjectivalization if high school students have some tendency to take the perspective of a fellow student rather than that of a professor, on the "closeness to ego" principle. The "closeness to ego" conflict should not generally arise in the competition between a professor and blocks for subjectivalization in the first scene—except perhaps in an aberrant and ungrateful few.

Tannenbaum and Williams (1968) also provide evidence for the role of topicality, or contextual focus. They asked subjects to produce descriptions in either passive or active sentence form. Syntactic sets were built up prior to these descriptions, using either declarative active or passive sentences. These purely syntactic sets had little influence on response times to produce the desired sentences, relative to baseline measures. On the other hand, response time was definitely influenced when the preliminary material set up a discourse focus or topic related to the test description. For instance, passives were slower than usual (and thus ostensibly harder) when the conceptual focus was on the subject; they were considerably faster (and easier) when the focus was on the object. The reverse was true of the active sentences subjects were asked to produce. Of course, the problem with this study is that subjects were asked to produce certain syntactic structure types. Thus, we do not know what types they might have produced on their own, i.e., we do not know how a change in focus naturally affects structure.

In a more recent test of topic or attentional focus that was designed to remove any potential syntactic confounds, O'Connell, McNew, Bates, and MacWhinney (manuscript in preparation) used a different stimulus type. A series of film segments that involved what would normally be considered to be an actor and an acted upon element (e.g., an apple bumping a stool, a dog chasing a zebra, or a flowerpot hitting a pig) were shown to college students. MacWhinney and Bates (also in preparation) have found that these segments have yielded an overwhelming natural or default descriptive preference for the active voice and first actor or causal agent as initial element or subject. (In this default condition, the experimenter does not set up topics for individual segments but simply gives general instructions to describe each segment after its presentation.) Only 1.8% of such unfocused descriptions in both English and Italian are given in the passive voice. The few passives that do occur do so primarily in segments in which practically every possible visual cue (i.e., a kind of looming visual saliency, givenness, and temporal priority) are focused on the acted upon element. O'Connell et al. found that this general preference for active voice sentences with agents as subjects could be dramatically altered with the simple discourse manipulation of setting up a topic via the general question frame "Tell me about the (actor/acted upon), "with the appropriate lexical item substituted. About 70% of the time, focus on the acted upon element led to production of a passive with the acted upon element as subject (e.g., "the pig was hit by the flowerpot"). Due to the use of the "tell me about" frame rather than active or passive frames such as "what did the flowerpot do?" or "What happened to the pig?" it is clear that the topical effect is independent of syntactic priming. Thus under default perceptual conditions, the grammatical devices such as initialization and verb agreement that we associate with "subjects" are actually associated with agents; under conflicting discourse constraints, those grammatical devices get resorted and are more likely to be associated with the discourse-established topics.

Topicality is psychologically important in adult linguistic processing in other ways. In recent work, van Dijk and Kintsch (in press) have found topic to be the most influential factor in interpretation and use of ambiguous pronouns in a paradigm in which subjects read one or more context sentences and then are asked to write a continuation sentence beginning with a specified pronoun. That ambiguous pronoun could be taken to refer to any of several elements in the preceding text, but subjects generally inferred that it indexed the discourse topic. This evidence seems to indicate that topics have a privileged place in short-term memory or discourse representation. In an experimental manipulation designed to check aspects of that privileged status, Fletcher (in press), found that changes in topic or departures from topic continuity require explicit marking. He presented students with two single clause sentences and asked the students to rewrite them as one sentence that sounded natural. The degree of topic continuity between the two sentences was varied and its effects on the form of the referent in the second clause was observed. For instance, if the topic changed from the first to the second sentence, as in the pair "Sam intended to go bowling with Pete last night" and "Pete broke his leg," the outcome was likely to be something like "Sam intended to go bowling with Pete last night but Pete broke his leg." The full noun phrase "Pete" tends to be required in the second clause, even though it was already made explicit in the first, in order to indicate a change in topic from Sam to Pete. On the other hand, if there was more topic continuity in the two sentences, as in "Pete intended to go bowling last night with Sam" and "Pete broke his leg," the combined sentence was likely to be something more akin to "Pete intended to go bowling with Sam last night but broke his leg" or "Pete intended to go bowling with Sam last night but he broke his leg." In other words, with topic continuity, "Pete" does not need to be explicitly mentioned twice and thus subject phenomena differ somewhat in the second clause. Choices in production among options like ellipsis or zero anaphora, pronominalization, and a full noun phrase thus respond to variation in pragmatic or discourse phenomena. In comprehension, ellipsis and pronominalization also indicate to the listener that the topic is being continued or is more of a "given," as Fletcher found in a second experiment. This experimental evidence buttresses evidence from naturally occurring speech samples in a wide variety of languages (Givon, in press).

Vande Kopple (1982) also reports that there are distinct processing and memorial advantages when expository paragraphs are structured so that sentences follow a given-new ordering structure of topic-comment relations. The same informational content with reversed order, i.e., with new information preceding the old, was considerably less satisfactory. Thus, on yet another level "grammar" seems designed to work best when it responds and conforms to other organismic and discourse constraints.

The implication of work with adults is that grammatical devices respond to or map onto nongrammatical motives. Turning to children, we can examine two kinds of evidence. The first includes demonstrations that the proposed pragmatic motives exist in the repertoires of children prior to the onset of syntax; the second involves a demonstration of the kinds of effects on grammar that they might have, including any evidence that they are indeed used in children's hypotheses about grammatical mappings, such as initialization, agreement, and the like.

Certainly, there is evidence that at least some aspects of the notion of agency emerge prior to language, in the sensorimotor period. A child's sense of his or her own causal properties or potential to influence events comes earliest (Piaget, 1954). The first manifestations of such a conceptualization of other humans seems to appear in sensorimotor stage five (Bates, 1976). At this point children begin to look to an adult for help in attaining desired objects. That is, for the first time they look back and forth between the goal and the adult who could help them achieve it. The onset of imperatives or explicit demands made of a human to behave causally begin on a nonlinguistic level during this period. Prior to this point, the same children focus directly and single-mindedly on the object, apparently not mindful of the agentive potential of adults vis-a-vis objects.

This evidence for some causal and human concept of agency is, of course, evidence for the concept on a sensorimotor level, not a linguistic level. In fact, linguistic evidence for agency does exist at the one word level (Greenfield & Smith, 1976; Greenfield & Zukow, 1978). However, in child language at the one-word stage, Greenfield and Smith and Greenfield and Zukow find that agents are not specified linguistically as often as other kinds of elements. These authors invoke another, and indeed competing, principle for what gets encoded in single word speech: informativeness. That is, they propose that a child will encode the aspect of a situation that cannot be taken for granted or presupposed, because it is undergoing the greatest amount of change. And they provide both naturalistic and quasi-experimental data that supports their view. Interestingly, the notion of informativeness is related to the given-new motive system for the functional topic-comment dimension. While old or background information (i.e., a motive for topicalization) remains implicit in the nonlinguistic context, children tend to encode comments for maximally new and changing information. Thus, if a block tower fell over, a child at the one-word stage would be likely to encode the new information or comment "fall," but less likely to encode the old information or implicit topic "block". (Adults can behave rather similarly if givenness is exophoric or contextual; for instance, a woman seeing a dress on a store rack and commenting "how pretty" would not need to encode the contextually obvious fact that she was talking about the dress.)

In the child's here and now world, comments or new information are not usually likely to be agentive. In that world, the child and parent are likely to be jointly engaged in some enterprise or shared context. As such, both are generally to be taken for granted and are nonconfusable in their agentive roles. If the mother were to knock the block tower over, for instance, the child would be more likely to encode the surprising action of knocking over or the result of falling than the fact that the default agent caused the event. In the view of Greenfield and Smith and Greenfield and Zukow, the only time that a child at the single-word stage should specify an agent is when there is conflict about who should do an action (e.g., who gets to put my shoes on, mommy or me?) or when an agent is not visibly present, as when a child hears a noise made in another room and can add information by encoding who made it. In the block tower example, had there been doubt about agency—for instance if the child had turned away and then turned around again to discover the block tower falling and her mother *and* her sister *and* her dog standing next to it—the child should be more likely to lexicalize an agent. But again, the lexicalization would conform to the operative informational or reduction of uncertainty principle. In most cases, an agent will be too unchanging, obvious and redundant to take up a child's precious one-word lexicalization space.

Interestingly, Snyder (1976) finds that this linguistic sensitivity to the given-new dimension or information value is lacking in language-disabled children. She compared normal children at the one-word stage and linguistically matched but older language-disabled children in situations in which action patterns remained the same but objects changed. For instance, after a child had put several blocks in a pail, the experimenter would hand her a doll. Normal children encoded the informative or changing element in the situation linguistically 50% of the time and indicated it with a nonlinguistic declarative performative (cf. Bates, Camaioni, & Volterra, 1975) just as frequently. Language disabled children, on the other hand, were only able to deal with informational value on the nonlinguistic level. Their linguistic output was not sensitive to this dimension. Thus, these language-disabled children had not caught on to the nature of the one-word language game; they had difficulty manipulating linguistic symbols in the service of the informativeness motive.

In this sense it is interesting that Bates, Benigni, Bretherton, Camaioni, and Volterra (1977) have documented a substantial correlational relationship between the Piagetian means-end scale and language in normal children. It is even more suggestive that, using multiple regression analyses, Snyder found that the deficient linguistic performance of her language-disabled children was predicted by exactly that scale. Furthermore, training in the means-end scale (along with the object permanence scale) has been found to be more beneficial in aiding profoundly retarded children to acquire language than more direct linguistic training has been (Kahn, 1981). This suggests that some sensitivity to language as a means to particular communicative ends is both missing in some language disabled children and critical for early linguistic progress.

If agency and informativeness are often at odds in determining lexicalization at the one-word stage, and if informativeness seems to be a much more potent motive, what can we say about the relationships of these motive systems at later stages of acquisition? Do they change? If so, what makes them change? A manipulation or contextual analysis of informativeness similar to that in the Greenfield studies would be useful in establishing continuity or change in motives for lexicalization. For instance, although a child may look as if he or she has the capacity to lexicalize all parts of an hypothesized agent-action-dative-object-locative chain, as in R. Brown (1973), could informativeness principles account in part for why some pieces get lexicalized sometimes and others get lexicalized at other times? For instance, when a child does lexicalize agent and action (as in "daddy work"), is the child more likely to do so because neither the agent nor the action are given? That is, is the child likely to specify particular relations when they are unavailable to the child or its listener in the here and now context, i.e., when each has comment-like aspects? Or does the child instead (or at a later stage) incorporate *both* topics and comments, distinguishing each from the other via word order or other means? The Greenfield and Zukow paradigm (1978) would allow us to actually manipulate aspects of situations so that we have specified and unconfounded notions of relative givenness and newness, and their relationships to semantic motives like agency. Such tests would be very useful in charting any roles these motives actually have in two-word speech and would be superior to suggestions of influence derived from less controlled naturalistic data (e.g., Gruber, 1967).

Although we do not have systematic information on the role of givenness at the two-word stage, we do have some information about agency. At the point of two-word utterances, children's sentence "subjects"—when there is an element corresponding to that designation at all—are far more likely to be of certain semantic types like agent (e.g., "daddy" in sentences like "daddy run") than they are to be less prototypical members of the subject class, such as gerunds (e.g., "running" in the sentence "running is good for you") or nonagentive entities like "work" in the sentence "work is wonderful." (Even some adults have difficulty producing these particular sentences, but that fact is probably not germane to the present discussion.) The point is that the concept "subject" generally seems *too* powerful early on; it predicts usages beyond those that children produce. Furthermore, there is abundant evidence (Bloom, 1970; R. Brown, 1973; Bowerman, 1973; deVilliers & deVilliers, 1974) that when both animate and inanimate objects are lexicalized, agents or animates almost always precede objects or inanimates. This suggests that some part of the set of devices that will be associated with subjects (e.g., verb agreement and word order) is controlled by aspects of agency early on.

At later stages this order relation also holds. For instance, working with 3- to 5-year-olds, Dewart (1976) found that her younger group tended to pick an animate toy as the referent for a nonsense noun in first noun position in a sentence. Choices for nonsense nouns in second noun position were inanimate. This was true regardless of sentence voice, which could be either active or passive. The older group of children behaved similarly to the younger on active constructions, but when sentences were passive their performance deteriorated toward chance levels. Thus, somewhere during this period the "agent first, object second" mapping seems to come under tentative revision in "odd" linguistic environments. But until that point, agency is apparently a primary motive controlling word order.

We do not have a great deal of cross-lingusitic evidence about agency as the functional basis for early syntax. We do know, however, that at one point Italian children seem to use one grammatical indicator (word order) to indicate topic-comment relationships and others (agreement and case-marking) to mark agency (Fava & Tirondola, 1977). The divisible status of "subject" here suggests the intriguing possibility that at least for some children acquiring some languages both functional motives are salient early on and form the bases for some grammatical hypotheses. More cross-linguistic work is obviously necessary to ascertain the generality of such findings—and generality is of course crucial for the substantiation of functionalist hypotheses.

Other evidence suggests change in the way certain motives control certain devices. For instance, Hornby and Hass (1970) find that older preschool children with more developed sentential grammars tend to acknowledge changing information (e.g., same agent and action but progressively changing object) by stressing the changed element, (e.g., "now the boy's kicking the *basketball*" if he has previously been shown kicking other things). Actually, stress is more likely to be used with changing *agents* than with changing objects or actions, and agents are in fact the default topics of these sentences. Thus children seem to be indicating some sensitivity to topicalization. They, like adults, apparently find more need to mark topic change than change in aspects of the comment. Hornby (1971) also finds that the range of grammatical devices controlled by a topic (e.g., the passive, clefts, etc.) does change with age. MacWhinney and Bates (1978) have also charted differences in how the given-new dimension controls devices such as stress, ellipsis, and pronominalization in several languages at several ages.

It appears then that there is considerable evidence suggesting that various functional motives influence various grammatical devices in various ways in adults and language acquiring children. But, of course, it has not been systematically established that these motives are operative in all languages at all points in time. A number of researchers are now beginning rather programmatic examinations of these motives in a wider variety of languages (e.g., studies and proposed studies by Ito in Japanese, Miao in Mandarin Chinese, McDonald in German, and MacWhinney and Bates in Italian, Hungarian, Serbo-Croatian, and English). Systematic and multivariate analyses of the interactions of such perceptual and discourse motives as movement, perceptual saliency, givenness, animacy, focus, and linguistic context are underway. An examination of their ability to control various devices at various ages in various languages seems basic to establishing the validity of functionalist models in language acquisition.

Another Emergent Model of Grammatical Categories

Some interesting criticism of semantic formulations has come from Maratsos and Chalkley (1980), who propose a process for grammatical acquisition that does not begin with universal innate syntactic primitives, but rather results in the emergence of grammatical categories that may be less universal and somewhat language-specific. The problem that Maratsos and Chalkley point to is that dependence on semantics (and presumably pragmatics) alone may not get the child to all of the grammar that the child does eventually produce. In essence, their criticism revolves around two points. One is the fact that children do seem to attend to form per se. Although many formal elements like "ed" and "ing" encode semantic meanings, gender marking represents a rather arbitrary assignment of words to classes. In some languages (e.g., German and Russian) children must use such gender information to assign the appropriate case-markings, since the marking for a given case varies with gender. Maratsos and Chalkley assert that the fact that children can do this well argues for some less semantic capacity for language organization that rests on attention to form differences.

Functionalists would not disagree that some parts of language are—at given moments in time, if not in their inceptions—impossible to grasp on a functional level. These "vestigial" elements of language would require a more special and indeed arbitrary kind of processor. But the argument is whether language is at base mainly rational and functional or mainly arbitrary, and whether the child enters it via a rational semantic and pragmatic route or via arbitrary mechanisms. From the functionalist perspective, the more arbitrary the formal mapping and the less valid as a cue to pragmatic and semantic function it is, the more difficult it should be to acquire. This is a testable hypothesis with the potential to establish or invalidate certain processing mechanisms as central in the language acquisition process.

Maratsos and Chalkley's second point is that many categorical boundaries that children observe are not fuzzy enough to be accounted for entirely by a semantic prototype model. For instance, suppose that the core semantic property of "verb" is "action" and the core of "adjective" is "state" or "property". Quite young children produce verbs that have "state" properties, like "want," "know," and the like (Bretherton, McNew, & Beeghly-Smith, 1981). They also produce adjectives which are not inherent properties of objects, but are closely connected to action implications, like "naughty" and "snoopy." In other words, the semantic notion "action" has the potential to cross grammatical categories, as does the notion "state." Maratsos and Chalkley then ask why, faced with such fuzzy categories, children do not produce many sentences like "she naughtied" for action-like adjectives and "he is know it" for state-like verbs. (Children do, of course, produce some sentences of this sort.) They suggest that to avoid systematic errors children must respond to other constraints, and that those constraints are formal and distributional co-occurrences. In their model children will note that a word that gets the past "ed" will also tend to get other parts of a complex of markers associated with verbs: "ing," "is," and the like. Attention to such packages of morphemes, which of course involve both meanings and the formal and phonological markers that indicate those meanings, will allow children to develop a more precise notion of formal class equivalence. In essence, as children begin to make connections among these grammatical morphemes, they will be able to develop a more complete notion of important language-specific grammatical categories.

Although Maratsos and Chalkley tend to focus on the role of formal co-occurrences, they specifically do not try to suggest that "grammar is all one thing or another." Semantics and indeed, agency, have critical and important roles to play in their analysis of English grammar. For instance, adjectives may take the "ing" which also characterizes verbs, although they do not take the whole complex of verb formalisms. However, although the "ing" construction may occur in "he is being careful" or "doting mother," it is not acceptable in "he is being red" or "prettying mother." In fact, it is limited to adjectives which are necessarily associated with agents: only agents can be "careful," but other things can be "red" or "pretty." Thus, for Maratsos and Chalkley, grammar seems to operate at an intersection between general semantic organizing notions and appreciation of constellations of fine-grained semantactic distributional properties. This is a critical point, because, as in the "subject" examples given in the functionalist section above, it again suggests that all members of a "grammatical" category are not equal, and that control over associated grammatical devices has a good deal to do with semantic and pragmatic, rather than grammatical, properties.

Functionalists would also be prone to suggestions that there are at least moments in acquisition at which the general semantic and pragmatic notions have primacy, e.g., the point at which Italian children seem to use one grammatical indicator (word order) to indicate topic-comment relationships and others (agreement and case-marking) to mark agency (Fava & Tirondola, 1977). What this may imply is that at some ontogenetic moments attention to the general semantic-pragmatic organization of language dominates and at other moments attention to their intersection with noncongruent formal markers or grammatical clusters does. In any case, eventually some rapprochement must be reached between the two, in order for children to assign to language its characteristic grammatical properties. One way in which this could occur is, of course, for extension of the category from the prototypes to take place on the basis of shared surface devices and distributional characteristics. But such patterns and processes remain to be charted and established ontogenetically.

Maratsos and Chalkley also suggest the relevance of more basic principles when they say that:

> we can for our purposes only assume whatever is needed, including notions such as activity, temporal and aspectual relations, animacy, shape, communication value, emotional state, number and so on. . .These may seem like very complex primitives to assume. But in fact, we know of no recent discussions of language acquisition, including those based purely on semantics, that do not presuppose them, in one form or another. (1980, p. 139)

This indeed seems to be the case. And these primitives and any capacity they have for driving the hypothesizing system for language acquisition need more attention if we are to have any adequate conceptualization of the entire process by which children acquire language. It is also clear that we will need precise and detailed and theory-driven cross-linguistic data to ascertain the generalities and universalities in the nature of the hypotheses that children make during the acquisition process. We are at present still rather far from being able to generate models of the original set of primitives and any epigenetic changes in them that will predict the actual acquisition data across time and linguistic groups, although we have several interesting lines of research to pursue.

Input and Output Characteristics

We will now turn to research that has focused on the linguistic environments that confront children. Historically, a series of studies on English (Broen, 1972; Phillips, 1970, 1973; Sachs, Brown, & Salerno, 1976; Snow, 1972) and Black English (Drach, 1969) established a number of properties that characterize talk to English-learning children. We know from them that input language is actually quite well-formed and articulated, in contrast to its adult-adult counterpart. A parallel observation that predominates in the anthropological and cross-linguistic literature is that processes in various languages serve to phonologically clarify speech, by supplying elided vowels, increasing and augmenting stress, and the like (Ferguson, 1977). Other properties of speech to children also seem unique, including grammatical ones. But two questions can be asked about these properties. The first is if register differences can make a difference to language learning children. The second is how register differences make a difference, a question that encompasses subquestions about how register differences interface with child capacities and whether any register properties are universal or necessary or sufficient for language acquisition in general or grammatical acquisition in particular. The question about direct influence on grammar per se has been asked in several ways. Here we will consider each of the several ways of asking that question and the implications of each.

Correlational Studies

We shall first consider the sort of parental adjustment that has often been presumed to be most suited to a direct test of whether pragmatic adjustments have implications for the acquisition of syntax. The studies involved are correlational; they test for relationships among general measures of syntactic input by parents and general measures of syntactic output by their children, such as mean length of utterance (MLU), general verb complexity, and the like. The question researchers generally want to ask is whether any syntactic change is tutorial or simply epiphenomenal; does it make syntax more transparent to children or is its existence both unrelated to children's needs and without implication for them?

Obviously one can answer such a question on a limited basis only. Since almost all children receive a certain amount of pragmatic adjustment (and we have little access to children who do not but whose lives are otherwise completely analogous to those who do), we have little opportunity to test for what would happen in the absence of any adjustments. The best information we have suggests that children who get their input from less contingent sources than parents (e.g., children whose parents are deaf and whose basic input has come only from sources like TV) do show deviance (Sacks, Bard, & Johnson, 1981; Sachs & Johnson, 1976). Similar children who get some degree of contingent input from nonparental sources—say for 20 hours per week—appear to be in a much better situation (Jones & Quigley, 1979; Schiff, 1979). Such incidental data suggest that language acquisition cannot really proceed fully or adequately without some general semantic and syntactic limits and certain amounts of responsivity in the environment. However, these input adjustments apparently need be neither continuous nor pervasive. A better understanding of such threshold effects in motherese would be helpful for theoretical specification of what it is about the child and what it is about the environment that is required for language acquisition, but obviously such information is not likely to be forthcoming in any great quantity.

More typical studies, those that simply attempt to correlate input that falls within the normal motherese range to child output, cannot provide answers to the question about what would happen if the child received no environmental supports for language acquisition. Instead they allow us to ask a secondary question: how does variation within an a priori restricted range affect outcomes? This is also an interesting question. By telling us how rate of acquisition is related to limited diversity in linguistic input, it could be a question with particularly practical implications. For instance, if one achieves a simple, unconfounded and unambiguous "more is better" result within the range usually available to children, one might be encouraged to test whether specific additional pragmatic adjustments by parents who already use some degree of motherese might be useful—either for children generally or perhaps more especially for children having difficulty acquiring language. On the other hand, the relationship of input to output could well be more complicated than the linear or "more must always be better" function that is the most obvious model to test. And, certainly, negative results (i.e., no correlation) would not logically imply that parents could dispense with "motherese" with impunity; some threshold degree of motherese could still be critical to normal language acquisition as the Sachs et al. results suggest, even though one cannot ethically rearrange contingencies to conclusively demonstrate that fact.

However, to make the best use of correlational results we would need to understand the mechanisms underlying them. The correlational studies themselves are preliminary and have certain limits. They certainly cannot provide direct evidence of causal relations or directions of effect, although they may suggest their existence. Thus, we need additional information to establish whether certain correlational linkages are likely to be the result of the mother's effect on the child, the child's effect on the mother, a more reciprocal or bidirectional process, or somewhat co-incidental. There are, however, a few experimental and behavioral genetics studies that bear on these questions. After reviewing the basic correlational evidence, we will turn to those and to questions of underlying mechanism.

Another point we should make before examining the initial round of studies on "motherese" in more detail is that the initial impetus to ascertain if these register differences make a difference came from two types of researchers. The first group had primarily cognitive notions of language acquisition but somewhat imprecise and sometimes empiricist approaches to syntax. Although most of these researchers would in principle undoubtedly grant the child an active cognitive processing role, they have not usually specified with any precision the sort of active mechanism that could process input with particular properties; instead they tended to invoke vague notions like learning by some unspecified form of analogy or to hope that the structure of the language environment itself would simply do the work. They have been roundly and probably rightfully criticized for this lack of precision by the second group of researchers (e.g., Shatz, 1982). On the other hand, as we have indicated, there is also some danger associated with taking any extant theory of the nature of the initial organizing structures as the default alternative to a fully empiricist solution, without verifying the relationship of established aspects of the environment and the child data itself to that hypothetical innate structure. To resolve the ambiguities it seems to us that one must look closely and simultaneously and from a number of perspectives at both the organism and the environment. Let us turn then to the rate of acquisition data, first examining the data themselves and then indicating what they can and cannot tell us about the *process* of language acquisition.

Two correlational studies are based on simultaneous sampling of input and output language (Cross, 1977; Harkness, 1977). When Cross tested 16 American infants ranging in age from 19 to 32 months, all of whom were making rapid progess in language, she found significant positive correlations between maternal mean length of utterance (MLU) and a number of child variables: MLU, longest utterance length, receptive speech scores, and age. Harkness, in her rural African study, sampled 13 mothers and 12 children 4 to 8 years of age who served as significant sources of language input to younger children aged 2 to 3½. This is of note because in many cultural groups motherese is not, strictly speaking *mother*ese. In those cultures, mothers are not the primary sources of input to language learners, and a universal model of language acquisition must be able to deal with that fact. There is, however, reason to believe that even in cultures in which siblings provide a major part of the linguistic data, "syntactic" and other tailoring will automatically occur. For instance, Shatz and Gelman (1973) found that 4-year-old American children changed speech registers when speaking to 2-year-olds; their speech became shorter and simpler and included more bids for attention. Sachs and Devin (1976) provide additional evidence that linguistic tailoring is not an ability limited to adults. Their young children were able to transform their speech in a fashion analogous to motherese even when they were simply speaking to a "baby" doll.

However, mothers and children may not be equally adept at pragmatically tailoring input to language learners, on syntactic, semantic, or other linguistic and paralinguistic grounds. When Harkness examined language acquisition in rural Africa, she compared the talk to language learners by adults and older children. In her Kipsigis community the speech of 4- to 8-year-olds did depart from maternal speech on mean length of utterance and number of verbs. It was the mothers who were significantly higher on both. Both maternal and sibling MLU were significantly correlated with the MLU of language learners, even though maternal and sibling MLU were significantly different from each other. Maternal correlations with infants were somewhat higher although, as noted, it was mothers who used significantly more complex utterances with language learners. Maternal complexity as measured by number of verbs per utterance was also significantly related to infant MLU; the less complex sibling verbs were not. Adults thus seem to be somewhat more sensitive and flexible providers of input; both the upper ranges of sibling input and its responsivity may be more limited. Perhaps in support of this, second-born American children tend to be slightly less competent language-learners than their firstborn siblings (Bates, 1975), potentially reflecting the liklihood that second-born children will get less adult attention and input than firstborns.

Although these two simultaneously sampled studies are of interest, they present problems for interpretation, particularly for a theory that maintains that it is precise and direct syntax to syntax matches that should determine syntax acquisition. Because the variable of age is not controlled, any relationship of child language with language input might be the result of mothers tuning into quite obvious cognitive and semantic differences in children of widely varying ages. While hardly unimportant or irrelevant to questions of language acquisition—particularly if grammatical processing works best when concurrent semantic and cognitive demands are not unduly high—such studies are not tests of whether mothers are doing any narrowly grammatical fine-tuning or tutoring. (Of course, it is hard to know what truly specific or isolated grammatical fine-tuning would be. We would hardly expect to find semantic constructs or vocabulary held constant at the level of adult-adult conversation, with only grammatical complexity varied. However, we can attempt to remove general cognitive and age-linked variance from general lingusitic variation.) More obviously, because the studies use simultaneous sampling, they do not provide any clear evidence that what mothers do has effects on later linguistic progress; mothers could simply be responding to their children's current levels, and such responses would not have to be linguistically progressive.

Two studies do at least address the prospective question, while controlling for age. One by Furrow (1979) looks at maternal language when children are 18 months of age; it correlates that with 27-month child language. Another by Pentz (1975) looks at mothers and their 28-month children; it takes a second language sample at 36 months. These are, of course, two very different time frames; the first corresponds generally to the onset and development of multiword speech and the second to the fine-grained grammatization of language, in which productive verb and noun inflections and function words are established.

For the younger children, Furrow finds a significant negative relationship of maternal MLU to later child MLU. In other words, mothers who used longer and more complex sentences early on had children with slower language development. This suggests the possibility that too much early complexity hinders development, and that general syntactic (and concomitant semantic) reductions in talk to children may be important to young language learners. Furrow also finds a negative relationship between the number of verbs per sentence a mother uses and her child's subsequent

MLU. Thus general reduction in syntactic measures seems to be helpful at this stage of language acquisition. Of note is the fact that Furrow's method does not address the question of whether mothers who provide the best *matches* to their children have children who then progress faster in language, since it simply looks at absolute levels of input complexity at initial sampling, and *not* matches. Within the complexity ranges that these mothers represent, however, it looks as if input can be too complex to be maximally effective.

On the other hand, Pentz, dealing with input that begins at the point when Furrow's study ends, finds no significant relationship between maternal MLU and either simultaneously sampled or later child MLU. Thus, by this point in time, it does not look as if reduction in complexity or matches on measures of general complexity like MLU are generally useful. Interestingly, Pentz does find that the larger the *difference* between maternal and child MLU at 28 months, the lower the child's MLU at 36 months. If maternal MLU was relatively uniform, this could mean that children were progressing independently of their mothers; in other words, children who were initially farther from the adult speech standard simply would not reach the same absolute MLU in a given period of time as children who were initially closer to adult performance. However, maternal MLU is highly correlated with the difference in MLUs. Pentz suggests that since mothers with lower MLUs have smaller differences in adult-child MLU, difference is in part a measure of sensitivity to the child's linguistic level. This seems to mean that in this age range, more tailoring or fine-tuning may have been going on for children at the *lower end of the scale* than at the higher, where children have already figured out a great deal about language and grammar. Children with initially small mother-child language gaps and high subsequent MLUs might thus be of two types: either those who were initially fairly far along and whose parents needed to do less tailoring or those who were not so far along but whose mothers had given them *a great deal of linguistic tailoring*. Linear correlations would, of course, be washed out if both the most advanced and the least advanced children showed the same surface pattern, albeit for quite different reasons. Thus, Pentz's evidence would generally follow the reduction of complexity and or fine-tuning line for children who have not yet attained such mastery, while suggesting that the productive language of mothers and children gradually becomes more unhooked.

Presumably any model emphasizing the efficacy of a parent-child match would expect maternal language to become less restricted by child limits and to vary more in terms of other situational and conversational demands at some point in the acquisition process. But the exact point would depend on the underlying notions of how grammatical acquisition works and what the child and the environment must each contribute to the task. These dimensions have not been well specified. On the other hand, it is possible that children who have worked out some basic ideas about grammar may be able to use those to figure out more; they may thus be able to direct their own attention and provide their own bootstrapping. Indeed, at some point they may have mastered enough of the rudiments of the syntax or grammar "game" to set up their own foci or problem-solving spaces using less tailored input (cf. Karmiloff-Smith, 1979a and b), actively searching for confirmations of their hypotheses about particular words or word combinations. It is also possible that such bootstrapping capacities may be what is unleashed on the semantic level as children begin to show bursts and spurts in naming after getting a certain number of names under their control. Perhaps at this point they have ascertained much of the essence of the "naming game" and are capable of setting up a problem-solving space in which they actively look for names of things or correspondences between words and objects.

Other researchers might instead presume that the environment has to provide some more absolute sort of step-by-step grammatical tutorial. There is no clear evidence for such a tutorial, and it is not entirely obvious what its nature would or should be. For instance, there is no reduction in number of grammatical forms addressed to children, and particular patterns are not focused on individually at particular times or in all-or-none fashion to the exclusion of all others. We do not see dramatic changes from one form to another as in "today, children, the plural, tomorrow the past." On the other hand, some particular forms or form-function mappings may rise in frequency above a background level in response to child initiatives (Sachs, 1979), providing a less dramatic form of tutorial and a more child-directed data base. Correlational studies using very general grammatical measures are not likely to clarify such process questions. Thus, after considering one final correlational study, we will turn to experimental studies and more fine-grained considerations of process.

This latter study (Newport, Gleitman, & Gleitman, 1977) attempts to answer questions about the adequacy of linguistic input by simultaneous partialling out both age and the child's initial linguistic level. But the Newport et al. study is by virtue of that clearly not a test of matching or fine-tuning. Since the child's initial linguistic level was actually partialled out, only maternal variation unrelated to children's initial linguistic variation is left in the equation. Thus the component of adult language that would theoretically be best tailored to provide data for the child has been statistically removed, and one may thus fear that this is a classic case of throwing out the baby with the bathwater. Nonetheless, the study is an instructive one.

Partial correlations on a sample including children varying from 12 to 27 months yielded few significant relationships between initial maternal measures and child level six months later, when general grammatical measures such as MLU and number of S-nodes per utterance were used. These partial correlation results are important as indications that there is *little effect of the general grammatical or linguistic environment that is independent of the child's effect on that environment.* Thus, the results probably preclude a radical empiricist perspective; the adult cannot in general pitch his or her language at any random and nonresponsive level and guarantee language learning. This is a critical finding. But it does not do two things: it does not establish what heuristics children do use to process input data nor does it tell us that they do not make use of *contingent* input. All it can suggest is that adults cannot generally be irrelevant and disrespectful of their child's linguistic level and still have any general influences on later acquisition.

On the other hand, the Newport et al. results do indicate some interesting things about the influence of frequent use of particular grammatical devices by mothers. For instance, maternal use of yes-no questions seems to predict acquisition of auxiliaries, even when partial correlations are used. Apparently the sheer frequency of a particular kind of linguistic event can have effects. We shall return later to some potential mechanisms by which frequency effects might work.

Although the Newport et al. procedure may be problematic, there are grounds for wanting to unconfound the relationship of initial child processing to later child accomplishment: a smart child or a good linguistic processor at one time may remain a smart child and a good lingusitic processor at another. In other words, a child's own performances over time could be correlated. However, if such a child's mother or father (who share the same "good" genes) also seem to be particularly good at tuning in to the child and providing the child a good data base, it may be difficult to disentangle what might be two independent contributions to language acquisition - intrinsic and extrinsic. We do not really know if good precessors *need* good data; they may be better than other children even with relatively poor data. On the other hand, good data may help even good processors. Probably the only way we can legitimately separate these influences is in a behavioral genetics study. For instance, in an adoption design, we can look at how child performance is correlated with that of genetic parents who do not provide any linguistic input, and we can look at how it is also correlated with the syntactic and other input provided by adopting parents, who do not genetically contribute either cognitive or specifically linguistic capacity. Such a design allows us to have some of our cake and eat it too, in that we can actually look at environmental influences unconfounded by just inherent good processing capacity and vice versa. Hardy-Brown (1980) has made a first pass at such a study, but her longitudinal design has so far only allowed her to look at 1-year-olds and their communicative competence, both gestural and vocal. One-year-olds are obviously not acquiring syntax. But Hardy-Brown finds significant effects of both genetics and environment on what they are acquiring. For instance, both the general cognitive ability and memory capacities of the biological mother are significantly related to several indices of infant communicative competence. Some environmental influences are also substantial; adoptive parents' contingent vocal responsivity to infant vocalizations and their vocal imitations are strongly related to infant competence. This suggests that there may be a significant role for genetics and a separable and significant role for the environment in language acquisition.

Of course, it is important to again keep in mind—especially in the context of behavioral genetic studies—that those children who do not get the benefit of the best environmental tailoring are rarely exposed to language that is not somewhat reduced in complexity. Studies in behavioral genetics cannot perform miracles; they can only apportion the variance that occurs within the gene pool and the environment that they actually test. They cannot provide information about the relative weighing of the genetic and environmental contributions outside of that gene pool or that restricted environment. In other words, they cannot tell us what would happen if a child was in the unusual position of having access only to language with the semantic and syntactic properties of adult-adult language, because they will generally not sample children in that range.

Furthermore, behavioral genetic studies will not necessarily tell us anything about the *process* of cracking the linguistic code or the specific biological preparation it requires. They may simply tell us that individual differences can be accounted for by differences in genes or environment or both, without telling us much about the specifics of the hypothesis base. For instance, a study indicating that the general grammatical facility of children is related to the general grammatical facility of their parents via some genetic link will tell us simply that good grammatical processing (whatever its essential nature) can be inherited. It will not necessarily tell us much about the fine-grained nature of the process or hypothesis base used to generate the grammar.

So what can we say about the correlational studies we do have? In essence they suggest that there may be some linguistic responsivity of mothers to children, as measured by general reductions in complexity like MLU, particularly in the earliest stages of acquisition, and of children to mothers in turn. Certain amounts of responsivity and general limits to complexity may be useful, particularly at early stages in the acquisition of communicative compentence and syntax, but more variety and complexity may be the norm later. On the other hand, behavioral genetics provides one of the few ways to disentangle the contribution of the child's own process-ing capacity from the utility of environmental supports, and until we have additional information from them we will not really have uncontaminated evidence for environmental or genetic effects on general syntactic measures. Furthermore, even established general relationships do not really elucidate how environmental supports are useful nor specify the processes by which language is acquired.

Particular Environmental Supports to Language: How Might They Work?

The relationships between general measures like MLU do not tell us much about how the environment supports particular acquisitions (e.g., what ac-counts for the child acquiring a plural or a passive construction). We shall now turn to the question of what more specific aspects of input to children suggest. For years psycholinguists took as gospel Brown's (1973) results showing no effect of environmental frequency on order of acquisition of 14 grammatical morphemes; order seemed to be determined only by gram-matical and semantic complexity. But very few noted or were fully aware of the method of determining frequency that Brown used. He did not in-corporate all parental input in his analyses; in fact, he omitted at least 30% of the input. The omitted utterances were exactly those which in an in-teractive model look particularly important: utterances that were either repeti-tions or expansions of child utterances. In this section we will focus on the evidence that expansions and other pragmatic adjustments can influence the acquisition of particular pieces of grammar, we will discuss the im-plications for a general model, and we will offer certain caveats that must limit those implications and that suggest the necessity for additional research.

It is clear that researchers find a great tendency of at least English-speaking adults to expand on or add to a child's utterance (Cross, 1977; Moerk, 1972). Expansions involve retaining the child's attentional focus and basic semantic and syntactic structure, while adding additional syn-tactic information. Thus, the child's "bear" might be expanded as, "yes, that's a bear" or "daddy home" as "oh, daddy's home?" Expansions have been singled out as particularly good pragmatic devices for facilitating syn-tax acquisition by Moerk (1972), Nelson (1977), and Nelson, Carskaddon, and Bonvillian (1973).

The power of expansions has been established experimentally. Although an initial experiment by Cazden (1965) showed no effects, others have been positive. Cazden's method involved restating (without additional information and in exactly the same sentential frame, but in full grammatical regalia) almost all utterances produced by a child. This is somewhat excessive, and it may have been quite boring. It also ran the risk of mistaken interpretations of unclear utterances. An even more important confound results from the fact that the expansions were provided to children speaking Black English by speakers of a different dialect. This could mean that their natural environment actually provided the children with contradictory exemplars, a situation that could certainly inhibit rule-based linguistic progress.

Nelson et al. (1973) and Nelson (1977) used a more flexible version of the expansion, the recast, in more pragmatically natural and varied ways. The first experiment with 32- to 40-month-olds used a variety of recasts, with the emphasis on changes in predicate forms. It yielded significant differences from initially equivalent controls on a verb index, auxiliary verb constructions, and imitations. Nelson then divided a second sample of children into two groups, one getting complex verb expansions and one getting complex questions. Each group was initially comparable on the two usages, and each served as the control for the other. After five one-hour play sessions over a period of two weeks, the effects were clear and selective. Children who got verb expansions improved significantly only on those; the improvement of children who got complex questions was equally selective.

These experiments establish that expansions or recasts *can* make a difference, at least under certain circumstances and for certain age groups. But are parents likely to be this focused on single targets for expansion? Even if they are not, the process could work, but Nelson (1981b) suggests that certain pragmatic motivations may bring certain forms to the fore at certain points. There is actually some evidence to suggest that there are moments at which certain form/function mappings do become foregrounded. Sachs, who provides it (1979), also shores up the dyadic perspective when she finds that the mother augments or "bumps" the frequency of certain usages when the child begins to provide utterances that indicate potential awareness of the meanings that underlie those usages. Thus, adult references to the distant (as opposed to the just-prior) past rise dramatically above a baseline level when the child begins to supply two-word utterances indicating that the child may have some cognitive notion of distant past, e.g., when the child says "daddy fall" when he or she sees the ladder from which the father fell the day before.

Other information on specific acquisitions may or may not be contradictory. For instance, Nelson (1981b) provides evidence that it is the *discrepancy* between mother and child in complexity of auxiliary verbs at initial sampling

(22 months) that is strongly and positively associated with the rate of auxiliary verb growth between then and 27 months. In other words, apparent disregard of fine-tuning would promote language, with larger gaps leading to more learning. However, if the Sachs and expansion work does generalize, Nelson's findings may argue *for* a fine-tuning perspective: mothers who look particularly discrepant on a given structure for a period of time may actually be quite responsive. Their children's behavior may lead them to "bump" those usages to provide additional data on how to realize a given grammatical function. Clearly, in order to ascertain any relationship of specific changes in child language to subsequent changes in adult input language and any influence of those on the child we will need more detailed charting of interactive language behavior than we have had heretofore.

Other data from expansions may also support the more-or-less fine-tuned hypothesis. Nelson (1981b) reports a study of children 22 to 27 months and their mothers; researchers found that the proportion of simple recasts (e.g., recasts that included structural changes in only one of the major sentence constituents—subject, verb, or object) was positively correlated with growth in MLU and auxiliary verbs. In contrast, the proportion of complex recasts (involving changes in two or three major sentence constituents) was negatively related to the two measures. Thus, even expansions may need to be tailored to facilitate language acquisition.

Even though we have experimental evidence that expansions or recasts can make a difference for language learners, we should ask some additional questions. First, we clearly need to ask how they work. Do they simply focus and direct attention and make relevant data more available to the child's processing apparatus? Or do they somehow "stamp in" small pieces of grammatical content? This is a critical difference—one between the environment simply providing an accessible data base versus the environment providing grammatical structure per se. Any mechanism for the latter alternative, providing grammatical structure per se, remains to be clarified. As we have indicated, the environment only provides particular instances or words that could logically be conceptualized in an infinite variety of ways—to see them as instances of a general type, the child ought to have some preparation to do so.

The second question we should ask is whether expansions are critical for language acquisition or not. Expansions might provide a particularly good source of data since they have the virtue of using the child's topic and thus referents and relations that the child controls. This could help in freeing up processing space and attention for grammatical or fine-grained processing by reducing other processing demands. On the other hand, there may be alternate routes to an acceptable data base, and we certainly do not know if expansions are either universal or necessary. We simply know that they can be helpful. In the English data base, frequency effects derived from noncontingent input language seem to be somewhat less influential than expansions. However, when Moerk (1980) re-analyzed Brown's (1973) frequency data, he did find noncontingent frequency effects on order of grammatical morpheme acquisition relative to age and similar effects on relative linguistic delay. Newport et al. (1977) also found some frequency effects for particular grammatical devices. It is thus possible that frequency per se helps to focus attention (i.e., the frequent and noticeable appearance of "a" or "ing" may make the child wonder about why and to what end they occur and may evoke interest in resolving that question.) But since frequency per se does not entail the match between child-established referents and adult referents that expansions do, it would probably not have the proposed added benefit of freeing referent-establishing capacity for other processing. If this is the mechanism by which expansions work, we are left with a sense that the environment counts in language acquisition—but by providing good and accessible data, rather than by providing grammatical structure itself.

The questions about universality, necessity, mechanism, and implications for syntax can be raised about other aspects of motherese also. We shall raise briefly a few of these questions, with examples, in order to indicate the scope of the approach. For instance, if the speech register addressed to young children is to serve as a helpful linguistic data base, one would need guarantees that it is preferentially and universally attended to. Such preferential attention does seem to occur both early on and later, and it appears to be in part a function of at least one prosodic dimension of speech to young children. There is essentially universal anecdotal evidence across languages for higher fundamental frequency or pitch. Ferguson (1977) and Sachs (1977b) have reviewed the substantial body of evidence for the phenomenon, and Garnica (1974, 1977) has substantiated the anecdotal evidence for English with systematic and objective measurement. In addition, there is evidence that children *do* selectively attend to talk addressed to them (Lewis & Freedle, 1973). Even 5-day-olds orient preferentially to sound pitched at about 500 Hz, the normal frequency of English utterances addressed to infants (Kearsley, 1973). At five days there has not been much time to learn to orient selectively, so it may well be that we are dealing with some mutual biological preparation of infants and caretakers. Older children also prefer to listen to samples of adult-child language rather than adult-adult language (Snow, 1972). Children at least seem to know how to find the subset of language that should be their best linguistic data base, although one might want additional information on the universality of this finding.

Other motherese phenomena may well not be universal. For instance, Garnica (1977) established that in English stress patterns change when the addressee is a child; the amount and level of stress increases, so that all of the referentially significant items receive stress. And there is some evidence for English that very young language learners may give particular attention to the meaning expressed by those stressed sentential elements (Shatz, 1975). An ability to preferentially sort out referents in comprehension may rest in part on the perceptual "grabbiness" of relative stress levels in American motherese.

Unfortunately, we have no direct evidence on whether augmented stress on referential elements is the product of a particular culture or is more universal, nor on whether some means of emphasizing referents is critical for establishing sound to referent linkages, nor on whether there are alternative means. We do have indirect evidence that the number of stressed elements and the physical level of stress does increase with lento speech in many cultures. In addition, we know that in numerous cultures, sentential elements are sometimes omitted in talk to children; they receive input equivalent to "baby hungry?" (Ferguson, 1977). Such utterances do more than emphasize the major meaning bearing constituents of sentences; those are the only utterances which are left intact. On the other hand, augmented stress has not been experimentally documented for languages other than English, and it seems possible that it would not be the route chosen to emphasize major meaning bearing elements by language providers who do not normally encounter stress as a device in adult language. We may well want more direct information about widely varying languages (e.g., tonal languages) than we can get by extrapolating from stress-accent languages such as English. Children may be biologically prepared to attend to many things; we need to ascertain the range.

But even if aspects of motherese are universal, their impacts on syntax could be indirect. For instance, some degree of early referent restriction may indirectly aid syntax if children can best process finer form/function mappings and acquire preliminary rules when they have considerable control over some much-repeated and well-automated referential meanings. The process might be analogous to learning how to play chess by observation alone. If the number of pieces was initially restricted, it might be easier to figure out how each was allowed to move than if one was simultaneously trying to direct attention to a great many poorly differentiated pieces. One of the most common observations about the semantics of talk to young children is that the range is very restricted. Ferguson asserts that the number of baby talk words normally used within a language is 100 or less. Rūke-Draviņa (1977) asserts that for Latvian a single family is not likely to use more than 30 words early on. It is also of interest that baby words can be categorized under a very few rubrics. Ferguson (1964, 1977) suggests that the following headings will encompass the known lexicons rather well: kinship terms, body part terms, food terms, animal names, and interesting or dangerous object qualities. Rūke-Draviņa (1977) adds a category for interesting objects of the immediate environment. The semantic base of early language does indeed seem limited.

Other work by Thomas (1979) on the remarkable consistency within and across parents in the use of certain linguistic routines in particular contexts adds to our sense that English language learners are exposed to predictable comments made in predictable ways about predictable topics in predictable circumstances. This may also be useful for establishing major meanings and for allowing children to see some of the grammar in the linguistic surround of well-known referents.

On the other hand, stress, reduction of referents and contextual supports may not provide grammatical structure per se. The controversy in the gestural literature is an especially instructive example, so we will use it to illustrate this point. Gesture has been suggested as providing a nonlinguistic entry or cognitive counterpart or prototype of grammatical structure—a suggestion worth examining briefly. In speech to young children referents are usually present when referred to; moreover, in a play situation Messer (1978) found that maternal reference to a toy usually coincided with manipulation of that toy, for 11-, 14-, and 24-month-olds. This held true for 73% to 96% of all references, with the proportion holding among all age groups. In other words, knowing what toy a mother had in hand reduced the uncertainty of what her speech was about enormously, either for children who were preverbal or for language learners of limited sophistication. In contrast, knowing the frequency of reference to a particular toy (in an array of seven) reduced uncertainty of reference only 1 to 4%. Speech and concurrent action do seem to be mutually relevant. But are they "grammatically" linked? Let us examine the likelihood.

Rodgon and Kauffman (1979) provide evidence that the gestural repertoire used by adults speaking to children is quite different than that which adults typically use to communicate with other adults. The gestural register for communication with children primarily involves deictic or symbolic gestures (e.g., pointing or pantomine demonstrations), with 2-year-olds receiving more of these than 4-year-olds. In samples of adult-adult speech, these two types of gestures are used sparingly and more "conversational" gestures are substituted (i.e., the typical flow of hand-waving that punctuates and accompanies utterances). The functional requirements of the two audiences obviously differ, with adults generally needing less nonverbal specification of everyday sorts of objects and actions. One can certainly conceive of situations in which this adult-adult bias against deixis and demonstrations would change: for instance, when an adult is trying to teach another adult the relevant objects and operations in a new technical domain. Like aspects of verbal motherese, gestural changes are thus not entirely age-specific but we do seem to have a nonverbal counterpart to verbal motherese.

The fact that gestural support, particularly pointing, guides attentional behavior and is minimally comprehensible to language-learning children has also been established in a number of recent studies. Infants begin to show the capacity for joint visual attention to objects quite early (Scaife & Bruner, 1975). Mothers of children under nine months do not point; instead they bring objects to the infant or the infant to objects (Murphy & Messer, 1977). Or, as Kaye (1976) has shown, they "mark" objects for attention in various ways, by direct touching, shaking, and the like. Pre-linguistic 9-month-olds are usually able to follow more distal cues like points, but only those that are in the same visual field as the hand that initiates them. They may be less able to comprehend the specific direction that the finger provides. Fourteen-month-olds, who are at the beginning of one-word speech, are much better at following points that cross visual fields (Lempers, 1979; Murphy & Messer, 1977). Thus, comprehension of pointing has some potential for aiding in the language acquisition process because it exists prior to much acquisition.

To evaluate this potential, Zukow, Reilly, and Greenfield (in press) sampled naturally-occurring maternal offers to transfer objects to the child or to allow the child to engage in a particular activity. They report changes in the amount of contextual support that six children at various levels of semantic-relational sophistication receive during the one-word stage. At first offers seem to be presented mostly on the sensorimotor level alone, then with a combination of language and sensorimotor support, and then with language in isolation. They also provide evidence from these naturalistic settings about what happens when referents are not contextually given and unsupported adult language misfires; adults who successfully "repair" their messages do so by providing gestural and other contextual support.

These studies suggest the possibility that gesture and other forms of contextual support have some role to play in language acquisition. The obvious question is: how could such a "motherese" of gesture be useful? One might suspect that its main role would not be specifically grammatical but would be helpful for establishing referents (e.g., in establishing that the word "bed" has something to do with beds) or reinforcing them when the child is not responding to linguistic cues alone. However, a number of other possibilities have also been tested.

To assess the notion that children might learn about other properties of language by analogy from nonlinguistic information, Shatz (1982) looked at maternal gestural data for eight children varying in age from 18 to 34 months. She examined several levels at which gesture might serve language acquisition: the syntactic, the semantic-relational, and the pragmatic. In her study mothers used seven basic types of gesture: two to present objects (holding out an object or putting it near the child), two kinds of tapping on objects (with finger or another object), points, and two illustrative gestures (actual demonstrations or implied demonstrations without objects). The most frequent gestures were holding out, pointing, and demonstrating.

At the syntactic level of analysis, gesture types did not map well onto particular sentence forms (e.g., questions or declaratives), since no gesture accounted for more than 50% of the gesture tokens for any sentence type. This result conforms to our intuitions; it is hard to imagine a child determining syntactic type from gesture. Gestures simply do not look as if they were made for the purpose of giving either general or specific information about form (i.e., about either general syntactic type or the internal organization of relationships like auxiliary fronting or subject-verb inversion within a particular type).

Shatz thus turned her attention to semantic relations within sentences (e.g., locative, recipient of action, etc.) to see if these categories might map directly onto gesture. They did not. Several gestures could be used with any type. For instance, a point or a tap might be used to indicate location, but either might also be used to indicate the object of a proposed action.

On the other hand, there were very interesting relationships at a discourse or intersentential level. As Shatz says, "Mothers concentrated mainly on two kinds of interactions, one involving object reference and the other activity with objects." She segmented the interactions of the eight mothers and children into reference or activity cycles; these accounted for 80% of all utterances. Each cycle was defined to encompass either one object or one activity.

Relative proportion of cycle types did not differ with age over these eight children. Over all children, the reference cycles involved gesture 67% of the time, while 72% of the activity cycles were gestured. Shatz then examined the consistency of gestural patterns. She did not look at each of her seven single gesture types per se but at groupings or patterns of gestural combination within cycles. Thus, if in one cycle a point was paired with a tap, that was counted as one pattern. A point occurring alone in a cycle would count as another pattern, as would a lone tap. These patterns were fairly reliable for each mother, although somewhat idiosyncratic. For each of the six youngest children, 82% of the gestured cycles were accompanied by patterns unique to the cycle type.

Actually, although Shatz differentiates among them, it seems plausible that points and the two kinds of taps are lumped together by children as functionally equivalent object-focused gestures. In fact, when children do not understand points, mothers usually decrease the distance to the object, often touching or tapping it, and mothers even cue the child by first tapping the child, and then the object (Murphy & Messer, 1977). In the normal acquisition of comprehension of points, as indicated earlier, the progression is also from very proximal maternal cues to more distal, thus suggesting that Shatz's three gestural types represent graded components of a single conceptual grouping.

However, the two-pronged focus on reference and activity cycle types by mothers is particularly interesting because the divisions may correspond to a rather basic linguistic distinction—that of noun and verb. Unfortunately, Shatz does not give us the gesture types used, but we would suspect that the action cycles tend to involve demonstrations and iconic indications of action while the reference cycles tend to involve the rest of the gestures (the pointing complex and the offers) which look quite object-focused. Interestingly, other things which are often pointed to, such as locations or places, may also be considered equivalent to objects by young children inasmuch as the "places" they deal with actually are touchable, concrete entities like "bed," "chair," "hole" and the like. All of these can be pointed to or touched. It certainly seems worth investigating the possibility that, in addition to specifying particular referents, gesture may help the English-speaking child to establish or concretize some of the first language appropriate *classes* of referents: objects and actions. In addition, it would be of great interest to see if gesture works in similar ways in diverse cultures and linguistic groups.

Although the results from these gestural studies are intriguing, the fact remains that none of them yield results that establish that gesture facilitates *syntax*. In general they seem to indicate that gesture helps to establish referents, or correspondences between particular words and their real-world counterparts. Such hypotheses may be so trivially obvious that they need no testing, although they could be tested directly via experimental manipulations in which new words were introduced with a variety of novel objects with and without gesture. Gesture might also have reassuring or motivational properties. For instance, demonstrations could provide evidence to children that certain actions are both safe and socially desirable. If gesture to American children does facilitate syntax it does so rather indirectly and on a rather basic level, by treatment suggesting that referents are of two types, object and action, which correspond to two potentially important linguistic divisions. Furthermore, since gesture seems to be a backup or support option for establishing sentence meanings, as in the Zukow et al.

study, one alternative model of syntax facilitation seems unlikely. A child who needs gestural specification of the major meaning elements in a given sentence would presumably have little leftover attention to spare for the fine details of the grammatical structure of that sentence. It seems more likely that when the child has relatively good control over particular lexical meanings and does not need them to be specified gesturally, that he or she will be in a reasonable position to work on the fine-grained grammaticization of language.

We are thus left with a preliminary sense that particular aspects of the linguistic and extralinguistic environment with which a language-learning child is faced may be useful, but in rather variable and particular ways. Some seem particularly useful for establishing referents; some (like expansions) seem to provide particularly accessible exemplars or instances of grammaticization. At this point there is no clear evidence that the environments themselves provide grammatical structure and no clear mechanism by which they could do so. On the other hand, there does seem to be evidence that various kinds of linguistic restrictions and environmental supports may help to provide a good data base, potentially increasing the rate at which children can acquire language and otherwise facilitating the process, but perhaps nonspecifically and regardless of the nature of the primitives that children themselves may bring to the process.

Conclusions

It appears to us that each of the approaches that we have examined here has a great deal to offer in exploring possibilities for a full conceptualization of the language acquisition process. But, to date, none has been tested across the range of cross-linguistic data that we see as necessary for specifying the universal and particular aspects of a general language acquisition model. Clearly, in order to establish any proposed sets of primitives as universal, a great deal of cross-cultural specification of the error patterns and organizing principles that seem to inhere in child language will be required. And to establish the utility and roles of particular environmental supports, whether universal or not, we will need concurrent and detailed specification of the environments in which particular hypotheses about grammar are made. We are far from having data that is both this specific and detailed and this generalizable. En route to attaining that data, we may want to heed the words of Oscar Wilde, who once said, "Arguments are to be avoided. They are always vulgar and often convincing." We are not yet at the point where we should be fully convinced by or fully committed to any general theory of language acquisition. For now, like children acquiring language, swamp sparrows learning song, and laughing gulls trying to feed, we may have to be content with rather provisional conceptualizations, subject to revision by more data.

Lynn S. Snyder

Cognition and Language Development

Introduction

The study of the relationship between language and cognitive development is like the carnival huckster's shell game. The player—try as he might to keep his eye on the pea—often finds that it is not under the shell he has selected. Unfortunately for the individual interested in the child's acquisition of language, the problem often becomes confounded by the addition of many more shells than the player can follow. When one looks for instances where the acquisition of linguistic and cognitive structures may be related, it is often difficult to discern with which cognitive shell the linguistic pea is located. Cognition represents such a broad domain that it adds many more shells to the game.

The impact of the scope of cognition and the question before us is better appreciated when we examine what we mean when we refer to cognition and its development. The word "cognition" is derived from the Latin verb *noscere*, to know. Definitions contained in dictionaries typically describe cognition as knowing. It represents, then, how a person knows the world.

At a simple level, cognition seems to have some relationship to language, the symbol system used by men for communication. Language symbols are thought to represent some information that people have of the world. The symbols stand for external states, conditions, activities, objects, people and events as they are known or apprehended by the minds of men;

©College-Hill Press, Inc. All rights, including that of translation, reserved. No part of this publication may be reproduced without the written permission of the publisher.

that is, words stand for concepts. Most theorists seem to agree that a relationship between cognition and language exists at this level. However, there seem to be differences of opinion regarding the extent to which cognition and language are related. Some, e.g., Fodor (1980) feel that the previously stated relationship is the only one that applies. It is generally agreed that the ability to understand complex syntactic structures requires specific knowledge of linguistic structures that concepts themselves cannot provide. Some researchers contend that information processing variables, attentional variables, conceptual and cognitive problem solving strategies play a significant role in how complex linguistic strings are apprehended (Bates & MacWhinney, in press). Consequently, the questioned relationship between cognition and language in general remains unsolved.

The debate is not a new one. It has been around for centuries. The Platonic school of thought held that principles such as one finds in language are immutable and unaffected by man's mortal mental structures. By contrast, Aristotelians felt that such principles were affected and defined by the constraints or limitations of the organism that must use them. Obviously, these same positions are represented today, articulated in our contemporary idiom.

Naturally, these two positions are reflected in discussions of the nature of child language development. On the one hand, Chomsky's (1975, 1980a) position asserts that cognitive mechanisms could never account for the development of the highly structural rules specific to language. Rather, children discover these rules because an innate language mechanism predisposes them to do so. By contrast, MacNamara's (1972) early interpretation of Piagetian principles suggests that specified cognitive abilities must develop prior to and are prerequisite for the acquisition of specified language skills. Between these two ends of the philosophical/theoretical continuum, lie many viewpoints regarding cognition and language development.

Recent Conceptualizations of the Problem

At the present time, there seem to be three major philosophical positions: the nativist, constructivist and behaviorist theories of language development. These viewpoints differ in where they place the source of the child's language learning ability and the mechanisms by which this language acquisition takes place. In recent years, however, the debate has been developed by and restricted to the nativist and constructivist camps. No doubt the behaviorists' inability to adequately respond to the concerns leveled by nativists and constructivists in the late 1960s and early 1970s has led to their recent lack of theoretical and empirical visibility on this question. Consequently, this discussion will review selected recent characterizations and contributions to the issue at hand, namely, selected nativist and constructivist approaches to the problem.

Nativist Language-Specific Rule Discovery Hypotheses

Generally speaking, the language-specific rule discovery or "little linguist" (Valian, 1979) hypotheses represent the nativist view that the source of the child's ability to acquire language is an innate language-specific rule discovery system. Chomsky's (1965, 1975, 1980a; Caplan & Chomsky, 1980) thinking initiated this trend in linguistic theory and developmental psycholinguistics. He suggested that the child is an active participant in the language development process who creates a series of successive hypotheses about language and "tests" them. This point of view is not unlike that of the constructivist who also regards the child as a little theorist.

The nativist viewpoint diverges from the constructivist with regard to the source of the child's hypotheses and the strategies that he uses to derive and test them. Chomsky (1980a; Caplan & Chomsky, 1980) regards language as a specific faculty of mind that can produce complex linguistic structures once it has been launched on that developmental path. He regards language as a faculty of man that is uniquely different from other mental faculties. Consequently, we should view the relationship between language and cognition just as a "neutral" scientist would view the relationship between the ear and the liver. Thus, investigations of language development should begin with a priori assumptions of uniqueness much as studies of the development of the organs of the body would. Chomsky feels that language is sufficiently rich in structure that viable parallels to its structurally dependent rules do not exist in other domains. Consequently, the child's ability to apprehend these detailed and rich structures in light of the relatively impoverished information available to the child must reflect an innate, genetically determined rule discovery mechanism specific to language.

In developing this hypothesis, Chomsky focuses his attention on the richness of the structures or rules of language. In particular, he develops his arguments with appeals to the acquisition of syntactic rules. The acquisition of word meaning, as influenced by conceptual development, seems to present fewer problems for many nativists, e.g., Fodor (1980). Rather, their arguments are played out around the question of the acquisition of syntactic structures. This chapter will look at three of the current nativist approaches.

The Little Linguist Hypothesis

Working in a manner consistent with the Chomskian nativist tradition, Valian (Valian, 1979; Valian, Winzemer, & Erreich, 1981; Valian & Caplan, 1979) has investigated the child's acquisition of syntactic structures. Essentially she proposes that the child learns a transformational grammar containing both phrase structure rules and transformational rules. Consistent with Chomsky's notions, she argues that the child possesses an innate *syntactic acquisition device*. This mechanism contains the organizing principles that form the common denominator in all languages, the linguistic universals. These principles make available to the child the elements and the operations which he will need to formulate hypotheses about the grammar of the language.

Valian suggests that the hypotheses formulated by the child are candidate phrase structure and transformational rules which the child then tests against the available evidence. Although the youngster makes use of the distributional regularities in the utterances he or she hears, the child uses this information only to test his or her hypotheses. Given the goodness of fit between the rule that the child has formulated and the data, the youngster may retain or discard his or her rule. Thus, Valian characterizes the child as if he or she operated in the scientific method. Unlike scientists who formulate their hypotheses through logical deductive operations, Valian suggests that the child has an inside edge. The child's innate rule discovery system guides the youngster toward his or her first hypotheses.

The Lexical Hypothesis

Roeper and his colleagues propose a somewhat different approach to language acquisition (Roeper, Lapointe, Binigi, & Tavakolian, 1981). They observe that children learn lexical items before they learn the rules that affect them. In contrast to theorists who would focus on the meaning component of the word, Roeper et al. (1981) suggest—in the Chomskian tradition—that the child learns the set of subcategorization frames associated with the lexical items. These frames characterize and restrict the types of syntactic relations into which these items can enter. Consequently, as the child learns lexical items, he or she learns something about syntax. The lexicon becomes a vehicle which introduces the child to syntactic categories and frames. Having become alerted to these relations, the child becomes sensitive to those syntactic rules that change subcategorization frames.

In some sense, Roeper et al. regard hypothesis formation as an activity which, once begun, leads the child to or triggers the child to the formulation of a successive series of hypotheses. Once started in the process of hypothesis formation for a particular rule, the child appears to gain increasing momentum until he has acquired a rule that will handle the information that he encounters.

The Learnability Hypothesis

Wexler and Culicover (1980) have proposed a learnability theory of language acquisition. They suggest that the child's learning of language, particularly syntax, can only be explained by making an appeal to the effect of specific linguistic constraints. Although they focus their discussion on specific syntactic principles, they also extend their consideration to semantic constraints as well. They suggest that the child uses these principles in learning language and such principles ultimately are what make a language "learnable." The thrust of their efforts has been to specify these principles of mind which make language learning attainable and feasible for the child. While they concede that ultimately these linguistic constraints may be cases of or reflect more general cognitive constraints, they suggest that such cognitive constraints have not been well-formalized or specified and that evidence is lacking to support this point of view. Consequently, they propose a nativist stance until constructivist evidence is found that will withstand their logical and empirical tests.

The preceding discussion has served to acquaint the reader with the major articulations of this theoretical orientation. Wexler and Culicover's hypothesis, as well as the other nativist hypotheses, are discussed in greater detail in McNew and Bates (this volume). We will now turn our attention to a very different approach to the problem, the constructivist point of view.

Constructivist Hypotheses

Constructivist hypotheses propose that the child is an active processor whose knowledge of the world serves as an interactive source for his hypotheses about language. Some constructivists might suggest that this source is *innate* (Slobin, 1979), others (Bates & Snyder, in press) suggest that it may be the *inevitable* result or outcome of the child's dynamic interface with the world. Regardless of this distinction, constructivists suggest that the child comes to know the world through his or her interactions with it. The child applies his or her schemas—sensorimotor or mental—to the environment and incorporates or assimilates that information. Or, the environment may give the child information which prompts the child to change his or her schemas. The give and take of this continuous interaction is the mechanism of the child's cognitive development. The gradual emergence of the structures of formal operational thought are the result of this process. Thus, the constructivist viewpoint suggests that the child's cognitive development—how the child knows the world and the language object at any one point in time and how the child responds as he or she interfaces with it—is related to the hypotheses that the child will formulate about language in an important way.

At this time, there seem to be three major types of constructivist hypotheses. These include the "strong" cognitive hypothesis, the "weak" cognitive hypothesis, and the correlational hypothesis.

The Strong Cognitive Hypothesis

The strong form of the cognitive hypothesis suggests that the development of specific cognitive factors is sufficient to account for the child's ability to apprehend and learn language (Miller, Chapman, & Bedrosian, 1977). In this form, the cognitive hypothesis often carries an implied direction of effects. For example, MacNamara (1972) contended that the notion of cognitive prerequisites presupposes that the nonverbal cognitive skill precedes the acquisition of its corresponding linguistic skill. However, we encounter difficulty reliably measuring cognitive and linguistic skills in young children, determining "productive" instances of linguistic skills, and deciding which nonverbal cognitive skills predict and are truly prerequisite for the attainment of specific linguistic skills. Some general cognitive abilities thought to be critical for the acquisition of language have been delineated by Bowerman (1974). These attainments have included the development of symbolic representation, the ability to order, classify, embed and conserve, the development of concepts of basic invariance, appreciation of object-action relations and the ability to construct a representation of perceptual space. No one would argue that they are necessary for the child's attainment of language. The individual interested in the strong form of the cognitive hypothesis, however, would have to demonstrate that they, in themselves, were sufficient to explain the child's development of language.

A vocal proponent of this position, Karmiloff-Smith (1979), focuses on the operative aspects of cognitive development or the development of strategies. She suggests that language acquisition requires the development of encoding and decoding strategies or procedures like other types of problem solving. Once the child can operate the strategy in an automatic and consistent manner, the child can reflect upon and analyze the strategy itself. The organism's tendency toward an organized equilibrium will lead the child to organize his or her system across strategies to a point where there is agreement among them and the system operates in a coherent manner. The child engages in this reorganization spontaneously. Karmiloff-Smith perceives that cognitive development results from the child's increased interactions with the world and that this change is reflected in the child's interaction with language. If the child interacts with, uses, or has the opportunity to use a specific strategy with increasing frequency, the child is likely to tend to automatize it and reorganize other strategies within his or her system so that they will operate in agreement and in coordination with it. Thus, it represents a version of the strong form of the cognitive hypothesis (Chapman, 1982).

Miller, Chapman, and Bedrosian (1977) point out that such a position implies that language development should be commensurate with cognitive development. Further, it cannot exceed cognitive development. In other words, this point of view implies a nearly perfect correlation between language and cognitive development.

The Weak Cognitive Hypothesis

The weak form of this hypothesis (Cromer, 1974, 1976) argues that cognitive developments are necessary and critical for language development but not sufficient in themselves to account for the development of language. Cromer suggests that cognitive development allows for the development of meaning content to be encoded by the child. However, skills specific to a linguistic system are necessary for the child to be able to express these meanings with language.

Miller et al. (1977) point out that the weak form of the cognitive hypothesis implies that language development would be equal to or less than cognitive development. It should not exceed cognitive development.

The Correlational Hypothesis

The third constructivist viewpoint articulated in recent years is the correlational hypothesis (Miller et al., 1971). In general, it suggests that cognitive and linguistic development will be strongly related to one another. They share this relationship because they are both served by common underlying structures. When developmental change takes place in specific underlying structures or mechanisms, the change may be observed in either the linguistic or the nonlinguistic domain. Basic to this position is the Piagetian notion of the horizontal decalage in development. This concept refers to the time delay between the expression of an operation in one content domain before its expression in another. Thus, the expression of the child's operative structure may be observed first in language or in nonlinguistic activities.

There are two well articulated points of view regarding the nature of this relationship: those of Bates (Bates, Benigni, Bretherton, Camaioni,

& Volterra, 1977, 1979; Bates & Snyder, in press) and Johnston (in press). Bates and her colleagues have argued for a "local homology" point of view. They argue that there is a relationship between specific developments in language and cognition. The relationship that they observe between specific achievements appears to be such that attainment will occur in either the cognitive or the linguistic domain first. Bates clearly states that the corresponding developments in both domains do not occur because the two attainments reflect the use of a similar task strategy. They are not related because they are analogous in some way. Rather, Bates hypothesizes—in a Piagetian fashion—that similar underlying cognitive structures or mechanisms subserve both the specific cognitive skill and the linguistic skill. Thus, if a cognitive skill required the development of "software" programs A and C and a language skill requires the development of programs B and C, they may appear correlated in development when program C—which subserves both of them—emerges. This is particularly true if programs A and B have already developed and program C is all that is necessary for the skill to emerge. Since specific language and cognitive attainments may require the input of more than one type of underlying "program," the correlations that one observes between language and cognitive skills are highly specific and often multidimensional. The number of different cognitive attainments that we must examine is often larger than that which we had anticipated. Further, the relationship between specific cognitive and linguistic achievements is not a constant one. As the child changes his or her way of knowing the world and language itself, the underlying software needed for subsequent development in both domains changes. More of software program C will not result in further development within seemingly linked cognitive and linguistic areas. Rather, subsequent developments are often subserved by a different set of software programs.

The Batesian point of view seems to stress the changing relationship between cognition and language development as well as the operations or strategies involved in both domains. Her work has concentrated upon those attainments taking place during the first 28 months of life. Johnston's (in press) characterization places a somewhat greater emphasis on exploring the way that concepts and their attainment constrain and correlate with the acquisition of highly specific linguistic structures, particularly spatial, locative, and dimensional terms. However, she also considers the effects of operative aspects of knowledge which she calls structural knowledge. Johnston's position seems to be that one cannot simply look at the relationship between the way that conceptual knowledge constrains and affects the acquisition of language. One also needs to consider the ways in which procedural and organizational knowledge (in a sense, operative knowledge) does the same. Her analysis of the acquisition of language thus considers both types of information from studies containing direct and indirect tests of the question. Johnston seems to play the shell game most astutely.

Johnston concludes that on the one hand specific cognitive achievements may not be implied in the acquisition of all linguistic forms, e.g., elements of the auxiliary system, nor may cognitive operations be necessary and sufficient for the acquisition of specific linguistic structures. On the other hand, some linguistic forms clearly require prior conceptual knowledge which constrains their acquisition. Thus, there seem to be relationships between some but not all aspects of language acquisition and specific cognitive development. However, Johnston sagely acknowledges many of the limitations under which our inquiries have had to function until this time. Her point of view seems to be quite reality-based in that she acknowledges both what we *do* and what we *don't* know, how far our data can take us.

Summary

Nativist and constructivist theories offer us a wide variety of ways to consider the relationship between linguistic and cognitive development. There are many types of linguistic structures and operations whose acquisition can be studied in comprehension and production. Similarly, there are many cognitive attainments that can be explored in relation to the linguistic.

To afford ourselves the best opportunity to observe whether language and cognitive development are related and whether the nature of that relationship is general or highly specified at different points in time, we will focus our attention on two very different stages of development. We will examine recent studies of the relationship between cognition and language from the sensorimotor period and the period of transition into concrete operations. Further, we will examine two very different aspects of language development: comprehension and production. Specifically, we will look at the child's development of productive communicative gesture, words and syntax during the first two and a half years of life and his development of constructive comprehension processes between 6 and 9 years of age. When possible, evidence will be reviewed from studies of both normally developing children and children with specific language impairment. The latter population provide a unique opportunity to examine the relationship between language and cognition. By definition, children with specific language impairment must demonstrate *general* intelligence within the normal range. Thus, if specific cognitive and linguistic attainments are linked, these youngsters should demonstrate delays in those targeted cognitive skills as well as in their language skills.

Exploring Possible Links

The acquisition of productive communicative gestural and linguistic milestones is perhaps most easily studied when children are in the earlier stages of development. It seems to be somewhat easier to establish criteria to determine what the achievement should look and sound like, as well as to determine how many times the gesture, word, or syntactic combination, must be used to establish that it is "productive." For such purposes, then, we will look at those studies of language and cognitive development during the first two years of life. Specifically, we will examine three major milestones of communicative development: the onset of the intentional use of prelinguistic conventional gestures at 9 to 10 months of age, the baby's first words at 12 to 13 months of age, and the child's production of two word combinations, the beginnings of syntax, at approximately 20 months.

These particular milestones also seem to hold some interesting promise for investigations into possible links between cognition and language. McCall, Eichorn, and Hogarty (1977) reanalyzed the Fels and Berkeley longitudinal studies. These investigations administered a variety of standardized psychometric measures, particularly cognitive, to a large sample of normally developing children and followed the youngsters for approximately 5 years. McCall et al's factor analysis of these data revealed four distinct moments in development when there appeared to be major changes in the pattern of relationship among the major variables. These shifts among the many cognitive and some verbal variables that were studied took place at 9 to 10 months, 12 to 13 months, 20 to 21 months and 30 to 36 months of age. The first three-time periods are precisely the points which we identified as reflecting major changes in the child's early productive linguistic and communicative development. These data suggest, then, that something more than linguistic development may be implicated at these developmental points and that it may be wise for us to examine them more closely.

Prelinguistic Intentional Communication

The nativist point of view may not regard the onset of the child's intentional use of communicative gesture as bearing any intrinsic relationship to linguistic communication apart from the fact that intent to communicate is shared by both. As such, it may be regarded as probably related to the development of social cognition. By contrast, many constructivist points of view would suggest that it is related to the development of social cognition and/or some specific subset of cognitive skills. The strong form of the cognitive hypothesis might predict that there should be a very high, positive correlation between language and cognitive developments. Further, the direction of this relationship should be the same across children. The weak form of the cognitive hypothesis would argue that specific cognitive developments must occur in order for communication to emerge. However, there may be a considerable time delay between the onset of the cognitive skill and the emergence of the communicative milestone. Lastly, correlational hypotheses might predict a link between the communicative development and specific cognitive skills. However, the communicative attainment may emerge just before the cognitive in some children and the converse sequence of events may be observed in others. Regardless of the theoretical stance that one takes, all points of view would agree that such findings should be verified by replication.

The problem posed by these generic descriptions of the outcomes possible from this line of research is the identity of the cognitive attainments to be studied. Fortunately, the development of the Uzgiris-Hunt *Ordinal Scales of Psychological Development* (1975) has made it possible to study those specific cognitive skills whose development Piaget (1963) observed during the infant's sensorimotor stage of development. These include:

(1)   object permanence, the development of the appreciation of the independent existence of objects;

(2)   construction of objects in space, the development of the ability to construct representations of objects as they move along a continuum and with memory for familiar locations of objects and people in space;

(3)   means-end relations, the development of the ability to use a tool to achieve a desired outcome;

(4)   operational causality, the development of the ability to appreciate mechanical causality;

(5)   vocal and gestural imitation, the gradual development of the ability to imitate novel vocal and gestural actions that had been seen or heard at some earlier date; and

(6)   schemes for relating to objects, the child's gradual acquisition of the ability to represent objects enactively.

These specific skills are considered good candidates with which to test the language/cognition hypothesis.

Studies of Normal Children

In a benchmark study, Bates, Camaioni, and Volterra (1973, 1975) describe the child's shift from the reactive use of natural signals, e.g., crying, for communication to his intentional use of signals, most of which are communicative conventions, e.g., pointing. They traced the emergence of this signaling from their early natural schemas through their subsequent augmentation with conventional phonetic sequences. In so doing, they were able to chart the child's development of functional communication. Specifically, they traced changes in the child's ability to get an adult to do something for him or *protoimperative* and to catch the adult's attention, establishing a shared point of reference or *protodeclarative*. When the protoimperative was produced with the child's intentional and controlled use of signals, Bates et al. observed their subjects use pointing and/or reaching toward the desired object or goal, paired with back and forth eye contact between the adult and the goal to communicate their intention. The babies intentionally gave, showed or pointed to objects to express their protodeclaratives.

The naturalistic observations made by Bates and her colleagues also allowed them to observe their subject's spontaneous play and object manipulation. They interpreted these instances in terms of Piagetian notions of cognitive development, finding an interesting parallel between the onset of their subjects' intentional use of signals and their object manipulation strategies. They found that at approximately the same time that intentional use of conventional signals emerged, the children also began to use Piagetian stage 5 tool-use strategies: using new means to achieve a goal. Bates et al. reasoned that sensorimotor stage 5 tool-use understanding was an attainment crucial to both the social tool-use of using a scheme to get an adult's attention and the object centered tool use of using one toy to reach another.

At approximately the same time, Sugarman (1973) also conducted a longitudinal study of babies' development of tool-use, operational causality, their ability to request objects from an adult, sensorimotor expressions of the agent case and social interaction. She found that intentional sensorimotor requests were characterized by what she termed a *coordinated person-object orientation interaction*. These were expressed by the child establishing eye contact with the adult and reaching and or pointing toward the goal object. Obviously, this schema is similar to that described by Bates and her colleagues. Further, she observed that this communicative development was concurrent with the child's development of sensorimotor stage 5 tool-use and instrumental causality at approximately 9 to 10 months of age. These cognitive achievements were observed in the babies' performance on the Means-End and Operational Causality Scales of the Uzgiris-Hunt battery of cognitive Piagetian tasks. Sugarman inferred that the structure of the agent case (Fillmore, 1968) has its roots in the child's sensorimotor awareness of external agents and the youngsters' ability to mobilize or signal this agency with his or her sensorimotor actions and vocalizations. Although the child may be summoning an active agent with his protoimperative, it is not clear that Sugarman was able to demonstrate that agent comments during the one-word stage were correlated with the sensorimotor interpretation of agency. However, the relationship between cognitive and communicative milestones observed by Bates et al. was replicated in this study, a piece of information relevant to the question at hand.

The initial study conducted by Bates and her colleagues contained three subjects. Sugarman's sample was somewhat larger. It is difficult to draw any robust conclusions from these limited samples. Consequently, Bates, Benigni, Bretherton, Camaioni, and Volterra (1977, 1979) conducted a larger longitudinal study, following 25 Italian and American babies from 9 to 13 months of age. They observed their social interaction, communicative and language behaviors. They assessed a variety of cognitive behaviors using the Piagetian assessment of sensorimotor intelligence, the Uzgiris-Hunt *Ordinal Scales of Psychological Development* (1975). All of these scales but the Operational Causality Scale were administered. During the prelinguistic period, their findings replicated the sensorimotor performatives—the protoimperatives and protodeclaratives—observed earlier by Bates, Camaioni, and Volterra (1975). At approximately 10 months, the babies engaged in giving, showing, pointing, and/or reaching communicative behaviors. These behaviors correlated closely with one another and with the babies' performance on the tool-use, gestural and vocal imitation scales of the Uzgiris-Hunt battery, and with social development. This, too, replicated their earlier observations as well as Sugarman's findings. These sensorimotor communication milestones did not correlate with the babies' performance on scales of object permanence and the construction of spatial relations. Thus, the pattern of relationship between intentional communication and cognition does not appear to be a general or global one. Rather, it seems to take place among localized and highly specified cognitive abilities.

Following Sugarman's approach to the relationship between intentional prelinguistic communication and cognition, Harding and Golinkoff (1978) conducted a cross-sectional study of infants from 8 to 14 months of age. They assessed their subjects' ability to use prelinguistic intentional schemes to get adults to help them and the development of causal thinking and object permanence. They used the object permanence scale from the Uzgiris-Hunt battery and causality tasks from the Mehrabian and Williams (1974) Piagetian measures. Harding and Golinkoff found that all of the children who had attained sensorimotor stage 4 on the causality tasks had not yet attained the ability to use intentional conventional signals. By contrast, approximately 71% of the infants who had attained sensorimotor stage 5 causal development had similarly developed the use of intentional communicative signals. They interpreted these findings as evidence for the weak cognitive hypothesis, that causal understanding is a necessary but not sufficient condition for communicative development. From our vantage point, it is difficult to understand why these results might not also offer support for the correlational hypothesis.

In the only training study conducted to date, Steckol and Leonard (1981) studied 32 infants who had reached sensorimotor stage 4 in Means-End relationships and schemes for relating to objects. Their subjects also had not yet begun to use intentional prelinguistic communication schemes or intentional protoperformatives. Each baby was randomly assigned to one of four groups. The first group received training in stage 5 tool-use behaviors. The second group was trained in stage 5 schemes for handling objects while the third received training in both sets of skills. The fourth group received no training per se but they received regular opportunities to handle, explore, and play with the same objects used by the children in the other groups. Only those children who received training in schemes advanced in their abilities in that cognitive domain. In addition, they demonstrated a corresponding increase in their use of protoperformatives. No other significant pattern of cognitive and or communicative gain was observed in any of the other groups. Interestingly, two of the children who had made gains in performative usage did not make corresponding gains in object schemas. Steckol and Leonard interpreted that this time lag may suggest that the relationship may be trivial. It could, however, be interpreted as support for a correlational hypothesis.

The milestone of the emergence of intentional communicative signals and its relation to specified sensorimotor cognitive abilities is rather impressive. The logic of this developmental point on the continuum of communicative development is appealing. However, it seems to be important to know—if we are examining the relationship between cognition and language development—whether this milestone is, in fact, related to later language development. There are times when our developmental logic does not meet the laboratory test, e.g., the relationship between the quality and harmony of early dyadic interaction to later linguistic communicative development (Kaye, 1981). Fortunately, this developmental milestone passes the test. Bates, Bretherton, and Snyder (in preparation) studied 32 infants, observing and assessing a variety of cognitive and linguistic behaviors at 10, 13, 20, and 28 months of age. They found that the prelinguistic gestural behaviors of giving, showing and pointing predicted language acquisition at later stages. In fact, it was one of five language variables from the 10, 13, and 20 month experiments that entered into a regression to predict language skills at 28 months of age, accounting for approximately 85% of the variance. Thus, these communicative behaviors appear to be intrinsically important milestones that relate to language development.

Thus far, the data from studies on normally developing children do not support the strong form of the cognitive hypothesis. Steckol and Leonard's (1981) findings present a problem for the weak version of the cognitive hypothesis. Although a specific cognitive ability did seem to be related to the attainment of a communicative milestone, it did not necessarily temporally precede the emergence of the prelinguistic milestone. The weak form of the cognitive hypothesis predicts that the cognitive attainment would exceed or meet but not lag behind the appropriate linguistic development. It would not predict that the communicative development would exceed or surpass the cognitive attainment. The evidence seems to lend more support to the hypothesis that there is some type of correlation between the emergence of prelinguistic intentional communicative behaviors and the stage 5 attainment of specific cognitive skills. Such a position does not commit itself to a lockstep temporal sequence of development. Rather it rests upon the notions of skill emergence in *either* direction and horizontal decalage.

There does seem to be some congruence observed in the identity of the specific cognitive skills implicated in this possible relationship. Clearly, tool-use and operational causality appear frequently in the data. Conversely, object permanence and the construction of spatial relations are not related. Unfortunately, methodological differences among the studies make it difficult to sort out this relationship with greater clarity. Studies of language disordered children, however, may provide us with some additional evidence.

Studies of Language Disordered Children

Language disordered children seem to provide a unique opportunity to the researcher interested in exploring the relationship between cognition and language. By definition, a child with specific language impairment, must demonstrate general cognitive abilities within the normal range and a significant deficit in one or more linguistic skills. That such a population exists—one whose language development does not appear to be related to cognitive development—was interpreted for years as robust support for the nativist hypothesis. This was clearly the case until researchers began to investigate specific cognitive skills.

In a study comparing matched normal and language disordered children, Snyder (1978) examined their specific cognitive skill attainments and their prelinguistic and early one-word performatives. The subjects were matched for sex, socioeconomic status, mean length of utterance (1.0) and roughly equivalent production vocabularies based on a maternal interview. She found that the language disordered children tended to use gestural signals that were consistently at an earlier developmental level than their normal counterparts. The normally developing children tended to consistently use stage 5 level performatives when they did not use words to communicate.

In addition to these differences, she also found that her subjects' level of communicative performance was predicted by their performance on the tool-use or Means-End Scales of the Uzgiris-Hunt battery. The level of the performatives produced by the children was accounted for by its relationship to their attainment of tool-use skills. The other cognitive scales from the battery, the Object Permanence, Operational Causality, Imitation, Construction of Objects in Space and Schemas for Relating to Objects Scales, did not account for any additional variance. She interpreted these findings as support for a specific relationship between tool-use and prelinguistic and early linguistic communicative behaviors.

Snyder's findings replicated a trend observed in the studies of normally developing children at this age. In addition, it demonstrated that children with specific language impairment may sustain a specific cognitive deficit. Interestingly, the deficit appeared to occur in a domain that had been identified as correlated to communicative development. On the one hand, this could be interpreted as lack of support for the nativist hypothesis that cognitive attainments do not bear an important relationship to language development. On the other hand, since we have confined our discussion to prelinguistic phenomena, the nativist might argue that since the data do not relate to linguistic phenomena, they are not admissable or relevant evidence for the question. Depending upon how one regards these prelinguistic performatives, these data can be taken as support for a cognitive hypothesis of language acquisition at this stage of development. Of interest, however, is whether such correlations between conventional communication forms and specific cognitive skills continue once the child begins to use language.

The Onset of Linguistic Communication

The crux of identifying possible links between specific cognitive attainments and early linguistic skills has often rested upon the child's attainment of representational or symbolic thought. This achievement characterizes the beginnings of Piaget's sensorimotor stage 6 (1962) and it is presumed to continue to develop throughout the succeeding years. The hallmark of this development is the child's ability to represent objects, events, and states that are no longer perceptually present. He may do this with verbal linguistic symbols, some types of nonlinguistic representation or mental symbols, and the gestural symbols of symbolic play. As the child develops this representational activity, he learns to mobilize it in the various cognitive domains of tool-use, object permanence, play, and so forth. The researcher interested in the language/cognition question tries to observe any links between linguistic representational achievements and nonlinguistic cognitive representational achievements. The same questions posed earlier by the nativist and constructivist theories for the relationship or nonrelationship between intentional gesture and cognition can be asked for the relationship between first words and cognition.

While the underlying general questions that motivate this inquiry remain the same, the content being examined has changed. The linguistic development studied at this point is the child's development of single word utterances. The cognitive achievement is the development of symbolic thought as it may be seen in the various nonlinguistic symbolic domains mentioned earlier. At first glance, this seems to be a straightforward task. Unfortunately, there seems to be very little agreement across investigators on a number of issues which appear to be both substantive and methodological in nature. First, some researchers, e.g., Ingram (1978), are reluctant to discuss a child's sensorimotor stage 6 abilities until that level of operation appears across several domains. Other investigators, however, focus on the notion of decalage and look for sensorimotor stage 6 achievement within specific cognitive skills. Second, some investigators seem to have different criteria for the attainment of cognitive stage 6 attainment in each domain. Obviously, such differences in stage assignment make it difficult to compare studies that differ with respect to these first two concerns. A more comprehensive treatment of these concerns appears in Corrigan (1979). If this were not enough cause for ambivalence, there are further problems. Third, investigators differ as to their criteria for what is regarded as a child's "first words." As Snyder, Bates, and Bretherton (1981) note, this can refer to the child's first word-like phonetic strings that are associated with highly specific routines and situation-specific behaviors to the emergence of true reference across contents or to the increased spurt in vocabulary development frequently observed around 16 months of age. Investigators seem to focus upon different points upon this developmental continuum of early language development. Fourth, there seems to be a difference of opinion as to whether one should examine the passage from qualitatively different milestones (e.g., from vocal routines such as "Mama" as an all-purpose request, to naming a referent class in many different contexts) or progress within a particular milestone class, e.g., the number of different vocabulary words produced. Last, investigators have been differentially entranced with the relevance of different cognitive domains to the language acquisition process. Consequently, some have focused on a single cognitive domain while others have examined the development of several or multiple domains. The net effect of these five problems is that it is difficult to draw a cohesive picture about the possible links between cognitive and linguistic development.

Keeping this in mind, we will examine the findings from studies of populations of normal and language disordered children. We will try to describe the focus and criteria for "linguistic" and "cognitive" development in each.

Studies of Normally Developing Children: Object Permanence

In one of the earliest observations of the relationship between cognitive and linguistic attainments in children, Bloom (1973) observed that her subject's first words were primarily functors. The child's substantive words or object names were few in number and were underextended or context-bound in use (Snyder, et al., 1981). When the child's lexicon underwent a shift toward a rapid acquisition of context-free substantive words or object names, it was accompanied by stage 6 or representational attainments in object permanence as observed in the child's object-related behavior. Bloom suggested that representational thought in object permanence may be a cognitive prerequisite for the acquisition of stable lexical representations of objects, i.e., object words. This early observation set the stage for and motivated many of the investigations of the relationship between language and cognitive development in the years that followed.

Ramsey (1977) studied the handedness, vocabulary development and development of object permanence in 24 infants. He found that most of the infants who had begun to use words had also attained an early sensorimotor stage 6 level of object permanence. Further, the infants' vocabulary development was characterized by a rapid acquisition of lexical items at the end of the second year. The infants' sudden acquisition of a large number of vocabulary words was accompanied by their completion of stage 6 object permanence.

Spawned by similar concerns and the same laboratory as Ramsey, Corrigan (1978) conducted a longitudinal study of the language acquired and used by children during the one-word stage and their attainment of stage 6 object permanence. She found a general relationship between the emergence of first words and early stage 6 object permanence. However, when age was partialled out, the correlation was not significant. She also explored whether the meanings being expressed by the children bore any relationship to the attainment or completion of stage 6 object permanence.

Corrigan found that the semantic categories of nonexistence and recurrence emerged at the same time the children were able to complete stage 6 object permanence. Like Ramsey, she also observed a burst in the children's total productive vocabularies at this time. The precise quantitative level correlated with the completion of stage 6 object permanence seems to vary considerably across children and across these studies. On the other hand, she did not observe the same functor/substantive word shift in her subjects' lexicons observed by Bloom.

More recently, Smolak (1982) examined the relationship between language comprehension and the production of first words to the attainment of object classification skills and object permanence in 48 infants from 9 to 15 months of age. She found that classification and object permanence scores and stages were related, but not significantly correlated to performance in language comprehension tasks. In addition, all of the children, but one, who used words had also attained stage 5 object permanence or better. However, there was no clear relationship between the level of object permanence attained and the children's level of productive language. Further, the comprehension of function words did not bear any interesting relationship to the attainment of object permanence level.

Veneziano (1981) followed six children over a six to eight month span of time. During her sessions, she observed their language production, symbolic play, and conversational interactions, and assessed their object permanence and gestural imitation behaviors. Focusing not on the meaning of the child's utterances, but their phonetic form and acceptability to the adult interlocutor, she observed a relationship between cognitive and linguistic behaviors. Specifically, Veneziano found that the linguistic acceptability of the children's productions increased over age. In four of her subjects, its substantial increment temporally coincided with the appearance of nonverbal representation or symbolic gestures for eating and feeding activities. She felt that her subjects' performance during these instances of symbolic play were more sensitive indices of their development of representational or stage 6 behaviors than their assignment to stage 6 by performance in other cognitive domains. Let us turn to this domain of cognitive development and examine its developmental relationship to language.

Studies of Normally Developing Children: Imitation and Symbolic Play

Much as Veneziano (1981) had observed that the emergence of symbolic play during the one-word period provided some meaningful insights into the relationship between language and cognition, other investigators before her had the same experience. Taking the Piagetian perspective, symbolic play is considered a form of representational activity. The child represents objects or activities that are no longer there with a gestured schema. For example, a baby may apply a drinking schema to an empty cup, or may pretend to stir a pretend cake batter with a hairbrush. The baby seems to gesturally represent events or objects that are not there. If we consider that symbols—both linguistic and nonlinguistic—are conventions that are used to "stand for" objects, persons, states, and events, such baby gestures can be regarded as a type of symbol or symbolic activity.

Volterra, Bates, Benigni, Bretherton, and Camaioni (1979) conducted an in-depth study of the gestural "symbols" produced by the 25 Italian and American babies that they had studied. In addition to finding a robust relationship between the frequency and repertoire of gestures and the children's lexical development, they also observed qualitative concurrences. Volterra et al. found content similarities between the words and gestures used by the infants. The babies used their symbols—words and gestures—to express the same meanings. Typically, the infants used both gestures and words to represent greeting, object transfer, eating, drinking, and so forth. In addition, as the children's early words began to be extended from ritualiz-ed context-bound situations to use across a variety of contexts, their gestures became *decontextualized* in a similar fashion. This interesting parallel may be more suggestive of the developing status of commonly shared concepts than of a shared operative strategy at this stage.

McCune-Nicolich (1981a) conducted a highly detailed longitudinal study of the relationship between symbolic play and language development dur-ing most of the second year of life in five children. Much like Volterra et al. (1979) she found that the emergence of first words was accompanied by early symbolic play behaviors. The infants' initial lexicons and the nature of their symbolic play were similar to those reported by Volterra et al. Their pretend play was characterized by what Nicolich terms *autosymbolic schemas* in which the child produces playful self-related schemas such as pretending to drink from an empty cup. McCune-Nicolich (1981b) also analyzed the emergence of relational words in the children's lexicon. Oc-curring some time after the emergence of first words such as object words, persons' names, and social routine words, the emergence of relational words seemed to be used to encode change in the environment. Relational words emerged during early stage 6 object permanence and coincidental with the children's sensorimotor operative understanding of those types of change.

Lastly, further support for the coincidence between early lexical develop-ment and the emergence of early symbolic or *autosymbolic* play can be seen in a study by Bates, Bretherton, Snyder, Shore, and Volterra (1980). They examined the language comprehension, production and elicited symbolic play in thirty 13-month-old children. Symbolic play was elicited with two tasks. One involved the experimenter's silent modeling of conventional gestures with objects, e.g., drinking from an empty cup, and counterconventional gestures with those same objects, e.g., driving the empty cup as if it were a car (Killen & Uzgiris, in press). In the other task, the experimenter modeled familiar "scripts" such as eating, drinking and putting a doll to bed (Wolf & Gardner, in press). The "props" for these scripts differed in their resemblance to the referent object, ranging from the drinking from a real cup sequence to a wooden dowel. Bates et al. (1981) found that the children's level of language comprehension and production was related to their ability to gesture with wooden dowels in a script and to produce counterconventional schemes or gestures with objects respectively. Thus there seems to be a relationship between the emergence of early symbolic play and the emergence of first words. Further, this relationship appears to be replicated across studies, irrespective of differences in methodological procedures.

Studies of Normally Developing Children: Multiple-Measure Investigations

A number of studies examined the problem of the relationship between cognition and language development at this level of development by assessing a variety of cognitive skills. If we suspect that more localized relationships seem to occur between language and cognition, we must examine them in a more detailed way.

Dihoff and Chapman (1977) took such an approach. They studied the relationship between the spontaneous language produced by their 20 subjects and the level of development that they had attained for object permanence, means-end relations and play schemas. Not unlike the results of the previously discussed studies, they found that the infants who were at early sensorimotor stage 5 level did not use any more advanced language than stereotyped vocal rituals, e.g., all-purpose request words. Those children performing at late stage 5 did engage in early naming activities but did not encode changing relations or absent objects. By contrast, those children who had attained stage 6 levels on the cognitive measures did produce words to encode relational meanings and absent referents.

In a cross-sectional study of 24 infants during the second year of life, Zachry (1978) examined the relationship between their language production and items from the Uzgiris-Hunt scales that were appropriate for children at this age level. He found that two-thirds of his sample were talking, 10 of whom had already begun to use multiword combinations. He analyzed the children's single word utterances for the semantic cases being expressed and their multiword combinations for the type of sentence represented (Brown, 1973). Scaling procedures were used to order the semantic and syntactic analyses of the children's productive language as well as representational stage 6 related performance on the cognitive scales. Comparison of the children's linguistic and cognitive performance revealed no clear relationship between the number of representational or stage 6 items passed and the level of the children's single word utterance development. In fact, all of the children had passed the object permanence items at the representational level. Only the oldest 10 children passed the causality items and six infants, the means-end items. All of the children who produced multiword utterances were able to pass at least four items at the stage 6 or representational level. Consequently, Zachry felt that stage 6 attainments were probably more closely related to the emergence of multiword speech than to the emergence of single word utterances.

The longitudinal research of Bates et al. (1979), parts of which have been discussed earlier, also employed the use of multiple measures. Examining symbolic and combinatorial play, imitation, means-end, object permanence, spatial relations and the children's language comprehension and production, they found that object permanence and spatial relations abilities did not relate to the emergence of first words. By contrast, imitation, tool-use, combinatorial, and symbolic play were closely related to language development.

Although there does appear to be some congruence in the findings across studies, there are sufficient differences among the methodologies employed to qualify these coincidences only as weak support. When we look only at those studies using *clearly identical methodology*, e.g., Corrigan's (1978) and Ramsey's (1977), and investigating some of the same aspects of language, we see far more agreement. Both Ramsey and Corrigan observed a "burst" in vocabulary development coinciding with the completion of stage 6 object permanence as they defined it. Unfortunately, it is not very clear—from psycholinguistic standards—what qualifies as a "burst." The descriptions of early symbolic play as articulated by Veneziano (1981) and Bates et al. (1979) and even McCune-Nicolich (1981a) appear similar. And indeed, these investigators have observed links between early symbolic play schemas and first words. We may find additional methodological similarities and support in the literature on language disordered children.

Studies of Language Disordered Children:
Multiple Measure Investigations

The Snyder (1978) study, described earlier, not only looked at the children's gestural performatives, it also examined their single word utterances in relation to their cognitive performance on the Uzgiris-Hunt battery. She found that the language disordered children used fewer of their available single words to communicate, despite the fact that they were matched with their normal counterparts for linguistic level. Further, her subjects' communicative performance overall was predicted by their performance on the means-end scales. These findings were interpreted as evidence for a specific representational deficit.

In a similar study, Folger and Leonard (1978) studied the linguistic and cognitive achievements of 20 normal and eight language disordered children. Half of their normal subjects were speaking one word at a time while the other half had begun to use two-word combinations. Similarly, five of their language disordered subjects had reached the multiword level of speech. They found that when the effects of chronological age were partialled out of the analyses, many of the children using two-word utterances demonstrated cognitive performance levels similar to those children at the one-word stage. Further, although the children had advanced well into the stage of referential use of words, many of them clearly demonstrated stage 5 means-end and what McCune-Nicolich (1981a) termed the "autosymbolic" level of symbolic play. These findings appear more supportive of those studies reporting a strong relationship between advances in lexical acquisition and symbolic play.

Recently, Rowan, Leonard, Chapman, and Weiss (1982) conducted a study comparing the performance of matched normal and language disordered children at the one-word stage of language development. Using Snyder's (1978) tasks to elicit communicative behaviors from their subjects and administering the Uzgiris-Hunt battery of cognitive measures, they found quite different results. Rowan et al. found that their language disordered children performed much like their normal subjects on the communicative tasks. Further, there were no significant differences between the normal and language disordered children's performance on all of the cognitive measures but one—the means-end scale. Oddly, the difference was not in the expected direction. The language disordered children had performed significantly better than their matched normals! The authors suggest that some of the differences observed between Snyder's and Rowan et al.'s findings may have been attributable to differences in the degree to which their subjects had advanced in lexical development during the one-word stage and differences in the chronological ages of the disordered subjects. Rowan et al.'s subjects appeared to be lexically more advanced than Snyder's subjects and were somewhat older.

At first glance, the study of language disordered children at the one-word stage seems to have muddied the waters. Snyder's (1978) study clearly appears to support the observed relationship between means-end behaviors and the emergence of first words. Rowan et al.'s more recent study observed nearly the converse relationship between the child's lexicon and the child's means-end skills. However, since Rowan et al. examined normal and language disordered children who were linguistically beyond the transition into "first words," while Snyder examined children at the earlier stage, it is inappropriate to compare these findings. These results, however, point to an important theoretical issue: transition points and differential skill levels.

When investigators look for links between skills or content areas in children, they frequently try to examine a transition point. They look at a point on the developmental continuum where some, but not all, youngsters are making the transition into a content area or skill of interest. In this way the hypothesized link can be clearly observed in those youngsters who have made the targeted transition. Similarly, those children who have not made the transition should not demonstrate the hypothesized developmental link. For example, the child who has made the transition into first words may show a level of development of tool-use that other youngsters still using phonetic sequences such as "hi" and "bye" as part of a ritual may not demonstrate.

While the transition into a new linguistic and cognitive skill level may be linked by a shared underlying input, this relationship does not imply that they will continue to grow at the same speed. Development or continued advancement in one domain will not necessarily be accompanied by concomitant advances in the other. Consequently, one would not necessarily expect continued lexical development to correlate with advances in means-end or tool-use behavior. Rather, studies repeatedly point to this language-cognition link *only* at the child's transition into use of words as reference. Once this stage is attained, the link often becomes masked by the accelerated development in one of the domains. Further, it seems that more than one specific cognitive skill is correlated with the emergence of first words. It appears that differential inputs form the underpinnings. And, although the emergence of first words appears to be correlated with attainments in more than one cognitive domain, children seem to differ in the rates at which they reach these attainments. Thus, some children seem to reach the critical stage of deferred imitation long before they develop in the means-end domain, while others demonstrate a converse pattern. Still other youngsters may progress in both domains at a more even pace. In sum, the differences observed among the studies seem to be most easily attributable to differences in methodology and the developmental point at which their subjects were studied.

The Beginnings of Syntax

Up until this point of linguistic development, the nativist could regard correspondences between observed language development and cognition as irrelevant to the argument. Many nativists contend that the most important question is whether the attainment of operative knowledge is in any way related to or relevant to the acquisition of syntax (Fodor, 1980). They perceive that one's unique and highly specified knowledge of language resides in insight into syntax. Fodor, for example, willingly concedes that one's conceptual knowledge constrains the semantic field one has for a particular word. The development of syntax, however, seems to require a unique knowledge which nativists feel is specifically linguistic in nature. They suggest that there does not seem to be any cognitive operations that are comparable to syntactic strategies. Thus, Wexler and Culicover (1980) suggest that while this link may be possible, it has yet to be demonstrated. For this reason, they and other nativists have described operations which are uniquely linguistic.

The challenge to the constructivist, then, is to find links between cognitive and syntactic development. To explore that question, we will examine studies on both normal and language disordered children. In particular, we will look at those studies which focus on the child's transition into syntax.

Studies of Normally Developing Children

The literature on normally developing children offers some interesting observations. In 1978, we find that McCall, Parke and Kavanaugh modeled arbitrary nonsymbolic actions consisting of single and multiple schema combinations to children 12, 15, 18, and 24 months of age. The infants' ability to imitate the single schemas increased in a linear fashion as a function of age. By contrast, their subjects were relatively unable to imitate multiple schemes even at 15 months. However, at 18 and 24 months—coinciding with the emergence of multiword speech—children could perform many of the multiple scheme combinations.

Similar findings can be noted in Sugarman's (1979) study of children's classification schemes between 1 and 3 years of age. She found a distinct change in the number of classification strategies that a child applies during one sorting. At the outset, the children could only apply one principle during the activity. However, somewhere between 18 to 24 months, they appear to shift to the use of multiple (two or more)"plans".

These types of links can also be seen in McCune-Nicolich's (1981b) analyses of the relationship between the level or type of symbolic play, the onset of syntax, and the point at which two-word combinations became dominant. In this previously discussed longitudinal study, she found that subjects produced their first observed multiword combinations at either the same testing sessions during which their combined symbolic play schemas were first observed or at a session following a demonstration of combined symbolic play schemas. She felt that the general ability to combine two symbols of any kind, as well as deferred imitation skills, were responsible for the children's advances in both symbolic play and multiword speech.

Looking at a larger sample, Lowe and Costello (1976) conducted a cross-sectional study of more than 100 children. Examining the relationship between the children's level of symbolic play and language development as assessed by the mean length of utterance (MLU), they found a significant relationship. After age was partialled out, they reported partial correlations between language development and symbolic play around .30.

In a factor analytic study, Fein (1978) examined children's language skills and types of play. She found that symbolic play and language loaded on the same factor while other types of play formed another factor. In addition, those children who demonstrated high language comprehension scores at 18 and 24 months of age also demonstrated more advanced symbolic play than children with lower comprehension performance.

Lastly, in Bates et al.'s (1980) longitudinal study described earlier, we reported that the experiment included an investigation of the children's ability to imitate "scripted" or scenario symbolic play. When these same 30 children were 20 and 28 months of age, elicited scripted symbolic play was studied again. However, the complexity of the scenarios presented increased at the subsequent test sessions. In a recent analysis of the subjects' symbolic play at 20 and 28 months, Shore, O'Connell, and Bates (1982) examined the average or mean length of the gestural sequences produced by the children (MLS). They compared this metric to the children's MLU. At 20 months of age, MLU and MLS were roughly equivalent. MLU was 1.13 and MLS was 1.25. However, at 28 months there was a marked difference between the two, with a significantly larger MLU than MLS. When Shore et al. considered the longest chains of different schemes that the child could produce, there was a significant correlation with their measures of syntactic development—even when the effects of total number of words and total number of play schemes were statistically removed.

The evidence from normally developing children, then, seems to suggest that there seem to be some fairly replicable events occurring in both language and cognitive development. Further, the data suggest that these coincidences are correlated. This relationship appears to be even more robust when we examine the literature on language disordered children.

Studies of Language Disordered Children

Symbolic Behavior in Language Disordered Children

Like the developmental literature, studies of the nonlinguistic symbols of language disordered children have examined their symbolic play. Looking first at those studies that have focused on play, we find that Lovell, Hoyle, and Siddall (1968) studied the play and verbal interactions of age-matched normal and language delayed preschool children, time sampling their play in an unstructured, nursery school setting. They analyzed the children's play in terms of the number of minutes spent in different types and levels of play as categorized by Piaget. They found no significant differences between the groups of 3-year-olds in the amount of time spent in different types of play. However, at the 4-year-old level, they observed that the normal children spent significantly more time in symbolic play. They noted that the language delayed children depended more upon concrete objects to maintain their symbolic play. Further, when the object or contextual support was removed, they found that the language delayed children were unable to maintain the symbolic play interaction, either with gestures or language. Lovell et al. also found a significant relationship between the amount of time spent in symbolic play and linguistic level. Although this study collapsed both gestural and vocal symbols within its category types and levels of play, it offered the pioneering observation that language disordered children may sustain deficits of both linguistic and nonlinguistic symbolization.

Exploring this issue in a more focused manner, Morehead (1973) compared the performance of normal and language disordered children matched for linguistic level on a series of symbolic play tasks. He varied the degree of contextual support or relatedness of the items given to the children for free play. Although the children were matched for linguistic level, and hence, the language disordered subjects were chronologically older than their normal counterparts, they demonstrated marked deficits in their symbolic play. In fact, linguistic level (mean morphemes per utterance) and performance on the symbolic play tasks correlated more closely than linguistic level and intellectual development as measured by a performance scale intelligence test.

A somewhat different approach to the question was taken by Brown, Redmond, Bass, Liebergott, and Swope (1975). They structured a series of play situations to elicit increasingly complex symbolic play behavior in preschool children. Comparing the performance of normal and language disordered preschoolers on these tasks, they found qualitative differences between their symbolic play. The language disordered children used less complex levels of symbolic play than their age-matched controls. They were less able to adapt different objects in the service of symbolic play as well as integrate and organize the objects, events, and themes in the play context. These findings, too, suggest that language disordered children sustain concomitant deficits in the development of nonlinguistic symbols.

Summary

The studies discussed here seem to reveal some trends. First, there appears to be converging evidence for the relationship between the emergence of the child's operative knowledge of tools and external causes and his ability to produce controlled intentional gestural signals. Data obtained on children in the single word stage show replicable links between specific cognitive skills *only* when the methodologies and the subjects' level of development are highly similar. When we examine the period of the beginnings of syntax, there seems to be distinct agreement on a relationship between symbolic play, particularly the ability to combine play schemas, and the ability to combine words.

It is difficult to imagine that such congruence across studies is accidental. At the very least, the data appear to provide support for a correlational hypothesis. The required temporal sequencing of a strong cognitive hopothesis in which the cognitive achievement closely predates the emergence of the linguistic milestone do not seem to be reflected in these studies. Nor has the similar criterion of a weak cognitive hypothesis in which the linguistic milestone must never predate the cognitive attainment been met by the observations reported here.

The studies discussed thus far have focused on the child's attainment of specific kinds of operative knowledge and their links with the production of gestural communication, first words, and early word combinations. Language production and comprehension are not, however, merely active and passive aspects of language. Rather, they seem to possess some differential qualities which allow them to develop at different rates in some individuals. The findings from the longitudinal studies of Snyder, Bates, and Bretherton (1981), Bretherton, Bates, McNew, and Snyder (1983) and Bates, Bretherton, and Snyder (in preparation) suggest that the development of language comprehension and production are somewhat dissociable. They have observed that across linguistic development in the first 28 months of life, achievements in language comprehension at one stage of development seem to predict different language developments from production at later stages. And certainly, factor analytic studies of language disordered children, e.g., Aram and Nation (1975), support this distinction. If these aspects of language are this dissociated, it may be important to determine whether any links have been found between specific cognitive attainments and language comprehension. A fruitful place to begin this search may be the child's acquisition of the constructive comprehension process of inference. This achievement appears to begin in the late preoperational stage and continue well into the stage of concrete operations.

Drawing Inferences

Inferring information from a message appears to be a language comprehension task with a unique set of properties and processing characteristics. As such, this comprehension skill provides a distinct contrast to the types of language production achievements reviewed earlier. This skill does not simply involve the comprehension of vocabulary words and/or syntactic structures. It includes these skills, but it also requires that the processor construct a comprehension bridge between two clauses or sentences (Kintsch, 1974) or even between the episodes of a narrative (Johnson & Smith, 1982). This type of language comprehension requires extra processing by the listener and the resulting demand is reflected in increased processing time. This can be seen when the comprehension for linguistic material requiring an inference is compared with that which does not. For example, when Haviland and Clark (1974) compared subjects' ability to comprehend the following sentence pair:

Horace got some picnic supplies out of the car.
The beer was warm.

and another pair in which the word "beer" had a definite antecedent, i.e.,

Horace got some beer out of the trunk.
The beer was warm.

they found that their subjects took longer to comprehend the first pair, the pair that necessitated the construction of an inference. This finding has been replicated in a number of experiments with many different types of language stimuli, e.g., Hilyard and Olson (1978); Keenan and Kintsch (1974): Kintsch (1974); McKoon and Keenan (1974).

More important, this example points out that inferencing involves the listener's comprehension or understanding of something to which no explicit reference has been made. Take another example, Johnson and Smith's (1981) illustration "John did not see the rock and he fell." We understand from this sentence that John fell because he tripped over the rock although that was never stated in the sentence. We draw the inference necessary for the comprehension of this sentence by using our world knowledge. Or, to return to the previously cited Haviland and Clark (1974) sentence pair, one must go beyond the information explicitly stated and infer that beer had been packed in the picnic supplies in order to comprehend this sentence sequence. Such information is clearly not contained in linguistic stimuli here. Yet, it is the understanding that one derives from the language. It appears then, that in comprehending such language, listeners draw upon and use their conceptual world knowledge to make the inference.

Individuals have a vast store of world knowledge. They can infer information about agents, spatial locations, consequences, instruments, and a variety of transitive relations (Bransford, Barclay, & Franks, 1972; Bransford & Franks, 1971; Johnson, Bransford, & Solomon, 1973; Potts, 1972). They activate this knowledge and use it to draw many inferences that are required and necessary for understanding the message. This comprehension process appears to be sufficiently unique to allow us to study its acquisition with somewhat greater ease than others. It is easily identified and seems to have highly specified operational characteristics. Consequently, it appears to be an ideal place to look for possible links between the transition into inferential processing and specific cognitive operations. We will examine the development of inferences and cognitive attainments, looking at studies of normally developing children. Factors such as attention and memory and reading level can affect children's ability to draw inferences over several sentences. Their reading level may affect their ability to infer across written material. Consequently, we will confine our discussion to those studies that have examined inferences drawn during listening comprehension tasks. Further, we will pay particular attention to those studies that focus on limited quantities of verbal information, i.e., those which present no more than three short sentences at a time.

Studies of Normally Developing Children

In the last decade, it has become clear that children acquire the ability to draw inferences. Although it was initially thought that this constructive comprehension process did not emerge until the period of concrete operations, more recent evidence, e.g., Gelman, Bullock, and Meck (1980), suggests that younger children are capable of such activity. So long as investigators control for general performance factors such as attention and memory, preoperational children can draw inferences.

Recognition memory tasks are often used in studying constructive comprehension processes. They take the form of a short paragraph such as the following taken from Paris and Carter (1973):

The bird is in the cage. (Premise)
The cage is under the table. (Premise)
The bird is yellow. (Filler)

After a short intervening task, the subject is asked to recognize new versus old sentences from the paragraph. Recognition items include foils such as the following (Paris & Carter, 1973):

The bird is in the cage. (True premise)
The cage is over the table. (False premise)
The bird is under the table. (True inference)
The bird is on top of the table. (False inference)

If a subject has constructed an inference from the test paragraph, he or she will recognize the true inference as an old sentence.

Since inferences seem to entail unique operations, the child's development of cognitive operations may be likened to the development of this process. Prawat and Cancelli (1976) studied the ability of conserving versus nonconserving first graders to draw inferences. Children were assigned to these groups on the basis of their performance on a standardized cognitive test. This measure assessed the children's ability to conserve two-dimensional space, number, substance, continuous quantity, weight, and discontinuous quantity. Using a recognition memory task of the type described earlier, Prawat and Cancelli assessed the children's ability to construct spatial inferences. They found that their conservers drew more true inferences and thus made more true inference errors than their nonconservers and made fewer errors on the other foils. They felt that their findings suggested that there was an effect of the general operative process of conservation than a highly specific directional effect. They reasoned that if conservation were specifically linked to the ability to draw inferences, they would have observed their nonconserving subjects making fewer true inference errors than they had. Thus, it appeared that their nonconservers were able to construct some true inferences, although not as many as the conservers with whom they had been matched.

A somewhat different study was conducted by Liben and Posnansky (1977). They examined the ability of kindergarten, first and third graders to make spatial inferences on a recognition memory task. They also assessed the children's ability on Piagetian transitivity tasks for length and number. Transitivity tasks are those in which the child is presented with information about a relationship between A and B and B and C, and then asked to infer the relationship between A and C. Liben and Posnansky found that the youngster's ability to make transitive inferences was not significantly correlated to their performance on the Piagetian transitivity tasks despite the similarity of the operations required.

Also using a recognition memory paradigm, Johnson and Scholnick (1979) studied third- and fourth-grade children's ability to construct class inclusion and seriation inferences and their specific cognitive attainments in those domains. Using verbal cognitive problems to assess their subjects' class inclusion and seriation skills, they were able to divide their subjects into four groups: includers-seriators, includers-nonseriators, nonincluders-seriators, and nonincluders-nonseriators. Johnson and Scholnick found that those children who could seriate were able to construct true seriation inferences significantly more frequently than those who could not. However, a similar effect did not hold for class inclusion. Liben and Posnansky (1977) observe that seriation or linear order skills may facilitate constructive processes more than a hierarchical order. In addition, class inclusion requires knowledge of both the intensional and extensional properties of classes in addition to logic. Consequently, it may be more difficult to acquire and activate class inclusion knowledge for inferences, and to assess it in subjects. Thus, their equivocal findings for class inclusion may be related to methodological problems and/or an extended horizontal decalage in this area. Or, it may be more symptomatic of our poor understanding of the developmental process and continuum for class inclusion, as Winer's (1980) review seems to indicate.

When we look across these studies, we find only limited support for links between the attainment of specific cognitive operations and the emergence of inferential comprehension. However, when we examine the specific stimuli used to assess the linguistic and cognitive attainments in question, serious concerns can be voiced. First, only Prawat and Cancelli and Johnson and Scholnick's studies demonstrated some similarity between the content area of the inference, e.g., spatial, and the content area of the cognitive attainment. Since inferences seem to depend not only upon one's ability to perform some transitive and or logical cognitive operation but also upon one's specific world knowledge of specific content, e.g., spatial relations, the link between cognition and this type of language processing may be revealed only in the presence of both operative and conceptual knowledge. Second, it is well known that the operative attainments of the concrete operational period, e.g., conservation, typically develop in a horizontal decalage. Thus, it may be highly inappropriate or even naive to expect to observe an all-or-none link between a specific cognitive operation from this developmental stage and a corresponding linguistic achievement. Third, Johnson and Scholnick assessed both the targeted linguistic and cognitive achievements verbally. Consequently, it is difficult to know whether their subjects would have performed differently on nonverbal tasks, allowing us to observe a different pattern of relationship.

Summary

The study of constructive comprehension processes in children has only begun. We can see some limited links between operative knowledge and this type of language comprehension activity. However, it has yet to be demonstrated in a particularly strong way. Unfortunately, there are serious problems with the studies reviewed. Some seem to ignore the relevance and or interaction of operative and figurative knowledge to this question. This is a critical consideration during the concrete operations period, a period in which horizontal decalage occurs frequently. Thus our studies may not be keeping track of all the shells in the game. We may not yet have figured out how many underlying "programs," or which "programs" one may need as input for particular tasks. Our search for relationships between language and specified cognitive ability may have taken our attention away from other relationships that may also be making differential contributions within a domain.

Some Shells to Watch

If we are to explore the relationship between language and cognitive development, it is not sufficient to just look at specific linguistic and cognitive attainments. Other aspects of the problem must be examined. In the last couple of years, the literature suggests that there may be some additional factors which are relevant to the question.

Parametric Considerations

The study of the relationship between cognition and language development is typically a study of how these skills or abilities "go together" at different points in time. Essentially, it is a study of correlation. Hence, the name chosen by Miller et al. (1977) to characterize a set of hypotheses.

Correlation is a statistical notion that carries with it some implicit assumptions and operational dynamics that we often forget in our interpretation of data. More careful attention to these notions may clear up some of our unrealistic expectations for the outcome of studies addressing the language-cognition question as well as help us interpret their findings more accurately.

A particularly important psychometric consideration for the cognition and language development question is the effect of regression to the mean along the continuum of general cognitive abilities. In the normal population of children at each age level, general cognitive abilities (as measured by a standardized intelligence test) are distributed normally. When one examines the relationship between general cognition as indicated by IQ and other skills such as academic achievement or even language skills, we see that achievement or language skills are distributed across the IQ continuum. The relationship between these variables, e.g., IQ and language, will tend to fall into a regression line in relationship to the size of the correlation that is found between them. In the normal distribution of IQ, the absolute direction of the relationship between IQ and language will be affected by *regression to the mean*. If, for example, the size of the correlation between IQ and performance on a given language measure is .6, there will be a very close relationship between the two variables for those children with average intelligence or scores clustered around the mean. However, the language scores of those children with much lower IQs will regress toward the mean of the sample (a higher score) and thus, be higher than their IQ or Mental Age scores. Conversely, regression to the mean affects children with much higher IQs in the opposite way. Their language scores also regress to the mean, a lower score. Thus, children with very high IQs tend to have language scores that are somewhat lower than their cognitive scores. A more comprehensive discussion of this effect can be found in Snyder (1982).

Studies of normally developing children often fail to remember this consideration. The effect of regression to the mean precludes the articulation of both strong and weak forms of the cognitive hypotheses. Assessment in a normal population simply does not result in any direction of effects that is predicted by the strong and weak cognitive hypotheses. Consequently, a correlational hypothesis appears to be the only psychometrically viable form of the cognitive hypothesis.

Language Learning Strategies

One of the caveats articulated by Wexler and Culicover (1980) is that specific cognitively oriented strategies or principles have yet to be defined that can account for the child's ability to learn specific linguistic structures. In the face of such lack of evidence, they can only conclude that these strategies are the specifically linguistic ones that Wexler and Culicover have delineated. This statement, however, blithely ignores the pioneering contributions of MacWhinney (1980). For some time, the cognitive operational strategies that children use in learning language (Slobin, 1973, 1979) have enriched our understanding of the acquisition process. In recent years, MacWhinney has investigated and delineated a series of strategies that children appear to use to acquire morphophonology (1975, 1978) and syntax (1980). His research has not only identified these strategies, but it has also tested them against data from child language acquisition and in artificial intelligence modeling.

MacWhinney's work in the area of syntax (1980) may be of special interest since it is the arena in which most nativists choose to make their claims. Although MacWhinney has identified a number of language learning strategies and the ways that they are applied, we will focus on three principal ones: rote, analogy and combination. *Rote* has been defined by MacWhinney as memorization of the target as a whole. In the syntactic domain, this means that the child commits word strings or whole sentences to memory despite the fact that he or she cannot productively use the particular forms. The literature on child language acquisition is replete with reports of such fixed order holistic memorization of syntactic forms. Among other evidence, MacWhinney cites Clark's (1976) report of a child's use of *I could easily do that*, when *could* was notably absent from the child's productive repertoire.

Given the limitations of our available memory and the evidence from neologisms and developmental errors, it is clear that one could not learn language simply by rote. Consequently, MacWhinney proposed that a second strategy, *analogy*, was available to the child. In syntactic development, MacWhinney uses analogy to refer to the child's ability to immediately recall an item with a pattern similar to the one that the child wishes to produce, extract the patterned relationship, and apply it to the new item. The child, then, seems to perceive the analogy or similarity between structures, extracts the pattern and applies it. For example, MacWhinney cites Clark's (1974) report of a child producing *wait for it to dry*, based upon analogy with *wait for it to cool* which was already in his repertoire.

The last strategy identified by MacWhinney to be discussed here is that of *combination*. In syntactic acquisition, MacWhinney uses *combination* to refer to the child's ability to form principles or rules from structures that may contain a number of complexities or irregularities. Thus, the child can figure out the rule even when the pattern demonstrating its application is not very apparent. For example, the child has to figure out (and does) the rule that places *do* into pattern of *why* + *tense* before the sentence subject in the case of wh-interrogative questions, e.g., *Why did she?*, and after the subject in other sentence patterns, e.g., *She did*.

These, and a number of other specific strategies have been identified, tested, and operationalized for both syntactic and morphophonological acquisition by MacWhinney. This abbreviated discussion does not begin to do justice to his impressive array of evidence. Over the years we have examined conceptual and operative development as defined in Piagetian terms in our search for the relationship between cognition and language development. However, we may be limiting and frustrating our search if we confine ourselves to these aspects of cognitive development. Our understanding and our findings may be enhanced by extending our considerations to another cognitive shell, cognitive language learning strategies, and observe the way that these interact with the development of specific conceptual and operative knowledge.

Resources and Their Allocation

A final concern that appears to be relevant to the question at hand involves the resources that the child has available to him or her at any one point in time. The last decade of research in cognitive information processing has taken a view of human performance as a single entity and tried to observe those situations in which a specific type of task performance can be enhanced and those in which it may be limited.

Considering this question, Norman and Bobrow (1975) examined the effect of data versus resource factors on human performance. The results of their studies of human performance in tasks of varying degrees of complexity, information, and output load suggested that the human processing system is best characterized as having a fixed or limited fund of *resources* or processing capability available to it. When an individual attempts whatever task placed before him or her, the individual must draw upon the available resources. If the demands of the task are greater than the resources available, the individual will fail to complete the task or do it well. For example, if one tries to edit a manuscript and give directions to a phone caller about how to find a book in one's messy office, the formulation of the explanation may use all of one's resources. Consequently, either the editing or the directions will go woefully astray. Norman and Bobrow call this *resource limited* processing. The individual's performance on the task is hindered because all of his available processing resources have been allocated. However, if by some magical force more resources were made available to the individual, he or she would be able to complete the tasks.

Norman and Bobrow also observed that human performance can be constrained by data limits. If there is insufficient information or data available to the processor to complete the task, the individual will not be able to complete it despite an unlimited fund of resources. Thus, his or her performance is *data limited*. For example, if one tries to lipread a conversation and the speaker suddenly articulates a series of phones that are not visible, the lipreader will not be successful no matter how many resources are available. If, on the other hand, the speaker suddenly articulates words containing a higher proportion of visible cues, he or she is providing the lipreader with more data. With increased data, the lipreader's performance will no longer be data limited and it is likely to improve.

Norman and Bobrow's (1975) conceptualization encountered some difficulty in determining those tasks which will constrain a human processor's performance and those which will not. Their point of view has been supplemented by the development of dual processing models of human performance. Dual processing models such as those proposed by Schneider and Shiffrin (1977) and Shiffrin and Schneider (1977) suggest that there are two different modes of processing which make different claims on the individual's resources. They suggest that there is *automatic processing*, an automatic, inhibition-free mode in which a task is highly learned and incorporated into the system. In other words, the individual knows how to do the task so well that he or she can do it automatically. This type of processing is thought to draw few resources. Consequently, it can occur simultaneously with or parallel to other kinds of processing. For example, most individuals can walk and talk at the same time.

Many tasks, however, require our conscious attention and require our direct control. This *controlled processing* is usually serial in nature and appears to make high demands on the system's resources. For example, it is difficult to accomplish a second task while one is trying to plan the winning move in a game of chess.

These models of attention or resource allocation have offered very cogent explanations of those activities that we, as processors, seem to be able to perform simultaneously and those which we cannot. However, these models have found it difficult to explain those instances in which performance in one task actually *improves* when another task has been added, e.g., Long's (1977) work. Conversely, sometimes performance may deteriorate despite the fact that we have ascertained that there are sufficient resources. To explain these events, some researchers have turned to multiple resource models.

The multiple resource model (Navon & Gopher, 1979) suggests that the human processing system houses a diverse set of mechanisms which are used to varying degrees in different tasks. Some tasks will require the use of the same mechanisms while others will require another set. The nature of the mechanisms needed to complete a task depends upon the task itself, the processor's skill and the environmental context. Each mechanism has its own set of resources with its corresponding set of limits.

If we think about these mechanisms as operative "programs" or "software," the dilemmas of unpredictable improvements and decrements in performance are more easily explained. It may be that performance may suffer from the accessibility of these mechanisms or programs. Consequently, if one program that is needed for a task happens to be stored with or adjacent to another program that is needed, accessing or activating one will automatically access or activate the other. To access only one of the programs may take extra resources which are used to separate the programs or inhibit the activation of the other adjacent program. This could result in what Navon and Gopher (1979) call a *concurrence cost* which is reflected in decreased performance. However, when both programs are activated by accessing only one, performance may improve dramatically. This would be an instance of a *concurrence benefit*.

The relevance of these notions of resource allocation to the question of cognition and language development is that as the child struggles to learn about the language object and the nonlinguistic aspects of the world, the child is prey to resource allocation constraints. The mastery level that he or she has attained for various linguistic forms will affect the resources the child may have available at any one time to learn new forms. As a child can produce more linguistic forms automatically, he or she will have more resources available for the controlled processing required for the acquisition of new forms.

Further, some forms may be learned or activated with other forms, offering the child a concurrence benefit and enhanced language performance. On the other hand, such concurrence benefits may, in fact, be only present for structures learned by rote. When the child begins to engage in analogy and appreciate the similarity of some structural forms, the child's performance may suffer.

Lastly and most important, the child is building a language system during his or her development. The child is organizing and reorganizing the system until that point at which it can operate in the most efficient, accurate and parsimonious manner. The child tries to characterize the language with the least number of rules or principles that will allow him to generate an infinite number of novel correct utterances. At the same time that he or she is constructing his or her grammar, the child is also building, organizing and reorganizing his or her knowledge of the world. Any account of language development, with or without cognition, must deal with and account for the demands that such activity places upon the child's resources. We need to be able to explain the *dynamics* of this system.

Summary Focus

This discussion of the relationship between cognition and language development has described some major points of view on the issue. Evidence from the study of the emergence of intentional communicative signals, first words, syntax and of the construction of inferences has been reviewed. The findings from studies of prelinguistic communication and the beginnings of syntax have lent some clear support to the correlational hypothesis for cognition and language acquisition. The data from the study of first words tend to be fraught with methodological differences. On the other hand, the data on the emergence of inferences are just in their infancy and are barely suggestive. Johnston (in press) examines the acquisition of specific lexical pairs such as spatial and locative prepositions and dimensional adjectives during the preoperational period, as well as of passive constructions during the period of concrete operations. Her review adds scope to the discussion of linguistics and cognitive achievements found here. In her review, Johnston found support for a constructivist point of view in some domains, but not others. At the very least, those instances of support observed in this discussion and in Johnston's suggest that the strong nativist position is not tenable.

Further, the parametric considerations discussed here suggest that neither the strong nor the weak form of the cognitive hypothesis is viable. The distributional characteristics of the normal population and the nature of regression to the mean given the correlation between IQ and language skills, make such a stance unrealistic. On the other hand, the specific language learning strategies identified by MacWhinney (1978, 1980) seem to present problems for those nativists who would discount "cognitive" strategies. We must begin to discern how such strategies interact with the child's operative and conceptual knowledge. Finally, the effect of resource allocation constraints on and as a result of language acquisition is virtually unknown. Yet it becomes increasingly apparent that this is an important consideration.

At the outset of this chapter, we likened the search for links between cognition and language development to playing the shell game. One must watch carefully to discern which cognitive shell the linguistic pea will "go with" or to which it will relate. Unfortunately, it becomes clear that we are at a great disadvantage in this shell game. In addition to the shells of all of the content domains and operations that we must watch, we must also keep our eyes on or consider some others. These include statistical considerations, specific language learning strategies and the allocation of resources. Just as the carnival huckster warns us that "the hand is quicker than the eye," the domain of cognition is so large and so dynamic that success often eludes us. On the other hand, just as the huckster's prize will often keep us playing the game, the question of cognition and language development will probably continue to tantalize us for centuries to come.

Acknowledgment

This work was supported in part by a Basil O'Connor Research Award 5-340 from the March of Dimes Birth Defects Foundation to the author.

Judith F. Duchan

Language Assessment: The Pragmatics Revolution

Ask any of your local language pathologists. They will tell you that their catch word of this decade is *pragmatics*. The term is packed with a variety of subcategories which come into play as clinicians and researchers examine the language of language impaired children. This chapter will be devoted to uncovering the historical roots of this pragmatics revolution in language pathology by looking at the literature in language sciences and language pathology over the last 20 years. The review is aimed at explaining the breadth and apparent lack of coherence in the changes that are taking place under the name of pragmatics. A critical stance will be taken throughout with the focus of the critique being: (a) to evaluate the older assessment procedures we are using in light of the recent pragmatic literature; (b) to ask whether language pathologists should be equally accepting of all aspects of their pragmatics revolution; and (c) to propose a set of categories for doing language assessment which derive logically from the research on pragmatics.

Twenty Ideas in Pragmatics: The Historical Threads

In order to identify the sources of conceptual overlap and distinction in the categories of pragmatics, and to clear up some of our present confusion, it might be useful to begin with examination of the history which

© College-Hill Press, Inc. All rights, including that of translation, reserved. No part of this publication may be reproduced without the written permission of the publisher.

led us to the set of ideas from which we are currently conducting our pragmatics assessment of our language disordered children.

The Linguistic Assessment Period

It was probably Chomsky (1957, 1965) who started it all. While his revolution in linguistics denied the role of context, it led to a counterrevolution which emphasized it. Chomsky also gave us the historical edifice for treating language as part of a speaker's conceptual system, leading us away from our engrained behavioristic notion that language was a set of responses to be evaluated in terms of its surface structure characteristics. Our endeavor in the 60's was to take a scientific look at language disorders by analyzing the linguistic regularities contained in the errors. We, like Chomsky, focused on syntax at first, but rather than analyzing language for its grammatical systematicities, we analyzed our samples of language impaired children's language for their departures from normal children's progress in language acquisition. Menyuk, for example, in an influential article (Menyuk, 1964), took a group of sentences representing different transformations and presented them to normal and language impaired preschoolers and first graders to imitate. Others of us followed her example and gave her sentences to our language impaired children having them imitate them or trying to elicit the sentence types more naturally (Leonard, 1972).

Just as did Menyuk, Lee (1966) also designed assessment procedures based on syntax in normally developing children. Her "Developmental Sentence Types" procedure evolved from research on developmental stages through which normal children progressed from single words to simple sentences. Lee's well known Northwestern Syntax Screening Test also borrowed from methodology in developmental psycholinguistics, specifically from Fraser, Bellugi, and Brown (1963) and is now used for identifying children with language problems. And lastly, Lee and Cantor's now popular Developmental Sentence Scoring Procedure for children who are speaking in full sentences was also built on her own and others' research on normal children. Her choice of syntactic structures such as question forms and negatives reflected the earlier choices of researchers who studied these forms in normally developing children (e.g., Klima & Bellugi, 1966).

Leonard's enthusiastic review article in 1972 reflects the themes of this early 1960's period. First he described our endebtedness to Chomsky's transformational paradigm and to Menyuk and Lee who followed it. Secondly, Leonard revealed his own commitment to the normative theme which is that our primary focus in language assessment and research should be to determine whether language impaired children use syntax differently or are just slower to develop syntax than their normal language learning peers.

The historical threads from that early syntax period which contributed to our current sense of pragmatics were four:

(1)   A sense that children's language comes from an underlying finite set of linguistic rules;

(2)   A methodology that viewed abnormal children through the lens of normal children acquiring their language;

(3)   A commitment to linguistics and the newly emerging field of developmental psycholinguistics as disciplines from which to derive our assessment procedures and categories;

(4)   A move away from normative formal tests to language sample analysis in natural contexts.

Following five or so years on the heels of the syntax period came an emphasis on relational semantics. This second trend in linguistic analysis in part originated from Fillmore's cases (Fillmore, 1968), which, in turn, fed those early influential normal language acquistion studies of Bloom (1970), Schlesinger (1971) and Brown (1973). All three researchers studied children's language at the two-word stage and devised short lists of semantic relations through which described how the first and second words of their subjects' utterances seem to relate. The lists impressively overlapped with one another and with Fillmore's cases, leading to our sense of comfort as we borrowed them and used them to compare our language impaired children with normal children (Curtiss, Prutting, & Lowell, 1979; Duchan & Erickson, 1976; Freedman & Carpenter, 1976; Leonard, Bolders, & Miller, 1976).

Besides the focus on semantic categories, what differentiates this second period from the syntactic era preceeding it is the acknowledged necessity for looking at the events embracing the utterances in order to classify those utterances. Bloom used the situational context to differentiate possible meanings for the child's ambiguous two-morpheme utterances. Her now famous example was "mommy sock" which was said in contexts which differentiated its possessive interpretation (That's mommy's sock) from its agent-object counterpart (mommy put my sock on me). This method whereby the analyzer uses the situational context to interpret the deep meanings of the child's utterances was first called "rich interpretation" (Brown, 1973) and has more recently come to be called "interpretive analysis" (Bloom, Capatides, & Tackeff, 1981).

The most elaborate and influential expression of this semantic relations era for language pathology was Bloom and Lahey's (1978) publication of

Language Development and Language Disorders. In it the authors present an assessment technique for discovering the developmental level of semantic relations produced by language impaired children. Bloom and Lahey include in their assessment some 21 categories along with the forms the categories tend to be expressed in, and their relative stage in normal acquisition.

Others, such as McDonald and Blott (1974) and Watson and Lord (1982), have trimmed the semantic relations list to a select few and offer them as more amenable assessment checklists for analyzing the meanings in the language of language impaired children.

As we passed through this semantic relations period, we picked up another idea that was later to become part of the pragmatics movement. It was the first explicit admission that context made an important difference in how we interpret language. It was to be another thread leading us toward the pragmatics revolution because it allowed:

(5)   A methodology of interpretive analysis that saw the legitimacy and necessity for using situational context to assign meaning to the utterances we hear and analyze.

A third wave of the linguistics period occurred in the late 1970's when we took a more in-depth look at language impaired children's phonological systems. Still reverberating from the earlier waves was our use of the data from normal language learners as a standard for language assessment (Ingram, 1981; Shriberg & Kwiatkowski, 1980; Weiner, 1979). In the same vein, research efforts were undertaken to determine whether language impaired children are like normal learners in slow motion, or of a different phonological ilk (Ingram, 1976, 1981).

What was additionally characteristic about this phonological period and significant for the pragmatics revolution that was to follow was its look at the sounds around the error sound. Context sensitive analysis in phonology requires that we examine the phonological neighborhood of the sound in question to see if processes such as assimilation or harmony are a source of a child's misarticulations (Ingram, 1976; Lund & Duchan, 1978).

Also consistent with this period of extending phonological analyses from isolated units to sound combinations, was a new emphasis on phonotactics, i.e., on the constraints which govern the way sounds combine with one another. These phonotactic constraints differed from the context sensitive phonological process analyses in that the adjacent features of sounds need not be implicated in the error production. Instead, it involves an overall constraint such as one which only allows for consonants and vowels (Panagos, 1974), or which inhibits dramatic phonological differences in single words (Waterson, 1978), or which results in highly constrained idiosyncratic phonological forms (Lund & Duchan, 1978). Some of these phonotactic constraints have been described as syllable structure processes (Ingram, 1981; Shriberg & Kwiatkowski, 1980; Weiner, 1979).

Another aspect out of this period also lending fodder to the pragmatics revolution was a set of context sensitive rules which presumed that words, just like sentences, have a derivational history in their production, moving from deep to surface productions via transformational rules (Parker, 1976).

So this third and most recent wave of our 20-year-old linguistic period went along with the idea that assessment was a normative question, and, furthermore, it emphasized the importance of linguistic context via context sensitive rules and rules which impose contextual constraints. These emphases led to:

(6)   A sense that a unit of language does not occur in isolation, but often varies and is determined by the surrounding linguistic context, or by abstract rules which place contextual constraints on how elements can combine.

There is a fourth change now going on in linguistics (*see* Morgan and Sellner (1980) for a succinct and clear account), which is beginning to be felt in language pathology—that of text analysis. Text analysts examine the linguistic connections between sentences, and they do this in two distinguishable ways. One is to discover abstract ways texts are organized, i.e., to do text grammars (Prince, 1973; van Dijk, 1977). And the second is to determine how components of the texts cohere, i.e., to discover cohesion devices (Halliday & Hasan, 1976).

The focus on text content uses a methodology modeled after generative syntax, with its hierarchical phrase structure and transformational rules (Hurtig, 1977). When applying the linguistic model to stories, Rumelhart (1975) and Stein and Glenn (1979) take as their basic constituents units such as setting, episode, and reaction. This work on text grammars leads to:

(7)   An effort to discover the units of discourse and their relationships.

Cohesion devices serve to glue the text together, and their study by various researchers with a linguistic bent has led to the understanding of how morphemes tie to previously mentioned elements in the text (anaphoric reference), and to what is yet to come (cataphoric reference), and to the uses of ellision, conjunction, subordination, and tense as ways of orienting the listener to the text content. The study of cohesion devices provides us with:

(8)   A set of devices by which language users can tie their sentences to one another.

The Cognitive Assessment Period

Once we began to plumb children's minds for the underlying syntax and semantic relations, it was only a natural next step to allow ourselves the luxury of looking beyond the language for the conceptual scaffolding which supported those language competencies. The first article leading us to ask about the cognitive bases of language was by Bever in 1970. In it he outlined a set of cognitive (i.e., nonlinguistic) strategies used by normal children and adults to comprehend language. A second early and influential article was by Slobin (1973) which presented some cognitive principles which normal children employ as they learn their native language. These two articles offered us the "cognitive strategies" theme later to be enveloped by the pragmatics movement.

One strategy of special relevance to that upcoming pragmatics revolution was the "probable event strategy" called that by Strohner and Nelson in 1974, but reported earlier by Bever (1970) under the rubric of semantic probability strategy and later by Duchan (1980) under the title of cognitive bias. These researchers asked normal preschool children to carry out improbable directions by giving them sentences that went against the child's ordinary life experiences. That is, the children were asked to demonstrate events such as fences jumping horses, animals petting people, and babies under beds. Two-and three-year-olds unflinchingly interpreted the sentences in their more probable sense, showing the horses jumping fences, people petting animals, and babies in their beds.

Deward (1979) found this reliance on language to convey ordinary expected events even more pronounced in the severely retarded children he studied.

While it was first investigated in the 1970's as part of the study of the cognitive bases for language acquisition, the probable event strategy can be seen as depicting the quintessence of the pragmatics revolution. Pragmatics, just like the probable event strategy, has as its main theme that language is interpreted in light of what speakers and listeners expect or want to have happen on a particular occasion. This probable event strategy was a precursor to the pragmatics movement because it contained:

(9)   A notion that what the speaker and listener expect to happen on certain occasions will be reflected in their interpretation of the language used on those occasions.

Besides the cognitive strategy approach, a second theme, the "cognitive precursors" theme, was also a strong part of this 1970's cognitive period. It was defined by researchers investigating what children needed to know before they acquired language. Those investigating this theme liberally borrowed from Piaget's discoveries of stages in sensorimotor development. In language pathology, researchers used assessment measures which classified their nonverbal children into one of the six stages of sensorimotor development. The cognitive areas most frequently examined were those defined by Piaget (1952, 1954, 1962) and later used by Uzgiris and Hunt (1975) in their well-known scale. They were: object permanence, means-end relationships, imitation, action schemes, and operational causality (Lund & Duchan, 1983; Miller, Chapman, Branston, & Reichle, 1980).

Piaget saw these sensorimotor stages as general and governing all aspects of children's cognitive acccomplishments, whereas other researchers, most notably Bates (1979), treated preverbal cognition as a composite of separable knowledges, with its various pieces developing at different rates and casting different influences on the subsequent emergence of language. For example, when examining correlations between sensorimotor stages and language acquisition, Bates found that children's ability to devise means to obtain desired ends was more highly correlated with beginning language than their ability to perform Piaget's object permanence tasks.

The differential correlation between early language acquisition and the two kinds of sensorimotor knowledge: means-ends and object permanence, led Bates and her colleagues to a new sense of language learning in normal children. They showed that when children begin to use language they use it as a means to achieve some desired end, rather than solely as a label for acknowledging the permanency of objects.

This shift from a conceptual view to a functional view of language learning was fathered by "speech act theory" which was being developed in philosophy by Austin (1962) and Searle (1969). Austin, its originator, evolved his early ideas that sentences were acts rather than statements of facts from the realization that some sentences could not be verified or falsified. The particular sentences he singled out were those with verbs which become enacted when they are spoken. Sentences which contain verbs such as promise, apologize, warn, name, and bequeath, may misfire, but they cannot be regarded as true or false. Austin called these verbs "performatives," since by saying them one also performs the act.

While performative verbs are explicit statements of acts, speech act theorists came to realize that all utterances perform some act, even when they do not contain performative verbs. Austin labelled this performance sense of utterances their "illocutionary force" or "illocutionary act" and contrasted it with what the utterance actually meant, its "locutionary act," and with the impact of the utterance on the listener, the "perlocutionary act."

This focus on the performative and then on the illocutionary force of utterances was translated by psycholinguists and language pathologists as the "speaker's intent" and known as the intentional or functional component of utterances. True to our usual form, we, in language pathology, waited for our hand-me-down taxonomies to be donated by those studying acquistion of intentionality in normal language learners, both in preverbal stages (Bates, 1979; Bates, Camaioni & Volterra, 1975; Dore, Franklin, Miller & Ramer, 1976; Halliday, 1975), and beginning stages of verbalization (Carter, 1979; Dore, 1975).

The lesson we learned from speech act theorists in philosophy and those in child language who borrowed the philolsophers' ideas was:

(10) A shift from viewing children's language as a representation of their thinking, to a view of children's language as a tool they use to achieve their desired goals.

A third theme of the cognitive period had historical antecedents in Piaget (1970) as well as Werner and Kaplan (1950). It was the idea of decontextualization. While there are many facets to its meaning, the most general use is to refer to the process by which children distance themselves from thinking or talking only about what is currently perceptible to them. Piaget studied children's cognitive progression toward decontextualization in each of the six sensorimotor areas. For example, for imitation, children developed from only imitating things immediately present to being able to imitate an earlier event; in means-ends they developed from using familiar means for obtaining obvious and immediate ends to using novel means to obtain temporally distant ends; and in the area of symbolic play they moved from using present and perceptually similar objects as pretense substitutes to making those substitutions with absent and perceptually dissimilar objects. This notion of cognitive advancement being manifested by children's movement away from context boundedness has its direct parallels in the pragmatics revolution. We see echoed later:

(11) A principle that thinking and talking about events in the here and now is less taxing for beginning language learners than referring to events which are temporally or spatially distant.

The most recent theme in this period which studies cognitive ties to language learning has given a number of labels, but most frequently "schema theory." The emergence of schema theory has already been profoundly felt in developmental psycholinguistics and in its subarea of reading disabilities (Spiro, Bruce, & Brewer, 1980) and assumes the form of studies of normal children's understanding and production of connected discourse (Mandler & Johnson, 1977; Nelson & Gruendel, 1979).

Schema theorists conjecture about what type of knowledge would be required to understand or produce discourse such as narratives, descriptions or expositions (Brewer, 1980: Rumelhart, 1980). The hypothetical schemata have been likened to a script of a play wherein the major events are indicated but the particular choice of words and secondary embelishments are improvised (Shank & Abelson, 1977). A restaurant script would contain knowledge of an ordinary restaurant scene about ordering, eating, and paying for a meal. The script would not contain idiosyncratic information such as what would happen when there is a fly in the soup.

Schemata have also been likened to grammatical structures because they contain indications for parsing a story into its major constituents, just as grammars do for sentences (Mandler & Johnson, 1977; Stein & Glenn, 1979). So, Stein and Glenn's depictions of story grammars used by children to understand, remember, and tell stories contain constituent nodes for initiating events, planned sequences, and consequences.

Additionally, schemata have been likened to scaffolds which provide the undergirding for the discourse structure (Bruner, 1975). Bruner describes children's acquisition of interactive routines such as peek-a-boo games as originating with the adult providing the entire scaffolding, enacting the whole event, and progressing to where the child can enact the prescribed parts.

Script, grammar, and scaffold all are metaphors designed to portray the same idea—that a speaker and listener must have knowledge about what ordinarily happens, and that knowledge provides language users with the between-the-line fill-ins around which they construct language meaning. Recent cognitive theory has thus offered the pragmatics revolution:

> (12) A new unit, a schema, that language users use to structure their discourse.

The Social Assessment Period

While certain origins of the pragmatics movement can be traced from the linguistic and cognitive periods, it is my prediction that the focus on the social interaction between conversational partners will launch the pragmatics movement as something more than an extension of what we have already been doing these last 20 years. It is this social focus that will make pragmatics seem like a revolutionary change. Under the linguistics-cognitive frameworks, our primary assessment concern has been to build models of what is going on in the minds of language impaired children; in the social framework we begin to ask what is going on in the interaction between the language impaired child and someone else. In the linguistic and cognitive frameworks we look for the source of the language difficulty in the knowledge system of the language impaired child; in the social framework we need to examine the interaction exchange for reciprocity, and for occurrences of breakdowns, and repairs. Under the linguistic-cognitive orientation, we confine ourselves to the consideration of children's understandings about their language and the way it is served by cognition; in the social period we become more concerned about the social knowledge and social conditions through which communication takes its shape.

One research tradition that has sparked the social period has been developed by sociologists who engage in a particular branch of sociology known as ethnomethodology. Garfinkel, its founding father, coined the term in 1945 to describe his study of people's practical common sense knowledge which they use to carry out their everyday lives (Garfinkel, 1974). Later, in the early 1970's Sacks began what was to become the most borrowed subarea of ethnomethodology—the study of practical knowledges involved in conversational interactions (Mehan & Woods, 1975; Sacks, 1972; Turner, 1974). The analytic techniques for discovering those knowledges make up what is now called "conversational analysis" (Coulthard, 1977; French & Maclure, 1981; Wootton, 1981).

Conversational analysts of the ethnomethodology camp see conversation as a type of work which the participants engage in together. The participants work together to open conversations (Schegloff, 1968), and to close them (Schegloff & Sacks, 1974), to make them run smoothly via rule governed turn taking tactics (Sacks, Schegloff, & Jefferson, 1974), and, when the interactions break down, the participants work together to repair them (Jefferson, 1972, 1974).

This "working together" to conduct a conversation has offered the social component to the pragmatics movement:

(13)   A contention that interactions are accomplishments which grow out of work done by both participants in negotiation with one another.

A second research tradition which turns us toward a social view of language learning comes from a segment of applied speech act theory—

the part which analyzes children's use of language or prelinguistic communication for social ends. As an example, Bates (Bates, 1979; Bates, Benigni, Bretherton, Camaioni, & Volterra, 1977), leading our way once again, offers a distinction between the set of gestures which preverbal children make to obtain an object, and a second set of gestures whose purpose is social. The first she called protoimperatives and the second protodeclaratives. Illustrative of protodeclaratives are actions children perform to show off. Indeed, such actions are prototypic examples of protodeclaratives because their force is purely social, as if they are saying: "look at me!"

Bruner (1975) has also emphasized the social side of preverbal communicative acts in his study of pointing and showing gestures used by children and their caretakers for purposes of mutual referencing. Continuing in this social theme are Bruner's studies of preverbal games such as hide and seek and picture naming through which children and adults engage in joint activities (Ninio & Bruner, 1978; Ratner & Bruner, 1978).

Communicative acts designed to achieve social goals become an important subset of skills developed by children. Our study of them in relation to speech act theory led us to:

(14) A recognition of the special importance for language learning of socially directed intentional acts.

Viewing children's utterances as socially intended acts leads to a question of how well the children can engineer the situation to accomplish their social goals. A third research literature which can be considered to have a social emphasis asks this question even more elaborately than speech act theory. Its focus is on listener perspective taking.

Young children are reputedly inept in gearing their talk to their listener's point of view. They make the mistake of describing things as "this one" or "right here" to listeners who can't see where they are pointing (Krauss & Glucksberg, 1969); they use vocabulary only to reflect their own perspective (Tanz, 1980); they underuse indirect or polite forms; they fail on tasks which require them to indicate what the other person may be seeing (Piaget, 1954). In a word, they fail to give their listeners the necessary background knowledge for understanding what they are talking about, or to provide their listeners their proper respect.

The literature on perspective taking has an important role in the pragmatics movement in that it has offered us:

(15) An emphasis on the speaker's need for making their talk acceptable to their listeners.

A fourth influence on our developing social consciousness about language has been Grice's cooperative principle and the maxims entailed within it (Grice, 1975). Grice, a philosopher of language, developed the cooperative principle to explain how speakers communicate information which is not present in the propositional content of the sentences they are using. How is it, for example, that we know from the response "There's fruit in the refrigerator" to the statement "I'm hungry" is a suggestion that the hungry person satisfies his hunger by getting the fruit from the refrigerator? Grice says this type of interchange works because we adhere to a cooperative design that says speakers should be informative, truthful, relevant, and clear. Thus, the hungry listener can assume that the comment about fruit in the refrigerator had something to do with his declaration of hunger. He can supply information that makes the response relevant to his statement. Grice called these inferential jumps between sentences "conversational implicatures," and his maxims have been elaborated (Gordon & Lakoff, 1971) and called "conversational postulates."

Grice's conversational postulates and implicatures worked their way into the normal developmental literature through the investigation of children's detection of indirectness in requests (Bates, 1976; Ervin-Tripp, 1977; and Shatz, 1974, 1976). Grice's work leads us to the realization of:

(16)   A cooperative effort through which children come to interpret indirect meanings.

A fifth contributor to the social period emanated from the research on adult-child interaction. Under radical Chomskianism the full responsibility for language learning was relegated to the child's inborn competencies. As a reaction to that strict nativism, researchers as early as 1972 (Broen, 1972; Snow, 1972) began looking at how adults talked to children. They immediately discovered that most adults tuned their language to be commensurate with their ideas of the children's language and cognitive competences. It came to be called the "fine tuning hypothesis" (Cross, 1977). These findings have been elaborated since (see Chapman, 1981b; Ferguson & Snow, 1977; and Snow, 1979; for a review) and have resulted in a conceptual change from holding the child's innate knowledge responsible for language acquisition to holding the adult responsible. The change resulted in:

(17)   A shift from looking at the child's language performance to examining the match between adult talk and the child's language competencies.

A sixth research trend adds to our historical picture of the pragmatics movement, and that is the research which recognizes the importance of adult attitudes toward the language learning child and toward the event which contains and defines the interaction. The most apparent distinction which emerges from the literature on adult to child interactions is that sometimes adults focus their attention on the child and nurturantly respond to the child's initiatives. Other times the adult directs the event, disallows initiatives, and works from a preconceived notion about what the child should say or do. I have called these modes of interaction the nurturant mode and the teaching mode (Duchan, 1983). The mode is selected by the adults to achieve some overall goal, or, as it is called in everyday language, some "hidden agenda," or "ulterior motive."

The agenda held by the different participants in the interaction appears to have a powerful influence on how the interaction is conducted (Lubinski, Duchan, & Weitzner-Lin, 1980), and brings another contextual influence into the interaction adding a new idea to the pragmatics movement:

> (18)   An agenda which governs the way people negotiate the interaction.

Adults not only have preconceived ideas about the event, and what they want from it, they also have notions about the child which influence their interactions. Evidence that adult attitudes guide their social approaches to children comes from at least two sources. One is from labeling theory in sociology, which indicates that abnormal children are socialized differently not only because they are abnormal, but because they carry a particular diagnostic label (Gove, 1975; Hood-Holzman, 1982; Mercer, 1973), and the second is from research done by those same ethnomethodologists who study conversational interactions (Frankel, 1982; Helm, 1982).

One can tell, even by our name, that language clinicians or pathologists have taken what Mercer (1973) dubs "the clinical approach to deviance." This stance is at the expense of ignoring insights we might glean from the "social system perspective" (Mercer, 1973) found in labeling theory in sociology. The clinical perspective regards language disorders as being within individuals, the social perspective looks upon the assignment of diagnostic labels as being socially determined, and at variance with the social setting (Mercer, 1965), social class (Hood-Holzman, 1982), and prejudices from those doing the labeling (Rosenhan, 1973).

But conferring the label is not the worst of it. Labeling theorists have found from their research that, once labeled, people behave in collusion with others according to their conceptual model of those who already have the label. Those labeled mentally retarded come to act as if they were mentally retarded (Mercer, 1973); those labeled late bloomers, become late bloomers (Rosenthal & Jacobson, 1968). The labels become self-fulfilling prophesies (Rosenthal & Jacobson, 1968; Rosenhan, 1973). Labeling theorists call this prophesy effect "secondary deviance" (Lemert, 1967).

Labeling theory has its own history in sociology in the more general study of power and status relationships among groups of people, not just those who have been stigmatized as deviant. The work by sociolinguists has dealt with how these status relationships are manifest in the language used by representatives from different social or status groups (Gumperz & Hymes, 1972; Williams, 1970).

The social view of interaction, with particular reference to deviance is in keeping with pragmatic sensibilities in several ways. First, it demonstrates how the same behaviors are interpreted as deviant under certain contextual conditions, and as nondeviant under others. Secondly, it suggests that role expectations on the part of the people in contact influence the ways those people interact with one another. And, thirdly, it moves the site of disorder from inside people to the culture, and to the social interaction (Duchan, 1982a). Labeling theory lends our pragmatics movement the sense that we must consider more carefully:

(19)   The role a diagnostic label has in the playing out of social interactions.

At the same time the labeling theorists were showing the effect of labels on interactions, the ethnomethodologists were doing detailed studies of interactions with people labeled deviant. Their goal was to see how the preconceived notions held by the co-participants were being enacted in their everyday lives.

Helm (1982) describes the effort interactants go through to understand what is going on with the other person as "strategic contextualization." He sees the effect of strategic contextualization as one where the interactant construes the inappropriate response of the "culturally incompetent" person as comprehensible and appropriate. The contextualizer tries to take the child's point of view in an attempt to figure out how the apparently inappropriate action makes sense for the child. The adult thereby conceptualizes the child as someone who is competent. The effect of the endeavor is to maintain the child in the interaction and to allow the interaction to proceed. The endeavor of having to provide such a context presumes that the children are trying to communicate, and that they are unable to do that conventionally. Helm's poignant example of strategic contextualization revolves around an autistic child who answered his mother's question "The belt goes in the what?" with "In the living room." The mother then proceeded to explain to an onlooker "Well, in fact, we were in the living room when I put his belt on" (Helm, 1982).

Frankel (1982) and Helm (1981) also offer instances where adults fail to strategically contextualize abnormal behavior. Frankel observed a mother who judged her autistic child's verbal responses as wrong, and ignored his appropriate nonverbal attempts to communicate with her, and Helm describes "cutting out" operations where the interactants fail to allow the partners to take an assigned or deserved turn in the interaction.

This ethnomethodological view of how participants work to keep one another in or out of the interaction presents us with:

> (20)   The creativity involved in making sense of other people's behavior, and the crucial influence this sense making has on the interaction.

Six Loose Ends

The twenty historical themes represent milestones in our move toward appreciating the influence of context on language interpretation and use. The themes have helped us direct our attention to designing a new methodology for analyzing children's language—that of informal assessment in natural contexts. They have also led us to a recognition that language is functional in that it is used by interactants to achieve preconceived goals. Further, we learned that we should not regard sounds, morphemes, or sentences in linguistic isolation, but must look at how the language around these units impinge on them. And, perhaps most importantly, we developed from the themes the idea that interactional partners are trying to make sense of what is going on in the interaction and their sense making depends on their ideas about the event and about their social partners as much as it does about the language being used.

What has been unenlightening about the 20 themes is that they have been presented as isolable categories giving the impression that all that need be done is to tie them together, in whatever way we want, and then we will have the full picture of pragmatics. What is actually the case is that the historical threads may sometimes represent different ways of expressing the same idea, but come from different sources. Other threads may not relate at all. And still others may be so closely intertwined that they can be best represented as an intricate conceptual web. This section will discuss some of these webbed ideas, adding six loose ends to what remains of the discussion of the pragmatics revolution and illustrating how our historical threads can be tied together in our current synthesis of the pragmatics revolution. They are: turntaking; topic maintenance; presuppositions; units of conversational exchange; nonverbal communication; and, deixis.

Turntaking

Turntaking is a category fall-out from ethnomethodology (Sacks, Shegloff, & Jefferson, 1974); and, in keeping with that "ethno" methodology, it has to do with how people negotiate interaction. In this case, the focus is on how people who are talking to one another manage to get and give away their talking turns. The turntaking system in conversation differs from that involved in ritualized exchanges, interviews, or meetings, in that the size and turn exchange in conversations are not predetermined. Instead, they are worked out in the course of the interaction. Speakers can decide who to give a turn to and when, and they give turns away by doing such things as asking questions, challenging, complimenting, and by using paralanguage or nonverbal cues. Another thing speakers can do to give turns is simply to stop talking, creating a gap during which the next speaker can claim a turn. The turn taking system described by conversational analysts Sacks et al. (1974) operates alongside other systems such as those which work to organize utterances within turns, or those which maintain control of topics. These authors as well as others who study nonverbal mechanisms associated with turn exchanges (Duncan, 1975; Duncan & Niederehe, 1974) talk about the mechanics of turntaking, but not as much about where in the discourse or interaction structure turns occur, and why it is that they occur there. The literature on topic maintenance and topic shift sheds more light on this issue of how those "transition relevant places" for turntaking come about.

Topic

"Topic" is a topic which resides in linguistics at the sentence level of analysis as well as at the discourse level of analysis. It also has found its way into psychology in discussions about sentence and discourse processes in comprehension (Bransford & Nitsch, 1978). The philosophers need the construct of topic to account for presuppositions and inferencing, and conversational analysts rightfully assign topic a central role in their study of sense making and turn taking.

The meaning of topic takes on different shades depending upon the theoretical context in which it is treated. Sentence topic is discussed by linguists interested in the distinction between subjects and predicates of individual sentences (Li, 1976). Subjects of sentences usually specify the topic of the sentence, and the predicate then comments on that topic. Similarly, sentence topics are regarded by psychologists who work in an information processing framework as marking the given information, with the rest of the sentence providing something new about what's given (Clark & Clark, 1977; Greenfield, 1979). Topics may be explicitly stated in the sentence (e.g., "The dress is beautiful"), or may be inferred or presupposed from the context ("Beautiful"). In either case, all sentences are thought either to have or to presume a topic.

Unlike sentence topics, discourse topics cross sentence boundaries and serve to tie the sentences together thematically. The organization along discourse topics might be preplanned, as would be the case in storytelling or preplanned narrative descriptions (Keenan, 1977), or they may be formulated as they go along, which would happen in natural conversation where one person initiates the topic and a second person maintains it. Discourse topics can end, or can fade or shade into one another (Hurtig, 1977), or can be shifted abruptly by means of topic shifting apologies such as "sorry to butt in" or "that reminds me.." Tellers of shaggy dog stories can lead their listeners down one topical garden path and shift topics at the end to reveal a second and more obscure topical path. Agendas can coincide with topics, when they are made explicit, as when salespeople try to sell their wares; or they may not be topic related, as with the well known hidden agendas of seduction behind the conversations in bar scenes. Topics can be controlled by the interactant with higher status or stronger personality, or by the person who is limited in his or her choice of topics. Successful conversations require topic sharing between partners, unsuccessful ones may break down because of topic problems such as disagreements about whose topic deserves featuring or because of lack of listener perspective taking on the part of one or more of the participants.

How, then, might turntaking relate to topic maintenance? The most obvious relationship, which I have alluded to is that turns are often taken and given when topics are ended. That's where the two categories coincide. But the management of turns and topics also differ. Some sentences seem unrelated to topic, and are designed, instead, to serve the turntaking system. "Your turn" would be the prototypic example of such a sentence. Less obvious examples would be topic-empty greetings, calling on someone to talk, and refusing a turn by telling the person who has the floor to go on talking. These utterances which have a turntaking focus have been called conversational moves (Goffman, 1969; Hurtig, 1977), and housekeeping moves (Weiner & Goodenough, 1977). Sometimes turns are taken but do not become real turns. These have been called back channeling (Yngve, 1970), or conversational passes (Weiner & Goodenough, 1977) wherein the listener makes noises, or nods knowingly, or echoes the speaker a la Carl Rogers, all to let the speaker know to go on, and that they are still listening. Topic has an integral relationship with turntaking. What about topic and presupposition? That brings us to the next topic, presupposition.

Presupposition

Is the following sentence true or false? "The king of France is bald."
This example was Bertrand Russell's (1905), and was designed to illustrate
that assigning truth value to such sentences presumes certain facts, in this
case making the wrong presumption that there is a present king of France.
Given these presumptions, such sentences ask that you evaluate the assertion which the sentence contains, in this case whether or not such a king
has hair. Another famous example with a built-in presupposition is "When
did you stop beating your wife?"

This use of presuppositions to handle logical assumptions in philosophy
has been extended by Bates (1976) to include psychological presuppositions, which are all those things which speakers and listeners presume as shared
tacit background knowledge to what they are saying. Topics which are not
explicit are presupposed under Bates' definition. "Beautiful" presupposes
that the listener has knowledge of the topic, say, "dress." Children who
speak one word at a time have been said to presuppose their listeners'
knowledge of their topic (Greenfield & Zukow, 1978). Conversational implicatures (as in "There is fruit in the refrigerator" in response to "I'm
hungry") are presupposed by their speakers. The cooperative principle is
presupposed, which leads listeners to perform strategic contextualization
of one another's apparent "off the wall" comments as when the autistic
child answered "in the living room" to "The belt goes in the what?"

Units of Conversational Exchange

There is a group of researchers who study conversational patterns, yet
who are not among those who call themselves ethnomethodologists. They
come from the structuralist orientation, some taking their models from
philosophy (Garvey, 1979), others from the adult-child interaction research
in psychology (Moerk, 1978), and still others include a rendition of schema
theory (Cazden, 1979; Ratner & Bruner, 1978). Their endeavor has been
to look for structural regularities across speakers, in the way those speakers
talk back and forth to one another.

One basis for analyzing conversational exchange clusters is to look for
who initiates, and who responds, and what comprises those single volley
initiation-response pairs. These analyses reveal a summons-answer pattern
which occurs in greetings, question-answer exchanges, and request compliance exchanges.

A second approach to conversational exchange is to focus on the adult's
role in the child's language learning, which leads to an emphasis on how
the adult responds to children's topics. Cazden (1975) classified these into

imitation, expansion, and modelings. Cross (1978) and Snow (1981) emphasized the semantic relatedness of the adult utterances to the child's.

A third emphasis has been on three step exchanges, where one or the other conversational partner asks for clarification and the initiator corrects accordingly (Gallagher, 1981; Garvey, 1979). These have been called contingent queries and clarification requests by Garvey (1979) and misunderstandings by Wilcox and House (1982).

Keenan offers a fourth focus which is on the role of children's repetitions in utterance exchanges, serving them as clarification requests, agreements, or self information (Keenan, 1977).

Fifth, there are a group of studies which report preparatory utterances which are designed to set up conditions several moves ahead in the conversation. For example, "You know what?" is a bid for a question "What?" which then can be taken as permission to have the conversational floor. Sacks calls this a "story preface" (cited in Coulthard, 1977).

Finally, some researchers have looked beyond the two volley and three volley exchanges for those which go to multiple volleys. They find turns which function as turnabouts, answering the last utterance and requesting another (Fine, 1978; Mischler, 1975).

The volleys in conversational exchange are often governed by those same organizational devices which I have described earlier under turntaking, topic maintenance and the presuppositions involved in perspective taking. The similiarity holds insofar as the responder must take the turn at the appropriate time, and recognize the summons to do so; the responses need to be topic relevant, and the initiator as well as the responder must carry appropriate suppositions about what the other knows and intends in order to have the exchange work.

Nonverbal Communication

Categories pertaining to nonverbal communicative exchanges are making their way into our category checklists under the headings of proxemics, synchrony, facial expressions, gestures, gaze, and kinesis and sometimes paralanguage (Higgenbotham & Yoder, 1981). This literature presents nonverbal communication as parasitic on the verbal exchange system in that it is regarded as either an indexical precursor to language (Bates, 1979) or an underestimated supplement to it (see Ochs, 1979; and Weitzner-Lin & Duchan, 1980, for more on this criticism). When not parasitic on the verbal system, the nonverbal system is seen as divorced of meaning or from the interaction, and is portrayed as separate behaviors.

The parasitic view of nonverbal communication minimizes the central role that it plays in the turntaking system through postural shifting, mutual gaze and gaze aversion, and movement synchrony. Nonverbal communication is as central to communication as is verbal communication and sometimes more so (see Kendon's 1979 literature review). Topics can be designated by a nonverbal point, a give, or a show. They also can be maintained via a nod, or rejected either by the issuance of a dismissal gesture or a movement out of face to face alignment (Duchan, 1982b). Mutual referencing can be done nonverbally; knowing glances and smiles are a means for showing that one shares knowledge with a conversational partner. These nonverbal communications serve to indicate mutual suppositions and presuppositions. The role of postural shifts, proximity, and gaze in the execution of turn exchanges is well known, and is crucial to understanding how turntaking works (Craig & Gallagher, 1982; Rosenfeld, 1978).

If nonverbal behavior is underregarded, timing in interaction is virtually ignored. Some have discussed its impact on turntaking by looking at the length of silences (Garvey & Berninger, 1981); others have documented the existence of interactional synchrony, where speakers and listeners move to the same beat (Byers, 1976; Duchan & Oliva, 1980; Kendon, 1970). But its role in social interactions as a signaling system has yet to be explored.

The separatist view of nonverbal behavior and timing in social interaction takes the behaviors as isolated events occurring outside the meaning network. They are seen as behaviors which should be counted or judged appropriate or inappropriate with no regard to their role in the interaction or the ongoing event. This is typically the approach to undesirable behaviors like the self stimulatory behaviors of autistic children. (For an argument against this approach, see Duchan, 1982b.)

Deixis

A sixth loose end is deixis. It refers to a particular set of words whose meanings are unknown unless you know something about the settings in which they occur. Deixis has been of concern to linguists dealing with semantic representation (Fillmore, 1973) and of psycholinguists looking at semantic acquisition (Tanz, 1980). There are deictic terms which refer to people, such as "I, you, them" whose referents require that you know who is talking ("I"), whom they are talking to ("you"), and who they are talking about ("them"). Similarly, there are place terms (here, there) and time terms (now, then) which require a contextual grounding. Deixis has obvious and intricate ties to turntaking, topic, presupposition, as well as to nonverbal communication.

In sum, I have been discussing the interweaving of six areas of pragmatics: turntaking, topic maintenance, presuppositions, conversational exchange, nonverbal communication, and deixis. These areas tie to one another in such integral ways that separating them fails to capture their nature. In fact, it is this intertwining of categories that makes pragmatics different from the other areas of language, and which challenges our sense of the efficacy of the whole enterprise these last 20 years to render language and language disorders as composed of separable units within separable levels. In the last section of this paper I will pick up this idea again, and make the case that the pragmatics movement is revolutionary and not a simple addition of another tier to our existing language assessment tool kit. But before I do that, I would like to test the coverage of the 20 themes in 20 years by matching them against taxonomies and topics from recent literature in language pathology.

Tying the Threads to the Literature in Language Pathology

In these meanderings through the last 20 years, I have pulled ideas from our work in language pathology and our sister disciplines, which I touted as our own cognitive precursors to the way we are currently thinking about pragmatics and pragmatics assessment. The historical account reveals a mixed academic heritage; it contains our special renditions of speech act theory in philosophy, of generative transformational theory in linguistics, and borrowings from cognitive theory in psychology and from the ethnomethodologists and labeling theorists in sociology. It also contains crossbred constructs, such as notions of presupposition and topic, which come from philosophy and linguistics, as well as sociology. Table 5-1 summarizes the twenty threads and six loose ends, and the times and terms which accompany them.

In order to insure that the whole pragmatics territory has been covered, the categories in Table 5-1 can be matched against the taxomomies forwarded in the review articles of research on pragmatics, and some pragmatics research and assessment checklists now being developed for assessing the pragmatics knowledge of language impaired children. The categories are numbered according to their place in Table 5-1.

Let's begin with Prutting's 1982 literature review of pragmatics. She presented four areas of research concentration, the study of cognitive and social precursors to language acquisition, the functions of language, conversational rules, and the ways speakers change their talk for different listeners (stylistic variation). Her cognitive and social precursors derive from the cognitive period, with its focus on sensorimotor origins of language (#11). Prutting's functions (#10) stem from speech act theory, which emerged during the cognitive and social eras. Also from the social era were her conversational rules a la Grice's 1975 article (#16), and the speakers'

TABLE 5-1
Historical pragmatics twenty threads.

Historical Phases	The Threads	Some Associated Terms
The Linguistic Period		
Syntax	1. Linguistic rules	Deep structures Transformations
	2. Normative Orientation	
	3. Parent Disciplines	
	4. Informal Tests, Natural Contexts	
Semantic Relations	5. Interpretive Analysis	
Phonology	6. Linguistic Context	Context sensitive rules
Text	7. Discourse Analysis	Conversational exchange patterns
	8. Cohesion Devices	Anaphora Cataphora
The Cognitive Period		
Cognitive Strategies	9. Situational Expectancies	Probable Event strategy
Cognitive Precursors	10. Functionalism	Illocutionary acts Performatives Functions
Decontextualization	11. Cognitive Distancing	Sensorimotor stages
Schema Theory	12. Schemata	Story grammars Scaffolds Scripts Routines

The Social Period

Conversational Analysis	13. Interactions as Accomplishments	Turntaking Breakdowns Repairs Negotiation
Communicative Acts	14. Socially Intended Acts	Protoimperative Protodeclarative Mutual attention Mutual activity
Listener Perspective Taking	15. Listener Acceptance	Code Shifting Polite Markers Background knowledge
Cooperative Principle	16. Conversational Maxims	Implicature Postulates Indirect meanings
Adult-Child Talk	17. Fine Tuning	Semantic contingency
Adult Attitudes	18. Agenda	Self fulfilling prophesy
	19. Labeling theory	Role, Status, Stigma
	20. Sense Making	Strategic contextualization Cutting out

And Six Loose Ends

E1	Turntaking	
E2	Topic	Comment New-old information
E3	Presupposition	Logical presupposition Psychological presupposition
E4	Conversational Exchange	
E5	Nonverbal Communication	Gaze Proxemics

---

adjustments from the literature on perspective taking (#15). So, Prutting selects from diverse literatures which have as their grounding diverse theoretical concerns.

Rees (1978) exhibits similar diversity. In her review article she includes as her major categories: the functions of language (#10); new and old information (E2); rules of conversion (#16); deixis (E6); and mother-to-child input (#17).

Bates (1976) takes a less eclectic stance in her composition of pragmatics and adheres closely to the literature in philosophy. She treats propositions and reference as pragmatics, regarding the words and sentences as spoken acts, rather than as having fixed symbolic ties. Bates also builds performatives (#10); logical and psychological presuppositions (E3), and conversational postulates (#16) into her pragmatics edifice.

Carrow-Woolfolk and Lynch (1982) include pragmatics in their "integrative approach to language disorders in children" and take functions (#10) and conversational postulates (#16) as their major headings. Under conversational postulates, they include presuppositions (E3), indirect speech acts (#16), turntaking (E1), and deixis (E6), thereby drawing from speech act theory, ethnomethodology, and semantic theory for their category conglomerate.

Lund and Duchan (1983) organize their literature review and pragmatics assessment approach around four contextual categories, *the situational context*, which attends to how the ongoing physical setting (#9), speech event (#12), and topic (E2) influences children's language performance; *the intentional context*, which includes illocutionary force (#10) and agenda (#18); *the listener context*, where they emphasize the role of listener perspective taking (#15); and *the linguistic context* where they discuss discourse cohesion devices such as anaphora and cataphora (#8). Carrow-Woolfolk and Lynch, and Lund and Duchan as well as Prutting and Rees, assume the multitheory stance, in contrast to Bates, who subscribes more closely to a single theoretical framework.

When we attend to how to bring theoretical pragmatics to our assessment or study of language disordered children, we find another set of articles, some trying to cover a broad spectrum of pragmatics categories, and others concentrating on specific areas of pragmatic competence.

An example of the broad view is Bernard-Opitz's (1982) evaluation of the pragmatics competence of an autistic child. Her general areas of concern are discourse functions, or what she calls communicative acts and responses (requests, responses, statements, answers, clarification, disconfirmation) (#7), and topic manipulations (introduction, continuous discourse, off-topic productions) (E2). Both sets of categories emanate from conversational analysis.

Miller (1978) also takes a broad view of pragmatics assessment, crediting Bates (1976) and Watzlawick, Beavin, Helmick, & Jackson (1967) as the sources for her category selection. From Bates, and therefore from speech act theory, Miller borrows the four categories of performatives (#10), propositions, presuppositions (E3), and conversational postulates (#16), calling all these "communicative strategies." From Watzlawick et al., she designs a way to analyze communicative interaction. She does this through the use of categories which derive more generally from the conversational analyses: turntaking (E1), topic maintenance/switching (E2), communication breakdowns (#13). Miller adds a fourth category under her communication interaction—the relative dominance of a speaker, which she measures as the amount of speaking in terms of total time and the number of utterances spoken (#19).

Corsaro (1981), a sociologist, takes what he calls a "social cognition view" of pragmatics, and structures his approach to assessing communicative competence accordingly. He suggests that we examine language disordered children's attention gaining competencies (#14), child and adult turntaking skills (E1), conversational skills in discourse (under which he includes topic relevance) (E2), and children's reluctance to interact with peers (#13). Corsaro's categories are general and are gleaned from his review of his own and other's research on social interaction between normal preschool children and their peers or their caretakers. His list represents an accumulation of ideas with a social focus on language learning and is a good example of what I described earlier as the third wave in our developmental history, the social focus.

The narrow perspectives on pragmatics assessment pick one particular domain of pragmatics to concentrate on. The most prevalent approach is to use category checklists which are engendered by studies of normal children. Under this approach, language disordered children are evaluated in terms of whether they are doing things which fit those category checklists, and if so, whether their performance is age appropriate.

The most commonly found checklists are those of pragmatic functions or intents (#10). Some are based on Dore's research (Coggins & Carpenter, 1981), others on Halliday's (Prutting, 1979). Some are combinations of Dore and Halliday (Leonard, Camarata, Rowan, & Chapman, 1982; McLean & Synder-McLean, 1978; McShane, 1980). And some use the protoimperative, protodeclarative distinction of Bates (Greenwald & Leonard, 1979; Snyder, 1978). Chapman, in her chapter on *Assessing Language Production in Children* (1981a), combines them all, advocating a rational selection depending upon the assessment goals.

Another checklist domain is of mother-to-child talk, (#17) (Russo & Owens, 1982) and yet another is conversational competence (#13) (Abbeduto &

Rosenberg, 1980; Bryan, Donahue, Pearl, & Sturm, 1981; Watson, 1977, cited in and Leonard, 1979).

Besides broad category and narrow checklist approaches, there is a third approach to studying pragmatics in children. That is to combine pragmatics assessments with either linguistic or cognitive checklists to look for correlates. Several researchers have combined their look at semantic relations and functions (Curtiss, Prutting, & Lowell, 1979; Skarakis & Prutting, 1977; Watson & Lord, 1982). Others, taking after Bates (1979), have looked at sensorimotor performance alongside communicative functions (Greenwald & Leonard, 1979) and a third group have looked at cognitive requirements for discourse (Blank & Franklin, 1980; Tough, 1977).

A fourth approach to studying pragmatics issues in relation to language disorders, and the one which is most often adopted by researchers interested in comparing language disordered children with one another is to examine their performance on limited domains of pragmatics. Below is a listing of articles on pragmatics and language impairment in specific pragmatic domains, and numerical indicators showing their ties to Table 5-1.

Situational Expectancies (#9)

probable event strategy	Deward, 1979
	Duchan & Siegel, 1979

Functions(#10)

issuing requests	Weitzner-Lin, 1981
	Donahue, 1981; Prinz, in press
understanding indirect requests	Shatz, Bernstein, & Schulman, 1980
functions of echolalia	Prizant & Duchan, 1981
declaratives and imperatives	Snyder, 1978
	Greenwald & Leonard, 1979

Topic (E2)

new information	Snyder, 1978
	Leonard, Cole, and Stekol, 1979

Discourse Analysis (#7)

discourse contingencies in echolalia	Curcio & Paccia, 1982
response to inadequate messages	Donahue, Pearl, & Bryan, 1980

revisions   Gallagher & Darnton, 1978
                                   VanKleek & Frankel, 1981

Nonverbal Communication (E5)

interaction synchrony   Duchan & Oliva, 1980

use of gesture   Wilcox & House, 1982

nonverbal interaction   Frankel, 1982

Schema Theory(#12)

memory for gist   Graybeal, 1981

comprehension of narratives   Johnston, 1982

Adult to Child Talk(#17)

responding to child's intent   Rondal, 1978
                                   Brinton & Fujiki, 1982

topic contingency of adult   Hurtig, Ensrud, & Tomblin, 1982

adjusting to the language
level   Cramblit & Siegel, 1978
                                   Wolchik & Harris, 1982
                                   Marshall, Hegrenes, &
                                   Goldstein, 1973
                                   Lasky & Klopp, 1982

The 20-plus-six areas of pragmatics gleaned from the 20-year history has, with some stretching for differences in terminology, been able to accommodate our literature in language disorders. That suggests that the 20-plus-six themes cover the territory, and understanding them in their respective histories is all that we need to understand what is going on in pragmatics and all we need to know in order to proceed to pragmatics assessment. Unfortunately, a closer look suggests that there are some problems involved in our reliance on the current approaches being developed for pragmatics assessment.

Some Knotty Problems

The effort in lining up the major ideas contributing to our pragmatics revolution was two-faced: to look back at our history in order to get a sense of its technicolored origins, and to look forward to try to weave the historical threads together into a coherent approach for language assessment. The hidden agenda in looking backward was to show that the themes came from their own theoretical contexts in their respective disciplines and that our stripping them from these contexts contributed to the disjointedness of our own pragmatics movement. That problem can be remedied by looking for a way to bind the ideas in pragmatics together by rewording and reorganizing the themes.

The look into the future will begin by examining some major obstacles which will need to be overcome.

A Priori Categories are Like Blinders

A discussion of this a priori category problem can begin with two exaggerated examples. The most famous is the example of the drunk who loses his watch in a dark alley and looks for it under the light where the alley intersects the street. He figures that he can see much better under the light.

Or have you heard the one about the language pathologist who witnesses the autistic child say "Don't throw dog off balcony," while throwing a block across the room. The pathologist concluded from the observation that the child's language problem is one of article omission.

These examples go together in that they both involve mistakes which are made because people have preferences for where and how to view their world, and those preferences involve looking for things where they can best be seen or understood. This is the a priori category problem, and it explains why we use category checklists to evaluate the language of our language impaired children. We would rather look under the street lights than to fumble about in dark alleys.

The perceptual distortion of the a priori categories is not just in the clinical arena, it is also felt in our research in language pathology. As can be seen by the above review, we typically take our research issues in language pathology from normal language acquisition, and that research literature typically designs its efforts around the ideas bouncing about in the parent disciplines of philosophy, psychology, linguistics, and sociology. We are the grandchildren who accept the category hand-me-downs as truth, and use them as the street lights under which we assess and research our language disordered subjects.

This a priori category focus not only leads us to take our parent disciplines as our sole models, it also leads us to regard language disordered children in terms of what they are not doing right, as opposed to asking why they are doing what they are doing. I have called this the deficit view, as opposed to the difference view (Duchan, 1982b).

Some further examples from my own research may make this point clearer. Rather than viewing autistic children's echolalia as a symptom of abnormal language, Prizant and Duchan studied how it might function for those children (Prizant & Duchan, 1981). Similarly, rather than viewing autistic children's self stimulatory behavior as something to rid them of, I examined the context of its use for a particular autistic child, concluding that the same behavior can serve him differently, and different behaviors can serve him similarly (Duchan, 1982a). Lund and Duchan reported on a child's idiosyncratic phonological structure which accounted for his misarticulation of two syllable words (Lund & Duchan, 1978). And in another study Lund and Duchan looked at the apparent erratic pattern in children's answers to questions of the form "What do you (verb) with?" We postulated a general rule: "Answer with what you need to carry out the verb" and presented this rule as a simpler and more predictive one than that their answers occurred because they lacked full knowledge of a semantic relations checklist (Duchan & Lund, 1979). Finally, I argued against the multilevel approaches offered by information processing and linguistic models by reconceptualizing those multilevel accounts of language disordered children described in the literature (Duchan, 1983).

The bottom line of these examples is that we may be finding out something about language disordered children by looking under our parent disciplines' light, but unless we take our children as a source for our own taxonomies and make aposteriori descriptions and explanations of what they are doing, we may never even know what it is they are about.

The Normative Focus has Led Us Down a Garden Path

The a priori category problem is unavoidable if one takes a normative approach to studying or assessing children with language disorders. That is to say, if disordered children are compared with normal children, they must be compared on preestablished developmental categories. Even if we base our normative questions on what the average language disordered child is like, we still are forced to compare the children with one another, and not in their own terms, thereby succumbing to the a priori category basis. Thus, normative concerns entail those same problems of intellectual blinding as are involved in any type of a priori categorization.

The most virulent form of the normative problem is found in the efforts of people to standardize their assessment procedures with the intent of creating contexts which allow them to compare children to one another. This standardization is antithetical to the pragmatics sensibility which holds context as all important rather than an outside intruder. Mishler (1979) captures the pragmatist disdain for such control by dubbing it "context stripping."

But there is another even more unyielding dilemma involved in comparing language impaired children with others like them or with their normal age or stage mates. That has to do with the excessive intellectual creativity of those doing the comparing. If I ask you to compare very different things, say an elephant and a pencil, your ingenuity will win out and you will be able to arrive at some dimension on which they are similar. Your ingenuity has even more room to operate in if I were to offer you the dimension and ask you to compare two things along it. This is what Osgood has done these many years in getting people to perform on his semantic differential technique (Osgood, Suci, & Tannenbaum, 1957).

What looks then like objective measurement when we compare children on a given dimension or checklist may be more a function of our ingenuity than some external degree of similarity. Said the other way around, if you were asked to contrast two things, you would use the same ingenuity to point out their differences, and your dimension of contrast may or may not have to do with the essential nature of what you are contrasting.

Now, to capsulize: in the process of normalizing we may be doing a mini Rorschach test, treating our language disordered children as ambiguous inkblots into which we ingeniously read our own preselected dimensions.

A shady example from our own literature may drive home the point. Many language pathologists have, in their test giving repertoire, a popular standardized test, the Illinois Test of Psycholinguistic Abilities (ITPA) that they use to diagnose children as language disordered and to determine their particular area of language deficit (Kirk, McCarthy, & Kirk, 1968). That test contains a subtest, the grammatic closure subtest, which supplies the children with a stimulus picture and asks them to complete sentences such as: Here is a dress. Here are two ____. Children who fail the subtest are considered to have grammatic closure problems and there are well worked out lesson plan kits for remediating their problem by teaching them automatic language skills. The test and teaching programs seem plausible to the clinician who believes that grammatic closure is an important skill (the dimension needs to be believable), that normal children perform with age defined competencies on the task, that children who do not perform at age equivalence are by definition deficient in that skill, and that the children can be brought up to par on that skill if given proper practice.

Unfortunately, nowhere do the test makers or curriculum makers talk about the skill as involving knowledge of inflectional morphology, which is differentially affected by different dialects (Duchan & Baskervill, 1977), and which subsumes subtle knowledge of discourse, irregular inflectional markers, etc., and therefore requires much more than automatic rehearsal. The ITPA led us down a garden path which had nothing to do with the children we were supposed to be helping, and it was believable because our task was to compare our language disordered children with normal children, without looking for the regularities contained in their own language system.

Language Disorders are Context Bound

We used to ask our questions about children with language disorders as if the disorder were caused by a germ in the child, a fixed entity, a disease to be diagnosed and then prescribed for. The pragmatics sensibility which has been evolving over these last 20 years points us toward thinking about language disordered children more ecologically. We are led by its tenets to think from the perspectives of the language disordered children. We study the children's knowledge system and try to construct how they make sense of the current scene through which they interpret and use language.

We are also led to examining the nature of the interaction, how language disordered children and their partners negotiate it, how they manage their turntaking, their topic selection, and so on. Finally, we are led to thinking about how children become designated as language impaired in the first place and how that diagnosis affects the interaction.

All these new sensibilities dictate a different conceptualization of language disorders, a much more context bound one which allows for thinking that the child may have a disorder under some conditions, and not under others; and a conception which entertains that the disorder may be in the interaction or in the attitude toward the child, and not in the child at all. (See Duchan, 1982a, for more on this point.)

The Pragmatics Movement Comes in Different Strengths

Like Buffalo chicken wings, pragmatics can be bought in its mild, medium or hot versions. The mild version takes pragmatics as a new aspect of language which needs to be assessed along with our traditional assessment approaches. It is also the case that those who select the mild version would hope that the new area of pragmatics will soon give birth to formal tests, or standardized informal assessment procedures, which will offer them ways to determine which areas of pragmatics children show deficiencies in.

Those with medium tastes see pragmatics as more pervasive, and movement which requires them to evaluate their children's language in natural contexts, even when the language problem is one of phonology or syntax, or has as its source a cognitive deficiency. This group will willingly abandon their standardized procedures and look at the child's language in light of its intentions, and listener and situational appropriateness. However, they still hold to the idea that language is what they are studying, and context is what is influencing it.

The hot version of the pragmatics movement is forwarded by the movement's revolutionaries, who opt for overthrowing our previous conceptions that language is what we are assessing, and propose that we move toward a new conceptualization which examines communication and context, and, if called for, the language within it. The hot view is the one that must be embraced if we are to take seriously what the literature in pragmatics has to tell us.

First, the literature in pragmatics says that children, normal as well as abnormal, regard language simply as an aspect of the more important endeavor of sense making. The children may produce sentences or narratives that only hint at what they mean, or that mean different things depending upon the context. Indications are that children also understand language in terms of their ongoing sense of the situation, and they often distort their interpretation of language to fit their sense making endeavor.

Besides sense making, these children are also concerned with making the interaction work. They are likely to accommodate to expectations regarding their social role and deviance which are given them through their label, and they are likely to act out their accommodations through active negotiation in face to face encounters.

And so we have the social view of human interaction, from the perspective of the particular child. Such a view leads us to a new perspective on assessment which looks to the interaction for its corpus, and, within the interaction, the aspects of the event which are most contributory to the mutual (or disjointed) sensemaking going on between the participants. The hot view involves interaction, sensemaking, and intentionality, and only peripherally the formal language system.

Weaving Together the Twenty Threads and Six Loose Ends and Removing the Knots

The threads and loose ends so far have been presented as equal contributors to the pragmatics movement and to pragmatics assessment. But, in practice, they have unequal status and differential affinities with one another. They can be spun into a six category suprastructure: methodology, sensemaking, linguistic rules, intentionality, and interactional management. Each category can be discussed in the suprastructure with an eye toward building overarching principles for doing pragmatics assessment in the future.

Methodology

There are two themes in the 20 plus six (Table 5-1), which directly pertain to how we should carry out our assessment approach; #4, which argues for informal assessment in natural contexts, and #5, which allows us to make interpretations from the behavior we observe. The a priori category problem cautions us about making our interpretations from our own presuppositions gleaned from our parent disciplines (#3), and against relying on a normative framework from which to assess our children (#2), thereby neutralizing the contributions of these last two trends to our pragmatics suprastructure.

Sensemaking

Sensemaking, the largest supracategory, guides us to focus on how the participants, particularly the language disordered child, are making sense out of what is going on (#20). The categories involving situational expectations (#9) and schemata (#12) produce a kind of sense making based on prior experience with events like the current one. They offer the participants a way of conceiving of the current event as a whole. If the event at hand involves discourse, the sensemaking will affect and benefit from the discourse organization (#7), and cohesion (#8) and shared presuppositions (E3), and deictic referencing (E6), and will provide a grounding for topic comprehension and elaboration (E2). If the sensemaking is only related to the objects in the presenting scene, the language and conceptualization going on is said to be contextualized, in contrast with the decontextualized sensemaking involved in distant events (#11).

Functionalism

While the functionalist concern must be a large part of sensemaking, it also has a life of its own. That life includes formulating intentions (#10) and overall agendas (#18) which may or may not have a social focus (#14). It also includes devising means for carrying those intentions out and for managing interactions in their behalf (#13).

Interactional Management

As the conversational analyses have so successfully shown, interactions need to be negotiated (#13), and this is done with strict conformance to rules of turntaking (E1) and cooperation (#16), and through use of both verbal and nonverbal signals (E5). Interactions are affected by the role definition of the participants, particularly when one of them is labeled deviant (#19) and the interactants need to consider where the listeners are coming from (#15, #16).

Linguistic Rules

The status of linguistic rules in a pragmatics framework will depend upon which version of pragmatics you buy: mild, medium, or hot; and upon the nature of the event. If you are a hot pragmatist, you will deemphasize rules as fixed entities (#1) and, instead, conceive them as variable guides to the sensemaking enterprise. The medium pragmatists' stance is to view linguistic rules in their lingustic context (#6, #7), as well as attending to their functional role in carrying out the communicative intent of the participants (#10) and in building toward discourse, (#7, #8). The mild pragmatist will see linguistic rules as the main assessment concern, and add linguistic contextual information to those rules when they feel it is warranted.

Conclusion

Now, after all this, what have we? We have a history of 20 plus six ideas reduced to a five category taxonomy which stands above the constituent ideas and has the potential to offer a less cumbersome way of approaching pragmatics assessment. It is not a checklist, nor is it an all inclusive container of the pragmatics sensibility. Rather, it is a set of categories around which to ask questions and think about how particular children are getting along in communicating and in making sense of their world. It is also a way of asking how the interaction is going. The category system differs from other taxonomies in that it came originally from the literature on pragmatics, but was then reformatted to capture what might be the orientation of language disordered children. Furthermore, it takes the perspective of the language pathologist in that it excludes aspects of the literature which I felt to be knotty and wrong headed. It conceives of the language disordered child in terms of the social context rather than in terms of circumscribed cognitive or linguistic deviance. It is a guide through which the warp and woof of particular interactions involving children diagnosed as language impaired can be examined. And that, after all, is the most a priori constraint we would want as we carry out our pragmatics assessment.

Daniel A. Dinnsen

Phonology: Implications and Trends [1]

Since the publication of *The Sound Pattern of English* (Chomsky & Halle, 1968), a variety of different approaches to phonology have been proposed. These alternatives can be categorized into three classes: (1) formalistic, (2) naturalistic, and (3) substantive. It is generally agreed that these different approaches uphold the basic tenets of Generative Phonology. Nevertheless, important distinctions can be made. The purpose of this chapter is to review the theoretical and practical implications of these three alternative approaches to phonology. This chapter examines discussions of the impact each approach has had on several theoretical controversies. The particular controversies addressed include the nature of phonological representations, the goals of linguistic science, and universal vs. language-specific properties of rules and rule interactions. Also discussed in this chapter are the practical contributions of certain approaches in explaining empirical data provided by perceptual and production studies. Relevant data comes not only from normal adult studies, but also from studies of language acquisition, second-language learning, and speech disorders.

Generative phonological theory has dominated much of the descriptive and theoretical research in phonology since the publication of *The Sound Pattern of English* (Chomsky & Halle, 1968). The early work within this framework was largely concerned with formalistic matters, e.g., rule ordering, notational conventions and the adequacy of particular descriptive

© College-Hill Press, Inc. All rights, including that of translation, reserved. No part of this publication may be reproduced without the written permission of the publisher.

devices. A broad range of phonological descriptions of particular languages was produced to test the theory's formal descriptive devices. As more and more languages were described, particular details of the theory were found to require some modification. The proposed modifications were typically of two general types:

(1) Proposals that increased the power of the theory and thus broadened the range of possible grammars and or increased the complexity of the characterization of phonological systems. Included in this category are: phonological conspiracies (i.e., functionally related rules as opposed to strictly formal relationships among rules, Kisseberth, 1970), global rules (i.e., rules that have access to derivational history, Kenstowicz & Kisseberth 1970), and local ordering (i.e., nonlinear extrinsic ordering restrictions on rules, Anderson 1969, 1974).

(2) Proposals that constrained the theory and thus limited the characterization of what is a possible sound system. Included in this category are: universally determined rule interactions (i.e., universal principles for predicting rule interactions, Koutsoudas, Sanders, & Noll, 1974; Koutsoudas, 1980), and constraints on the abstractness of underlying representations (Kiparsky, 1968, 1976).

Despite these proposed modifications to the theory, generative phonology remained fundamentally generative. It eventually became known as the "standard theory" or the "revised standard theory." The basic tenets of the theory that remained intact and widely accepted included the following:

(1) Phonological descriptions can be formulated in terms of precise and explicit statements and notations.

(2) Segments are analyzable as a complex of features.

(3) There are two levels of representation, one corresponding to the underlying (abstract) level and the other to the phonetic level.

(4) Phonological rules mediate between the two levels.

(5) Phonological rules interact.

See Anderson (1979) for a detailed review of the theoretical issues that lead to the development of the "revised standard theory" as well as a review of the literature prominent through a large part of the 1970s.

By the middle of the 1970s, a number of seemingly different approaches to phonology appeared on the scene. Questions soon arose as to how different these approaches actually were from one another or from the standard theory. The Conference on the Differentiation of Current Phonological Theories (held at Indiana University during the Fall of 1977) was organized to address such concerns. One outgrowth of the conference was the volume *Current Approaches to Phonological Theory* (Dinnsen, 1979b). Some of the approaches represented in the volume include: Natural Generative Phonology (Hooper), Natural Phonology (Donegan & Stampe), Autosegmental Phonology (Goldsmith), Metrical Phonology (Schane, a), Atomic Phonology (Dinnsen, a), Up-side-down Phonology (Leben), Equational Phonology (Sanders), and Functionally Constrained Phonology (Houlihan and Iverson).

Despite the different names for these various approaches, there is general agreement that many of these and other approaches are essentially modifications and/or elaborations of standard generative phonology. The basic tenets of generative phonology noted above prevail, with the possible exception of the linear character of phonological representations (to be discussed below). This is not to say that there are no differences among the various approaches, nor that these differences are unimportant. However, before concerning oneself with such differences, it must be recognized that since the basic tenets of the standard theory are so general and fundamental, any approach that has a reasonable chance of being correct could be characterized as generative.

Substantive differences between the various approaches do exist. For example, the alternative approaches differ in their views of the very nature of phonological representations, the goals of linguistic science, and universal versus language-specific properties of rules and rule interactions. Interestingly, inspite of the proposed alternatives to standard generative phonology, the current leading textbook (Kenstowicz & Kisseberth, 1979) published more that 10 years after *The Sound Pattern of English,* is an explication of standard generative phonology. This reflects the overwhelming influence that generative phonology has had on phonological research over the years. The result of this influence has been a coherent tradition within the field of phonology not evident within other linguistic subdomains (e.g., syntax) or within the history of linguistics generally. Because of this relative stability in the field, there has been a healthy, fundamental questioning and refinement of some basic assumptions and constructs, making some real advances possible.

In what follows, I will discuss some of the different approaches, both within and outside of generative phonology proper, that represent either significant advances in phonology, or major current concerns in the field. I have chosen in some cases not to take a position on whether our understanding of phonology has been advanced. There have been three recent general approaches to phonology which have produced rather different results. These approaches may be described generally as follows:

(1) *Formalistic*—the postulation of hierarchical or nonlinear structures for phonological representations (Autosegmental and Metrical Phonology).

(2) *Naturalistic*—the appeal to physical (phonetic) and psychological plausibility for the explanation of various phonological constructs including phonological rules and underlying representations.

(3) *Substantive*—the establishment of typological universals concerning segmental inventories and phonotactics, the specification of substantive and functional constraints on phonological rules, and the applications of phonological theory toward the understanding of, for example, speech disorders and second language acquisition.

Each of these approaches is elaborated below.

Formalistic

The first general approach to be considered in this chapter will be termed *formalistic*. This approach, while consistent with the standard theory's preoccupation and emphasis on formal representations and devices, promotes representations quite different from those available within the standard theory. This approach focuses on elaborating the formal representation of the phonological structures comprising lexical representations. These more elaborate structures then serve as representations on which phonological rules can operate.

The operations performed by phonological rules have been understood to include, for example, changing feature specifications within a segment, deleting segments or adding segments. The key concept here is the "segment". The contention within generative phonology has been that words or morphemes are comprised of discrete *segments* linearly arranged one after the other, and that segments are further analyzable into a complex of features. No other phonological structures that would distinguish meanings or that would group segments or parts of segments together would be necessary either for the proper representation of lexical items or for the proper application of phonological rules.

There have been two general challenges to the contention that phonological representations are comprised of a linear sequence of segments, both constituting what has been called a "nonlinear" approach to phonology. The challenges come from Autosegmental Phonology (most notably, Goldsmith, 1976, 1979; Clements, 1981) and Metrical Phonology (most notably, Liberman & Prince, 1977; Selkirk, 1980). While nonlinear approaches radically reconfigure the conception of phonological representations, proponents of these approaches contend that their proposals are fully consistent with the basic tenets of generative theory and are offered as refinements to the theory and are thus presumed to be generative.

Autosegmental Phonology

Within an autosegmental approach, a phonological representation is comprised of several parallel tiers. Each tier represents a feature or set of features which is independent of other tiers. Within a tier, there may be one or more sequentially arranged segments (partial segments) called "autosegments." The number of autosegments in a tier may differ from the number in some other tier of the representation and are thus autonomous segments (hence the term "autosegmental").

Figure 6-1 presents a typical illustration of an autosegmentalized phonological representation with tonal features on one tier and nontonal (segmental) features on another. Note that there are only two tonal autosegments, while there are more autosegments on the nontonal tier. Also note that autosegments on one tier are connected with or related to autosegments on the other tier by means of "association lines". Different patterns of association lines result in different phonetic patterns, as can be seen in the two illustrations in Figure 6-1.

The initial motivation for autosegmental representations came from tonal and other suprasegmental phenomena. The nature of that motivation focused on (1) contour tones and (2) tone stability. Falling tones and rising tones are examples of contour tones. They represent a problem for the standard theory since the internal structure of a segment is presumed to be timeless. It is not possible within the standard theory for a single segment to have consecutive internal components.[2] Moreover, transitional gestures from one event to another are presumed to be linguistically irrelevant and otherwise derivable. Under an autosegmental account, contour tones are derived from level tones where the association between vowel and tone feature is not simply one-to-one, as in the second illustration of Figure 6-1. An explanation is thus provided for why a low tone would be changed to a falling tone under these circumstances as opposed to being changed to some other (complex) tone.

The phenomenon of "tone-stability" also motivates an autosegmental representation. This phenomenon refers to an observed stability in certain

FIGURE 6-1
Autosegmentalized representation.

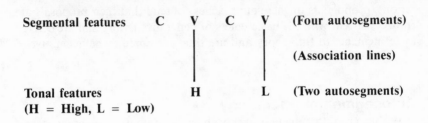

Segmental features   C   V   C   V   (Four autosegments)

(Association lines)

Tonal features   H   L   (Two autosegments)
(H = High, L = Low)

TONE ASSIMILATION

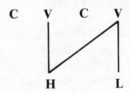

Contour (falling) Tone

Different associations result in different tone patterns.

tones despite phonological operations on an associated segment. For example, a vowel could be deleted, but its associated tone would simply be reassociated with an adjacent vowel. In such cases, while the segmental pattern is altered, the tonal pattern is unaffected. Such a characterization is not available within the standard theory since it is not possible to delete part of a segment.

The motivation for autosegmental representations is not, however, limited to suprasegmental phenomena. Goldsmith (1981) explicitly argues for extending this approach to certain segmental phenomena, such as the common assimilation of nasals to the point of articulation of the following consonant, i.e., /...np.../ → [...mp...]. The argument is that the features describing point of articulation typically function together, and the nasal

FIGURE 6-2
Autosegmental nasal assimilation.

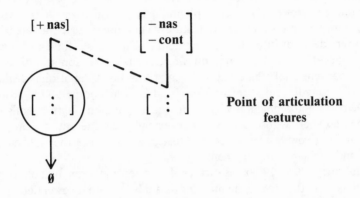

Point of articulation
features

Deletion of nasal point of articulation features and reassociation of nasal autosegment with remaining point of articulation features.

appears simply to take on those features as a whole from the adjacent consonant. Under an autosegmental account, the point of articulation features would constitute a single tier separate from the other segmental features. A phonological rule would delete the point of articulation features that had been associated with the nasal. The remaining nasal autosegment would then be reassociated with the point of articulation features of the following consonant.[3] See Figure 6-2 for an illustration.

Another example of segmental phenomenon is offered by Goldsmith (1981) in support of an autosegmental account, namely the aspiration of *s* in various dialects of Spanish. The rule converts *s* into *h* in the environment between a vowel and a consonant. In a standard generative account, the rule can be formulated roughly as follows:

$$s \rightarrow h \; / \; [+\text{syll}] \; \text{_____} \; [-\text{syll}]$$

While it is possible to formulate a rule to affect the appropriate change, no explanation is provided for why *s* should change specifically to *h* as opposed to any other segment. An autosegmental representation, on the other hand, would allow the laryngeal features, e.g., [spread glottis], to be separated out from the other segmental features describing the oral gesture. The two sets of features· would constitute autosegments on different tiers. The process would then be characterized as the deletion of the oral gesture alone. The resulting laryngeal features would describe the outcome as *h*.

Autosegmental phonology as developed by Clements (1981) offers an account of "vowel harmony" phenomena. In such cases the vowels throughout a word share certain features. They appear to assimilate to one another despite intervening segments. This assimilation between nonadjacent segments is sometimes referred to as "action at a distance". Given conventional segmental representations, no explanation is available for why nonadjacent segments should affect one another. This problem is overcome autosegmentally by letting the tongue-body features constitute a separate tier, whose domain may extend over the entire word. The assimilating vowels are adjacent autosegmentally since they all relate to one and the same autosegment.

McCarthy (1976, 1979) has further elaborated autosegmental phonology by suggesting that the segmental tier be analyzed into a vowel tier, consonant tier, and a syllabic skeleton in order to account for problems in Semitic phonology. Many of the details of autosegmental phonology are still to be worked out. It is not clear, for example, to what extent languages can differ in the autosegmentalization of a representation, in the associations between tiers, etc. Also, it is disappointing that many of the arguments for autosegmental analyses are based on issues of "elegance" with little concern for what the *facts* of the language would have to look like in order to reject an autosegmental analysis. Note, for example, Goldsmith's comments:

> In sum, I think the criteria for choosing a theory have little to do with falsification directly. Rather, we must adopt a theoretical viewpoint which allows for the elegant interaction of hypotheses and data that have typified science. Of course, to the extent that the hypothesis and the data must mesh to be elegant, falsification plays a role--but very much a secondary one. (1979, p.221)

There are nonetheless a number of areas that could conceivably benefit from considering further this rather different conceptualization of phonological structure. In particular, phoneticians have observed that speech is not segmentable, i.e., that all of the properties making up a sound do not begin and end in the same unitary domain. Such an observation fits well with an autosegmental representation, although proponents of autosegmental phonology assume conventional "segments" as the terminal elements of autosegmental representations. It may be fruitful to extend autosegmental representations into phonetics for the purposes of articulatory modeling. The geometry of phonological representations afforded by autosegmental phonology may be a more appropriate representation from a phonetic perspective.

Another area that might benefit from an autosegmental account is the characterization of child phonology, both in terms of normal development and speech disorders. For example, it is commonly observed (Ingram, 1976; Macken & Ferguson, 1981; Vihman, 1978; and Smith, 1973) that a child "backs" his word-initial consonants to agree with the word-final consonants, e.g., 'dog' is pronounced [gag]. Consonantal harmony of this type involves "action at a distance" similar to that observed for vowel harmony and as such may be amenable to an autosegmental account.

Metrical/Hierarchical Phonology

The other nonlinear approach to phonology is referred to generally as metrical phonology. Metrical phonology is actually a specific approach under the generic heading of hierarchical phonology. It was first proposed by Liberman (1975) to account for stress or 'prominence'. Since then, there have been a number of suggestions for elaborating this approach (most notably, Cairns & Feinstein, 1982; Halle & Vergnaud, 1980; Kahn, 1976; Kaye & Lowenstamm, 1979; Kiparsky, 1979; Liberman & Prince, 1977; Prince, 1980; Selkirk, 1979, 1980, 1981). The basic claim of all these varieties of phonology is that phonological representations are hierarchically structured, much like the familiar tree structures in syntax. In addition, then, to the conventional structures (such as segments and features), metrical (or hierarchical) phonologies postulate higher order structures or constituents that serve to group segments together and relate them to one another in a hierarchical fashion. Some of these higher order structures include the "syllable," the "foot," and the (prosodic) word." More specifically, segments group together to form syllables, syllables group together to form feet, and feet group together to form words.

In order to understand the presumed contribution of metrical phonology to the treatment of stress, we must first note the conventional treatment. Within linear frameworks such as standard generative phonology, "stress" is assumed to be a property of segments assigned by rules (e.g., the Compound Stress Rule and the Nuclear Stress Rule). These stress assignment rules apply cyclically reducing stress with each application. The domain of application on each cycle is determined by syntactically motivated surface structures. Readjustment rules could be invoked to modify the syntactic structures in order to derive correct results. Other rules could also serve to modify the results.

The innovation of metrical phonology was to characterize stress as a *relation* between elements—not a property of an individual segment nor even an individual syllable. The relation is expressed by means of a binary branching tree with one node labeled *strong* and other *weak*. The strong/weak relation is determined by principles of prominence. It is generally possible to derive the strong/weak relation from the branching properties of the metrical tree, although it has been argued that certain details of prominence must be stated language-specifically (Selkirk, 1979). The principle of prominence for English at least specifies that, within the prosodic word, the right hand node is strong just in case it branches. The principles that specify the branching properties of metrical trees are similar to phrase structure rules in syntax. They specify language-specifically the set of well-formed underlying structures, whether they are left or right branching, etc.

The principles of structure and prominence for English may be described generally as follows (Selkirk, 1981). First, there are three basic types of syllables in English:

CV=Lax vowel in an open syllable.
CVC=Lax vowel in a closed syllable (closed by one or more consonants).
CV:=Tense or long vowel which may be closed by one or more consonants.

Second, the next higher order metrical structure, the foot, has three characteristic structures in English:

a. [[CVC]s] or [[CV:]s]
b. [[S]s [CV(C)]w]
c. [[[S]s [CV]w]s [CV(C)]w]

The above statements of foot structure include the specification of the strong/weak relation and may be interpreted as follows:

a. Monosyllables are strong.
b. Bisyllabic words—The first syllable may be of any type and is strong, and the second syllable (open or closed) with a lax vowel is weak.
c. Trisyllabic words—The first syllable may be of any type and is strong, the second syllable which is CV is weak, and the third syllable which is either CV or CVC is weak.

From these principles of structure and prominence, it is possible to make the very general claim:

A syllable of English is stressed if it is the strong element of a stress foot.

FIGURE 6-3
Structure of symbols.

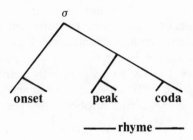

The foot may also serve as the domain for segmental phenomena. The English Flapping rule, for example, weakens certain consonants which are ambisyllabic (i.e., where a single segment is part of two adjacent syllables bounded by a superordinate domain, the foot). Such a weakening rule may be formulated as follows:

$$C \rightarrow [+\text{lax}] / {}_{\phi}[\ldots[-\text{cons}]\underline{\hspace{2cm}} \ldots]_{\phi}$$
$$\phi = \text{Foot}$$

(A consonant is weakened after a nonconsonant in the same foot.)

The syllable is also presumed to have its own metrical structure, constituted as in Figure 6-3

The value of such a structure is argued to facilitate the statement of phonotactics and to simplify the formulation of numerous phonological rules (Kahn, 1976). For example, the sequence [atktin] is excluded as a possible word on phonotactic grounds since it cannot be parsed as a well-formed syllable. That is, *tk* cannot close a syllable, and *kt* cannot begin one. Similarly, the rule of aspiration in English is actually most complex without reference to the construct 'syllable'. The various contexts for aspiration are unified, however, in the following rule formulation:

$$[-\text{voice}, -\text{cont}] \rightarrow [+\text{asp}] / {}_{\phi}[\underline{\hspace{2cm}} \ldots]_{\phi}$$
$$\phi = \text{Syllable}$$

There can be little doubt that metrical structures do afford substantial simplification of a sort in the formulation of a variety of phonological

rules. It is difficult to evaluate this resultant simplification in rule formulations, however, since the representations on which the rules operate have
been substantially elaborated and enriched. The structures available to rules
include features and segments as always, but also hierarchical relations,
labeled nodes of various different levels, prominence relations, etc. Many
questions remain to be worked out regarding, for example, the
language-specific versus universal character of the prominence principles,
the cyclicity of syllable structure assignment rules, the number and type
of metrical structures, the integration of segmental features with
higher-order structures, etc. For an alternative to metrical phonology as
presented here, *see* Schane (1979b,c). Also, *see* Bell and Hooper (1978) for
a variety of alternative approaches involving the syllable.

Naturalistic

Another currently dominant approach to phonology could be described
as 'naturalistic' because of its reaction against highly abstract and
formalistic accounts in favor of accounts that are in accord with physical
or psychological plausibility. This approach has focused on two general
concerns: the abstractness of underlying representations and phonetic
explanations for phonological rules.

Abstractness of Underlying Representations
Underlying representations (as a level of representation distinct from the
phonetic level) provide a means for relating different phonetic realizations
of a morpheme. Variation in the phonetic form of a morpheme is considered to be derived from the postulation of one underlying representation
for that morpheme and the operation of phonological rules. The problem
here is that early generative phonology specified no limits on what could
be related in this way. Questions arise about the semantic relatedness of
different phonetic forms. That is, despite the fact that it may be possible
to establish a phonological relationship between two different phonetic
forms, is it proper to relate them semantically, i.e. derive them from the
same underlying representation? This problem is evident in works such
as Lightner (1975), where, for example, forms such as "furnace," "ther-
mal," and "warm" are derived from the same underlying representation
by phonological rules which recapitulate sound changes in the historical
development of English. While such forms may be etymologically related,
it is not at all clear that speakers of English today relate these forms
phonologically.

There appears to be general agreement about what contributes to the abstractness of an underlying representation, even though not all linguists agree about how abstract underlying representations can be. Representations are judged to be abstract if, for example, they include segment types or distinctions that never occur phonetically. Also, the representation of a particular morpheme is considered abstract if its postulated features are not evident in at least one of its allomorphs.

The concern for what speakers could possibly know or what is learnable by speakers about a sound system has given rise to numerous proposals which would constrain or limit the abstractness of underlying representations. Such a concern was the very basis for the development of Natural Generative Phonology (Hooper, 1976, 1981). The abstractness of underlying representations was constrained in Natural Generative Phonology by the imposition of universal constraints on the formulation of rules (e.g., the requirement that all phonological rules be exclusively conditioned by phonetic properties and express surface true generalizations) and the exclusion of extrinsic rule ordering statements governing the application and interaction of phonological rules. There have also been proposals within generative phonology proper to limit abstractness, e.g., Kiparsky (1968, 1976). For a general review of this issue and an examination of a range of proposals for limiting abstractness *see* Kenstowicz and Kisseberth (1977).

While some linguists have proposed constraints limiting abstractness and others have argued for abstractness, the issue appears nowhere close to a resolution due to the absence of empirical arguments. Psychological investigations would seem appropriate, yet the concept of 'psychological reality' has been most elusive even for those aspects of linguistic structure about which linguists agree. In the meantime, all that is clear is that nonabstract accounts raise fewer questions about the appropriateness of relating different forms phonologically. Empirical evidence can be brought to bear in support of claims about nonabstract underlying representations. Abstract accounts raise more questions and thus require further or more extensive justification. The nature of evidence in support of abstract accounts is necessarily nonempirical, i.e., formal and *a priori* considerations. The evaluation of abstract accounts compared to nonabstract accounts seems to depend on the role nonempirical arguments can play.

Phonetic Explanations for Phonological Rules

The other major concern of the naturalistic approaches has been an enhancement of the role of phonetics in phonology. This has resulted in a focus on the "naturalness" of phonological rules. A phonological rule is judged to be natural if it is phonetically explainable or otherwise derivable from universal constraints on human anatomy, physiology, and or perception. This view of naturalness is different from a reaction to the view evident in standard generative phonology.

The standard theory view of naturalness as first put forward was a formalistic matter whereby "plausible rules" should be formally statable in simpler terms than less plausible rules (cf. Chomsky & Halle, 1968, Chapter 9). What constituted the plausibility of a rule was never made explicit, but apparently a rule's incidence of occurrence was a major factor. To achieve simplicity in the formulation of certain rules, interpretive devices were developed, i.e., marking and linking conventions, which permitted certain feature specifications to be ignored (not counted) in the determination of complexity. This move was made necessary because of various admitted inadequacies of the feature system. The sole purpose of these devices was to yield a formal measure for evaluation of relative simplicity. Nowhere, however, was there any concern for the explanation of phonological rules such that they were derivable from physical or phonetic constraints. Also, there was no attempt to exclude certain rules as possible rules of grammar or otherwise constrain rule formulations. The only concern was to render certain rule formulations simpler, and thus more highly valued, than certain other rule formulations.

Some of the naturalistic approaches (e.g., Hooper's Natural Generative Phonology and Stampe's Natural Phonology), on the other hand, have attempted to constrain phonological theory or the domain of phonology by limiting phonological rules to only those that are phonetically explainable. Naturalness is equated with phonetic explanation. The following statements from both approaches are representative:

> **From Hooper (1976)**--P-rules describe processes governed by the physical properties of the vocal tract...Their form and content can be predicted on universal principles. Thus it is further claimed that all P-rules are natural rules. (pp. 16–17)

> The hypothesis is that all of these processes are phonetically explainable or natural. (p. 133)

> **From Donegan and Stampe (1979)**---Natural phonology properly excludes the topic of unmotivated and morphologically motivated alternations. (p. 127)

> There is no evidence that the processes which govern phonetically motivated alternation and variation, children's regular sound-substitutions, and phonetic change are learned. On the contrary, there is massive evidence that they are natural responses to phonetic forces...implicit in the human capacity for speech perception. (p. 130)

> Although processes are mental substitutions, they are substitutions which respond to physical phonetic difficulties. (p. 136)

Naturalness is a matter of phonetic motivation, not formal simplicity. (p. 141)

Processes have synchronic phonetic motivation and represent real limitations on speakers' productions.... Processes are 'innate' in the sense that they are natural responses to innate limitations or difficulties. (p. 144)

By its nature, it [Natural Phonology] is ultimately accountable for...everything language owes to the fact that it is spoken. And by its nature, it must follow from the character of the human capacity for speech. (p. 168)

While both approaches make strong appeals to phonetics for understanding aspects of phonological structure, there is a striking absence of references to experimental or instrumental phonetic studies. The references to phonetics that are made are typically impressionistic phonetic studies. The cited studies employ such ill-defined and unsubstantiated concepts as 'ease of articulation', 'phonetic difficulty', and 'articulatory and acoustic incompatibility' as the bases of their explanations. It is, however, difficult to accept these putative explanations since the factual bases of these concepts are only assumed and nowhere established. These concepts find their basis only in the phonetician's intuitions, constituting impressionistic phonetics.

In view of the lack of empirical support for the very basis of Natural Phonology and Natural Generative Phonology, it is surprising to me that they have had the impact they have.[5] There can be no denying that these approaches have had an impact, especially in connection with their appeal to phonetics. It is not at all uncommon to find in the literature statements to the effect that some rule is 'phonetically explainable' or has a 'natural phonetic basis' or is a 'natural process' in the sense required of the naturalistic approaches. This is evident in even those approaches which would appear to reject Natural and Natural Generative Phonology, e.g., Kenstowicz and Kisseberth (1979). A rule's presumed phonetic naturalness is then used as an argument for the correctness of an analysis including such a rule. This is especially evident in the speech pathology literature. *See,* for example, Ingram's (1976) influential book, *Phonological Disability in Children,* and the numerous other works which have drawn extensively from Natural Phonology and have accepted 'natural processes' as established (e.g., Edwards & Shriberg, 1982; Ingram, 1981; Shriberg & Kwiatkowski, 1980; Weiner, 1979). For criticisms and an alternative to the work within speech pathology which has adopted "natural processes" along with abstract underlying representations, *see* Dinnsen (1982a); Dinnsen and Elbert (1982); Dinnsen, Elbert, and Weismer (1979, 1980); Maxwell (1979, 1982); and Weismer, Dinnsen, and Elbert (1981).

While the above approaches fail to provide any empirical support for their claims about phonetics, there have been efforts by others (most notably Ohala and his students) to establish the facts experimentally and instrumentally as they might bear on the explanation of phonological rules. In a long series of articles (e.g., Ohala, 1971; 1972a,b; 1976; 1978a,b,c; 1981a,b; 1982a,b), Ohala has attempted to explain particular sound patterns and sound changes by appealing to putative constraints on the mechanisms of speech production and speech perception. Ohala's accounts are generally plausible, but they fail to be convincing when examined more closely. For detailed criticisms, *see* Dinnsen (1980), Lass (1980), and Anderson (1981).

Some of the difficulties associated with the purported explanations of phonological rules are evident in the following cases. For example, Ohala (cf. references above) argues that some common sound changes (or rules) come about and have the form they do, because of an interaction between misapprehending acoustically similar sounds and resultant changes in pronunciation. A case in point is Ohala's (1978a) explanation of the common sound change whereby palatalized labials are changed to dentals. He argues that palatalized labials and dentals are acoustically very similar, especially in terms of the second formant transitions. Because of this acoustic similarity, a hearer may misperceive the intended (palatalized labial) sound as a dental. When hearer turns speaker, his production will reflect his (mis)perception, resulting in a sound change. Despite any questions about the plausibility of such a scenario, it must be noted that while palatalized labials can become dentals, there are no attested cases of dentals becoming patatalized labials. [6] That is, it should be equally possible for the reciprocal process (dentals becoming palatalized labials) to occur given the acoustic similarity of and potential confusion between the two classes of sounds. The fact is, however, the reciprocal process is unattested in any natural language. Consequently, while Ohala's account makes some correct predictions, it also makes some incorrect predictions. The rule producing dentals and the reciprocal process are both predicted to be phonetically natural and expected rules according to Ohala's explanation; yet the reciprocal rule type does not occur.

Similar false predictions follow from others of Ohala's putative explanations. For example, Ohala (1972a,b, and elsewhere) has attempted to explain the devoicing of obstruents in word-final position in terms of aerodynamic factors. It is shown in Dinnsen (1980), however, that an aerodynamic explanation of this phonological rule also predicts that certain other devoicing rules should be phonetically natural and should occur. In particular, it follows that there should be empirically defensible word-final devoicing rules restricted by point of articulation. The hypothesis predicts that there should also be word-final devoicing rules that must apply only to velar stops but not dentals and labials. The fact is no such rule has been attested in any natural language (Anwar, 1974; Dinnsen, & Eckman, 1978). The most severe restriction that has been motivated for a word-final devoicing rule involves limiting the rule to the more general class of stops (Dinnsen & Eckman, 1978). Consequently, if word-final devoicing is phonetically natural in terms of an aerodynamic explanation, then certain other empirically indefensible rules must also be natural.

A similar and interesting case is put forward in Houlihan (1982). She establishes that the intervocalic voicing of obstruents is a phonetically natural rule, again, in terms of the aerodynamics of voicing. She notes paradoxically, however, that this natural rule rarely occurs in natural languages; it occurs in only 20% of the languages in which it could. [7] Moreover, this rule occurs less often than the phonetically implausible rule of aspiration.

The preceding discussion is intended to show that while some rules may in some sense be explained phonetically, [8] these same explanations predict that certain other rules should also occur as phonetically natural rules. These predictions are often not borne out. In the case to follow, it can be seen that the difficulties with such explanations extend in the other direction as well. That is, if certain rules occur because they are phonetically natural, then certain other rules should not occur because they would be phonetically unnatural. The fact is, however, that such 'phonetically unnatural' rules do occur.

A case in point involves the putative natural rule accounting for the intrusion of an obstruent stop between a nasal consonant and a fricative evident at least in English. The rule accounts for the homophony of such pairs as 'prince'/'prints' and 'once'/'wants' in various dialects of English by epenthesizing a homorganic stop between *n* and *s*. This rule is argued to be phonetically natural in Ohala (1974) and Harms (1973). The explanation for the rule is essentially articulatory:

> If, during the articulation of the nasal, velic closure precedes oral release, an oral stop will appear.

The presumption is that there is a mistiming of the motor events, that it is difficult to syncronize these articulatory gestures. Harms is quite explicit about the phonetic necessity for the epenthetic stop as can be seen in the following statement:

> A nasal plus fricative sequence as the output of the phonological rules will *automatically* lead to an inserted stop at the level of sound production owing to the disparity in timing between the neural commands and the motor events. [Emphasis mine.] (p.5)

According to Harms at least, it should be impossible for any language to realize phonetically a sequence such as [...ns]. Catalan is, however, such a language. Nasal plus fricative clusters not only appear phonetically, but they are also derived by an empirically well-motivated, exceptionless phonological rule of homorganic stop deletion (cf. Dinnsen 1980; Walsh, 1977a,b; Roca, 1977). The following data exemplify the alternations motivating the rule and appropriate underlying representations.

FIGURE 6-4
Stop deletion in Catalan.

	fem.		masc.	
	sg.	pl.	pl.	
	[santə]	[santəs]	[sans]	'saint'
	[blaŋkə]	[blaŋkəs]	[blaŋs]	'white'
	[kəlentə]	[kəlentəs]	[kəlens]	'hot'
	[primə]	[priməs]	[prims]	'thin'

	diminutive		masc.	
	sg.	pl.	pl.	
	[kəmpɛt]	[kəmpɛts]	[kams]	'field'

What is especially striking about this data is that in the masculine plural forms a stop obstruent is already present between the nasal and fricative underlyingly; yet, this alleged phonetically optimal sequence is changed by the rule of homorganic stop deletion into what is supposedly either phonetically impossible (according to Harms) or what is phonetically unnatural (according to Ohala).

What we are left with regarding the phonetic explanation of phonological rules is that currently available explanations predict:

(1) that certain nonoccurring rules should occur, and
(2) that certain occurring rules should not occur.

Consequently, the predictions which follow from these explanations are either false or without empirical support. Moreover, if the above evidence and arguments do not serve as valid tests of phonetic explanations (cf. Ohala 1982a), it is difficult to see how even in principle phonetic explanations are falsifiable.

Substantive

The third general approach to phonology recently has focused on substantive properties of phonological systems. In contrast to the other approaches, it has not been so concerned with developing a formalism, for example, that will yield an elegant account of such highly problematic phenomena as have been associated with suprasegmentals. Nor has it been concerned with *a priori* treatments of such issues as abstractness. Instead, it has been concerned with discovering and establishing the facts of fundamental structural principles which relate to phonetic inventories, phonemic contrasts, positions of contrasts within a word, substantive constraints on rule formulations, etc. The focus has been on the substance of those principles that relate to elements of grammar which have been essential to virtually all theories of sound structure.

The major contributions along these lines come from investigations of typological and implicational universals. The findings from such studies typically take the form: 'All languages evidence X,' or 'Any language which evidences Y also evidences Z.' The value of such statements to phonological theory and to applications of theory will be illustrated below.

There has long been an interest in phonological universals (e.g., Jakobson, 1941, 1968). In recent years, the most intense study of universals has come from the Stanford Universals Project and the Stanford Phonology Archive (most notably Ferguson and Greenberg). For a representative, yet detailed, summary of this research, see Greenberg's (1978) edition on phonology.

The following are some examples of well-established universals concerning inventories: [9]

a. The presence of voiced stops implies the presence of voiceless stops, but not vice versa.

b. The presence of voiced fricatives implies the presence of voiceless fricatives, but not vice versa.

c. The presence of fricatives implies the presence of stops, but not vice versa.

d. The presence of aspirated stops implies the presence of unaspirated stops, but not vice versa.

e. The presence of a bilabial nasal implies the presence of a dental or alveolar nasal, but not vice versa.

f. The presence of mid vowels implies the presence of high vowels, but not vice versa.

g. The presence of voiceless vowels implies the presence of voiced vowels, but not vice versa.

Given implicational universals of this type, it is possible to establish a 'markedness' relation between segments. The conventional definition of markedness is as follows:

A segment X is considered to be 'marked' with respect to a segment Y just in case the presence of X in a given language implies the presence of Y but the presence of Y does not imply the presence of X in that language.

The markedness relations for the segments involved in the above implicational universals are as follows:

a. Voiced stops are marked with respect to voiceless stops.

b. Voiced fricatives are marked with respect to voiceless fricatives.

c. Fricatives are marked with respect to stops.

d. Aspirated stops are marked with respect to unaspirated stops.

e. The bilabial nasal is marked with respect to the dental or alveolar nasal.

f. Mid vowels are marked with respect to high vowels.

g. Voiceless vowels are marked with respect to voiced vowels.

Implicational universals of this sort and associated claims of relative markedness are independently valuable for the characterization they provide of what a possible phonetic inventory can be. Moreover, they are valuable for the implications they have in specifying substantive constraints on rule formulations. In particular, the very interesting observation is made by Houlihan and Iverson (1979) that certain rule types produce only unmarked segments, while certain other rule types produce exclusively marked segments. The distinction between rule types corresponds to the classic distinction between 'neutralization rules' and 'allophonic rules'. Neutralization rules affect the merger of a distinction in a well-defined context; allophonic rules account for the complementary distribution of sounds.[10] Houlihan and Iverson advance the following constraint and corollary:

Phonologically-conditioned neutralization rules convert relatively marked segments into relatively unmarked segments.

Corollary: Phonologically-conditioned rules which produce exclusively marked segments from relatively unmarked ones are
allophonic. (p. 61)

It follows from this that (1) all neutralization rules produce unmarked
segments, (2) all rules that produce unmarked segments are neutralization
rules, (3) all allophonic rules produce exclusively marked segments, and
(4) all rules which produce exclusively marked segments are allophonic
rules. An explanation is thus offered, for example, for why all intervocalic
voicing rules are allophonic, and for why the neutralization of the voice
contrast in word-final obstruents is always in the direction of devoicing
(and not voicing). Such a constraint imposes severe and substantive restrictions on permissible rules of grammar. While there are certain problem
cases for this principle (cf. Dinnsen, 1979a, p. 47; Kaye, 1979), it constitutes
a fundamentally correct insight into the nature of phonological rules.

Other substantive constraints on rules have been revealed through
typological studies investigating the distribution of certain contrasts within
a word for various classes of sounds. For example, in Dinnsen and Eckman
(1978) it is observed that there are languages with the following properties:

A. A voice contrast in medial obstruent stops and fricatives,
   a voice contrast in word-final fricatives but not in word-final
   stops, and an alternation between medial voiced stops and
   final voiceless stops.
B. A voice contrast in medial stops and fricatives, no voice contrast in word-final obstruents, and an alternation between
   medial voiced obstruents and final voiceless obstruents.

It is further observed, however, that there are evidently no languages
with the following properties:

C. A voice contrast in medial stops and fricatives, a voice
   contrast in final stops but not in final fricatives, and an
   alternation between medial voiced fricatives and final
   voiceless fricatives.
D. A voice contrast in all medial obstruents, a voice contrast
   in all but word-final velar obstruents, and an alternation
   between medial voiced velars and final voiceless velars.

The properties listed in A-D above constitute logically possible language
types and would motivate word-final devoicing rules with the following
restrictions, respectively:

A. Devoice stops only.
B. Devoice all obstruents.

C. Devoice fricatives only.

D. Devoice velars only.

A and B are empirically attested, while C and D are unattested. Consequently, the most severe restriction needed for a rule of word-final devoicing is the substantive restriction to stops. [11] The claim is that no other substantive restrictions on word-final devoicing will be necessary, like the logically possible, but empirically unsupported restrictions based on point of articulation. This prediction can be compared to the empirically un-supported predictions of an aerodynamic account (see above). Similar substantive restrictions on rules have been revealed through typological studies on, for example, palatalization (Bhat, 1978) and on spirantization (Ferguson, 1978)

The value of identifying substantive constraints on rules is that they specify what is a possible rule formulation. This is especially critical in evaluating, for example, arguments about the presumed necessity of ex-trinsic rule ordering statements. There are currently so few restrictions on what is a permissable rule that it is generally possible to simply reformulate the rule to avoid an extrinsic ordering restriction. Real advances in the con-troversy over the necessity of extrinsic ordering are most likely when the range of alternative rule formulations is limited.

On The Relationship Between Second-Language Learning and Substantive Approaches

A somewhat more applied concern, although still related to substantive properties of rules and typological investigations, has been the attempt to characterize interlanguage phonologies and make predictions about areas of difficulty for second-language learners. An interlanguage is presumed to be a second-language learner's internalized system of rules which may be different from either the native language (NL) or the target language (TL).

It has long been known that differences between the native and target languages may be a source of difficulty for second-language learners. Recently, Eckman (1977) demonstrated that not all differences are a source of difficulty. It appears that certain differences result in a characteristic directionality of difficulty, i.e., certain differences will present difficulties when learning one language after another but not vice versa. In an effort to explain the observed difficulties that second-language learners have, Eckman advanced the following hypothesis which makes essential reference to markedness and associated typological universals:

Markedness Differential Hypothesis (MDH)

Those areas of the TL which will be difficult are those areas which are (1) different from the NL, and (2) relatively more marked than the NL.

This hypothesis explains why, for example, German and Spanish speakers have difficulty learning to produce the word-final voice contrast in English. Specifically, whereas English exhibits a voice contrast in final position, German and Spanish do not. In order for German and Spanish speakers to learn to produce the voice contrast in final position, they must acquire a more marked phoneme, namely voiced obstruents. On the other hand, English speakers do not have difficulty suppressing the voice contrast in the acquisition of German or Spanish because, according to the MDH, a less marked property is called for relative to the native language.

The MDH along with other typological findings also explains why word-final position represents such difficulty in the acquisition of the voice contrast. More specifically, it has been observed in Dinnsen and Eckman (1978) that there are languages which evidence:

(a) no voice contrast,
(b) a word-initial voice contrast, but none in medial or final position,
(c) a voice contrast in word-initial and medial positions, but not in final position, and
(d) a voice contrast in word-initial, medial, and final positions.

There are, however, evidently no languages that evidence:

(e) a word-final voice contrast, but none in initial or medial position, and
(f) a medial voice contrast, but none in initial position.

These general findings allow relative markedness relations to be specified for voice contrasts in different word positions. That is, the maintenance of a word-final voice contrast is marked relative to medial position. Also, the maintenance of a medial voice contrast is marked relative to initial position. These markedness relations, like others referred to in this paper, are based on observed structural properties of primary languages. The MDH appeals to these independently established markedness values to explain observed difficulties in second-language acquistion. In this particular instance, the MDH predicts that it is more difficult to acquire the voice contrast in final position than in medial position. It also predicts that it is more difficult to acquire the voice contrast in medial position than in initial position. These predictions are borne out in Eckman (1977, 1981).

Through the analytical techniques of generative phonology, it has been possible to develop descriptions of interlanguages. These descriptions can serve as the basis for determining whether interlanguages are in fact distinct from, or independent of, the native language and or the target languages. They also may be compared with systems that are learned as first languages. Eckman (1981) empirically demonstrates that interlanguages are, at least in part, independent of either the native or target languages by motivating interlanguage rules which are independently necessary but which are not motivated in either the native or target language. That is, certain properties of interlanguages cannot be explained by simple transfer. These findings underscore the importance of conducting phonological analyses of interlanguages where these analyses are independent of assumptions about the native and target languages. The independently motivated properties of interlanguages would not otherwise be revealed.

Comparisons between interlanguage systems and natively acquired first-language systems are possible if empirically well-motivated descriptions of interlanguages are available. Since interlanguages can evidently be independent systems, the possibility exists that they could differ in significant ways from first languages. Eckman (1981) presents evidence that indicates in at least some instances interlanguages require rule types which are not motivated for any known first-language system. His explanation for rule types unique to interlanguages is that such rules follow from the postulation of (1) underlying representations appropriate to the target language and (2) surface phonetic constraints appropriate to the native language.

On The Relationship Between
Speech Disorders and Substantive Approaches

The characterization of interlanguages and principles of second-language acquisition have interesting implications and parallels for speech pathology. The case could be made that speech disordered children have acquired a system at least superficially different from the surrounding speech community. It must be determined, just as with interlanguages, if these disordered systems are independent of the target system. It is also reasonable to ask whether these disordered systems are different in any respects from other natively acquired first-language systems. Speech pathologists, too, are interested in predicting areas of difficulty for the child in learning the target system. Aspects of phonological theory, techniques of phonological analysis, and the findings of typological studies are thus equally relevant to speech pathologists.

It may, for example, be possible to bring principles like the MDH to bear in training studies. For instance, it would be interesting to see if a child who evidences no voice contrast, when trained on the contrast in final position (i.e., the most marked and thus the most difficult), generalizes his or her learning of the contrast more readily to other less marked positions. Addressing this question depends, of course, on having determined first what the child's system is through a proper phonological analysis.

Much of the current research yielding descriptions of disordered phonological systems shows that these systems are distinct from the ambient target system in several respects. Not surprisingly, these disordered systems require phonological rules not evident in the target system. For example, a common, well-motivated rule in disordered systems deletes final obstruents. The same rule is not motivated for English as a target system. It has generally been assumed that disordered systems are characterized by underlying representations appropriate to the target system. More recently, however, evidence has been presented which suggests that children may postulate underlying representations quite distinct from the target system (Dinnsen & Elbert, in press; Dinnsen et al., 1979, 1980; Maxwell, 1979, 1981, in press; Weismer et al., in press).

These most recent findings have interesting implications for speech pathology and for phonological theory. The claim that children may postulate underlying representations quite different from the ambient system embodies the further claim that children may be differentiated in terms of their knowledge of underlying representations. If this claim is correct, it should be possible to correlate individual differences in the results of training with individual differences in children's phonological knowledge prior to training. The value of phonological analyses that permit individual differences to be revealed is demonstrated in Dinnsen and Elbert (in press), where individual differences in phonological knowledge are related to individual differences in learning as the result of training.

The study of disordered systems (made available through the techniques of generative theory) also has interesting implications for the theory itself. One issue is why or how these children learn a system so different from the target system. It has generally been assumed within the linguistic community that given the constraints of universal grammar and exposure to some language, learners will arrive at roughly identical grammars. Clearly, these children have come up with different grammars. This raises questions about what the range of possible learnable grammars is given exposure to a particular language. Linguists may argue that grammars of disordered systems are not relevant to this question on the grounds that disordered systems are not otherwise like primary languages. There appears, however, to be no convincing evidence that disordered systems are different in any crucial respects from other first-language systems.

Phonological descriptions of disordered systems present further challenges to the theory. In particular, those descriptions that postulate underlying representations quite different from the target system raise questions about the child's receptive (perceptual) knowledge and the relationship between production and perception. The problem is that claims about underlying representations are motivated in terms of the child's production of morphophonemic alternations, contrasts, etc. The key point here is the appeal to *production*. In the analysis of primary languages, appeal to production data has not been problematic since it has been assumed that grammars are neutral with respect to speaker and hearer. Production and perception data should render identical descriptions. The correctness of this assumption for primary languages will be challenged below.

For those disordered systems requiring unique underlying representations, the tendency is for these underlying representations to provide fewer distinctions than the normal system. The child's productions suggest that the child does not have knowledge (even at the level of underlying representations) of all the distinctions existing in the ambient system. This is certainly the claim embodied in the underlying representations. Nevertheless, these same children give the impression of understanding speakers of the ambient system. There is very little research available on this point that would establish the facts. As more descriptions become available providing for the empirical determination of claims about underlying representations, it should be possible to address this question experimentally. The anecdotal evidence certainly suggests that children's perceptual knowledge fully coincides with distinctions in the ambient system (Locke, 1980a,b). Thus, there appear to be differences between the child's knowledge of production and his knowledge of perception. These differences motivate very different phonological descriptions. No grammar is neutral with respect to both perception and production in these cases.

The distinction between perception and production arising out of descriptions of disordered systems raises some interesting questions. Is the inability here to arrive at a description that is neutral with respect to perception and production a characteristic of disordered systems that would distinguish them from first-language systems? The answer to this question appears to be "no". Recent research by Labov (1981) and Labov, Yaeger, and Steiner (1972) on language change and variation reveals critical differences between perception and production, differences which support the independence of perception from production. All of the logical possibilities obtain. That is, speakers perceive differences in others' speech while not producing those differences in their own speech. This corresponds with the speech disordered children's abilities. Also, speakers produce distinctions that they perceive. This represents the normal, expected case. The most interesting case, however, is the finding that speakers produce distinctions that they themselves do not perceive. Similar findings supporting the independence of perception and production are reported in Connell and Parks-Reinick (1982) for normally developing children and in Sheldon and Strange (1980) for second-language learners. Disordered systems do not distinguish themselves from other language systems on this point.

The question remains concerning what the proper phonological description of disordered systems is? Should the description be perception-based or production-based? This question is also relevant to other language systems. It is argued in Dinnsen (1982b) that there has been a bias toward perception-based phonologies, at least in the characterization of primary language systems. This was only revealed, however, after experimental and instrumental phonetic research was brought to bear on determining the facts of, for example, putative phonological neutralizations. That research shows that the descriptions that have been developed fail to account for the production facts. Just because the bias has been toward perception-based descriptions does not mean, of course, that these descriptions are to be preferred. In fact, it is shown in Dinnsen and Elbert (1982) that the learning patterns of speech disordered children can be predicted based on phonological descriptions that are production-based. The suggestion is that production-based phonologies may be more useful in certain instances. Clearly, more research needs to be done on perception and production in phonology on all types of language systems. This is essential to determining the relationship between perception and production and determining the nature of phonological descriptions.

To summarize, the approach to phonology discussed in this section, the substantive approach, has focused on establishing substantive properties of rules and constraints. An important element of this approach has been the role of typological universals and their implications for other aspects of phonology dealing with second-language acquisition and speech disorders. There are moreover extensive applications for the findings derived from the substantive approach.

Conclusion

While there are currently a number of differing approaches to phonology, it must be recognized that generative theory has had an enormous impact in one way or another on all approaches. Most of the basic tenets of generative theory are found in all approaches, e.g., the analyzability of segments into a complex of features, rule interactions, levels of representation, etc. While approaches may differ in terms of their concern for formalism, they do not necessarily represent opposing empirical predictions. Often the phenomena examined under different approaches are unrelated and thus would not serve as points of conflict. Finally, the fundamentals of phonological structure and analysis are sufficiently well-established within a relatively stable theoretical tradition that it should be possible now for real advances to be forthcoming. The contributions are most likely to come from collaborations between researchers in related fields who are willing to share and learn about each other's field, e.g., phonologists collaborating with phoneticians, psychologists, and/or speech pathologists. Any one of these fields represents more than any one specialist can command. The advances that will be the most valuable to phonologists, and have the widest applications to other domains, will be those conceived in interdisciplinary research ventures.

Acknowledgment

This work was supported in part by grants from the National Science Foundation (Grant No. SPI 8165061), the National Institute of Health (Grant No. HD 12511-04), and the Office of Research and Graduate Development at Indiana University.

Notes

[1] I am grateful to Michelle Blank, Fred Eckman, Judy Gierut, Kathleen Houlihan, Gregory Iverson and Rita Naremore for their comments and assistance during the preparation of this manuscript.

[2] The standard theory could, of course, account for such phenomena by increasing the number of tone features to include contour-tones in addition to level tones.

[3] There remains the question, of course, of why the point of articulation features should have been deleted.

[4] Within Natural Phonology, a distinction is made between 'processes' and 'rules'. For discussion of this distinction, *see* Donegan and Stampe, 1979; and von Miller and Yallop, 1981. These two terms are used interchangably throughout this chapter. Wherever reference is made to Natural Phonology, however, the terms are to be interpreted in the Natural Phonology sense of 'process'.

[5] Natural Phonology has had an impact for more reasons than its presumed reliance on phonetics, namely its implications for phonological development and acquisition. *See,* however, Hastings (1981) and Leonard, Newhoff & Mesalam (1980) for a demonstration of the failure of Natural Phonology to account for the facts of acquisition.

[6] Such a scenario does not conform well with what is known about phoneme restoration experiments (Blank, 1979).

[7] The languages surveyed were drawn from the entire Stanford Phonology Archive.

[8]Whether even the above rules are explained seems questionable since typically the putative explanations fail to explain either why the rule occurs, or why it has the particular structural change that it does. See Dinnsen (1980) for a more detailed discussion of this point.

[9]Adapted from Houlihan and Iverson, 1979, pp. 54-55.

[10]The merger of two classes into a third class, while neutralizing in some sense, is categorized as allophonic. For further discussion of this point, *see* Houlihan and Iverson, 1979.

[11]For a detailed discussion of how such restrictions are to be accommodated theoretically, see Dinnsen (1979a).

Helen Smith Cairns

Research in Language Comprehension

It is perhaps wise to begin this chapter with a consideration of what is meant by the term *language comprehension*. Minimally, it should refer to the process by which meaning is ascribed to some physical representation of a sentence (auditory, orthographic, or gestural); indeed, in the early days of psycholinguistics, research tended to concentrate on the interpretation of single sentences. As the field has evolved, however, more attention has been given to the comprehension of sets of sentences, organized as sequences of text or discourse. Twin issues have emerged from this shift of emphasis: We have become concerned about the effects of context on the interpretation of individual sentences and, conversely, about the processes with which individual sentences are integrated into and become part of the larger context.

Closely related to the issue of the domain of language comprehension is the question of what constitutes the meaning of a sentence. This is not a linguistic question about the formal semantic representation of a sentence. It is, instead, a psycholinguistic question about the kinds of information included in the cognitive representation of a sentence after it is understood. Early research tended to concentrate on our ability to assign a literal meaning to individual sentences, based solely on the meanings of individual lexical items and the structural relations among them. More recently, research has both demonstrated and investigated a much richer cognitive representation of sentences and their contexts—a conceptual representation

© College-Hill Press, Inc. All rights, including that of translation, reserved. No part of this publication may be reproduced without the written permission of the publisher.

containing information based on real world knowledge, inferences, and pragmatic considerations.

Based on these observations, an informal contemporary definition of language comprehension is that it consists of the assignment of a conceptual representation to strings of sentences, which are physically represented in some way. This chapter will be concerned with research into very general processing mechanisms, which are relevant to the comprehension of either spoken or written (or probably even signed) language. It is, of course, beyond the scope of this chapter to address the peripheral, modality-specific processes involved in the perception of speech and orthography. It is assumed, however, that the comprehension model developed here receives as input the output of one of those systems.

The principle theoretical issue in language comprehension which has surfaced for the 1980s is the question of the autonomy, or modularity, of the language comprehension system. The theoretical position that will be developed here is that the comprehension system consists of autonomous subprocessors of two very different kinds. One set of subprocessors is highly constrained in its operation, analyzing only the purely linguistic properties of the input and responding only to linguistic information. The output of this set of subprocessors is a representation of an individual input sentence which depicts the structural organization of its individual lexical items, a representation closely akin to the sentence's literal representation. The other kind of processor is unconstrained in the kinds of information on which it can operate. It has access to real world knowledge, so it can make inferences, assess the plausibility of relationships within sentences, and use both linguistic and nonlinguistic context to resolve ambiguity or determine nonliteral meanings. This unconstrained processor takes as raw material the linguistic analysis of individual sentences and integrates them into an enriched conceptual representation of a string of sentences, which form a text or a discourse. The most basic claim of such an autonomous (or modular) view of the comprehension system is that there exists a set of processors whose operations do not respond to real world knowledge. In the model presented in Figure 7-1, two linguistic subprocessors are hypothesized, one lexical and one structural. The autonomy claim is that the former processor initially retrieves items from the internalized lexicon using only phonological information, and that the latter creates a structural analysis of the sentence using only grammatical information. In this model, only the Interpretative Processor has access to real world knowledge for its operation.

The position that the comprehension system includes an autonomous component that is limited to linguistic processing (Forster, 1979; Garrett, 1976, 1981) can be contrasted with more global processing theories

FIGURE 7-1
Model of an autonomous comprehension system.

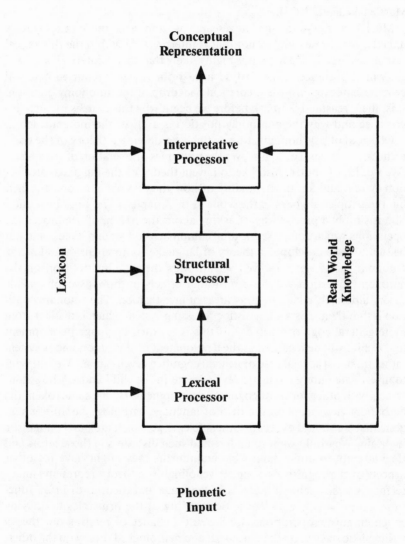

which essentially claim that a central system operates on all kinds of information, either doing most of its interpretation based on real world knowledge and expectations (Riesbeck & Schank, 1978) or allowing real world knowledge to intervene to assist lexical and structural processing (Marslen-Wilson & Tyler, 1980; Marslen-Wilson & Welsh, 1978; Tyler & Marslen-Wilson, 1977).

Much recent psycholinguistic research has addressed the autonomy issue directly; other research has not, but is interpretable within the theoretical framework developed here. It is highly likely that this theoretical issue will grow in importance in the next decade, so the research reported here will be represented against the theoretical backdrop of the autonomy question. It is, then, reasonable to ask before we begin why this issue is of such importance and why the autonomy position is a priori the more attractive.

One goal of psycholinguistic research is to develop a theory of the comprehension system, i.e., to discover the principles of operation of the system. (We would, of course, also like to have a theory of the language production system and an understanding of how the two relate to one another, but these topics are beyond the scope of this chapter.) The autonomy question is simply a precise way of asking about the nature of the processing operations which comprise the total comprehension system. One could not be said to have developed a theory of language comprehension unless the autonomy issue were resolved within one's theory. Our decision on the autonomy question will have profound effects on how psycholinguistic theory ultimately relates to other areas of investigation. The autonomy position is that there exists a linguistic processing system which is distinct from more general cognitive activity. If this is so, then language development in the child will be regarded as the development of this autonomous system rather than as a special case of general cognitive development. We will want to investigate purely linguistic development in the child and ask how it interacts with other forms of cognitive development. By the same token, the autonomy view bears on the field of language pathology because it suggests that we should expect disorders to emerge which are purely linguistic in origin. We would want to understand such disorders in those terms and then attempt to understand what entailments they might have for other aspects of the cognitive system. Psycholinguistic theory represents an interface between general theories of language and theories of brain function. Unless we have a clear understanding of the principles underlying psycholinguistic operations, we haven't a chance of relating our theory to linguistic theory, on the one hand, and neurological theory on the other.

There are a number of reasons for expecting a priori, that the comprehension system will consist of autonomous components. Most compelling is that all complex biological systems are organized this way. The human organism, for instance, is composed of interacting subsystems (neural, pulmonary, cardiovascular, gastrointestinal, etc.) which are in turn composed of autonomous modules. Each carries out its own function within the context of its unique structure and biochemical activity. Any system more complex than a sponge can only be understood as the interaction of autonomous subsystems. Surely the psycholinguistic system is one of the most complex in nature. Another reason to expect modularity of some sort is that the other theories to which psycholinguists must ultimately relate do appear to have their own modularity. Linguistic rules are organized into autonomous subsets with unique principles of operation, and the brain certainly consists of a collection of highly specialized processing systems, separated both structurally and functionally. This observation does not mean that we need expect an isomorphism among the autonomous elements of linguistic, psycholinguistic, and neural theory. It would, however, seem odd (if not impossible) for two autonomous systems to be mediated by a global one. Further, it does seem to be the case that there are numerous purely linguistic aspects of language development and language pathology which can only be understood adequately within the context of an autonomous theory of language processing.

There is yet another reason to adopt an autonomy position, initially, as we approach the task of developing a theory of comprehension. On general philosophical grounds, among a set of theories, the most highly constrained is the most desirable, all other things being equal. Further, empirical findings may force us to relax constraints, but they cannot force us to impose them. Thus, if we begin with a highly constrained, autonomous theory which is wrong, data can force us to relax our constraints and move toward a global theory. If we begin with an unconstrained global theory which is wrong, data will not force us back to a more constrained theory. On more practical grounds, it is unlikely that experiments organized around confirming a global theory would produce data suggestive of an autonomous model. If we start with an autonomous model, however, and attempt to falsify it, we can produce data which will move us toward a more global one. Put very simply, we can never discover autonomous subprocessors unless we look for them.

The remainder of this chapter presents some of the major lines of recent research in language comprehension. It is organized within a processing model that includes a Lexical, a Structural, and an Interpretative Processor. The operation of these processors is assumed to be independent, but not necessarily serial. Some aspects of their operation may be serial and others may not be. For instance, the Structural Processor cannot begin its analysis until it knows the form class of the items it is dealing with. Therefore, it must await lexical retrieval for this information to be available; thus, this sequence of operations is serial. On the other hand, the Interpretative Processor may be developing expectancies based on real world knowledge at the same time lexical and structural processing is proceeding. Those expectancies will, then, play a role in the integration of the most recently processed sentence into the developing conceptual representation. To the greatest extent possible, the research reported here will be analyzed in terms of how it relates to a unified theory of language comprehension.

The Lexical Processor

The term *lexical processing* includes a number of distinct stages of operation that a lexical item must undergo in sentence comprehension. At this point that number appears to be about three: A retrieval stage during which the lexical item is located in the lexicon; a post-access decision stage during which the contents of the lexical entry are checked against the input signal to determine the accuracy of the retrieval operation; and an integration stage during which information associated with a particular lexical item is fused with that of other items according to the syntactic relations among them in order to form an integrated conceptual representation of the meaning of the sentence. The first two types of operations are carried out by the Lexical Processor itself, while the integration stage is part of more general integrational processes accomplished by the Interpretative Processor. The vast majority of experimental research in lexical processing has ostensibly investigated the retrieval stage, although I will argue below that it may well be the case that experimental tasks believed to be tapping retrieval were, instead, tapping higher levels of lexical processing.

Ambiguous Lexical Items

The interest in the processing of lexically ambiguous sentences bloomed with the observation that while only one meaning of such a sentence seemed to be the output of processing (Cairns, 1971, 1973), the presence of a lexically ambiguous item seemed to complicate the on-line processing of a sentence (Foss, 1970). The account of these processes was straightforward and compatible with the hypothesis that the Lexical Processor is autonomous. Based on phonological information alone, there is exhaustive retrieval of all stored meanings of a homophone, followed by a decision process during which one meaning is selected by a higher-order processor for incorporation into the meaning of the sentence. Cairns and Kamerman (1975) determined that this decision process was completed by two syllables following an ambiguous lexical item (in roughly 500 msecs). Yates

(1978), in an elegant interpretation of the Cairns and Kamerman findings within the framework of the two-factor attentional theory of Posner & Snyder, (1975), suggests that the initial retrieval stage is automatic, unattended, and thus unconscious. The transfer of one meaning to working memory requires the recruitment of attentional processing. Among other things, Yates' theory explains why the ambiguity of natural language, which is rampant, is rarely noticed and does not perceptibly impair processing (think of the selective disadvantage of a creature designed otherwise).

Having developed a plausible account of how ambiguous words are handled in semantically neutral sentential contexts, the obvious next step was to determine how those processes are altered in sentential context which bias toward one meaning of the ambiguous item. Since we know that context effectively determines the outcome of the comprehension process, there are, logically, two possible on-line mechanisms for selection of the contextually appropriate meaning: One is that context allows only the appropriate meaning to be retrieved in the first place; the other is that context participates in the postaccess decision stage only after exhaustive retrieval of all meanings. On the first view, the mechanism postulated for prior selection has typically been semantic priming. Schvaneveldt, Meyer, and Becker (1976) showed that executing a lexical decision for a word related to only one meaning of a lexically ambiguous word seems to cause the retrieval of only the related meaning of the ambigous item. Schvaneveldt, et al., offer a priming interpretation for their results, compatible with the logogen model of Morton (1969). According to this theory, retrieval of a lexical item requires that its associated logogen be activated beyond a certain threshold level. Prior activation by semantic or associative priming brings a lexical item nearer its threshold, so that less activation provided by the phonological input is required, and retrieval of the primed representation of an ambiguous lexical item reaches threshold faster than its unprimed representation. This interpretation follows from a general theory of priming, by which every time one lexical item is activated, other semantically and associatively related items in the lexicon are also activated, or primed. Priming is a pervasive phenomenon in lexical decision tasks; not only have semantic and associative priming been demonstrated, but phonetic and even orthographic priming, as well. The theoretical issue raised by the ambiguity question was whether the priming phenomenon is used in the comprehension of sentences.

The importance of this question for the autonomy issue is clear. If the priming account is correct, the autonomy hypothesis is falsified, for we would have a lexical processor whose retrieval stage is affected by semantic and real world information. But if biasing context only operates at a postaccess stage, after exhaustive retrieval of all phonologically determined meanings, then there is no reason to abandon the hypothesis of an autonomous lexical processor.

The first empirical question was whether biasing context relieves the adverse effects of ambiguity in on-line processing. This turned out to be a difficult question to answer; experiments demonstrated that it did (Cairns & Hsu, 1980, Swinney & Hakes, 1976), others that it did not (Conrad, 1974; Foss & Jenkins, 1973; Holmes, Arwas, & Garrett, 1977). Even among those whose research demonstrated ameliorating on-line effects of biasing context, some argued that the findings reflected postaccess processing (Cairns & Hsu, 1980), while others argued that they were the result of prior selection due to priming (Foss & Hakes, 1978, p. 123; Swinney & Hakes, 1976).

The debate seems to have been settled by several ingenious studies conducted by Swinney (1979), Onifer and Swinney (1981), and by Tanenhaus, Leiman, and Seidenberg (1979). Basically, what all these studies show is that an ambiguous item appearing in a sentence will prime words which are related to both its meanings for a very brief period of time. This is true even though sentential context biases toward one or the other meaning of the ambiguity. Following this brief period (which is within the time frame identified by Cairns and Kamerman (1975) as comprising the postaccess decision operation), only the contextually appropriate meaning is primed. These results indicate that all meanings of an ambiguous item are initially retrieved, even in biasing contexts, but that one meaning (the contextually appropriate one) is immediately selected. They demonstrate, then, that context intervenes, not in the retrieval phase of lexical processing, but in a postaccess process.

Swinney's experiments dealt with ambiguous nouns which were biased by real world context occuring in either the same or a prior clause (as did Cairns & Hsu, 1980; Swinney & Hakes, 1976), while those of Tanenhaus et al. (1979) dealt with words such as "watch" which are ambiguous not only in meaning, but also in form class (noun/verb ambiguities) and were biased by syntactic context. Since both types of experiment demonstrated that contextual bias takes effect only after lexical access, it would seem that the lexical processor does not operate on semantic, syntactic, or real world information. Rather, the processor is autonomous in the sense that it retrieves items on the basis of phonological information alone.

Unambiguous Lexical Items

If the only function of context in lexical processing were to select contextually appropriate readings for homophones, then we would expect that context would not affect the processing of unambiguous lexical items, but, of course, this is not the case. The literature is filling with studies which report the effects of context on numerous dependent measures in experiments involving unambiguous lexical items: Phoneme monitoring latency (Blank & Foss, 1978; Cairns, Cowart, & Jablon, 1981; Foss, Cirilo, & Blank, 1979); comprehension time (Cairns et al., 1981); speed to detect mispronunciations (Cole, 1973; Cole & Perfetti, 1980); accuracy of mispronunciation detection (Marslen-Wilson & Welsh, 1978); restoration of mispronounced phoneme in a shadowing task (Marslen-Wilson & Welsh, 1978); latencies for rhyme and word monitoring (Marslen-Wilson & Tyler, 1980); and lexical decision speed (Schuberth & Eimas, 1977). The theoretical task is to develop a unified model of lexical processing which will account for the effects of context on both ambiguous and unambiguous items. The crucial question for the autonomy issue is whether such a model can be constructed so as to preserve an autonomous retrieval process or whether (as some have argued) the evidence from unambiguous lexical processing forces us to move to a global lexical processor operating simultaneously upon phonological, syntactic, semantic, and real world information.

Key to this enterprise is to identify the processing stage to which each task responds. Marslen-Wilson and Welsh (1978) attribute their shadowing results to retrieval processes, but they report average shadowing latencies of around 800 msecs. Since we know from the work of Cairns and Kamerman, Tanenhaus et. al., and Swinney, that retrieval and post retrieval processes are completed within 500 msecs, it seems likely that the shadowing task taps stages of processing beyond lexical retrieval. The mispronunciation detection data are neatly explained by the postaccess decision stage postulated by Forster (1976), in which retrieval accuracy is assessed by checking the contents of the retrieved lexical item against properties of the input. That syntactic, semantic, and even real world information should also enter at this stage is to be expected because once an item has been retrieved from the lexicon, all information related to it is available to subsequent processors. Similar processes can account for responses on word and rhyme monitoring tasks in which the subject's job is explicitly to test the hypothesis that the word(s) he or she has just heard matches another on some specified parameter.

Below, I will review three competing theories of lexical retrieval: Priming, cohort, and search theories. It appears at this time that some version of cohort theory will turn out to be the most likely to account for our current data related to lexical processing.

Priming Theories

Priming theory was discussed above in relation to the particular issue of ambiguous lexical items. It is, however, a much more general theory relating to the retrieval of all lexical items, ambiguous and unambiguous, alike. Researchers such as Morton and Long (1976) and Blank and Foss (1978) have appealed to the notion of prior activation to predict retrieval facilitation of unambiguous items in context by the same mechanisms that produce only prior activation of contextually appropriate readings for ambiguous items. There are, however, two strong objections to priming as an active mechanism in sentence comprehension. First, sentences rarely contain words which are close associates of one another. Indeed, it is easy to imagine that in ordinary discourse the effects of priming would be to activate most just those words least likely to be called upon for retrieval (for instance, "dog" rarely follows "cat" in casual conversation). A second, and more serious objection comes from the time span of priming effects. While these effects have been reported to last as long as 4 seconds, severe attenuation seems to take place after less than a second (Blank & Foss, 1978; Swinney, Onifer, Prather, & Hirshkowitz, 1979). If priming is of such short duration, it is difficult to see how it could account for context effects over as long a temporal span as has been observed in the experiments cited here. Perhaps to overcome this objection, Foss, Cirilo, and Blank (1979) proposed that in sentential processing, activation may be maintained for long periods of time by the attentional system. To this proposal there is still a serious objection. Even if activation can be maintained for long periods of time, so many new items are being freshly activated with each retrieved lexical item that activation would cease to be sufficiently precise to be helpful. This problem is compounded if one makes the reasonable assumption that activation spreads to related sets of lexical items.

Cohort Theory

On this direct access model, articulated by Marslen-Wilson and Welsh (1978), Perfetti (1980) and Norris (1982), incoming phonological information activates a cohort of lexical items, the initial syllables of which match the input phonetically. Members of the cohort deactivate as further information produces a mismatch. For many input items, all but one member of the cohort will have deactivated before the final syllables are received. In the absence of context, a lexical item will be selected as soon as it is uniquely determined by incoming phonetic information (hence, retrieval speed of unambiguous items will vary according to their phonetic structure relative to that of other items in the language). In the case of an ambiguous item, phonetic information will be insufficient to select a single entry, and two (or more) members of the phonetically defined cohort will remain activated after all the phonetic information is in. On this type of theory contextual information can be recruited to deactivate semantically ineligible members of the cohort after they have been activated by phonetic information, predicting earlier retrieval of some unambiguous and all ambiguous items in context which renders them more predictable or at least more plausible than other members of their phonetic cohort. This type of theory is not necessarily nonautonomous, for it does postulate activation processes which are sensitive to only phonetic information and selection processes which are sensitive to other types of information. What remains is to formulate a version of cohort theory in which the selection process is adequately constrained. Unfortunately, the proposal presented by Marslen-Wilson and Welsh involved an "active" lexicon in which each lexical "cell" was capable of evaluating the incoming speech signal to determine its relevance based on every available kind of information. Cowart (1978) correctly pointed out that such an arrangement would require that each active lexical cell embody its own language comprehension system, each including its own active lexicon, and so on, to an infinite regress. A further problem with cohort theory as currently formulated is that the deactivation of semantically irrelevant items suggests an inhibitory process. Semantic relatedness, however, is typically associated with facilitory, rather that inhibitory activity. What is needed, then, is a cohort theory containing a passive lexicon and only selective processes.

A coherent theory can be formulated if we assume that the higher level processors project highly constrained on-line predictions of certain properties of the continuing signal for matching against each lexical item. Note that this projection process can begin even before members of the cohort are activated phonetically. (This account is very similar to those of Cowart, 1978, and Norris, 1982.) By way of illustration suppose the Syntactic Processor projects, following the receipt of an article, with a high probability (although not certainty) that the next item will be an adjective or a noun; it will then select from a phonetically activated cohort just those items which are either adjectives or nouns. Other matching parameters could further narrow the set of appropriate items. The interesting question then becomes (as it probably should have been all along): What types of information are projected for match? Phonetic information surely would not be projected because only in very unusual situations (and surely not in ordinary discourse) would a unique word be specified by context. We would expect, however, that information available in the grammar, relating to syntactic organization and selection restrictions, would be included in the projection. For example, it seems reasonable that a context containing the verb "frighten," should predict animate nouns as objects. Such a mechanism is plausible because it postulates that the projection and matching system operate over a relatively restricted domain and exploit units of information that must be assumed, for independent reasons, to be present and accessible in all lexical representations. It is less plausible to suppose that real world information would be projected for a match at the level of lexical retrieval, since such information would tend to be idiosyncratic and available only by inference. This is, however, an empirical question. In any event, thinking of the problem in this way raises the possibility that retrieval and selection in lexical processing operate on separate and highly constrained sets of information.

Search Theories

The best articulated search theory of lexical access is Forster's (1976) autonomous theory. On this view there is a master lexicon, with a number of access files organized in different ways. For auditory comprehension, there is a phonetically organized access file in which the phonetic representations of all the items in the lexicon are organized into "bins" of phonetically similar items. Phonetic input triggers a search of the appropriate access bin (the bin being organized in such a way that the most frequent items are checked first). When a phonetic match is discovered, a marker directs the processor to the master file and retrieval of the item is effected. All phonetic, syntactic, and semantic information about the item is then available for the postaccess decision process to make sure that the retrieval process has been carried out accurately.

There are two differences between cohort theories and search theories as they have been articulated in the literature. First, search theories delay retrieval until phonetic input is complete, rather than until it defines a unique lexical item (as in cohort theory). This delay is not a central feature of search theory, and it would seem perfectly compatible with the theory to allow a partially, but uniquely specified item in the access bin to direct the processor to the master file. (*See* Forster, 1979, p. 269, for an example of just such a process.) Even with this modification, however, search theory has no way to account for any selection process that depends on information other than phonetic before the input has uniquely specified an item in the access file. Thus, the second difference from cohort theory is that search theory cannot accommodate a nonphonetic retrieval process. This is simply because syntactic and semantic information are not available for the selection process before the master file has been entered. If search theory were to allow simultaneous entry to the master file from a cohort of phonetically similar items from the phonetic access file, then it and cohort theory become notational variants of one another. (It may be that search theory is able to provide a better explanation of data relating to the rejection of nonwords in lexical decision tasks than is cohort theory, but a review of this issue is beyond the scope of this chapter.)

If data force us to postulate selection from among a set of phonetically similar items, then we must go to some version of a direct access cohort theory. The relevant data are not yet in.

Integration Theory

This theory, offered by Cairns et al. (1981), is not so much a theory of the Lexical Processor as an attempt to locate the effects of context on lexical items in processing levels beyond that of the Lexical Processor. A thorough discussion of integration processes must be deferred to a full discussion of the Interpretative Processor, so only a brief sketch of the theory as it applies to lexical processing is appropriate here. The one feature that all psycholinguistic theories have in common is the claim that the output of the entire comprehension process is some representation of the meaning of the processed sentence or set of sentences. I have referred to this representation, after Forster, as the "conceptual representation" of the sentence. This representation constitutes an integration of information associated with individual lexical items—an integration governed both by the grammatical relations specified by the syntactic organization of the sentence, and by the nonlinguistic plausibility relations that unite them. Each lexical item, then, can be said to be integrated into the final conceptual representation. In fact, the act of integration can be characterized as the goal of the sentence comprehension process.

Cairns, et al., (1981) suggest that the facilitating effects of context are located in the integration processes and that a lexical item received in a highly plausible context will be more easily integrated with the other lexical items in its sentence than will be a less plausible (or less predictable) item, all other things being equal. They have shown an inverse relation between ease of initial processing of a lexical item and the speed with which it is recognized in a probe task. Thus, an item that has been processed in a predictive context will take longer to recognize in a probe task (presented after an intervening sentence has been processed) than does the same item processed initially in a nonpredictive context. One explanation for these (at first glance, counterintuitive) findings is that the context not only affects the ease of integration of sentential information, but also affects the quality of the resulting conceptual representation. Sentences of which the initial part provides a context which predicts a later lexical item can be integrated with little elaboration. A less predictable lexical item would require a sequence of inferences for integration into the sentential context. The existence of such a set of inferences (to be discussed in more detail below) would render the item more elaborated, hence more salient, in the resulting conceptual representation.

Integration theory also offers an account of the effect of context on the processing of ambiguous items. Following exhaustive retrieval of all phonetically allowable readings, only the contextually appropriate one will be integrated into the conceptual representation of the sentence. If this is the correct interpretation of the disambiguation process, then we can assume that the integration process is well along within 500 msecs following the retrieval of a lexical item.

In summary, we can view the Lexical Processor as a dedicated subprocessor whose sole function it is to retrieve lexical items from the hearer's internalized lexicon based on the phonological information that is its input. Information available at the higher processing levels, Structural or Interpretative, may, however, have an effect on the selection and integration of lexical information. Following the retrieval of a lexical item from the internalized lexicon, information about its structural properties is available to the Structural Processor.

The Structural Processor

The task of the Structural subprocessor is to produce a representation of the formal organization of the lexical items which have been retrieved by the lexical processor. On the autonomous model within which we are working, the Structural Processor uses only syntactic information to create its analysis and produces an analysis which is purely formal in nature. That is, its processing operations are describable only in a syntactic vocabulary, not in a semantic or conceptual one. It can perform no operations which cannot be described in purely formal terms. Therefore, it cannot use real world knowledge to facilitate its operation, nor can it perform any operation for which real world knowledge would be required.

We can identify at least five separate (but not necessarily independent) operations attributable to the structural processor: The segmentation of input into processing units; the computation of the internal organization of the processing units; the matching of fillers and gaps; the identification of missing constituents; and the marking of items which may or may not be coreferential on structural grounds.

Segmentation

A key task of the Structural Processor is to group the incoming lexical items into hierarchically organized constituents (such as sentence, noun phrase, verb phrase, embedded sentence, etc.). This is called parsing and involves both the identification of the structural units and the computation of their internal organization. Thus, the operations described here and those of the next section are both parsing operations performed by the Structural Processor. Obviously the most basic information which the Structural Processor has in its possession is the grammar of the input language, which defines the possible syntactic structures to be constructed. Associated with the lexical representation of each input word is its form class and the sentence frames into which it can be inserted. Thus, a transitive verb such as "hit" will be identified as requiring a direct object noun phrase to follow the verb in a verb phrase of which it is a part. Verbs which take complement sentences, such as "believe," will be so marked, etc. Also included in the lexical representation will be information about the selectional properties of lexical items. Thus, the verb "kill" will require that its object be animate. Finally, the function words and grammatical markers in the input string provide cues to structural units. Articles will begin noun phrases; prepositions, prepositional phrases; and subordinating conjunctions signal the beginning of an embedded sentence, as do complementizers and relative pronouns. Numerous studies have demonstrated that the presence of such markers in the input string facilitate the processing of sentences (Hakes, 1972; Hakes & Cairns, 1970).

Thus the Structural Processor uses internalized grammatical knowledge, lexical information, and surface cues to segment the incoming signal. The parsing function of this processor also consists of the computation of the internal organization of the segmented units.

Internal Organization

Two early lines of research into the structural organization of sentences have been extended in more recent work. Bever (1970) articulated the Canonical Order Hypothesis and Kimball (1973) identified a number of parsing principles attributable to the structural processor. Recent research has built on this work and allowed the formulation of an array of hypotheses regarding the functioning of the Structural Processor that will undoubtedly be addressed for years to come.

The original formulation of the Canonical Order Hypothesis was that any Noun-Verb-Noun sequence would be interpreted as the Subject, Verb, and Object of a single processing unit. This analysis would go through only if there were no marked clause boundaries and if the Verb agreed with the Subject noun. Such an internal analysis would simultaneously identify the sequence as a processing unit, so the Canonical Order hypothesis is an hypothesis about both segmentation and the assignment of internal structure. Bever's famous sentence "The horse raced past the barn fell" cleverly illustrates the dual predictions of this hypothesis. The correct interpretation of the sentence is that the subject, "horse," is modified by a reduced relative clause "raced past the barn." Thus, there are unmarked clause boundaries between "horse" and "raced" and between "barn" and "fell." In the absence of a marked clause boundary, "raced" is incorrectly identified as the main verb (since it agrees with the subject, "the horse"). The adverbial phrase "past the barn" completes the structure, producing segmentation (or closure) after "barn." When "fell" arrives, there is nothing to do with it. We should note in passing that this sentence also illustrates that "canonical order" need not refer only to Subject-Verb-Object constructions, but to other sequences, such as Subject-Verb-Adverbial Phrase, which are allowable in the basic sentence structures of English.

The Canonical Order hypothesis is closely related to some of the parsing principles identified by Kimball (1973) and elaborated by the more recent work of Lynn Frazier and Janet Fodor (Fodor, 1979; Fodor & Frazier, 1980; Frazier, 1978; Frazier & Fodor, 1978). Two of these principles ("Late Closure" and "Minimal Attachment") state that as the parser is organizing a linguistic unit, every new constituent that can be a member of the larger constituent is so analyzed; thus, no new high-order constituents are constructed until structurally necessary. According to this principle, the local ambiguity occurring after "Jane's date" in the sentence "Everyone believed Jane's date was an idiot" should be resolved by the parser with an analysis in which "Everyone believed Jane's date" is a single clausal constituent, an analysis which must be rejected when "was an idiot" is received, just as the analysis of "The horse raced past the barn" as a single clausal constituent must be rejected when "fell" is received in "The horse raced past the barn fell." Hakes (1972) had shown that such sentences with the complementizer "that" deleted were more difficult to process than sentences in which they were not (e.g., "Everyone believed that Jane's date was an idiot."), but the source of the additional processing difficulty remained controversial. It could arise because the parser must produce and store two structural analyses, one as in (a) and another as (b), or it could be because the parser initially constructs analysis (a), which is more plausible according to both Canonical Order, Minimal Attachment, and Late Closure, but turns out to be incorrect. On the latter view the added complexity resulting from deletion of the complementizer arises from the necessity of revising the structural analysis from (a) to (b) as more of the sentence is processed. Frazier and Rayner (1982) report data which may bear on this question from an experiment tracking the eye movements of subjects reading sentences such as "Since Jay always jogs a mile and half seems like a very short distance to him." According to Late Closure,

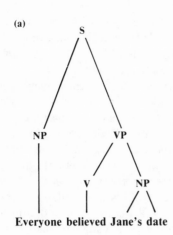

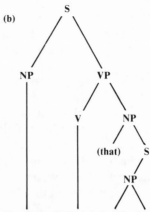

Minimal Attachment, and Canonical Order, "a mile and a half" will be initially parsed as object to the verb "jogs," only to require reanalysis as the subject of "seems" later on in the sentence. Confirming these predictions, longer fixations were observed in the area of "seems like" than in sentences such as "Since Jay always jogs a mile and a half this seems like a short distance to him" in which the initial parse does not have to be revised. Further, more regressive eye movements were observed in the former sentence than in the latter, indicating that subjects were reprocessing the initial sequence. The Frazier and Rayner data suggest that the source of difficulty in the complementizer deletion cases is that an incorrect structural analysis is initially projected. The two cases are not truly commensurate, however, because the Hakes experiment used verbs which take complementizers, while the Frazier and Rayner experiment did not. Recent research shows that verb structure is one of the most important determinants of structural analysis, so it is impossible to make inferences about the processing of one type of verb from data gathered using another type.

Another parsing principle related to the internal organization of constituents is that of "Right Association," or "Low Attachment." In a structurally ambiguous sentence such as "Joe called the friend who had smashed his new car up," the particle "up" is more likely to be associated with "smashed" than with "called." And the adverb "yesterday" is more likely to be associated with "taken-out" than with "said" in "Tom said that Bill had taken the cleaning out yesterday." Frazier and Fodor account for this principle within the context of their two-stage parsing model "the sausage machine." On this theory several lexical items are processed at a time by the initial stage and sent to the second stage for further processing. Thus, late-occurring sentential material is associated with immediately preceding material because the earlier sequences have already moved on to the second parsing stage, and are no longer available for association. Compare, for instance, the following sentences. "John bought the book for Susan" seems to violate the principles of right association and low attachment, since "for Susan" is more likely to be interpreted as a benefactive adjunct to "bought" than as a modifier of "the book" (as in "the book that was for Susan"). "John bought the book that I had been trying to obtain for Susan," on the other hand, follows the principles of Right Association and Low Attachment in that "for Susan" is attached to "obtain" rather than to "bought." Acccording to Frazier and Fodor, the differential parsing preferences in these two ambiguous sentences are attributable solely to their length differences. In the first sentence, "bought" is still available to the parser when "for Susan" is received for analysis, but in the second, longer sentence, "bought" has been sent away to the second stage of the parser when "for Susan" arrives. The sentences above illustrate the operation of the Frazier and Fodor "sausage machine," but, as we shall see below, length alone clearly does not account completely for all preferred structural analyses. Verb structure is an equally important factor.

A number of other theories attempt to account for the parsing principles identified here (see, for instance, Wanner, 1980, who attempts to account for these principles within his Augmented Transition Network theory of parsing), the most interesting of which has been proposed by Ford, Bresnan, and Kaplan (1982) and is based on Bresnan's Lexical Functional Theory of Grammar (Bresnan, 1978; Bresnan, 1981; 1982). According to this account, each verb is represented in the lexicon with its preferred argument structure, which has entailments for the syntactic frame into which that verb is most likely to be inserted. This lexical representation, then, guides the parser. Ford et al. (1982) show that principles such as Right Association can be varied depending upon verbs even if sentence length is held constant. Compare, for instance, the ambiguous sentences "The woman wanted the dress on that rack" to "The woman positioned the dress on that rack." In the former sentence, Right Association seems to dictate the parse, in which "on that rack" is a modifier of "the dress." In the second sentence, however, "on that rack" is preferred as an adverbial complement to "positioned," apparently violating Right Association. According to Ford, et al., this difference arises from the fact that the verb "position" is entered in the lexicon with a preferred structure which includes a locative adverbial complement, while "want" is not. One can think of the Lexical Functional theory of parsing as a highly evolved version of its ancestor, Canonical Order. The early hypothesis was essentially saying that sentences are processed according to the least marked structure in the language. The Lexical Functional theory is saying that the least marked structures will differ depending upon lexically specified properties of sentential verb.

Relating Fillers and Gaps

Sentences in which elements have been moved will contain "gaps" representing the original location of the moved element and "fillers" that represent the moved elements themselves. Examples of this phenomenon are the following sentences, in which the filler is underlined and the gap is indicated by an asterisk: "Who did John hit * ?" "This is the girl John hit * ." In order for comprehension to take place, the Structural Processor must identify the gaps in a sentence and the fillers that are associated with them (Fodor, 1979; Frazier, Clifton & Randall, in press). Clearly, the structural properties of sentential verbs again play a role. In the sentences above, "hit" requires an object, so a gap must be identified following the verb, to be associated with the only available filler. Things become a bit more complicated when a verb, such as "visit" in the following sentence, can either be transitive or intransitive. Thus, the sentence "Who did John want to visit?" is ambiguous; the gap can either precede the verb, as in "Who did John want * to visit?" or follow it, as in "Who did John want to visit * ?" The latter seems to represent the preferred interpretation, indicating that the preferred structure of the verb "visit" is transitive.

Other factors play a role in matching fillers and gaps and these factors are just beginning to be investigated experimentally. One hypothesis is that the Structural Processor associates the nearest available filler with each gap that it identifies. On this hypothesis, a sentence such as "This is the girl the teacher decided * to talk to * ", in which "the teacher" is associated with the gap in the subject position of "talk" and "the girl" is associated with the gap in the object position of "to," should be easy to process. More difficult, however, should be the similar sentence "This is the girl the teacher forced * to talk." By hypothesis, the latter sentence is more difficult because "the teacher" (the nearest possible filler) will be considered and rejected as the associate of the gap in the subject position of "talk." Clifton and Frazier (1982), using a reading time measure to compare the comprehension difficulty of sentences such as the two above, confirmed the hypothesis by obtaining longer reading times for sentences of the "forced" type. It is undoubtedly the case that many variables affect the Structural Processor's identification of gaps and their related fillers. A complete theory of the operation of the Structural Processor requires that these variables be identified and their operation understood.

The Identification of Missing Constituents

In a sentence such as "Sue interviewed Evelyn after arriving at the studio" the Structural Processor must identify the subject of "arriving", which is, unambiguously, "Sue." This must be ascertained by structural analysis, since there is no other type of information which can identify the missing subject. To my knowledge there has been no empirical investigation of the processing of such sentences by adults (*see* Hsu, 1981, and Hsu, Cairns, & Fiengo, 1980, for an investigation of the development of the child's ability to comprehend such sentences), but the fact that we can do so indicates that the Structural Processor obeys the constraints imposed by the structural principle of C-Command (Reinhardt, 1976). One constituent is said to C-Command another if the first branching node which dominates it also dominates the other. In the above sentence, which in organized as (c) below, "Sue" C-Commands the missing subject position of "arriving"because the S-node, which is the first branching node above "Sue," also dominates the missing subject Noun Phrase.

(c)

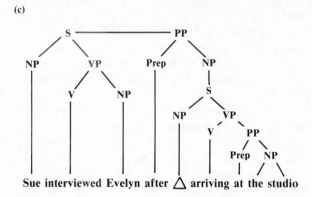

Sue interviewed Evelyn after △ arriving at the studio

Since the Verb Phrase which dominates "Evelyn" does not also dominate the missing Noun Phrase, "Evelyn" does not C-Command the missing Noun Phrase. There is a general principle in English that a missing constituent must be C-Commanded by the constituent with which it is identified; thus, only "Sue" and not "Evelyn" can be associated with the missing subject of "arriving." We assume, then, that the Structural Processor incorporates operations which allow it to relate missing constituents to other sentential elements based on structural principles such as C-Command. As we shall see below, the principle of C-Command also relates to another operation of the Structural Processor, which is its evaluation of the structural constraints on pronominal reference.

Pronominal Reference

Essential to the comprehension enterprise is the assignment of referents for all pronouns which occur in a sentence. First and second person pronouns refer to the speaker and hearer(s), respectively. There are a few types of pronouns whose referents are determined structurally, viz. reflexive pronouns ("John shaved himself") and reciprocals ("The men hated each other"). Third person personal and possessive pronouns, however, are unusual in that they may be prevented from coreference with Noun Phrases within the same sentence, but they can never be required to be coreferential with a particular Noun Phrase on structural grounds. For instance, in the sentence "John hit him" or "He said that John was tired," "John" cannot be coreferential with the pronoun. In the first instance, coreference is blocked because the pronoun is not reflexive and "him" and "John" are in the same clause. (Note that some idioms represent an exception to this rule, such as "John had a knife on him".) In the second instance, "he" and "John" cannot corefer because "he" C-Commands "John." Pronominal reference also makes use of the C-Command principle, but in a manner opposite from the principle which assigns identities to missing constituents. In the case of pronouns, if the pronoun C-Commands a lexical Noun Phrase, then the pronoun and the Noun Phrase cannot corefer. If, on the other hand, the lexical Noun Phrase C-Commands the pronoun, as in "John said that he was tired," then the pronoun is free to refer either to "John" or to some Noun Phrase in another sentence, or, indeed, to a nonlinguistic entity, i.e., some male in the physical or conceptual environment. In all cases of third person personal and possessive pronouns, coreference is never assigned by structural factors, but will be determined by a variety of plausibility and contextual factors related to real world knowledge. Since, by hypothesis, the Structural Processor cannot operate on such knowledge, we assume that assignment of coreference is done by the Interpretative Processor. In fact, we shall see that the final processor must be concerned with issues of coreference which go far beyond pronouns. But more about this later.

The Autonomy Issue with Respect to the Structural Processor

The hypothesis that the Structural Processor is autonomous says simply that there are a collection of processing operations which it performs based only on the form of the message to be decoded, and not on its content. If the Structural Processor is indeed autonomous, then it will use information about the grammar of the language on which it is operating, formal information derived from the lexicon (stipulating the form class of individual words and the sentence frames in which they may appear, ordered by preference), and structural cues from the input sentence, such as function words, clause boundary markers, etc. What it cannot use is nonlinguistic information derived from general conceptual knowledge, real world knowledge, or the conceptual representation of previously analyzed linguistic material. Thus, real world knowledge should not facilitate structural analysis (although it will certainly facilitate the operation of the final processor, as we shall see later on.) Forster (1979) and his colleagues (Forster & Olbrei, 1973; Ratcliff, 1978) have done a great deal of work on this question. They first addressed the old findings of Slobin (1966) and Herriot (1969) that irreversible passives are not more difficult to process than matched actives, while reversible passives add processing complexity. This finding obviously controverts the autonomy hypothesis in that the real world knowledge which makes the passive irreversible is said to operate to facilitate the structural analysis of the passive sentence. In a series of four experiments involving a number of different tasks to measure comprehension complexity, Forster and Olbrei (1973) were able to show that irreversible passives, like reversible ones, involve more comprehension time than do their corresponding actives. (It is not really a surprise that Slobin's picture verification task produced inaccurate information about comprehension time. After Gough's experiences with it in 1965 and 1966, it was no longer used as a measure of comprehension speed.) The new data from Forster and Olbrei, then, confirm the hypothesis that all passive constructions require common processing operations no matter what their internal plausibility constraints, thus confirming the autonomy hypothesis that real world knowledge plays no role in the syntactic analysis of passive sentences.

In their experiments with passive sentences, Forster and his colleagues have shown that the manipulation of the syntactic properties of a sentence affects its processing independent of plausibility constraints. They have used this same general device successfully in numerous ingenious experimental paradigms to demonstrate the autonomy of syntactic processing (Forster, 1979). For instance, pairs of sentences are judged to be the same or different with greater facility if they are syntactically coherent than if they are not. Semantic plausibility, however, does not significantly improve judgment latencies. The rearrangement of lexical items interferes with the processing of plausible sentences as severely as it does with that of implausible sentences, indicating that there are syntactic operations which depend on word order which are insensitive to plausibility information (Forster, 1979). Further, an early experiment of Forster and Olbrei (1973) demonstrated that two-clause sentences involve more processing complexity than do one-clause sentences regardless of their internal plausibility characteristics; another demonstrated that a significant amount of the shared variance among plausible and implausible sentences is attributable to their common syntactic structures.

There have been few experiments dealing with the effects of context on syntactic ambiguities, an area which has proved so fruitful for investigating the autonomy issue as it relates to lexical processing. The studies of syntactic ambiguity (Cairns & Berkovits, 1975; Hurtig, 1978; Tyler & Marslen-Wilson, 1977) have produced varying results and some have been methodologically flawed, so the results are difficult to interpret. If it is the case that the parsing principles mentioned above influence the initial analysis of many syntactic ambiguities, then future explorations of the effects of context must take them into account.

It is clear that the Structural Processor can operate independently of real world knowledge. We can, for instance, impose a structural analysis on a string of inflected nonsense words ("The rolper proked the melp") and we can interpret sentences which, when processed by purely structural criteria, appear bizarre when confronted with our real world knowledge ("The patient consulted the doctor after performing the appendectomy"). The autonomy question is whether the Structural Processor must operate independently of real world knowledge. A recent study by Rayner, Carlson, and Frazier (1983) concludes that the general parsing principles described above operate even if the resulting parse is pragmatically implausible. Thus, they claim that real world plausibility factors are not available to the Structural Processor for its initial structural analysis. This issue is emerging as an important theoretical question to be addressed by future research.

The Interpretative Processor

The processes described so far operate in the absence of real world knowledge and produce a representation of the structural organization of lexical items in individual sentences. This representation underlies the literal meaning of the sentence that is being comprehended and constitutes the input to the Interpretative Processor, whose task it is to construct a nonlinguistic, conceptual representation of the meaning of the sentence.

This final processor, which has free access to the entire range of real world knowledge, both factual and conventional, must carry out two tasks. First, it must construct a nonlinguistic conceptual representation of the sentence which is being comprehended (Goetz, Anderson, & Schallert, 1981). This representation will integrate information from the individual lexical items based on their structural organization and also on inferences based on real world knowledge. The second task of the Interpretative

Processor is to integrate representations of individual sentences into a conceptual representation incorporating the linguistic and nonlinguistic contexts in which they occur (Walker & Meyer, 1980). People do not go around understanding lone sentences. Rather, sentences occur in conversations, lectures, plays, stories, etc. While the processing of an individual sentence must precede its integration into a larger context (Clark, 1978; Kintsch & van Dijk, 1978), a complete account of language comprehension must address the use to which sentences are put after they are processed. Much early research by Bransford, Franks, and their colleagues (Barclay, 1973; Bransford & Franks, 1971, 1972) demonstrated the integration of related sentences into a single conceptual representation. More recent work in this area, however, has dealt with the comprehension of connected sentences in written texts. The findings of this research are not necessarily limited to the reading of texts, however; indeed, they can be taken to reveal very general cognitive operations.

In the next section we will return to a description of some of the properties of the conceptual representation of sentences, but first let us examine some of the organizational principles to which the Interpretative Processor appears to respond.

A number of factors facilitate the integration of segments of linguistic material. More plausible sentences, for instance, are processed with greater facility than are implausible ones. Forster (1979) has demonstrated quite convincingly that plausibility does not affect the Structural Processor, but instead facilitates integration at a higher level. As noted above, Cairns, Cowart, and Jablon (1981) argue that the presence of predictive context facilitates integration at the level of the Interpretative Processor. These variables are clearly related and are themselves related to the fact, discussed in some detail below, that inferential activity complicates processing. In any event, it is clear that ease of integration facilitates processing and, furthermore, that when processing is facilitated, it is speeded. We assume that initial processing takes place in some sort of short-term (or working) memory buffer, in which material is held while it is being analyzed. A sentence whose processing is being facilitated will remain in working memory for a shorter period of time than will one for which processing is more difficult. It has been demonstrated experimentally that lexical items are recognized more quickly when they are being held in working memory than they are when they are part of an integrated conceptual representation (Cairns & Berkovits, 1975; Cairns & Blank, 1976; Caplan, 1972). Other studies have shown that the linear ordering of items in working memory is more salient than that of items in an integrated representation (Carroll, Tanenhaus, & Bever, 1978; Townsend & Bever, 1978). Experiments such as this not only give us some insight into the differential properties of representations at various levels of analysis, they also allow us to identify properties of sentences which allow them to be integrated more quickly. Bever and his colleagues have shown, for instance, that multiple-clause sentences with initial subordinate clauses are more difficult to process than are those with initial main clauses (Townsend & Bever, 1978). This is because the initial subordinate clause cannot be completely processed (integrated) until the information from the main clause is received. (This research also suggests that this effect varies with the identity of the subordinating conjunction.)

The observation was made years ago that sentences are processed in clausal units (Bever, Garrett, & Hurtig, 1973; Fodor & Bever, 1965; Garrett, Bever, & Fodor, 1966; Caplan, 1972). At one time this was believed to be purely a structural phenomenon, relating to the presence of an embedded sentence which would form a processing unit. It is undoubtedly the case that clause boundary markers are among the surface cues used by the Structural Processor in its parsing operations, but the optimality of the clause as processing unit appears to be attributable to higher-level processes. Recent work has shown that the psycholinguistic segmentation unit is not simply a linguistically defined clause, but one which is functionally complete. Carroll et al. (1978) defined a functionally complete clause as one which "...contains a complete, explicit, and coherent set of grammatical relations" (p.192). They showed that functionally complete clauses, such as "After the crook stole the woman's bag..." are better segmentation units by a number of measures than less complete clauses such as "Meeting the pretty young girl..." The former contains a complete complement of grammatical relations, Subject, Verb, and Object, while the latter has only a Verb and Object. Marslen-Wilson, Tyler and Seidenberg (1978) have further elaborated the completeness notion by demonstrating that the best segmentation units are not only functionally complete but also informationally complete. The clause "Because he didn't like it" is functionally complete in that it contains a Subject, Verb, and Object. It is also informationally complete in the sentence "John threw the book away, because he didn't like it" but not in the sentence "Because he didn't like it, John threw the book away." In the former case, referents for the pronouns are provided by the initial clause, while in the latter, that information must await a following clause.

It appears, then, that the most plausible explanation for the well-known "clause effect" is that the Interpretative Processor integrates most smoothly configurations of lexical items which form semantically cohesive units. The idea that informational completeness relies in part on the ability of the processor to determine referents across clauses relates to other principles of organization which will be described below.

Texts or stretches of connected discourse can be described in terms of their cohesiveness (Cirilo, 1981; Kintsch & van Dijk, 1978), and it is generally true that the more cohesive a text, the easier it will be to process (Cirilo, 1981; Vipond, 1980). Text cohesion arises from considerations of organization at the global level (its macrostructure) or the local level (its microstructure). The local cohesion of a string of sentences or propositions depends upon common references among them. In order to integrate an individual sentence with the discourse which has preceded it, referents must be discovered for its content-bearing elements; the more accessible those referents, the greater the referential cohesion of the text. There are three processes by which referents can be located (Cirilo, 1981; Kintsch & van Dijk, 1978; Lesgold, Roth, & Curtis, 1979). The easiest is to locate the referent in the most recently processed prior sentence. A key assumption is that short stretches of discourse are held in short term memory and (all other things being equal) the most recently processed sentence is more available than are earlier ones which have been discharged from short-term store. The second referential process is the retrieval from long-term store of a referent from a less recently processed sentence. This process is called "reinstatement." The final, and most difficult referential process is one which requires an inference to discover a referent in prior material. An example from Clark (1978) is the sentence pair: "I went to a wedding yesterday. The woman was a doctor." In order to discover the discourse referent for "the woman," the hearer must use the real world knowledge that the cast of characters at a wedding includes a woman to infer that "the woman" refers to the bride.

This process of discovering referents across stretches of discourse has been referred to by Clark (1977, 1978) as "bridging" and the inferences which are required, "bridging inferences" or "bridging assumptions." Experimental evidence abounds that the ease of processing a target sentence varies according to the accessibility of its referents (Cirilo, 1981; Clark & Sengul, 1979; Lesgold et al., 1979; Manelis & Yekovich, 1976); *see* Black and Bern, 1981, for a note on the facilitative effects of causal cohesion. This principle forms the basis for Haviland and Clark's "Given-New Hypothesis" (1974). In a series of studies they demonstrated that a sentence is more easily processed if a common referent exists between it and an immediately prior sentence than if such a referent is absent. By hypothesis, the common referent allows for ease of integration between the given information in the first sentence and the new information in the second (target) sentence. Thus, the sentence "The beer was warm" is understood more quickly if it follows the sentence "We got some beer out of the trunk," which establishes the existence of some particular beer to serve as a referent for "the beer," than if it follows the sentence "Andrew was especially fond of beer," which does not establish such a referent. A number of studies have subsequently shown that increasing the distance between referents increases the complexity of processing (Cirilo, 1981; Clark & Sengul, 1979; Lesgold et al., 1979), confirming the hypothesis that a distant referent must be reinstated before bridging can take place. Keenan and Kintsch (Kintsch, 1974, cited by Clark, 1978) demonstrated that sentences which require bridging inferences to establish referential cohesion between sentences require longer processing times than those which do not. Thus, the sentence "The fire destroyed many acres of virgin forest" is understood more quickly following "A carelessly discarded burning cigarette started a fire" than following "A burning cigarette was carelessly discarded." In the latter case, but not in the former, the bridging inference must be made that the discarded cigarette started a forest fire. In an experiment investigating all three types of referential processes simultaneously, Lesgold et al., (1979) confirmed the hypothesis that the availability of an immediate referent facilitates comprehension more than a reinstated one, which is, in turn, less facilitating than one which must be constructed by a bridging inference. Extending the notion of local referential cohesion to the construction of texts and conversations, it is clear that speakers and writers use not only their own real world knowledge but the knowledge that they believe their interlocutors to possess in constructing strings of sentences which can only be related via bridging inferences.

The global cohesiveness of a text or sequence of discourse derives from its more general structure, and this in turn may either be known to the reader (or hearer) in advance or may emerge from the reader's analysis of the text itself. In the first instance, the extent to which a text adheres to the conventional structure for texts of its type will determine its global cohesiveness. An article in experimental psychology, for instance, will consist of an introduction, which includes a statement of theoretical issues, a description of the reported experiment, and a conclusion which relates the results of the experiment to the original theoretical issues. The experienced reader approaches the task of reading such an article with the anticipation that it will conform to this organizational frame. A number of researchers have postulated the existence of organizational frameworks for stories (sometimes called "story grammars") and have shown how such global cohesiveness facilitates the cognitive activities of comprehending and recalling narratives (Mandler & Johnson, 1977; Rumelhart, 1977; Thorndyke, 1977; Yekovich & Thorndyke, 1981). The notion of global organization has been extended to encompass systems of real world knowledge, called "frames" (Minsky, 1975) or "scripts" (Shank & Abelson, 1975). Accounts of this sort, frequently used in work in artificial intelligence, rely on the observation that people know many things about conventionalized activities which need not be stated to be activated. For instance, when I hear that someone ate a steak at a restaurant, I know that they ordered the steak, paid a bill, etc. since a "restaurant frame" is part of my real world knowledge. Thus, frames can, among other things, form the basis for bridging inferences in strings of discourse.

Global cohesion in a text can also arise as the text is processed and its hierarchical organization is replicated in the cognitive system of the reader. Referential cohesion is relevant here, as higher level propositions are those which are relevant to greater numbers of other propositions than are lower-level ones. On the account of Kintsch and van Dijk (1978), whose work forms the basis of much of the work on text cohesion, propositions are processed in a short term memory buffer, in which they are related to other relevant propositions. (Further confirmation of this proposal can be found in Miller and Kintsch, 1980, and Fletcher, 1981). Previously processed propositions can be returned to the buffer if necessary (as in the reinstatement process mentioned above). It will turn out that higher-level propositions will be returned to the processing buffer more often that lower-level ones, since they bear relevance to many propositions that follow them. Typically, a higher-level proposition will introduce a textual theme which will be elaborated by lower-level propositions that follow. Many researchers have demonstrated that higher-level propositions are recalled better than are lower-level ones (Kintsch & van Dijk, 1978; Thorndyke, 1977; Waters, 1978; Yekovich & Thorndyke, 1981). This is, presumably, because they have been elaborated during the course of text processing.

Cirilo and Foss (1980) investigated the effect of propositional level upon ease of initial processing. Using a reading time measure, they demonstrated that higher-level propositions are more difficult to process initially than are lower-level ones. It is not clear why this should be so, since the fact that higher-level propositions are recalled better than lower-level ones is attributed to processing activities which take place following the high-level proposition. A plausible explanation (one which seems to be preferred by Foss and Cirilo) is that the high-level proposition is difficult to process initially precisely because it introduces new information that cannot be immediately integrated with preceding information in the text. (A similar explanation is proposed by Yekovich & Thorndyke, 1981). Lower-level propositions are processed with relative ease because they have cohesion with the higher-level proposition.

The ease of processing individual sentences is, then, related to both micro- and macrostructural properties of the texts in which such sentences are embedded. It is possible to manipulate the extent to which subjects in psycholinguistic experiments engage micro- vs. macroprocesses by the formulation of experimental task demands. Cirilo (1981) demonstrated the effectiveness of experimental instructions in the manipulation of such processing demands. In Cirilo's experiment, subjects who were told that they would participate in a recall task engaged microprocessing strategies, while subjects who thought they were engaging in text processing as a distractor exercise engaged only macroprocesses. Thus, the recruitment of these two types of cognitive processing activities are dependent upon the outcome toward which subject are directing themselves, hence are mutable by the task demands of the experimental situation. (See also Just & Carpenter, 1980, and Vipond, 1980, for further evidence of the separability of micro- and macroprocesses.)

In summary, the Interpretative Processor takes incoming sentences and organizes them into an integrated conceptual representation. A number of variables affect the ease with which this representation can be constructed. It is generally true, however, that the ease of processing any individual sentence will depend on two factors: The ease with which its sentence-internal information can be integrated and the ease with which it can be integrated into the larger conceptual representation of which it is a part.

Characteristics of the Integrated Conceptual Representation

The conceptual representation which results from the activities of the Interpretative Processor has a number of properties which reveal its integrated and nonlinguistic character. For example, the uniqueness of information associated with individual lexical items is effaced. We have already seen that the lexical items in a completely processed sentence or clause are less accessible than are those from a more shallowly processed clause (Bever & Townsend, 1979; Cairns & Blank, 1976; Caplan, 1972). This suggests that in the conceptual representation of a sentence the phonetic information associated with individual lexical items is less available than it is at earlier stages of processing. One should expect, then, that semantically similar lexical items should be more confusable after integration than they are before. Jenkins and Strange (1977) have, in fact, demonstrated this phenomenon.

Another consequence of the integration of individual lexical items is that the meaning of nonspecific noun phrases is enriched in response to their sentential roles. Anderson, Pichert, Goetz, Shallert, Stevens, and Trollip (1976) refer to this phenomenon as the "instantiation of general terms." They point out, for instance, that the verb "eat" will play a very different role in the conceptual representation of a sentence depending upon its object (compare soup to an artichoke). The representation of a noun such as "container" will differ depending upon what is being contained (compare wine and apples). Anderson, et al., illustrate this phenomenon experimentally by showing that the noun phrase "the actress" is a better memory probe for the sentence "The woman was outstanding in the theater" than is "the woman." This is not true, however, for the similar sentence "The woman lived near the theater." In the former case the general term "the woman" has come to take on meaning from the rest of the sentence, so that it is stored in memory as the more specific "actress." Another way to characterize the process is to say that the hearer infers from the entire sentential context that the woman referred to is an actress and he stores this inference as part of his conceptual representation of the sentence "the woman was outstanding in the theater."

There is abundant evidence that many kinds of information not available in the literal meaning of a sentence emerge by inferential processes and are present in its conceptual representation (Corbett & Dosher, 1978; McKoon & Ratcliff, 1980; Morris & Bransford, 1982; Thorndyke, 1977). Illustrative of this process are the intriguing findings of Brewer (1977) who showed that a sentence tends to be recalled in a form describing its pragmatic entailments rather than in its literal form. So, for instance, "The hungry python caught the mouse" is recalled as "The hungry python ate the mouse." Obviously, an enormous range of inferences are available in everyday language use. The simple inferences demonstrated in experimental procedures are replaced in the real world with far more complex and idiosyncratic systems of inferences. So compelling is our interpretation and recall of events—both linguistic and nonlinguistic—in a form enriched by inferences, serious disputes and misunderstandings may occur. This is especially true because the surface form and literal meaning of individual sentences are lost as the integration process proceeds. I was told of a bilingual woman, for instance, who rarely remembers in which language she heard a newscast; she only remembers what's news. Several studies have demonstrated in particular that subjects store the meaning but not the surface form of sentences (Cairns & Jablon, 1976; Sachs, 1967). The former experiment also demonstrated that some syntactic forms are retained longer than others. The ability to distinguish between "there-insertion" sentences and simple declaratives ("There was a dollar bill on the sidewalk" vs. "A dollar bill was on the sidewalk") is of shorter duration than is the ability to discriminate sentences which differ in indirect object movement ("John gave the book to Sue" vs. "John gave Sue the book.") The inability of individuals to store verbatim information has profound implications not only for cognitive psychology, but for legal processes as well. Loftus (1975, 1977) has conducted a number of experiments which have disturbing implications for our belief in the veracity of eyewitness accounts of events.

A topic that is just beginning to be investigated is the relationship between aspects of the initial processing of an item and its salience in the final conceptual representation. For instance, high-level propositions, which are more difficult to process initially than lower-level ones (Cirilo & Foss, 1980) are yet easier to recall (Yekovich & Thorndyke, 1981). Lexical items that are received in unpredictable (although not bizarre) context are more difficult to process initially than those which appear in more predictable contexts, but they are recognized more quickly in a probe task (Cairns et al., 1981). These findings suggest an inverse relationship between initial processing difficulty and salience in conceptual representation, a relationship demonstrated earlier in the learning of word lists (Jacoby, Craik, & Begg, 1979). The best current explanation for this phenomenon seems to be that successful initial processing of certain items requires the application of operations (such as creating a system of inferences) that increase the item's salience in the final representation. Further research will, undoubtedly, improve our understanding of this phenomenon.

In summary, we note that the surface form of a sentence is available to a listener or reader for only a very brief period of time. It seems to serve as raw material for the creation of a conceptual representation in a process which adds some kinds of information (that based on inferences, knowledge of macrostructure, etc.) and destroys others (such as syntactic form, unique lexical representations, and literal sentential meanings). The high-level cognitive processes which construct conceptual representations are powerful operations which extend over a domain far greater than linguistic messages. It is at this level that we find common operations (such as those associated with integration and inference) applying to virtually all cognitive activities. A complete theory of the Interpretative Processor would of necessity include a very general theory of cognition, including memory and thought.

Conclusion

In this chapter I have attempted to develop a highly constrained model of the language comprehension system in which two dedicated subprocessors, the Lexical and Structural Processors, perform all aspects of analysis that are uniquely linguistic. These two processors together, in fact, can be thought of as a Linguistic Processor, which is specialized and probably unique to man. It interfaces with the highly unspecialized Interpretative Processor, which employs very general cognitive operations, such as integration and inference. The major distinction between the Linguistic and Interpretative Processors is that the operations of the former respond only to linguistic information of various kinds while the latter is able to respond to real world knowledge.

Such a modular model provides us with a framework for analyzing language development and language pathology and for exploring the relationships between the autonomous theories of linguistics, on the one hand, and neurolinguistics on the other. Best of all, it provides an explicit and constrained theory which informs our empirical investigations of language processing.

Acknowledgments

Many thanks to Michael Studdert-Kennedy, Merrill Garrett, Bob Fiengo, and Lyn Frazier for comments on an earlier version of this chapter. Their suggestions have been invaluable, but any errors that remain are, of course, my own.

Hugh W. Buckingham

Localization of Language in the Brain

Introduction

This chapter provides an overview of some of the most recent attempts at localizing the cerebral regions of the human brain that seem to be particularly involved in one way or another with various of the functions of man's language faculty. The studies that will be at issue are for the most part neurophysiological and neuropsychological; they are not linguistic. As a rule linguists take the position that it makes little sense to try to localize the neural structures that mediate abstract functions until it is understood what those functions are. In spite of this, however, the neuropsychology of language has forged ahead in its search for anatomical substrates, leaving theoretical linguistic research, at least in the realm of syntax/semantics, aside. These anatomical substrates have, for the most part, been correlated with macrofunctions, or psycholinguistic tasks (Arbib & Caplan, 1979)—tasks such as speaking (articulation), comprehension of speech, reading (silent and aloud), writing (copying, dictation, spontaneous), providing spoken labels for objects (naming), repeating, completing sentences and the like. Nowhere will we find anatomical substrates and neural networks that will only parse strings generated by context-free or context-sensitive grammars (Berwick & Weinberg, 1982) or localizations of neural mechanisms that are in any way sensitive to syntactic structures that disobey recently proposed conditions on rules (Chomsky, 1973, 1980).

© College-Hill Press, Inc. All rights, including that of translation, reserved. No part of this publication may be reproduced without the written permission of the publisher.

Specifically, this chapter will treat several recent studies of cerebral dominance and laterality and will then turn to left versus right hemisphere linguistic abilities. Many of the nondominant hemisphere language functions will be shown to have resulted from shifts subsequent to left lesions. Thus we will have a better idea of what the right brain *could* do—not what it does do in the normal case. Various extralinguistic functions, however, do seem to be the province of the right hemisphere. Humor, metaphor, antonymic response, connotation and emotional affect have been assigned to the right hemisphere by several researchers. In addition, there has been an upsurge of work with different techniques for actually specifying circumscribed regions for language or for the lesions that exclusively disrupt language. These techniques include the measurement of cortical asymmetry, cortical excision, cortical stimulation (direct versus scalp), regional cerebral blood flow, computerized axial tomography and position emission tomography.

Strict localizationism has several critical obstacles to confront, and these will be outlined towards the end of the chapter. Ontogenetic dynamics, vicarious function subsequent to brain damage and analytic/holistic induced functional shifts in processing all call for a weaker form of the localization position. This chapter will further consider the philosophical obstacles to be faced when inferring functional localization from neurological evidence, and it will try to elucidate the distinctions between what we learn about language from looking at the brain as opposed to the computer, to the computer program, or to the mind.

Cerebral Dominance and Laterality

The search for the location of language in the human brain is usually embedded in the larger issue of laterality in man. Corballis and Morgan (1978) suggest that there is a left-right maturational gradient that forms earlier or more rapid development on the left. They also suggest that the dominant side exerts an inhibitory influence on the right. Any early damage to the leading side will reverse the gradient. In general, they suggest that handedness and cerebral dominance for language quite likely involve cytoplasmic as well as genetic factors. In a followup paper, Morgan and Corballis (1978) emphasize that the polarity of laterality seems more to be determined by cytoplasm than by genetic code. It is difficult, they maintain, to demonstrate clear examples where *direction* of laterality is under genetic control. Alternatively, it is relatively simple to find cases where *degree* of laterality (not direction) is under genetic control.

Familial Sinistrality

Hardyck (1977) and Hardyck and Petrinovich (1977) have developed a model that is sensitive to *familial* handedness. Laterality for them is a question of degree as well, and four different populations are found: right-handers with no familial left-handedness (FLH), right-handers with FLH left-handed with no FLH (many of whom are the so-called "pathological left-handers"), and left-handers with FLH. In terms of degree, the right-handers with no FLH are the most strongly lateralized while the left-handers with FLH are the least lateralized, i.e., most bilateral. FLH is defined by Hardyck (1977, p. 238) as "the presence of left-hand preference in at least two generations." To be considered left-handed, one must have either a strong preference or at least demonstrate an ability to use either hand for a variety of tasks. Interestingly enough, left-handers with no FLH are like right-handers with no FLH. On the other hand, right-handers with FLH are closer on the laterality continuum to the FLH left-handers. Hecaen and Sauget (1971) demonstrated that, like FLH sinistrals, right-handed subjects with FLH were more likely to recover from aphasia (secondary to left sided lesions) than were right- and left-handers who had no trace of FLH. These investigators further found that for left-handers with no FLH the frequency of language difficulties of all types is always greater with left sided lesions. Hardyck alludes to one crucial caveat for interpreting laterality differences, which is agreed upon by practically everyone in the field. It is that whether laterally specialized or bilateral, the vast majority of people have motor speech production controlled by the left hemisphere (Hardyck, 1977, p. 240; Zaidel, 1978, p. 258-9; Studdert-Kennedy, 1981, p. 76).

The above laterality distinctions make certain predictions which generally obtain according to Hardyck, and they will be briefly outlined here, since they have obvious repercussions for language location (or degree of location). On certain tasks the magnitude of interhemispheric difference is most pronounced for right-handers. McKeever, Gill, and VanDeventer (1975) studied visual field reaction time differences to single letter stimuli. The right-handed subjects revealed a statistically significant advantage in vocal reaction time to letters projected to the left hemisphere as compared with letters projected to the right (36.9 msec). The left-handed subjects had only a 13.6 msec difference favoring the left hemisphere. However, when those left-handed subjects were further divided according to FLH, the non-FLH group was found to have a significant left hemisphere advantage (21.3 msec), whereas the left-handed group with FLH had no left hemisphere advantage at all (-0.57 msec). The left-hander with FLH can accept stimulus input, process, and output a response easier within the same hemisphere. The bilaterally organized person can better judge identity of identical but nonsymmetric patterns introduced to each hemisphere, and, for him, direct interhemispheric comparison of data is easier because each hemisphere has some degree of ability to process a wider range of stimuli types. However, the bilaterally organized person will make more errors in identity comparison where the stimuli presented to each hemisphere are mirror-images of one another. According to Hardyck (1977, p. 245) this suggests that visual information is reversed as a consequence of callosal transmission. Such mirror-image reversals may be involved in early reading disabilities and quite likely involve a "hyperactive" right hemisphere (Witelson, 1977a) or at least some variable cerebral organization of the hemispheres (Dalby & Gibson, 1981).

The fifth prediction of this model is that for problem solving that requires interhemispheric integration of information, the less lateralized subject will perform more efficiently. Hardyck (1977, p. 246) cites evidence that left-handers seem to be superior on paired-associate learning tasks, where one member of each pair is presented to each hemisphere. Goldberg and Costa (1981) suggest that the right hemisphere is more involved in learning new descriptive systems and in general in processing novel stimuli, and so it makes sense that a more actively functional right hemisphere will be superior during acquisition. This certainly holds for learning in children, and it may very well hold for the acquisition of a second language (Obler, Zatorre, Galloway, & Vaid, 1982, p. 52). Although the right hemisphere will be active during learning for the "early" bilingual (native and second languages learned before 6 years of age) and for the "late" bilingual (second language after age 6), eventual lateralized left representation for both languages will take place with the early bilinguals only. In some recent finger tapping experiments Sussman, Franklin, and Simon (1982) have demonstrated that early bilinguals have left dominance for both languages, whereas late bilinguals reveal left dominance for only the native language. Finally, left-handers with familial left-handedness will suffer linguistic impairment from either right or left lesions, but they will ameliorate faster and more completely than the strongly lateralized individual.

Other Views

Levy (1973) suggests that right hemisphere dominance represents an evolutionary retrogression (also see Levy, 1977). Although less lateralized dominance may have some advantages, it allows a greater degree of "overcrowding" of function and therefore does not favor the specialization for behaviors that call for fine-tuned sensorimotor control such as distal limb movements and speech. Further studies on all these issues can be found in Harnad, Doty, Goldstein, Jaynes, and Krauthamer (1977) and in Segalowitz and Gruber (1977), and Segalowitz (1983).

Another recent study on the nature of hemispheric specialization in man has appeared in Bradshaw and Nettleton (1981). These authors claim that strict dichotomies between hemispheric functions tend to break down and that the distinctions are more quantitative than qualitative. A rigid verbal/nonverbal separation into left versus right hemispheres is problematic. For example, sung digits yield an REA (right ear advantage) under dichotic conditions when the subject's attention is directed to linguistic content, but those same stimuli yield a LEA (left ear advantage) when the subjects listen for tonal quality. In general, the same stimuli may be geared to evoke left or right functions depending upon how the experimenter can manipulate the task (and therefore the cognitive set of the subject) at hand (Bever, 1980). The consequences of this for strict localization will be discussed at the end of this chapter.

The right hemisphere, however, seems more adept at less analytic acoustic mediation of intensity, timbre, environmental sounds, nonverbal vocalization, sonar signals, emotional tones and intonation patterns. There is little doubt that the right hemisphere contributes to suprasegmental production, despite the fact that there is prosodic disruption in patients with apraxia of speech (Kent & Rosenbek, 1982). The left motor disruption could override an intact prosodic mechanism in the right hemisphere. Note that severe left posterior damage causing a Wernicke's aphasia with neologistic jargon will not affect intonational patternings in the least (Brown, 1981). In sum, Bradshaw and Nettleton (1981, p. 54) attribute to the right hemisphere a "richly endowed lexicon, although it is likely to be a lexicon that is connotative, associative and imaginal rather than precise, denotative and phonological." The right hemisphere, however, does not appear to have the sophisticated neural circuitry for the unilateral coordination and control of a bilaterally innervated vocal apparatus. As mentioned above, the most salient characteristic of the left hemisphere is its capacity for the motor control of speech. Bradshaw and Nettleton (1981) provide a wealth of support for assigning a quantitative superiority for duration, temporal order, sequencing, and rhythm to the left hemisphere.

Analytic Linguistic Abilities

Unlike visual-spatial gestalt processing of the right hemisphere, linguistic processing is an analytical ability of the left (Bever, 1975). Articulatory control by the left hemisphere has been studied in depth by Sussman (e.g., Sussman & MacNeilage, 1975). The "Sussman paradigm" (Bradshaw & Nettleton, 1981, p. 61) involves pursuit auditory trackings where subjects are required to match a continuously varying pure tone (delivered to one or the other ear) with a second tone presented to the opposite ear by moving some muscle group. The muscle groups tested were the hand and the articulators (tongue, jaw, lips, and respiratory muscles). The movements were unidimensional and were transduced as input to the generator of the "cursor" tone. In the earlier studies, it appeared that the ability to track was better when the matching tone was controlled by an articulator and only when the cursor went to the right ear. The hand (right or left) showed no REA. This led Sussman to conclude that the effect was exclusively speech related. Later work (Sussman & Westbury, 1978), however, succeeded in demonstrating this REA effect for the right (not left) hand as well. This argues for a more general view of left-hemisphere function for control of all sequential, coordinated movement, limb as well as speech articulators.

Articulation as an Overlaid System

These findings better accord with the recent work of Kimura (1976), Mateer and Kimura (1977), and Mateer (1978b) that left hemisphere mechanisms are particularly well adapted not for symbolic function so much as for the transition from one ordered gesture to another. Several sources of data lead Kimura and Mateer to consider right-hand control and articulatory control as depending upon one system. First are the long observed relationships between handedness and cerebral dominance for speech. Second is the frequent occurrence of dominant hand movement during speech. Related to this is the disruptive effect that speaking has on finger tapping of the right hand but not of the left hand, the "verbal-manual interference paradigm" (Kinsbourne & Hicks, 1978; Sussman et al., 1982). The theory here is that if two tasks are programmed in contiguous cerebral zones, one will interfere with the other when simultaneously activated. That is, "...the degree of interference will be inversely related to the functional distance between the cerebral centers controlling each activity. " (Sussman et al., 1982, p. 127)

Mateer and Kimura (1977), have also observed that hand apraxias and the impairment of nonverbal oral movements quite often occur with fluent aphasia from left hemisphere pathology. The nonverbal oral movement sequences were: (1) bilateral lip retraction, lingual protrusion, upper teeth on lower lip; (2) lingual sweep across upper lip, clench teeth, clear throat; (3) lingual protrusion, lip protrusion, hum; (4) lingual lateralization, mandibular depression, lip protrusion; and (5) lingual protrusion, clench teeth, upper teeth on lower lip. As would be expected, anterior frontal aphasics had difficulty achieving the isolated, individual movement; fluent aphasics did not. The fluent aphasics, however, had significant problems when required to imitate sequences of three. This suggests that one system controls for the production of single discrete oral movements, and that system is more likely to be in the frontal speech area of the left hemisphere. Yet another system seems to program the transition from one discrete movement to another in a smooth and orderly way, and this system is more likely to be in posterior speech areas of the left hemisphere. It has been argued elsewhere (Buckingham, 1983) that disruptions of the anterior system result in apraxia of speech, while disruptions in the posterior system result in apraxia of language. In addition, fluent aphasics will often be able to repeat [ba] or [da] or [ga] individually but not the sequence [badaga].

Finally, Kimura (1976) cites evidence from the association of signing disorders in the deaf with left sided lesions. Although, as she states, some cases are more convincing than others, the picture that emerges is that manual signing systems in the deaf are disrupted subsequent to left hemisphere damage only. In some of the cases she reports on, however, precise and detailed clinicopathological descriptions were lacking, and in a few others the time of onset of deafness was not made clear. If it is the case that the deafness was not congenital or prelinguistic, then the manual system would likely be built upon an already existent vocal system. Nevertheless, one clear case reported by Kimura involved not only a congenitally deaf male subject, but one whose parents were also deaf. It was not until the subject was 8 years old—after he had begun to use manual signing—that he learned any vocal speech whatever. In addition, since he grew up in a deaf family, he was originally introduced to basic sign rather than finger spelling. After his stroke, this patient was administered extensive examinations. There was a transient weakness of the right arm and leg, which cleared. The detailed pathological report revealed that the lesion associated with the signing disturbance was located in the left angular and supramarginal gyri and involved the subjacent white matter as well. However, as it has been pointed out before (Buckingham, 1981, p. 283), counter evidence for Kimura's claims would be forthcoming if it could be shown that a fluent aphasic with left posterior lesions could learn a complex system of distal finger signing—especially finger spelling and other complexly coordinated finger movement patterns. Kimura's position would rule out the possibility of fine-tuned sequential finger manipulation in an unparalyzed left fluent aphasic.

In sum, we can agree with Bradshaw and Nettleton (1981) to the effect that "...the left hemisphere is closely involved in time dependent praxic movements of the limbs, hand, and fingers and the achievement of target oral configurations, even when unrelated to phoneme production, all in terms of a sequentially-ordered kinesthetic proprioceptive body schema." (p. 61)

Lexical Retrieval as an Analytical Process

Concerning the syntactic system (i.e., the mechanisms for the ordering of lexical units), next to nothing is known about its cerebral correlates except some very preliminary findings from Ojemann, which will be discussed under the heading of "Techniques for specifying where language is represented" elsewhere in this chapter. Providing *spoken* labels for items in the mental dictionary is a highly analytical as opposed to holistic or gestalt behavior and as mentioned above is practically an exclusive property of the dominant hemisphere. Again, as will be shown later, Ojemann has some significant findings concerning the cerebral localization patterns for naming. Recently the neurologist, D. Frank Benson (1979), has summarized a host of anomic disturbances resulting from brain damage and has outlined exhaustively the cerebral correlates for each. A set of recent psycholinguistic studies of labeling and lexical retrieval has shed light on the cognitive processes that must be involved in naming (Forster, 1978; Miller & Johnson-Laird, 1976), but typically these studies do not attempt to localize the functions physically in the brain. In addition, work has begun to focus on *why* brain damaged subjects have the access problems so often described but left unexplained (e.g., Caramazza, Berndt, & Brownell, 1982). Since, as we will later see, there is a good deal of lexical representation in the nondominant hemisphere, the truly analytic aspect of naming must be reserved for the provision of the label through motor speech production.

Perception/Comprehension

In contrast to production as a dominant left hemisphere analytic capacity, perception and comprehension is rather more elusive, since it seems to demand a great deal of analytic and holistic processing simultaneously. Essentially, though, there is abundant support for crediting the left hemisphere with mediating judgments of sequencing and temporal order (Bradshaw & Nettleton, 1981). Specifically, the left has a leading role in processing rapidly changing acoustic information (formant frequency shifts) which enables hearers to make fine (phonemically distinctive) discriminations among minimally distinct sounds. Strict, all or none, lateralization of these functions would be however, an unsound move, since most of our evidence on the acoustic properties of the left hemisphere comes from dichotic listening experiments, which rarely if ever show complete extinction of left ear effects. Those studies usually only show right ear advantages under neural competition and do not rule out the possibility that the right hemisphere *could*, under other circumstances, perform the function. Zaidel (1978) in his studies of split brain patients and left versus right hemidecorticates has found that for perception of CVC or CV syllables, the right is inferior to the left but only significantly so under "noise" conditions. These findings led Zaidel to suggest that the normal right hemisphere might not specialize in phonetic analysis of the auditory signal in noisy, everyday situations perhaps because it is generally not an efficient separator of signal from noise. Also he found that the right hemisphere confusions involving words that differed in one feature revealed that nasality was most likely to be confused, with voicing next. Whether a sound was an oral stop versus something else was next, while the easiest feature for the right to handle was place of articulation. Again we are left with a quantitative distinction between left and right. Consequently, even though the left is superior at processing rapid changes in the acoustic information containing the cues that allow for feature extraction, a good deal of the system is probably also represented in the right. Perhaps the neural thresholds are higher for activation there or perhaps activation is somehow inhibited during normal dominant hemisphere operation. One of the principal cautions for all-or-none assignment of comprehension strategies to the left is the ability of the right to subsume comprehension secondary to left damage—far outstripping the right's facility with vicarious production function.

One final analytic capacity in comprehension involves syntactic parsing. Little is known about this ability as it is related to the nervous system. Most of what we understand here has come from formal, mathematical linguistics (e.g., Berwick & Weinberg, 1982; Langendoen, 1975) or from work in artificial intelligence (e.g., Marcus, 1980). So, although we know in a metaphorical sense that the human must have a highly efficient, rapid processing, parsing algorithm (or program) which is somehow represented in the nervous system, we have no idea of the actual physiology or neuroanatomy except in the most indirect way. Work seems to be proceeding only on the logico-mathematical characterization of the algorithm. Nevertheless, from what we can understand of its metaphorical characterization at this point, the capacity must be an analytic one and accordingly must be largely a dominant hemisphere function (see Bever, 1980, pp. 196-202).

Right Hemisphere Linguistic Abilities

Non-Dominant Capacities, Callosal Function, and Split Brains

Witelson (1977b) in an "empirical and theoretical review" has surveyed early hemisphere specialization and interhemisphere plasticity. She concurs with previously mentioned studies that for language the left leads throughout life, but that during acquisition the right side is more involved than in later life. Nevertheless, what is learned there is likely to remain—albeit dormant due to left inhibition—throughout life. Her evidence comes from reported cases of childhood aphasia and recovery from it. The younger (even strongly lateralized with no FLH) are more likely to suffer mild aphasia from right-sided damage, not unlike the left or right-handed adult with FLH. These adults and the children tend to recover more rapidly and more extensively than do strongly lateralized adults.

Kinsbourne (1971, 1975) and Moscovitch (1976) have examined right hemisphere language in depth. From a series of laterality experiments, Moscovitch found that if a task calls for pictorial encoding of visually presented verbal material (alphabetic letters) the right is better. If, however, the task forces a linguistic analysis, then the right cannot handle the performance. Split brain patients, however, could perform the linguistic analysis with the right hemisphere. Moscovitch invoked the notion of callosal inhibition to account for these differences by proposing that language functions can be represented in the right hemispheres of normals but only functionally localized in the left. Then, when the left control over the right is weakened by commissurotomy, right-sided linguistic function may be more readily operable. Moscovitch later notes, however, that even in split-brain patients, if the task at hand is such that the callosally disconnected hemispheres compete with each other for some linguistic decision, the left will win out in the ultimate direction of the response. This suggests that the dominant hemisphere can gain its leading control over the nondominant side through extracallosal tracts, presumably through subcortical thalamic relay systems that cross hemispheres. Kinsbourne suggests (1975, p. 111) that the inhibitory effect could possibly take place at the level of the brain stem.

In his 1975 study, Kinsbourne agrees with most of the claims we have mentioned regarding language in the right hemisphere. He assigns an inhibitory role to the callosum but admits the possibility of some degree of right participation during language production and comprehension (clearly demonstrated by the regional cerebral blood flow studies to be discussed later). He further concurs that the nondominant hemisphere is for all intents and purposes mute in the adult normal and in the commissurotomized patient and that secondary to left lesions, right takeover of speech production is highly problematic for perhaps two reasons. The first could be that speech output programs are either absent or are the most weakly represented of right sided linguistic dormant capacities and must consequently be built up. The second suggestion of Kinsbourne is that the already existing, but unused or dormant, programs take time to gain access to the brain stem output facility, since they would have to displace competing neural connections from the left. The theory here is that synaptic connections not developed will be established only slowly, later on after left damage.

Zaidel (1978) has provided many insights into right hemisphere function for language in split-brain patients. He has improved the study of the split-brain patient dramatically by the use of a contact lens apparatus (pp. 231-234) and an occluding screen that allow for a prolonged lateralized visual presentation. Still, characteristically, the commissurotomized patients could not name verbally nor verbally describe the left field stimuli even though they could point to them promptly and correctly in response to auditory stimuli. Nevertheless, Zaidel has shown that, based largely on correct blind tactile retrieval with the left hand, and in response to the examiner's verbal description, subjects have a right hemisphere capacity for auditory language comprehension. Further probing revealed that the right hemisphere can comprehend verbs and action nominals. This accords with clinical data collected by the present author on left damaged aphasias with object noun word-retrieval deficits who can nevertheless provide responses such as "that's driving," "that's running," etc. for action pictures. Zaidel also demonstrated that on the auditory word discrimination subtest of the Boston Diagnostic Aphasia Examination, the disconnected right hemisphere showed the same pattern of deficits for specific semantic word categories as do fluent and nonfluent aphasics: letter name errors > number name errors > color name errors > geometric form name errors > object name errors. With aphasia, Goodglass, Klein, Carey, and Jones (1966) found that objects were one of the most difficult categories to name but one of the easiest to comprehend auditorily.

All this lexical comprehension on the part of the right hemisphere, which at the same time performs poorly on phonemic discrimination, suggests that the perception of meaningful words is less lateralized than the perception of single phonemes.[1] Recently, Zaidel and Peters (1981) have shown that a disconnected right hemisphere can even "evoke the sound image" of a word. Proof of this was that the subjects could match pictures flashed to the right hemisphere of objects whose labels were homophones, and they could match printed words that rhymed. This is quite significant since the subjects were not able to name either the pictured objects or the printed words when presented to the right hemisphere. There is no proof however that the right hemisphere can perform grapheme-phoneme conversions to evoke sound images of words from their orthographic representation. Zaidel and Peters showed that the right side cannot match a spelled word with a picture that has a rhyming name. Neither could they match two orthographically dissimilar words that nevertheless rhymed. The authors concluded that the nondominant hemisphere reads ideographically by decoding words as wholes without phonetic recoding or grapheme-to- phoneme mapping.

These findings offer support for characterizing right hemisphere reading comprehension as an analysis-by-synthesis process rather than an analysis-by-analysis. So-called "top-down" processing would allow comprehension to bypass initial surface grapheme-phoneme conversion and allow the subject to generate hypotheses for matching the input directly. "Bottom-up," or analysis-by-analysis, would force the right hemisphere to initially grapple with grapheme-phoneme translation in reading, which it apparently cannot do.

The right hemisphere is definitely inferior in syntactic processing. Although Zaidel (1978) claims it has "substantial syntactic competence" (p. 253), on the Carrow test of syntax it attained a mental age of 5;0. However, as Zaidel later notes, the right hemisphere fails to analyze correctly longer sentences where order is crucial and where context is not helpful. There is also much literature (e.g., Dennis & Whitaker, 1976, 1977) that right hemidecorticates perform substantially better than do left hemidecorticates on syntactic tasks. In addition, Kohn (1980) has suggested that the integrity of some very early processing in the diseased left cerebrum could actually contribute to and support eventual right sided acquisition of language. In fact, early partial left function may even be a precondition for intact right hemisphere syntactic comprehension. For example, Kohn (1980) provided evidence that early onset of seizure activity in the left has a more deleterious effect on ultimate right hemisphere linguistic proficiency, than do later seizure onsets. Not only does this finding demonstrate early left involvement for ultimate right hemisphere language, but it also suggests that the seizure activity itself—as opposed to the actual left tissue destruction—can disrupt language acquisition in the early years. The implication here is that the earlier in life the child's seizures begin, the worse off he will ultimately be linguistically.

Even though the right hemisphere cannot provide spoken labels for lexical items, Zaidel (1978, p. 237) claims that it, ". . . is at least able to construct or synthesize the meaning of the more general supraordinate from exemplars or co-hyponyms, i.e., instances of it." That is, the presence of an object in the right hemisphere could allow the function of its semantic and pragmatic spheres, i.e., semantic activation. A recent study addresses this active semantic spread in an interesting way.

Sidtis, Volpe, Holtzmann, Wilson, and Gazzaniga (1981) report on an extremely interesting case of interhemispheric cognitive interaction after a staggered callosal section that provides evidence for transfer of semantic activation. The patient was a 26-year-old right-handed male with intractable epilepsy. The initial section involved the posterior half of the callosum including the splenium so that the posterior cortical sensory areas were split. Tactile, visual, and auditory stimuli presented to the right hemisphere exclusively could not be named. Nonverbal responses indicated perfect appreciation by the right of what the stimuli were. Stimuli presented to the left were named correctly. As the 10-week interoperative period progressed, the patient gradually increased his ability to express in articulated language cognitive, semantic and memorial aspects of objects presented to the right hemisphere. By the 7th week, the subject had developed a self-generated inferential strategy based upon his description of a mental image for the object or printed word shown to his left visual field. Initially, though, the spoken label was not forthcoming, but after self-elicited verbal descriptions the correct label would finally be retrieved. These initial descriptions the patient would provide were rarely of the stimulus itself but were more like functional contexts or some type of associate. For instance, when the word "Knight" was flashed to the left field (right hemisphere), the patient's verbalization went as follows. "I have a picture in mind but I can't say it...Two fighters in a ring...Ancient wearing uniforms and helmets...on horses...trying to knock each other off...Knights?" (p. 345). This study demonstrates that the anterior portion of the callosum can play a role in the interaction between cognitive rather than sensory systems of the two hemispheres. There was no direct sensory transfer to the spoken label in the left. Rather, the verbalized inferential process reflected an active search through an aroused semantic and memorial structure for the identity of the spoken label of the original stimulus. Actually, Sidtis et al., (1981) at the end of the article, appear to forget that the subject knows the identity of the object in the right hemisphere, rather it is the label he doesn't have. They write, "The inferential process appeared to reflect a search through an already activated semantic field for the identity of the original stimulus" (p. 346). If the patient can identify nonverbally, then it is not the identity he is really searching for, but again it is the articulated label. Finally, after the second operation completing the commissurotomy, the patient could no longer transfer semantic, memorial information from right to left and was thus left completely mute when required to name stimuli presented to the nondominant hemisphere.

Clearly, the next question that must be addressed is what would result from an initial section that involved the anterior corpus callosum. One could then test to see whether intact posterior interhemispheric connections could facilitate spoken labels for objects presented to the right hemisphere better than do anterior connections. If the theory is that the left angular gyrus or other dominant hemisphere posterior structures are critically involved in the storage and manipulation of phonologically coded labels for production, then the prediction would be that the patient with a sectioned anterior callosum would name better since the interhemispheric posterior sensory connections would be intact.

Pragmatics and Affect

Aside from the numerous assessments of what the right hemisphere could do under this or that condition in terms of analytical linguistic processing, there has been a marked increase in recent years in the study of nondominant hemisphere mediation of pragmatic, extralinguistic functions—functions that appear to be more gestalt-like than labeling or phonemic discrimination. In general, these studies have illustrated unique right hemisphere effects in the mediation of humor and narration (Gardner, Ling, Flamm, & Silverman, 1975; Wapner, Hamby, & Gardner, 1981), metaphor (Gardner & Winner, 1979; Winner & Gardner, 1977), antonyms (Gardner, Silverman, Wapner, & Zurif, 1978), connotation (Gardner & Denes, 1973), and emotional affect (Heilman, Scholes, & Watson, 1975; Ross & Mesulam, 1979).

The essential finding of Wapner et al. (1981) was that right hemisphere patients were significantly poorer than normals, the aging, and aphasics (left damage) in appreciating narrative materials (inferring moral of a story, setting, major plot lines, etc.). In summarizing stories, right hemisphere damaged subjects provided an abundance of embellishments that were unnecessary or extraneous. Often, the extraneous commentary would yield to confabulation (see also Mercer, Wapner, Gardner, & Benson, 1977). These subjects could not make inferences about emotionality in order to appreciate a specific story or scene. Unlike the other control groups, the right damaged subject did not react quizzically to inappropriate—even bizarre—elements injected into the narratives. They did not jolt at, laugh at, or challenge these "noncanonical" story elements. Rather, they accepted them and would provide some justification. Moreover, the subjects performed poorly in tests of humor in that they could not appreciate the fit of a punchline to the body of a joke. Instead of selecting a correct punchline for some joke, they would typically select some non sequitur ending—rather than tailor it to the body. Wapner, et al. noted that the patients actually seemed to be more drawn to the bizzare anomaly of the non sequitur. They do not appear to distinguish between the joke or cartoon world and the real world. These findings relate to those of Heilman, Scholes, and Watson (1975), who showed that subjects with right temporoparietal lesions (as opposed to fluent aphasics with analogous left lesions) could not match tone of voice (angry, happy, sad, indifferent) with line drawings of faces corresponding to each of these moods. The neural basis of affective behavior has been recently studied in patients with localized cortical excisions (Kolb & Taylor, 1981). Again, the right hemisphere is shown to be crucially involved in appreciating emotionality in ways that the left is not.

Appreciation of metaphor seems also to be disrupted secondary to nondominant hemisphere disease. The subjects here have great difficulty in connecting a figure of speech with a situation that would call for its use. Unlike normals, or even aphasics, right damaged subjects will choose literal depictions for metaphors as often as not. For example, for the predicative metaphor "John is a snake in the grass," there could be a picture of boy, ostensibly John, doing something crafty or underhanded and another picture with a snake, say with the head of a man, slithering around in the grass. The damaged right hemisphere will be insensitive to how each picture maps onto the sentence. This situation is not unlike that of the youngster of 6 or 7 years who quite often will select literal interpretations of metaphors (Gardner & Winner, 1979).

From this brief outline it should be obvious that although the nondominant hemisphere does not perform to the level of the dominant hemisphere in analytical linguistic processing of phonological and syntactic strings or in articulatory output processing, it plays a crucial role in all that surrounds the strictly logical/analytic aspects of the language. Without it, much of the message will not be comprehended.

Let us turn back to some of the more analytical language processes at this point and to some of the recent technology that allows us to more closely pinpoint where in the left hemisphere these processes are likely to be mediated.

Techniques for Specifying Where Language is Represented

CT and PECT Scanning

Naeser and her associates (Naeser & Hayward, 1978; Naeser, Alexander, Helm-Estabrooks, Levine, Laughlin, & Geschwind, 1982; Naeser, Hayward, Laughlin, Becker, Jernigan, & Zatz, 1981a; Naesar, Hayward, Laughlin, & Zatz, 1981b) have been carrying out a series of studies aimed at correlating computerized axial tomography (CAT or CT) scanning with aphasia producing lesions as well as with aphasic symptomatology as measured by the *Boston Diagnostic Aphasia Examination* (Goodglass & Kaplan, 1972). This technique involves the scanning of the head in successive layers ($\pm$ 8-10 mm thick slices) by a narrow beam of X-rays, and a digital printout for lesion perimeters. The display appears on which brightness correlates with the extent of tissue damage. CT scans are best used in stabilized patients beyond the acute period (up to 8 weeks post-trauma). Kertesz (1979) points out that the "...effects of edema or other pathochemical or histological changes in the acute stage may not be evident on the scans." (p. 185) He also notes that initially negative CT scans may change to positive within 48 hours during the acute period. The radionuclide (RN) scan, however, shows a maximum uptake in the period of 7 to 21 days post-onset, but as Kertesz points out, the RN brain scans should not be employed beyond 6 to 8 weeks post-infarct for reliable localization.

The CT scans in Naeser and Hayward (1978) were sliced at angles of from 15° to 25° to a generally accepted anatomical atlas lateral reference line (referred to as the canthomeatal line). The outstanding feature of the CT scan is that it provides clear indications of the depth and direction or extent of the lesions. Crucial slices for locating lesions causing aphasia have been labeled by Naeser et al. (1981a) as B (showing Broca's area 44), B/W (showing area 44 and Wernicke's area 22), W (showing Wernicke's area), SM (showing supramarginal 40 and angular 39 gyri) and SM+1 (one cm above SM showing both gyri 40 and 39 again). Slices such as these show many subcortical regions as well. Slice W is a very important section in terms of significant correlations between the relative amount of left hemisphere tissue damage and severity of aphasia. Naeser et al. (1981b, p. 159) found that 28 of their 30 patients had focal lesions somewhere on this slice. Figure 8-1 shows the relations of cortical language areas, the ventricular system (used as reference points to locate the language areas) and the 20° slices from the lateral plane. Figure 8-2 presents cross-sectional views of these slices showing the spatial relationships of the language areas to the ventricles.

Subcortical structures such as the internal capsule and the putamen of the basal ganglia are best shown at slice B/W. Recently, Naeser et al. (1982) described three different types of subcortical aphasia, all involving capsular/putaminal lesions with distinct extensions that give rise to the different syndromes. Lesions with anterior-superior white fiber extensions produced a Broca-like aphasia. Lesions extending from the basal ganglia in a posterior direction gave rise to a fluent Wernicke-type aphasia but, quite unlike fluent aphasics, with marked hemiplegia. The intact anatomical pathways for the fluent speech in these patients are not well understood, since there should nevertheless have been some dysarthria with speech. The authors leave the answer for future experimentation. The third subcortical syndrome was global-like, where the capsular/putaminal damage extended both anteriorly and posteriorly.

The noninvasive methodology of the CT scan (although Kertesz, 1979, p. 169 notes that in some cases contrast enhancement can increase the diagnostic yield, hence the need for injection of contrast material) has significantly improved our ability to locate and measure aphasia producing lesions, although as John Hughlings Jackson (1874) (cited in Taylor,

FIGURE 8-1
Relationship of cortical language areas to ventricular system (lateral view) with slices marked at 20° to the canthomeatal line, similar to CT scan slices. Numbers refer to Broadmann areas as follows: 44, Broca's area; 22, Wernicke's area; 40, supramarginal gyrus; 39, angular gyrus. (From Naeser & Hayward, 1978, p. 546)

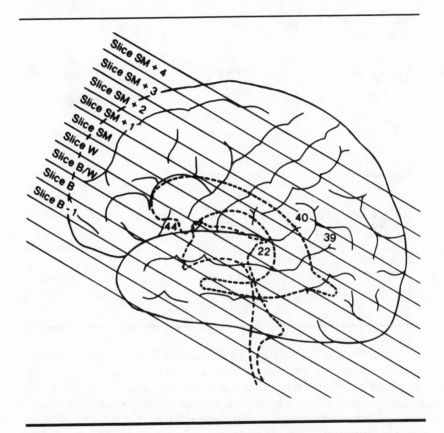

1931) wrote, "To locate the damage which destroys speech and to locate speech are two different things" (p. 130). There is another drawback with CT studies that has been emphasized by Kertesz (1979, p. 185). As noted above, the CT scan is best for use in chronic stages, while the RN scan is best for use in acute stages. In chronic stages, however, one syndrome may very likely have evolved into another syndrome (e.g., Broca's to an anomia or a Wernicke's aphasia to a conduction aphasia, Kertesz, 1979, pp. 263-282) without any change in tissue destruction. This means that

FIGURE 8-2
Relationship of cortical language areas to parts of ventricular sytem (cross-sectional view) with brain slices cut at 20° to the canthomeatal line, similar to CT scan slices. (From Naeser & Hayward, 1978, p. 546)

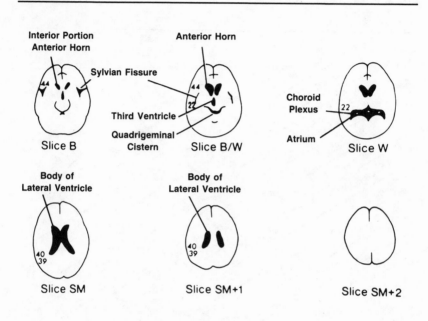

it is quite possible for patient X to be classified as a conduction aphasic at, for example, 1½ years post-onset, while that very same patient may have been a typical Wernicke's aphasic one year before. In addition, CT scanning is not likely to pinpoint undamaged but abnormally functioning tissue (in terms of abnormal glucose metabolism or regional cerebral blood flow) in aphasics. If the abnormality gradually ameliorates, functional recovery could take place with no demonstrable change in the lesion as measured with the CT scan. CT studies, therefore, should be supplemented by metabolic evaluation whenever feasible.

Cerebral metabolic activity for glucose can be measured in patients with aphasia. Metter, Wasterlain, Kuhl, Hanson, and Phelps (1981) studied five patients with chronic aphasia by using PECT (positron emission computer tomography) scanning. With an intravenous injection of a radioisotopic label, glucose distribution and absorption can be quantified by positron emission, and areas of diminished activity can be mapped. Since metabolic rate correlates with neuronal firing rates and with basic brain function, the PECT process provides yet another way in which to localize aphasia producing lesions. The findings of Metter et al. (1981) correlate with other localizing techniques. In addition, the PECT scanner will show accompanying metabolic suppression in areas that turn up normal on the CT scan. For instance, one of Metter et al.'s patients demonstrated thalamic aphasia, but the CT scan revealed lesions in the basal ganglia (left caudate and internal capsule) and a small lesion in the right caudate. The cortex appeared normal. On the other hand, the PECT revealed a 24% decrease of glucose metabolic activity in the left thalamus with major depression in the left striatum. Also, there was a 15% decrease in the left middle and inferior temporal gyri. In general, this method can localize the reduced cerebral metabolism in the noninfarcted tissue as well as point to the more widespread functional depression secondary to cerebral insult. Metter et al. (1981) have also demonstrated that left posterior cortical lesions will affect thalamic metabolic rate on the left. Since the posterior cortex and the thalamus have different vascular supply systems, the thalamocortical metabolic interaction supports theories that postulate thalamocortical language connections (Ojemann, 1976). Metter, et al. also point out that their findings of depressed metabolic rate in nondamaged regions accord well with findings from regional cerebral blood flow (rCBF) studies that show a generally reduced flow throughout the involved hemisphere, although not all the tissue is destroyed.

Regional Cerebral Blood Flow

Soh, Larsen, Skinhøj, and Lassen (1978) studied rCBF in aphasia. Blood flow distribution was measured using intracarotid injection of xenon 133 and a 254-detector gamma camera system. It had previously been shown (Lassen, Ingvar, & Skinhøj, 1978) that speaking essentially activates three centers in *both* hemispheres: the motor articulator area on the rolandic strip (sensory and motor), the auditory cortex, and the supplementary motor zones in the upper-mesial part of the frontal lobe low down in Broadmann area 6. In nonfluent aphasics Soh et al. (1978) observed flow abnormalities in the lower section of the rolandic area. A few of the patients classified as motor aphasics did not reveal complete flow disturbances in Broca's area, but there were always flow disruptions in the motor regions. Soh et al. do not indicate the amount of apraxia or agrammatism their motor aphasics had. Perhaps the less apraxic subjects had less specific involvement of area 44. While there was no significant increase in flow to the articulator strip along the rolandic strip, there was an increase in the upper posterior temporal region for 3 of the 4 patients. Also, some motor aphasics showed an increase in blood flow in other frontal areas and in the supplementary motor region when speaking (or attempting to do so). These studies provide striking support for Penfield and Roberts' (1959) inclusion of this zone in the overall cortical language system. As would be expected, sensory aphasics showed very little increase in flow into Wernicke's area.

As with the positron emission method, rCBF allows the study of dysfunction as separate from actual tissue destruction, unlike RN and CT scans; the latter techniques only reveal tissue destruction. The former techniques, therefore, should be used in investigating vicarious takeover and recovery phenomena. In addition, one can gain an appreciation of the bilateral rCBF activation during speaking and listening, but as Wood (1980) writes, "When feasible, one desirable strategy is to deconfound the cognitive from the sensory and motor components of a task, by holding sensory and motor components constant and varying only the instruction" (p. 5). This, of course, is advice well taken, since Bever (1980 and elsewhere) has shown that controlling stimuli while changing instructions can evoke distinct hemisphere effects. Therefore, what may underlie the shifts Bever obtained could be distinct blood flow and metabolic rate garnered for the distinct cognitive tasks—analytic or holistic. Wood, Taylor, Penny, and Stump (1980) have observed that semantic classification (linguistic) versus recognition memory (nonlinguistic) tasks, holding stimuli constant, will induce different rCBF patterns. The semantically sensitive task produced more left hemisphere cortical activation; localization within the left cortex, however, could not be further delineated.

There is one additional finding that has stemmed from rCBF investigations—the "hyperfrontal" response (Lassen et al., 1978, p. 63; Wood, 1980, p. 2). In normals, there exists a hyperfrontality of rCBF in many resting states and in certain conditions of psychological activation. These large frontal lobe flows, according to Risberg (1980) reflect the adoption of set and attention to task and surroundings. Actually, similar functional roles for the frontal lobe have been proposed earlier (see Damasio, 1979). Wood, Stump, McKeehan, Sheldon, and Proctor (1980) tested rCBF in stutterers on and off haloperidol medication. The two subjects improved substantially with the drug, thus permitting testing under stuttering versus "essentially" no stuttering conditions for each subject. When reading aloud in the no stuttering condition, rCBF's showed a left hemisphere advantage. While reading aloud without the haloperidol effects, i.e., with stuttering, the subjects showed higher Broca's area flow in the right hemisphere. These findings support the view that stutterers likely suffer from inadequate left cerebral dominance for speech production. Pinsky and McAdam

(1980) working with EEG and dichotic measures, however, demonstrated consistent patterns of cerebral laterality and left dominance for speech in five adult stutterers. These conflicting reports mean that more work remains to be done on dominance in stutterers.

Electrophysiology

Turning away from X-ray scanning, metabolic, and blood flow studies, we will now treat electrophysiological work, including electroencephalography, electrocorticography, and electrocortical stimulation.

Evidence of localized neuroelectric correlates of language functions have long been studied via scalp recorded evoked potentials. The complete readout of all ongoing and continuous electrical activity produced by the brain is referred to as the electroencephalogram (EEG), while "time locked" portions of the EEG that coincide with onsets of specific stimulus events are referred to as event-related potentials (ERP). ERPs generally fluctuate as a function of intensity, duration, sensory modality, meaning, and cognitive task. The recent group of studies from scalp recordings in Molfese (1980a) provide additional information on general auditory versus speech perception, auditory versus visual perception of linguistic versus nonlinguistic information as well as syntactic and semantic processing. For example, Molfese (1980b) has found a temporal detection mechanism in the *right* hemisphere that is involved in the perception of voice onset time (VOT). This right sided effect for temporal sensitivity is observed for nonlinguistic tonal onsets as well, and the functional asymmetry exists from 2 months of age to adulthood. Molfese further suggests that there is likely to be a differential distribution of various acoustic processors across both hemispheres rather than a special left hemisphere speech processor per se. He observes that there is a left hemisphere specific mechanism sensitive to F_2 transition cues, which are the cues for discriminating place of articulation. This contradicts Zaidel (1978) (see above), who found place of articulation easiest for the *right* hemisphere to discriminate.

Other researchers, such as Thatcher (1977), have shown left-right asymmetries with ERPs during semantic information processing, but not during nonlinguistic processing of similar stimuli. However, as Thatcher (1977) admits, "The precise meaning or significance of the asymmetries in terms of language processing is currently unknown" (p. 446). One reason for this puzzlement over the "meaning" of the pattern asymmetry is perhaps that no one has really developed formal pattern recognition algorithms for the tremendously complex total brain responses to human cognitive powers (see Wood, 1980, p. 5).

A more confined and problematic offshoot of electroencephalography is electrocorticography (ECOG), where the cortex is exposed and electrodes are placed directly on the cortical surface. The advantages are direct cortical recording as opposed to scalp recording. The disadvantages are the obvious ones; the subjects must be undergoing surgical operation, and *something* (usually epileptogenic lesions) must be abnormal in their nervous system. Subjects in these experiments will, of necessity, be fewer in number.

Fried, Ojemann, and Fetz (1981) studied six adult patients undergoing left-hemisphere craniotomy for resection of epileptic foci. Amytal testing had previously demonstrated left dominance for language. After the epileptocenters were identified, 1 mm silver ball electrodes were placed at eight to ten randomly selected sites—not in epileptic zones—in the cortex around the Sylvian fissure (four patients) or in the frontal lobe (two patients). During recording, the subjects were given two tasks. The linguistic task involved so-called "silent naming" where the patient had to state aloud whether labels for the pictured objects rhymed or not. On the nonlinguistic task the subjects were simply to indicate aloud whether or not two lines had the same orientation. As with EEG, cognitive functioning must be ferreted out from sensorimotor "noise" in brain activity. This required a series of three slide presentations. The first slide in each trial was the same for *both* tasks: a picture of a common object with a line superimposed across it. The second slide in each trial differed for both tasks. In the name match condition, the second slide was a picture of an object (whose label either rhymed with the first object or not) without a line. For the nonlinguistic line match condition, the second slide had only a line (whose orientation either matched the first line or not) without an object. The patients were instructed to wait for the presentation of the third slide (a uniform blue). This "cue" slide was the *same* for both operations, and thus the cuing stimulus was held constant while the cognitive processing it elicited was distinct. Furthermore, the patients were instructed to delay their vocal responses upon presentation of the cue in order to avoid components related to overt motor speech. One must not confuse a motor evoked potential with cortical motor activity directly locked to the onset of muscular contraction. For this reason, most EEG studies of evoked potentials in speech simultaneously record electromyographic (EMG) activity at the periphery. ECOG recording began with presentation of the cue.

Two important findings concerning the event related potentials were presented, which clearly demonstrate language specific activity. In frontal language cortex, slow potentials were observed in motor and premotor sites only when the cue was linked to linguistic processing. The authors claimed that the potential shift (680 msec before vocal onset) may have been related to some prior stage of subvocalization, inner speech, or effector readiness. Although the authors did not routinely measure EMG activity, they cited another study which showed that EMG activity will begin at 300 msec before vocal onset. Therefore, a shift at 680 msec could likely be dissociated from direct motor firing. Fried, et al. nevertheless caution that its onset in relation to speech muscle activity is uncertain. Nor could they exclude interactions with cerebral respiratory potentials. They further noted that the potential shifts begin approximately 100 msec earlier in premotor cortex, suggesting that premotor areas have some sort of preparatory function for speech before the primary motor cortex becomes involved.

The other crucial result was an ERP change exclusively locked to the silent naming task in posterior language sites, which involved a flattening of the ECOG waveform with suppression of rhythmic activity (desynchronization). This activity lasted approximately 800 msec. Interestingly enough, reading silently in rCBF studies also shows activity in Broca's area and the supplementary motor zones as well as in the posterior angular gyrus region (Lassen et al., 1978, p. 69).

These coordinated ERP shifts in frontal and posterior cortex specific to a language task appear to occur in parallel. Their occurrence argues for focal cortical activation at distinct sites rather than for general cortical mass activation. Fried et al. suggest that a subcortical thalamic mechanism could be at work in "alerting" variously located cortical regions for linguistic processing. On this view, activation is not seen as spreading across the cortical mantle but rather as spreading upward through thalamocortical tracts. Recall the metabolic evidence for cortical-thalamic connections that was provided by Metter et al. (1981, p. 182).

The Fried et al. (1981) study was actually part of a much larger enterprise on the electrophysiological localization of language in the brain being carried out by Ojemann and his associates in the Department of Neurological Surgery at the University of Washington (see Calvin & Ojemann, 1980). In fact, the sites chosen for the ECOG study by Fried et al. were subsequently shown to be functional for naming by Ojemann's electrical stimulation mapping. However, note that the so-called silent naming task in the Fried et al. study was precisely what Zaidel and Peters (1981) had shown a right hemisphere to be capable of carrying out. And yet, that right hemisphere could not provide a spoken label. Ojemann's studies of naming require the subjects to produce the spoken name, but since Fried et al.'s subjects had only to match pictures with homophonous labels it is doubtful that the two functions should be interpreted as the same.

Reviewing some of the studies by Ojemann (e.g., Ojemann, 1978; Ojemann & Mateer, 1979; Ojemann & Whitaker, 1978a, b; Whitaker & Ojemann, 1977), we find that the patients in these experiments were going through preparatory cortical language mapping prior to resection of medically intractable epileptic lesions; all were under local anesthesia. The great majority of the cases studied had anterior temporal lobe foci. As a consequence, the surgical exposure usually subtended the region of the peri-sylvian cortex. Practically all experimentation was performed on left hemispheres, but there were also right hemisphere operations, allowing Ojemann to collect comparative data from the nondominant side. A few of the right hemisphere patients were right dominant, thus permitting further comparisons. Ojemann and his co-workers regularly tested initially for language dominance by sodium amobarbital injection (Wada test). Regions within the perisylvian left language cortex usually included the lateral temporal lobe, the inferior posterior frontal lobe, and the inferior parietal lobe. Threshold currents for after-discharges were initially established for each site, so that all stimulations could be calibrated at a single current level, just below the lowest of these thresholds. In the experiments, 60 Hz trains were used with 2½ msec total duration biphasic square wave pulses. A Nuclear Chicago constant current stimulator was used, and current was delivered through bipolar silver ball electrodes, 5 mm apart (e.g., Ojemann, 1978, p. 333). Some experiments involved verbal labeling only (Ojemann & Whitaker, 1978a; Whitaker & Ojemann, 1977), while others tested short-term verbal memory in language (Ojemann, 1978), or a combination of memory, syntax, phoneme identification, and single versus sequential orofacial movements (Ojemann & Mateer, 1979).

The principal finding reported in Whitaker and Ojemann (1977) is that there were sites where each time there was a stimulation the patient's naming ability was disrupted. As little as ½ cm or less distance from these sites, stimulation would evoke no such deficit. The discrete nature of the effect is one of the most astonishing aspects of these studies. Furthermore, the outer limits of sites sensitive to naming indicated that the linguistic system is probably represented in a somewhat larger than expected area of the left lateral cortex—including, but extending beyond the classical language centers. Also, these findings illustrate that different cortical zones can mediate the same mental function. Unlike what one sees with the non-contiguous parallel processing in rCBF studies, the regions observed in the Ojemann investigations are infinitely more discrete. The different nature of the techniques involved seems to ensure this; rCBF is a more gross measure than minute electrocortical stimulation.

This discreteness is found as well in the bilingual brain. Ojemann and Whitaker (1978b) have shown that bilinguals will have certain sites where

FIGURE 8-3
Variability in naming changes within primary language zone in eight left-brain-dominant patients. After aligning these cases by the motor strip and the end of the Sylvian fissure, naming error data were determined for eight cortical zones which are indicated by dashed lines; each zone is represented by a circle graph. The number beside each circle graph indicates the number of patients with language mapping at one or more sites within that particular cortical zone. Each circle graph shows the number of patients with 100% errors (solid filled-in portion) and partial errors (vertical bar portion) in that particular cortical zone. (From Ojemann & Whitaker, 1978a, p. 249)

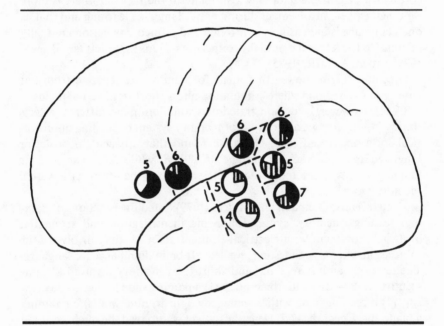

stimulation will block naming 100% of the time in only one of the languages. In the same brain, there will be sites where the opposite holds. Even more importantly, stimulation at these 100% sites for naming disruption in language X, will not hinder naming in language Y. In all these cases, however, there are sites where stimulation at times does, and at other times does not, disturb naming. These variable sites may indeed be those which assume an increased functional role subsequent to damage of the 100% sites, and accordingly they should be spared from surgical excision.

Other findings from stimulation mapping of the cortical naming system have given us further insights into right hemisphere function. For example, Ojemann and Whitaker (1978a) showed an even larger region for naming in the right hemisphere of right dominant subjects, demonstrating that the right hemisphere, when it is dominant for language, is more diffusely organized. Furthermore, in bilinguals (whose second language was learned later in life, i.e., not a totally balanced bilingual), the second, or less controlled, language has naming sites scattered over a larger region of left cortex. This suggests that there is more cortical involvement for less controlled language behaviors, and it supports the general notion that as behaviors are refined and come under more skillful and controlled coordination less cortex is utilized. The data may also relate to the fact that there is more right hemisphere involvement during native language learning and that as one's language is increasingly controlled and refined, mediation gradually migrates to the left and eventually to specific regions in the left (see Brown, 1978; Brown & Jaffe, 1975).

Ojemann (1978) showed that areas for naming are separate from but contiguous to regions where stimulation alters short-term verbal memory (STVM). However, he demonstrated that stimulation has different effects during input, storage, and output of memory system depending upon cortical location. Specifically, Ojemann found that adjacent to posterior language areas are sites for storage of STVM, while sites near anterior language areas seem to mediate retrieval from the short-term verbal memory store.

More recently, Ojemann and Mateer (1979) tested the functions of naming, reading, memory, syntax, phoneme identification and sequential orofacial movement with electrical stimulation. The study involved four subjects, in whom Wada testing revealed left brain dominance for language. The tests of naming, reading, and short-term memory involved 25 consecutive trials—each with three sides: (1) a naming slide (object to be named); (2) a reading slide with a sentence (eight to nine words) containing a blank space near the end. Here, the patient was to read the sentence aloud and generate the specific syntactic forms needed for completion; and (3) a slide with the instruction "recall," which cued the patient to say aloud (again) the label of the object previously pictured on slide 1. Stimulation was applied for the duration of one or another slide. No one site was stimulated consecutively, but three samples of stimulation at each site were obtained during each test condition.

Orofacial movements were elicited by slides of gestures, such as mouth opening or tongue lateralization, that the patient had to mimic (also see Mateer, 1978; Mateer & Kimura, 1977). Phoneme identification was tested at the sites identified with orofacial movements. Here, patients were to report aloud which of six possible oral stops (/p, b, t, d, k, g/) they perceived in the tape recorded carrier context /a__ma/.

The significant result was that four cortical functional systems clustered around the Sylvian fissure region. The first system appears to be the final cortical motor pathway for speech. At most sites in the premotor or motor region, stimulation impaired all facial movement and in general arrested all speech. A second system emerged, where stimulation hindered sequences of facial movements but not the production of single isolated facial movements. Very importantly, it was shown that at nine of the ten sites where sequencing was disrupted, phoneme perception was disrupted as well. What we see in this system are sites *common to* these crucial motor and sensory (acoustic) functions required for human language—but probably involved in nonlinguistic functioning as well. The sites in system 2 are in inferior frontal, superior temporal and parietal peri-sylvian cortex. Their existence could be used as support for either a motor theory of speech perception, as the authors claim, or it could justify an auditory theory of speech production (Ladefoged, DeClerk, Lindau, & Papcun, 1972). Ojemann and Mateer (1979) do not mention this second alternative. It is important to note that in system 2, we have different functions mediated at the same discrete sites. Coupled with the earlier studies of naming, we can claim that one function can be mediated in different circumscribed sites and also that different functions may be performed at the same site.[2]

Yet another system involves sets of sites where stimulation evokes disturbances in naming, reading, and syntax (specialized language faculties). The outer system involves focal sites that, when stimulated, give rise to disruptions in short-term memory. As noted above, parietal and temporal lobe zones appear to mediate storage into memory, while frontal sites are more involved with retrieval from memory for output processing. The overall short-term memory system, therefore, surrounds the specialized language system.

In summary, the peri-sylvian organization is composed of an output system, an auditory-motor system, a specialized language function system, and a short-term verbal memory system.

There are several conclusions to be drawn from the work of Ojemann and his associates. The first is that the primary zone for language is the peri-sylvian region of the dominant hemisphere in the distribution of the left middle cerebral artery. The various systems interlock in an anatomically feasible manner. The discreteness of the sites is indicative of focal cortical operation; the distribution of sites mediating the same function supports the notion of co-temporal parallel processing. Moreover, the fact that structures at one site can mediate different functions at different times argues that the human brain is like a general purpose computer. Cortical sites related to a particular function have a mosaic or macrocolumnar pattern. In fact, Ojemann's findings provide support for theories of columnar organizational units that form functionally distributed systems in the cortex (Mountcastle, 1978). Finally, the simultaneous parallel processing indicates that some subcortical mechanism could in a sense be alerting or directing the cortical zones. Ojemann suggests that the mechanism is most likely thalamic—more specifically, the left ventrolateral nucleus. This, again, was suggested in the Fried et al. study. Moreover, there is a wealth of information on the thalamo-cortical connections and on left thalamic language function (Ojemann, 1976).

Nevertheless, when one takes a close look site by site and subject by subject, one sees a great deal of variability, which Ojemann claims may be due to the gross morphology in the gyral patterns at the end of the Sylvian fissure of the dominant hemisphere or possibly due to the architectonic variability there. There are clear hemispheric asymmetries of cortical volume, and it is worth attending to some recent work on cortical cytoarchitecture and size as it relates to the linguistic system.

Cortical Asymmetries/Architectonic Variations

There is a rich history of cerebral measurement from ancient time (Clark & O'Malley, 1968) through the work of the phrenologists (Marshall, 1982; Young, 1970) up to the present. The influence of Geschwind is recognized in the study of cortical asymmetries (Geschwind & Levitsky, 1968) as well as in modern work on cerebral connectionism (Geschwind, 1965). Geschwind and Levitskty (1968) demonstrated that in 65% of their sample, the left plenum temporale (cortex behind Heschl's gyrus) was larger on the left. The collection they used was comprised of 100 adult human brains at postmortem, none of which had any significant abnormality. This study revealed also that the plenum was larger on the right side in only 11% of the brains. In another study, Sanides (1975) showed that there has been an increase in the size of the temporal lobe within the evolution of primates from prosimian to man. The expansion has been in auditory temporal integration cortex. According to Sanides, the evolutionary development of human language correlates with a significant development of left hemisphere temporal language areas.

Both the Geschwind and Levitsky and the Sanides studies demonstrate correlation of size of cortex with language, but it is logically impossible to infer causation from correlation. What is more, the size measurements in these investigations were performed on adult brains. It is certainly a logical possibility that some other mechanism could cause the language function to evolve to the left during ontogeny. Subsequently, the size would increase due to the increased sensorimotor stimulation. However, left-right asymmetries of temporal lobe speech areas in the brains of human fetuses were examined by Chi, Dooling, and Gilles (1977). They found that, during the gestational period of from 10 to 44 weeks, the transverse gyri were larger in number and size on the right in 54% (out of 207 serially sliced brains) of the brains, but that the plenum temporale was larger on the left of those brains. No asymmetries were observed in the plenum in 28% of the cases examined. Therefore, larger left temporal planes are recognizable in fetal brains. Two additional reports indicated that temporal asymmetries exist in auditory regions as well as in the plenum. Galaburda, Sanides, and Geschwind (1978) suggest a strong positive correlation between plenum asymmetry and auditory cortex asymmetry, and they claim that the previously demonstrated left plenum sizes reflected increased size in the auditory temporal area as well. Galaburda, LeMay, Kemper, and Geschwind (1978) supply additional data on structural asymmetries and suggest that, from the study of endocasts of early human forms, these Sylvian asymmetries may even have existed in Neanderthal man. They also remark that asymmetries are also found in these regions in some apes. Rubens (1977) also provides a good summary of findings on cerebral asymmetries, and discusses Sylvian fissure differences in other primates as well.

In recent reports, Galaburda (1980, 1982) discusses work that uses the technique of pigmentarchitechtonics, where the lipofuscin granules in neurons can be selectively stained. Certain very crucial areas containing large pyramidal cells in layer III are isolated by the technique. There are zones containing these cells in preoccipital, inferior parietal, temporal, and opercular frontal cortex. Except for the preoccipital region, the others are clearly in the language system. The frontal opercular zone for these magnopyramids on the anterior half of 44 according to Galaburda may indeed play a special role in language processing and may represent an anatomical pivot point of Broca's anterior speech region. This frontal opercular area may be larger in the left hemisphere as well. It corresponds to a small area in the frontal operculum found to be highly vulnerable to aphasic disturbance after stimulation (Ojemann & Whitaker, 1978a; Whitaker & Ojemann, 1977). Notice the solid filled-in portions in the cell of Figure 8-3 that corresponds to area 44, and recall that the solid portions represent sites for 100% errors with stimulation. Furthermore, area 44 is an intermediate specialized (specialization in frontal cortex meaning increased pyramidalization) cortex—more specialized than area 45, but less specialized than area 6. Even more important for Galaburda is the fact that 44 alone receives direct posterior auditory projections—at least in the rhesus monkey.

In addition, there is another layer III magnopyramidal zone in posterior temporal cortex in the region labeled Tpt (Figure 8-4). Tpt is located on

FIGURE 8-4
Schematic representation of the left human cerebral hemisphere.

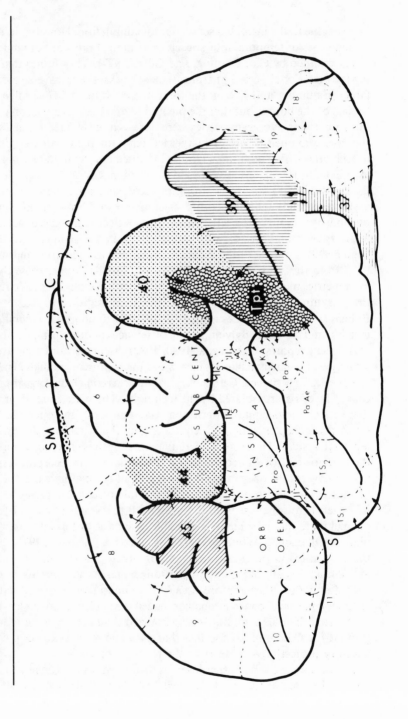

The Sylvian fossa, which is bordered by the Sylvian fissure (S), has been opened to show the opercular portions and the insula. The anterior speech area occupies roughly the pars opercularis (44), the posterior half of the pars triangularis (45), the anterior portion of the subcentral region lying below the central sulcus (Rolandic fissure), not shown in this figure, and the supplementary motor region (SM). A magnopyramidal zone, which corresponds closely to an area of greatest physiological sensitivity, is found on the anterior half of 44, posterior to the Y-branching ascending limb of the Sylvian fissure that separates pars opercularis from pars triangularis.

The superior temporal gyrus and the superior temporal plane, which includes Heschl's gyrus, contains a central core of primary sensory cortex. The plenum temporale is the part of the superior temporal plane lying posterior to Heschl's gyrus. In the posterior temporal region, another zone is delineated (Tpt). It is found on the caudal-most third of the superior temporal gyrus and on the posterior outer edge of the plenum temporale. This area is of particular relevance due to its temporo-parietal structure, its involvement in language (lesions here most often result in Wernicke's aphasia), its tendency to be larger in the left hemisphere, its prominent pyramids in layer III, and its apparent connections to frontal area 44. See text.

The supramarginal (40), angular (39) and temporo-occipital regions (37) contain areas that are functional for language, although 37 less so. The additional detail in this figure refers to the differentially specialized cortical zones (primary and association cortex) as well as to other Brodmann landmark areas not relevant to the discussion in the text. The arrows show general trends of differentiation of cortical structure. (From Galaburda, 1982, p. 439) the caudal most third of the superior temporal gyrus on the posterior outer edge of the plenum temporale. Area Tpt turns out to be an extremely important posterior language region, and Galaburda demonstrates its structural and connective relation with 44 in the frontal lobe. Like 44, Tpt represents an intermediate stage of specialization (specialization in temporal cortex meaning granularization, which in turn refers to the acquisition of stellate cells). It is less specialized than area 41 (primary auditory cortex - Heschl's gyrus), yet it is more specialized than areas 40, 39, and 37 (supramarginal, angular, and preoccipital gyri, respectively). Accordingly, Galaburda (1982) claims that, "...44 and Tpt are equivalent transitional areas between the paramotor and generalized cortices of the prefrontal area, and between parakoniocortex (primary sensory cortex—HWB) and the temporoparietal occipital junction areas respectively" (p. 442). As with 44, Tpt is usually larger in the left hemisphere, and where the plenum temporale is larger on the left Tpt is usually larger as well. In addition, the homologues of 44 and of Tpt in the rhesus monkey are "...neatly and separately connected (...) by fibers most likely coursing in the arcuate fasciculus." (Galaburda, 1982, p. 442)

It is tempting to suggest that 44 and Tpt match up with the sites Ojemann and Mateer (1979) delineated which mediate both sequential movement and phoneme identification. The cytoarchitectonic organizational similarities would then reflect the sensorimotor nature of those sites, and they indeed would represent the most critical regions within the more broadly defined Broca's and Wernicke's areas. As Galaburda points out, the strong connectivity and evolutionary similarity of 44 and Tpt would predict a certain degree of functional overlap, and for him, in fact, it is rather surprising that lesions in either region produce such distinct aphasic syndromes. Furthermore, if we follow the reasoning from form to function, the large magnopyramidal zones in layer III of 44 and Tpt indicate additional overlap of function.

If there is one overriding correspondence in all the localization studies treated in this chapter, it is that the left perisylvian region *is* the principal cortical substrate for human language. The improved technology for scrutinizing this area has allowed us a more microscopic view of its anatomy and physiology. We can now observe blood flow and glucose metabolism in well-defined regions. Noninvasive neuroradiological techniques allow not only a three dimensional view of lesion extent, but they also provide a way to measure the sizes of certain brain structures. The general picture that is emerging is that the classically defined perisylvian left hemisphere language cortex is more complexly structured than heretofore appreciated. Rather than a grossly characterized Wernicke's area connected to a Broca's area by the arcuate fasciculus white fiber tract, etc., this language region would appear to be structured more as a series of mosaic patterns of discrete zones functioning simultaneously and in parallel. The classical view generally held that the language regions processed information in series rather than in parallel. This no longer appears to be the case. Furthermore, there is likely to be more involvement of subcortical mechanisms in the overall direction and orientation of cortical processing. These innovative techniques of localization hold much in store for the future.

Dynamic Factors

Most studies of localization of function are synchronic—carried out at one point in time. Therefore, the principal caveat that must be expressed is that the nervous system is not static, although at the later stages of life the dynamism will have lessened. Nevertheless, as Brown (e.g., 1978) has proposed, the maturational history of the brain unfolds from bilateral organization to lateral organization (cerebral dominance) to contralateral representation. Linguistic representation tends to lateralize to the left focal centers (posterior-anterior). Throughout adult life, there is an increase in the discreteness of the representation sites, and functional localization tends towards a miniturization. Not only does maturational dynamism give rise to the "age-graded" nature of aphasic syndromes (Brown & Jaffe, 1975; Obler, Albert, Goodglass, & Benson, 1978), but it also makes it necessary to consider very carefully the age range of subjects in localization studies.

The dynamics will no doubt be different depending upon the genetic/cytoplasmic factors involved with handedness. Localization studies must control for this by consideration of the four populations: (1) right-handers with no familial left-handedness (FLH, see above); (2) left-handers with no FLH; (3) right-handers with FLH; and (4) left-handers with FLH. This grouping forms a continuum of laterality with group one being the most strongly lateralized and group four being the most bilaterally organized.

Lesion studies aimed at the ultimate localization of functions are notoriously problematic, not only because of Jackson's edict, but also because of the dynamics involved in the recovery patterns of aphasic patients. Kertesz (1980) states that, "Those of us who have followed patients over a long period of time learn to think of lesions as initiating a dynamic process rather than static symptoms." (p. 1)

Experimental studies of language localization with EEG, dichotic listening, tachistoscope, etc., must appreciate the fact that the *kind* of processing that subjects are set up to do generally determines which hemisphere will be dominant for the task. The actual stimulus may not be the crucial variable (Bever, 1975, 1980). If a subject switches from holistic to analytic (Bever, 1975, p. 256) or relational (Bever, 1980, p. 193) strategies for decoding a stimulus, then it is highly probably that the stimulus will accordingly evoke not a right but a left hemisphere effect. The overriding factor, then, is whether the task requires analysis or gestalt processing; hemispheric localization will result as a consequence of these different cognitive sets.

Philosophical Obstacles and General Conclusions

There are two types of philosophical arguments that can be raised concerning the issue of localizing language in the brain. The first set of obstacles deals with statements that infer functional localization from neurological data (von Eckardt Klein, 1978; Caplan, 1981). von Eckardt Klein (1978) outlines a series of steps in logical reasoning that must hold before any valid functional inference can be made from lesion data. First, the pathological behavior must be interpreted as the failure to exhibit a complex capacity of humans. Also included under the heading "pathological behavior" are all those disturbed functions induced by electrical stimulation of the brain. In fact, stimulation and ablation studies are in effect lesion studies, since something abnormal exists in the nervous system which presumably correlates with whatever disrupted behavior is being investigated. Stimulation, however, does not actually create a lesion but rather evokes different neuronal firing patterns during behavior. Further, although currents are controlled and applied at thresholds that are very low, it is often difficult to know whether the stimulation is releasing excitatory or inhibitory nervous reactions. All these studies should have in mind some complete model of the linguistic system, of which the capacity that is disrupted is but a subcomponent; that model should be the best available. The nature of the specific function under analysis should have already been characterized for *normal* functioning. For instance, before we look at disturbances in naming, we must understand basically how labeling behavior takes place in the normal language user. The lost capacity must be understood as it relates to other nondamaged capacities of the model. In addition, the pathological behavior should be characterizable as the output of all undisturbed components minus the damaged capacity. Finally, there must be no better explanation for the deficit. The basic lesson to be learned here is that until one completely understands the function in question, its localization in the brain will be premature. Herein lies the problem. One group (the linguists, the cognitive psychologists, the psycholinguists, the cognitive simulators, and the artificial intelligence experts) is searching for the best functional characterizations (i.e., the models) of behaviors, in our case language. The characterizations consequently will be couched in the essentially mentalistic vocabulary and terminology of these various disciplines. Another group (the neurophysiologists and neuroanatomists) is doing the actual localization, together with the clinical neurologists and neurosurgeons who have direct access to patient populations. There seems to be little doubt that the localizers are proceeding with their search despite the fact that little if any consensus has been achieved regarding the "best"overriding model for language. The problem is, of course, that the consensus will have to come from somewhere within the first group (Caplan, 1981, p. 134). The best one can hope for, however, is a truly interdisciplinary effort.

A large part of the obstacles relates to the differences in the vocabulary of the two groups. In fact, there is great variation even within the first group itself. The first group uses mentalistic terms such as *noun phrase, program, store, transformation,* etc., while the second uses physical terms as *neuron, cell, impulse, synapse, ganglia, gyri,* etc. The logical impasse involves the fusing of the two scientific jargons such that the resulting statements give rise to category mistakes. One simply does not find *words* in the *angular gyrus.* Surgeons do not extirpate *nouns* along with *gray matter tissue.* John Hughlings Jackson (1878) said as much over 100 years ago (Taylor (ed.), p. 155).

Most psychologists working in the area of cognitive simulation are of the opinion that we must go after the logic of cognitive systems not by looking at how the brain works but rather by constructing programs that will allow a computer to simulate the cognitive function in question (Pylyshyn, 1978, 1980).[3] In so doing, the researcher actually learns more about the function he or she is attempting to program. The effort, however, is divorced from the computer hardware as well as from the human hardware of the nervous system. For instance, Pylyshyn (1978) writes, "For psychologists, computational systems should be viewed as functional models quite independent of (and likely not reducible to) neurophysiological systems, and cast at a level of abstraction appropriate for capturing cognitive generalizations" (p. 93). In order to do this, of course, one cannot use the terminology of hardware systems (see also Harnad, 1982, and references therein).

Searle (1980) argues against too literal an interpretation of the computer metaphor for human linguistic capacity. The computer is an efficient and rapid string manipulator, and clearly string manipulation is crucial for linguistic performance. But, as Searle cleverly demonstrates, an organism can be programmed to provide answers to questions by manipulating formal symbols that it nevertheless cannot interpret. Therefore, the computer can answer questions without understanding what is going on in any way like a human. The crucial phrase is "like a human," since it is not at all obvious that a computer that simulates function X does it "like a human" would. Pylyshyn (1978) provides in-depth treatment of just this issue and concludes that if a computer can simulate some human behavior, then *at least at some level of description* it can be said to be doing it "like a human" (also see Dennett, 1978).

As we saw with Ojemann's results, at least at some level of description we can view the brain as a general purpose computer, since identical neural structures seem to be able to mediate different functions (sequential orofacial movement and phoneme identification) at different times, and the same function (labeling) may be mediated by different neural structures. At the level of hardware description, however, the computer and the human brain are not alike. Arbib and Caplan (1979) have indicated the way in which the study of language and the brain can become more computational. They suggest that techniques from artificial intelligence (which they do not appear to distinguish from cognitive simulation) can be utilized to model the "cooperative computation" underlying language processing. With findings such as those of Ojemann, this seems imminently possible. It would represent a very powerful union between the mental and the physical, and this, of course, is what language localization in the brain is all about.

Notes

[1]It is interesting to note that Blumstein, Cooper, Zurif, and Caramazza (1977) found the reverse case for Wernicke's aphasics. These patients did not reveal a selective deficit in phonemic hearing, but they nevertheless had great difficulties in utilizing the phonological information in a linguistically relevant manner in order to comprehend lexical items.

[2]Fodor (1975, p. 17), from a philosophical position of antireductionism, suggested that this may indeed be the case. To Fodor, then, this implies that higher organisms are analogous to general purpose computers, where functions subserved by a given structure may change from instant to instant depending upon the nature of the program and upon the computation being performed at the moment. (See Note 3.)

[3]Note that, in present-day cognitive science, when we describe human function *in terms of* a computer, we are following a centuries-old tradition of drawing from concurrent technological constructions for mechanical metaphors.

As far back as the 6th century B.C., scholars felt that many phenomena in the universe could be understood in terms of the functions of rather simple technological gadgetry of the times such as a potter's wheel, a lathe, a level, etc. (Marshall, 1977). In the Alexandrian period, tubular systems for water distribution were metaphorically invoked as models for nerve fibers conceived of as hollow pipes through which flowed the "pneuma." Hydraulic pumps were metaphorically extended to the realm of blood circulation. For centuries, libraries have been used as metaphors for human memory storage and retrieval. Aristotle, in his studies of movement, claimed that the movement of animals could be compared with those of automatic puppets (Marshall, 1977).

The development of toy animals that moved eventually motivated scholars to construct them not simply to produce moveable machines or trivial toys but rather as "simulacra" for demonstrating the manner of different types of actions. The artificial duck of Jacques de Vaucanson (Fryer & Marshall, 1979), an 18th century psychologist, allowed its inventor to characterize movements of different specifications. In fact, Vaucanson was acutely aware that, by constructing the duck in such a way its parts could move, he was actually *learning* about movement. This, of course, is the claim of modern researchers in artificial intelligence. By constructing programs so that a computer can recognize visual scenes or understand questions, one is simultaneously learning about scene recognition or comprehension.

More recently, telephones, thermostats and holograms have been used metaphorically to characterize human psycho-physiological functions (Pribram, 1981). Telephone systems are the sensorimotor centers connected by white fibers, thus characterizing information transfer. In addition, the thermostat can be used to characterize feedback systems, and the hologram can serve as the metaphor for nonlocalistic cerebral representation of memory, if that is how one wishes to view memory. Nevertheless, the technological metaphor of the day is the computer.

Acknowledgment

I would like to thank George Ojemann, Marney Naeser, and Al Galaburda for their kind cooperation in supplying me with materials pertaining to recent work in their laboratories. Without their assistance the present chapter would not have the scope it has. The description of the data and the judgments of it, however, are entirely the responsibility of the present author.

Raymond D. Kent

Brain Mechanisms of Speech and Language with Special Reference to Emotional Interactions

Introduction

Emotion, language, and speech are related in some powerful but as yet, poorly understood ways. The relationships among these three aspects of human behavior are fundamental to an understanding of speech and language—their development in children, their vulnerability to pathological conditions, and the likelihood for their recovery following damage to the brain. A central concern of this chapter is with speech as a means of expression of both language and emotion. Speech presents a variety of experimental and theoretical challenges to the student of human behavior. Many of these challenges relate directly or indirectly to the temporal structure of speech. Speech is a nearly maximal-rate motor performance slaved to the expression of meaning and emotion. The description of speech as *maximal-rate* comes from evidence that even normal conversational speech is produced at a rate that rivals well-rehearsed repetitions of simple syllable strings—a rate of about 10 to 14 phones per second (Tiffany, 1980). Performance at this decision rate requires sophisticated and reliable mechanisms of phoneme selection and sequencing. The rather common occurrence of sequencing errors such as spoonerisms serves to emphasize the fragility of the selectional and sequencing operations (Boomer & Laver, 1968; Fromkin, 1971; Shattuck-Hufnagel & Klatt, 1979). Speech also incorporates a rhythmic or melodic base, part of the prosody of language. Although this prosodic component is not well understood, it has been

© College-Hill Press, Inc. All rights, including that of translation, reserved. No part of this publication may be reproduced without the written permission of the publisher.

the subject of a great deal of research and speculation (Kozhevnikov & Chistovich, 1965; Lashley, 1951; Martin, 1972).

The interrelated mechanisms of emotion, language, and speech become particularly evident in speech behavior as we consider data from two primary areas, the development of speech and the deterioration of speech following damage to various parts of the brain. Speech usually has a privileged access to language because speech is the primary, and first-learned, modality of language. But speech also has roots that run deeply into our emotional being, and there are those who argue that the human infant engages vocalization to express emotion long before the vocal folds and tongue are harnessed to the work of language (Ploog, 1979). Damage to certain parts of the brain appears to spirit away the meaning or emotion while leaving an ostensibly fluent string of sounds. These pathologic states may shed some light on the organization of emotion, language, and speech.

One point of inquiry is the apparent dissociation of the voluntary control of movements and spontaneous emotional activation of the same coordinated movements (Gatz, 1970; Monrad-Krohn, 1942; Peele, 1961). Several reports, mostly anecdotal, describe a transient improvement in communicatively impaired patients under conditions of emotional stimulation. Clinical reports have indicated that although the apraxic patient is unable to speak fluently and intelligibly on command or during ordinary conversation, the same patient may produce a much more fluent and more intelligible speech when excited or highly emotional. This discrepancy of performance, apparently related to the emotionality of the situation, has been related to Jackson's (1864) writings on the "speechless patient" who has "power in his muscles and in the centers for the coordination of muscular groups, but, he, the whole man or the 'will', cannot set them agoing" (pp. 36-37). Mlcoch and Noll (1980) conclude that, "What is left to this type of patient is speech induced by limbic or emotional stimulation or speech not consciously controlled, as in reciting the alphabet, the days of the week, or counting to ten" (p. 225).

The capability for movement, including speech movements, also can vary markedly for akinetic patients. One of the "negative symptoms" of Parkinson's disease is akinesia, which refers to "a neglect of (or disinclination to use) the affected part" (Young, 1977, p. 216). Young comments that "With suitable provocation, even a severely akinetic patient, who has not moved out of his wheelchair for months, may walk or run from a burning building, for example, only to relapse thereafter back into total immobility" (p. 217). Transient improvements in speech have been similarly noted (Critchley, 1981). Although this "kinesia paradoxica" (Schwab, 1972) is rare, most patients with this disease show a varying severity of akinesia. Thus, they are not truly paralyzed. Similarly, Whitaker (1976) remarks that patients with akinetic mutism and lesions of the periaqueductal gray and reticular areas may produce speech—without dysarthria—under conditions of strong stimulation. Whitaker concluded that the deficit associated with these lesions is one of profound sensory neglect. (Because projections from many forebrain areas converge on the periaqueductal gray, Mantyh, 1982, proposed that this structure is an important site of functional interaction, possibly serving as a "focal interface" between limbic areas of the forebrain and the structures of the brainstem and spinal cord that generate the desired reflex or response.)

Brown (1979a) described the preservation of some thematic material in patients with jargon aphasia: "Commonly, patients lapse into these islands of speech reservation when asked to produce utterances that would otherwise result in jargon. *The affective element in such phenomena should not be overlooked*" (p. 164, emphasis added).

A more carefully documented instance of an apparent emotional facilitation of motor capability was described by Hixon (1981) for a 17-year-old female with Friedreich's Ataxia. She was nonambulatory and had severely disordered speech. Using a kinematic method for analyzing behavior of the chest wall, Hixon showed that whereas this patient's expiratory activity for conversational speech was accomplished by rib cage alone, her expiratory activity for spontaneous laughter was accomplished by both rib cage and abdomen, predominantly the latter. The respiratory pattern for laughter indicates the risks of assigning paralysis or weakness to muscles that appear to be inactive for certain kinds of voluntary movements. Similarly, Hixon (1976) reported that some cerebral-palsied children, who seemed unable to perform major inspiratory or expiratory efforts because of paresis of the chest wall, managed remarkable inspiratory and expiratory movements during crying.

Another demonstration of the potential interaction of emotion and language lies in the emotional value that individual words themselves come to have. The potency of this emotional weight is shown by reports that the emotional value of stimulus words influences language abilities in aphasic patients (Boller, Cole, Vrtunski, Patterson, & Kim, 1979). This finding holds the potential that the emotional valences of words can be an important variable in the management of speech and language disorders. The factor of emotionality also emerges as a potent factor in studies of verbal recall in normal subjects. Rubin (1980) concluded from a factor analysis of 51 properties of 125 words that associative frequency, emotionality and pronunciability were among the best predictors of commonly used tasks.

If it is true that emotional states can influence communicative ability, then such influences may give some clues about the neural organization of emotional and communicative functions. The purpose of this chapter is to review evidence for cortical and subcortical mechanisms that may be the basis for the interaction of speech and language with emotion.

Developmental and Evolutionary Considerations

Recent proposals by Jürgens (1979) and Ploog (1979) may help to relate infant vocalizations to maturational processes in the central nervous system. To appreciate these proposals, it is helpful to review three major conclusions concerning phonological development in infants and vocal behavior of nonhuman primates.

First, Ploog (1979) stated that from birth, the development of vocalization in humans differs from that of nonhuman primates. The nonhuman primates seem to have an innate repertoire of sounds that is only slightly affected by experience or developmental processes. In contrast, the vocalizations of the human infant expand in range and change in nature "in a process that begins in the first few weeks of life and proceeds through a number of genetically determined stages before the development of actual speech" (p. 87).

Ploog's second major conclusion was that despite the unique development of human vocalization, the vocalizations of human infant and nonhuman primates do bear certain similarities during the first year of life. First, the vocalizations possess great variety and therefore make possible fine differentiations of *emotional expression*. Another shared feature is the apparent inability to imitate sounds in the face of a capability to recognize species-specific vocalizations (Beatty & Devitt, 1975; Hupfer, Jürgens, & Ploog, 1977; Kuhl, 1979; Sinnott, Beecher, & Stebbins, 1976).

The third major conclusion is that the pattern of phonological development is fixed or determined by the maturational processes in the central nervous system (Figure 9-1). Ploog based this conclusion on the fact that phonological development does not vary with the language of the baby's caretaker; however, see Freedman (1979, 1980) for arguments for some genetically based differences in vocalizations of infants of different races. Ploog hypothesized that the pontine-mesencephalic region controls vocalizations of the human infant during the first few weeks of life. However, with the onset of cooing at about 2 to 3 months, function of the limbic cingulate areas was supposed to begin. Apparently, Ploog believed that subcortical control predominates over cortical regulation during much of the babbling period. The evidence for this position is that whereas myelogenesis of the motor roots of the relevant cranial nerves and several brainstem structures is largely complete by the onset of babbling, the

FIGURE 9-1
Progression of maturation and functional significance of the central nervous system controlling vocal function. I = pontinemesencephalic region; II = cingulate region; III = motor cortex.

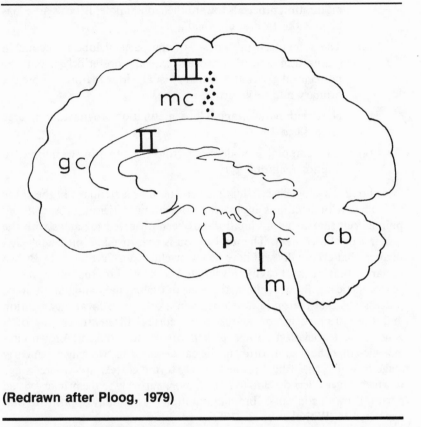

(Redrawn after Ploog, 1979)

myelogenetic cycles have only begun for the corticobulbar pathway, the association fibers, and the thalamocortical projections (excepting the visual system, which has an early myelination). Milner (1976), Whitaker, Bub, & Leventer, (1981), and Netsell (1981) have reviewed neural maturation as it relates to the development of speech and language; see their papers for a more complete treatment of this topic.

Knowledge about cortical maturation is based largely on the work of Flechsig (1901), Conel (1939, 1941, 1947), Yakovlev (1962), and Yakovlev and Lecours (1967). Whitaker et al. (1981) concluded from these reports that maturation of the brain is multidimensional rather than monolithic.

Generally, maturation proceeds from the primary motor and sensory areas to the secondary and association areas. Whitaker summarized the overall sequence of maturation as follows, from earliest to latest:

(1)   Within the frontal lobe, the motor cortex develops earliest and maturation proceeds toward the frontal pole; Broca's area lags behind the frontal eye field.

(2)   The somatosensory cortex of the parietal lobe is second in maturation and the process extends posteriorly from the postcentral gyrus; the primary visual cortex matures before the primary auditory cortex.

(3)   Next, within the occipital lobe, maturation progresses from area 17 to 18 to 19.

(4)   The temporal lobe develops from the superior, to middle, to inferior temporal gyri.

Although myelogenesis often has been used as a standard in the study of brain development, this approach is not without criticism. Brown (1979a) pointed out that early myelination has been observed for areas with the heaviest myelin content. The implication is that myelination begins first in areas that eventually will have heavy myelination. Furthermore, Brown remarks that these heavily myelinated systems are the most *recent* phylogenetically. Brown's alternative view of evolutionary and maturational processes is that the brain develops from a diffuse to focal organization and that primary motor and sensory cortex differentiates out of a generalized association cortex. In support of this concept, Brown cites evidence that the visual cortex in the cat develops in two stages: an early stage in which fine fibers project widely to the cortex, and a later stage in which larger fibers develop to project more narrowly to the primary visual cortex. Brown's concept of brain maturation is essentially opposite to that expressed by Whitaker et al. (1981).

The polar views on cortical development lead to different ideas on how and to what extent early cognitive and emotional experiences are represented in the cortex. Brown's formulation is consistent with an early affective-cognitive investment in the cortex, as development proceeds from limbic cortex to premotor area to percentral (motor) area. Of particular importance is the possibility that limbic processing of sensory and affective information is available to the cortex before the primary sensory and motor areas are substantially myelinated.

Jürgens and Ploog (1981) concluded that the neural control of mammalian vocalization and human speech is in the form of a hierarchically organized system [1]. They determined that some structures critical for the production of speech (including sensorimotor cortex, thalamus, and cerebellum) are not involved in nonhuman vocalizations, but that some neural structures considered unimportant to learned utterances (such as limbic cortex, amygdala, and hypothalamus) exert control over nonhuman vocalizations and emotional human vocalizations like laughing or crying. Thus, control of sound production can be widely distributed within the central nervous system. A related observation is that vocalization and emotion often seem to be controlled from similar brain structures such as the cingulate gyrus in monkeys. Ploog (1979) attached great significance to early sound production by proposing that vocalization is the earliest and most effective means to an infant's discovery of self. This idea bears directly on the interaction between vocalization and emotional development.

But the control of sound production differs in important respects between humans and nonhuman primates. Although electrical stimulation experiments on monkeys do not show involvement of the motor cortex in controlling monkey vocalizations, studies by Hast and Milojevic (1966) indicate that stimulation of the monkey cortex can result in distinct movements of laryngeal muscles, such as the cricothyroid, thyroarytenoid, and the extrinsic muscles. Stimulation of these areas produces muscle action but not vocalization or the arrest of vocalization. One hypothesis to be considered in this connection is that the monkey can exercise cortical control over the relevant muscles but not the behavior of vocalization. Similarly, Sutton (1979) concluded that the control of phonation in nonhuman primates is regulated largely by the periallocortex and rather little by the neocortex. He speculated that humans may have "a neocortically organized speech system overlaid on a more primitive periallocortex vocal regulatory system." (p. 65)

However, any direct comparison of the vocalizations of man and the nonhuman primates is immediately weakened by the differences in the nature and function of the vocalizations. Some writers have been adamant that propositional content is unique to human communication. Cassirer (1944) stressed that whereas man alone is capable of propositional speech, animals can utter only emotional "speech." Waszink (1978) draws the distinction even more clearly when he states that, "The fact that man is able to utter both propositional speech and emotional speech while animals utter only emotional 'speech' distinguishes man from animal" (p. 61). Waszink also asserts that there are no creatures capable of uttering propositional speech without also having the capability of uttering emotional "speech" at the same time. However, exceptions to this principle arise in several areas, including the neurologic disorders discussed above, where there does seem to be a splitting or discoordination of the propositional and emotional capabilities.

The neural pathways that influence vocalization allow for considerable complexity. Figure 9-2 illustrates how various brain structures connect with the nucleus ambiguous, the cranial nerve nucleus supplying motor innervation to the larynx. Notice that the motor cortex can work through the cingulate cortex and the pons-mesencephalon, or it can bypass the cingulate cortex, or bypass both the cingulate cortex and pons-mesencephalon. For the monkey, the cingulate area is very important in control of vocalization, and in the opinion of some investigators, it is responsible for a "readiness to vocalize" (Aitken, 1981; Jürgens & Muller-Preuss, 1977). Aitken has shown that damage to the anterior cingulate cortex in monkeys severely disrupts both conditioned and spontaneous vocal behavior, but has no effect on nonvocal social behavior or on a conditioned discrimination requiring a nonvocal response.

In human beings bilateral lesions of the anterior cingulate cortex result in akinetic mutism (Barris & Schuman, 1953; Buge, Escourolle, Rancurch, & Poisson, 1975; Jürgens & Von Cramon, 1982; Rubens, 1975). Kirzinger and Jürgens (1982) comment in summary of these reports that recovery of essentially normal speech is possible and that utterances produced during recovery are neither dysphasic nor dysarthric. They note that the one permanent speech impairment is a reduced voluntary control of *emotional intonation*. The importance of the cingulate gyrus to emotional and personality characteristics in man is well attested by reports of cingulate disease and cingulectomy (Angelini, Mazzurchi, Picciotto, Nardocci, & Broggi, 1981; Tow & Whitty, 1953; Whitty & Lewin, 1960). The Angelini et al. report of a 10-year-old boy with a focal lesion of the right cingulum notes that the presenting symptoms were serious behavioral abnormalities, including a lack of social restraint, heightened sexuality, bulimia, and aggressiveness. The boy also had a history of seizures accompanied by sensations of alarm and groundless fear. These abnormalities ceased following surgery. In view of considerations that (a) bilateral cingulate lesions greatly impair monkey calls and emotional expression in human speech, and (b) monkey calls have been regarded as homologous to human emotional intonations, Kirzinger and Jürgens (1982) concluded that this structure "plays an important role in the volitional control of emotional vocal utterances in both monkey and man (p.311).

Affective regulation is a central factor in MacLean's evolutionary model of the brain based on an hierarchy of three fundamental brain types: reptilian, paleomammalian, and neomammalian (MacLean, 1949, 1962, 1970, 1982). The reptilian brain consists essentially of the reticular system, midbrain, and basal ganglia. The paleomammalian brain is marked by the development of the limbic cortex. The last evolutionary stage includes the highly differentiated neocortex of the higher mammals. MacLean points

FIGURE 9-2
Pathways of neural control over vocal fold movement. Several alternate pathways feed to the nucleus ambiguous, the cranial nerve nucleus supplying motor innervation to the vocal folds.

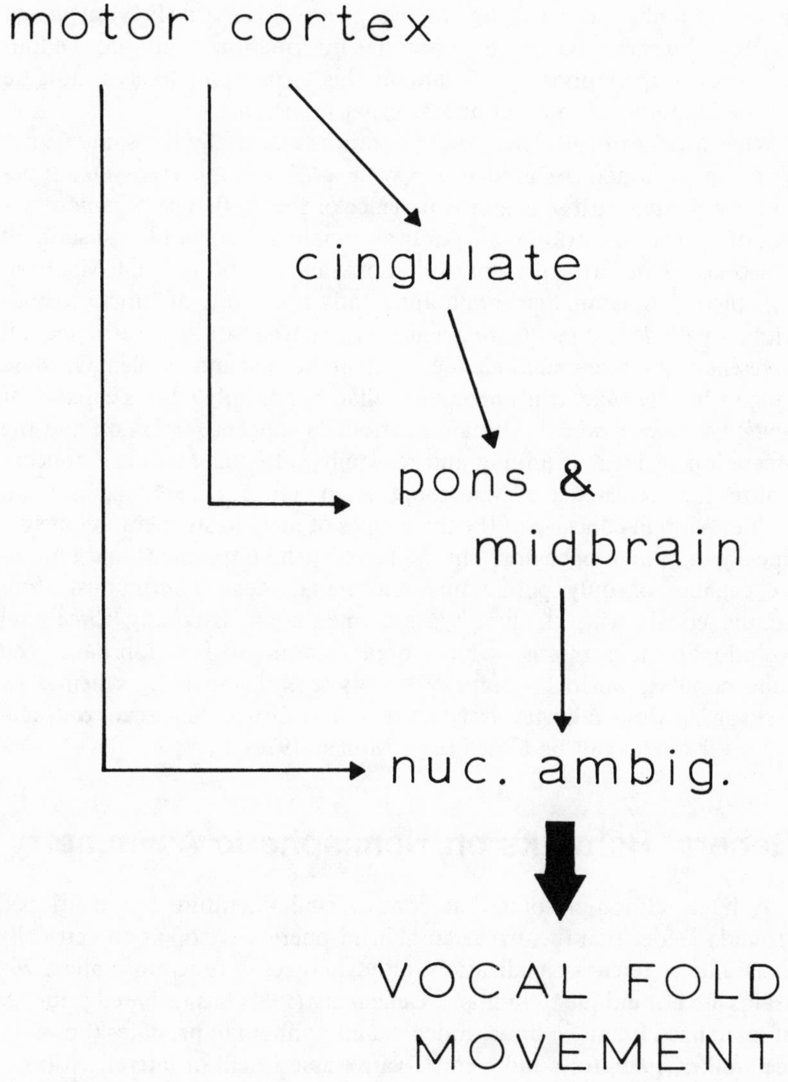

motor cortex

cingulate

pons &
midbrain

nuc. ambig.

VOCAL FOLD
MOVEMENT

to the limbic system as an important governor of emotional state. Electrical stimulation of this system produces a variety of vivid affects ranging from basic affects such as hunger, thirst, cold, or warmth to more general affects such as sadness, depression, foreboding, anger, reality or unreality. MacLean also points out that disturbances of affect, personal awareness, and recognition of reality also have been noted in persons with damage to limbic structures, e.g., limbic epilepsy. MacLean (1949) suggested that both interoceptive and exteroceptive information is fed into the limbic cortex of the hippocampus, making this formation a likely candidate for the blending of internal and external experience.

What MacLean calls the reptilian brain is essentially the same neural system that Altman (1978) identifies with *pathic mentation* (psychic functions associated with sensuous experience or feelings). The organic function of pathic mentation is for arousal, mobilization, and the sustaining of actions, as well as to prevent neglect of vital operations. What MacLean calls the paleomammalian brain apparently is capable of functions that Altman calls *iconic mentation*, which is patterned or structured mental representations in several modalities, both immediate and recalled. Of those animals having MacLean's neomammalian brain, only man is capable of *neotic mentation*, which Altman describes as concept formation and the generation of ideas (thinking and reasoning). Just as MacLean conceptualizes the coexistence of, and cooperation among, three brains in man, so does Altman conceive of the three types of mentation operating hierarchically in human behavior. Thus, whereas fish, amphibians and reptiles are capable of only pathic mentation, man deals continuously and simultaneously with all three types of mentation. (Actually, three-level evolutionary descriptions of brain organization and function have been quite popular; van der Vlugt, 1979, lists several, including schemes by Jackson, Pavlov, Yakovlev, & Lecours, Luria, Eccles, MacLean, & Isaacson. Still others can be added, e.g., Milner, 1976).

General Remarks on Hemispheric Asymmetry

A huge, although somewhat controversial, literature has developed around the idea that the two cerebral hemispheres develop asymmetrically to assume different specializations or advantages in function. Lateralized brains are not unique to humans. Denenberg (1981) has reviewed evidence of lateralized brains in birds, rodents, and nonhuman primates (however, see Walker, 1980, for a more conservative assessment of lateralized functions in the vertebrate brain). Denenberg's conclusion bears directly on the interaction of communication and emotion:

> Asymmetry is an initial condition of brains. The left
> hemisphere is preferentially biased to receive and transmit
> communication; the right is selectively set to deal with
> spatial and affective matters; and both often interact via
> activation-inhibition processes in the affective-emotional
> domain. (p. 20)

Morphological asymmetry of the hemispheres has been shown primarily in the posterior areas (Rubens, 1977). Recent studies by Seldon (1981a, 1981b) have revealed an interesting hemispheric asymmetry in the arrangements of the columnar clusters of neuron somata of the auditory cortex. Specifically, measurements of column diameters and their intervals were significantly larger in the left hemisphere (Seldon, 1981a). To some degree, these differences might be predicted from an overall size asymmetry of the cortices (Galaburda, Sanides, & Geschwind, 1978; Geschwind & Levitsky, 1968); for example, if essentially the same number of columns occur on both sides, then a wider spacing of the columns would be expected for the larger (left) auditory cortex. It is noteworthy that the larger planum temporale of the left hemisphere stands in contrast to an overall size asymmetry in which the right cerebral hemisphere is larger than the left, whether measured by brain weight or surface dimensions (Crichton-Browne, 1880; Kolb, Sutherland, Nonnemann, & Wishaw, 1982). Seldon (1981b) interpreted this asymmetry of the auditory cortices as the basis for laterality effects in speech perception. The morphological differences were believed to allow the spreading of afferent information to more columns in the right than in the left hemisphere. Consequently, the auditory cortex on the left is better suited to the analysis of brief acoustic stimuli (like stop consonants), and the auditory cortex on the right is better suited to the analysis of longer acoustic stimuli. The possibility that the hemispheres differ in temporal resolution for input is supported by a review of the clinical and experimental literature (Hammond, 1982; Mills & Rollman, 1979). Most reports show that the left hemisphere is capable of finer temporal acuity. Moreover, when patients with either right or left brain damage are compared, those with damage to the right side usually have a slightly depressed performance for temporal tasks whereas those with damage to the left side have a severely depressed performance on such tasks.

These structural and functional differences between the posterior regions of the hemispheres may relate to Brown's (1979a) proposal that language per se and the associated neural asymmetry is vested primarily in the perceptually oriented posterior zone of the hemisphere. That is, cytoarchitectonic asymmetry in the primary and secondary auditory cortices may be one factor contributing to the eventual lateralization of language. Rogers (1981) discussed the significance of lateralized perceptual input in determining lateralized forebrain function in avian species. Although anatomic studies on human brain development related to altered perceptual input are rare, some information does exist. Donaldson (1892, 1891), described anatomic maldevelopments of the auditory and visual areas of the brain of Laura Bridgeman, who lost her hearing and vision at the age of 2, but lived until the age of 60. She learned sign language and became noted for her mental abilities.

Perhaps lateralization for language "spreads" through the brain, beginning in the auditory cortex, then influencing Wernicke's area, and subsequently affecting Broca's area. A spreading lateralization is a feature of Brown's (1975, 1979a) ontogenetic model, in which the extent of hemispheric dominance is determined by the degree of completion of a process ("core differentiation") that occurs in focal zones of the generalized neocortex of the left hemisphere. Basically, these focal zones underlie the development of both language and neural structure, and develop in parallel for both anterior and posterior regions. Thus, the appearance of a language-related zone such as Broca's or Wernicke's area is accomplished by a core differentiation of a specialized region within a larger and more generalized field. According to this hypothesis, hemispheric dominance is an intermediate stage between bilateral and contralateral representation. With respect to Broca's area, Brown suggests that this area "undergoes a development out of a homotypical (generalized) isocortex," and that this "development occurs to a variable extent and determines the degree of lateralization in a given individual" (Brown, 1979a, p. 188). (There is some evidence for an evolutionary trend toward asymmetry, at least in the primates: Giurgea, 1981, notes that a longer sylvian fissure on the left side is observed in 44% of rhesus monkeys, 80% of chimpanzees, and 84% of humans).

Other writers have attributed the lateralization of speech and language functions to sensory and motor capacities. Semmes (1968) concluded from studies of brain-injured subjects that sensorimotor organization is represented more focally in the left hemisphere and more diffusely in the right. The focal representation was interpreted as favoring the integration and specialization of behaviors requiring fine sensorimotor control. Unless the cortical control of movement is essentially prefigurative and therefore relatively free of the details of temporal regulation, the cortex must use precise timing information in forming motor sequences. Nottebohm (1970) has argued that lateralization of motor function may be a condition for a flexible and efficient programming of movements: "A behavioral sequence has to commence, and unless it is rigidly programmed, it must incorporate a continuous decision-making process. Control of the commencement of behavior and decision making might be inefficient under equipotent and simultaneous bilateral representation" (p. 953). Nottebohm (1981) suggested that fine temporal resolution is a necessary feature of an executive network. Studdert-Kennedy (1981) also argued for a motoric explanation of lateralized language function, basing his argument on the two observations that (a) the most remarkable feature of the left hemisphere is the preeminence that it assumes in the motor control of speech, and (b) the fact that about 95% of the population has a left-hemisphere dominance for manual praxis. Studdert-Kennedy concluded that language was attracted to the left hemisphere because of the availability of the neural circuitry for unilateral coordination of the two hands. He argued that exactly this type of circuitry would be needed to control the bilaterally innervated vocal apparatus.

But Walker (1980) took quite a different view on the matter, concluding from a review of studies on lateralization in the vertebrate brain that, "if there is any form to the comparative evidence at all, it is that human asymmetries in vocalization and hearing may have evolutionary precedents, if not primate beginnings; whereas human right-handedness lacks any obvious animal precursors" (p. 361). Walker therefore proposed that "handedness is secondary to language.." and that "right-handedness arose only when vocalization, already lateralized, became associated with manual skills" (p. 361). A neurobehavioral basis for lateralization emerges from Walker's assertion that the strongest evidence of hemispheric lateralization exists for humans and birds—both of which have highly developed vocalization abilities. His hypothesis is along the lines of an ontogenetic and phylogenetic law of least effort: "hemispheric space is not used if it can be managed without, and vocalization—unlike, for instance, locomotion—does not require left-right differentiation usually achieved by the symmetrical employment of both sides of the brain" (p. 361). (However, evidence will be presented later in this chapter to show that the human cerebral hemispheres have complementary specializations of vocalization, rather than vocalization being vested solely in the left hemisphere.)

Experiments on rhythmic tapping with either hand individually (Wolff, Hurwitz, & Moss, 1977) and with both hands simultaneously (Ibbotson & Morton, 1981) have shown superior performance of the right hand in both sinistrals and dextrals. Wolff et al. interpreted their results as evidence of left-hemisphere specialization for precise timing control of movements of either hand. Similarly, Ibbotson and Morton concluded that handedness biases in rhythmic tapping are governed "not by ordinary handedness factors but by the language hemisphere" (p. 136). LeDoux (1982) argued from a neuroevolutionary perspective that the inferior parietal cortex of the left hemisphere underwent adaptive changes facilitative of the regulation of manual dexterity. This advantage was gained at the expense of spatial ability, which was assumed by the inferior parietal cortex of the right hemisphere. LeDoux supposed that language was biased toward the left inferior parietal lobe because of an early gestural phase in the evolution of language.

Evidence for a developmental interaction of manual praxis and vocalization comes from a study of infants by Ramsay (1982). He reported that unimanual handedness essentially co-emerges with duplicated syllable babbling but that approximately four weeks after the onset of babbling, the infants showed a weakening or reversal of the handedness preference. These results were interpreted to indicate a developmental change in hemispheric specialization at about the time of onset of duplicated syllable babbling. Links between babbling and maturation of the cerebral cortex also have been proposed by Milner (1976) and Whitaker (1976). Milner speculated that whereas mere vocalization is subcortically controlled, preverbal babbling represents the functioning of the lower three layers (4 to 6) of the speech areas of the cortex. Similarly, Whitaker (1976) proposed that babbling entails increasing phasic control of the vocal tract by motor circuits of the cerebral cortex. He suggested that babbling reflects both the maturation of Broca's area and the increasing interaction of Broca's area with Wernicke's area by means of the fibers of the arcuate fasciculus.

An interesting population to consider here is the deaf, who are deprived of the normal auditory language channel (and its potential lateralizing influence, as discussed above) but have normal manual praxis. McKeever, Hoemann, Florian, and VanDeventer (1976) reported that left hemisphere dominance for language is difficult to demonstrate in the prelingually deaf, a finding which would seem to mean that the auditory channel of language is a more potent lateralizing force than is manual praxis. However, Poizner and Battison (1980) concluded from their review of the literature in this area that cerebral asymmetries are common to the deaf and that auditory experience is not necessary for the development of cerebral specialization. Although the deaf often showed a weaker asymmmetry than do normal-hearing subjects, the asymmetry is in the same direction, that of a left hemisphere advantage for language. This conclusion also is supported by reports of aphasia for sign language as the consequence of left-hemisphere damage (Burr, 1905; Chiarello, Knight, & Mandel, 1982; Leischner, 1943; Meckler, Mack, & Bennett, 1979; Tureen, Smolik, & Tritt, 1951; Underwood & Paulson, 1981). Chiarello et al. concluded that a visual/gestural language is processed in the left hemisphere and, in agreement with Leischner (1943), that the supramarginal and angular gyri are the critical regions for the decoding of sign language.

It also has been suggested that bilateral representation may have caused interhemispheric conflict when purposive, internally generated actions such as bird song and language evolved and began to interact with earlier behaviors (Corballis & Beale, 1976). When a predominantly unilateral system such as language, bird song, or manipulative skills is superimposed on a bilaterally symmetric system, the result could be a complementary asymmetry for other functions which had an earlier bilateral representation (Corballis, 1981).

Correlational studies of several lateralized behaviors should help to resolve some of the thorny questions about the origin of lateralization. For example, it appears that several lateralized behaviors that supposedly reflect right-hemisphere dominance in the general population are not related to traditional measures of lateral dominance such as handedness or footedness. Among these behaviors are emotional tone perception (Safer & Leventhal, 1977), conversion reactions (Stern, 1977), face perception (Gilbert, 1977), and facial expressivity of emotion (Borod, Caron, & Koff, 1981). Thus, it appears that the right hemisphere is dominant for some nonverbal or paralinguistic functions regardless of the lateralization for other behaviors. A second approach that might be helpful is through the investigation of both absolute and relative measures of lateralization. Lauter (1982) reported that in the dichotic identification of complex sounds, there were significant individual differences in respect to absolute ear advantage for a given stimulus, but listeners were consistent in respect to relative ear advantage for a number of stimuli. The overall pattern of lateralized functions may reflect a conspiracy or complex interaction involving several factors rather than a simple determinism based on one behavior such as manual praxis or ear advantage for verbal stimuli. A mechanism of complex interaction seems consistent with the fact that there are a tremendous number of exceptions to the standard laterality pattern for humans. Levy (1980) commented that 85% of the population deviates from the standard pattern in some respect.

A comment by Altman (1978) makes a suitable postscript to this discussion. He noted that the most striking trait of man in the picture of brain evolution is the dramatic increase in the mass of the cerebral cortex (a trebling in weight from Australopithecus to Homo Sapiens); much less remarkable are evolutionary variations in cytoarchitectonics and appearances of morphologically distinct brain structures. Altman notes that along with this increase in mass of the cerebral cortex there occurs one other distinctively human feature—the assignment of one entire hemisphere to a new function, that of noetic processing. (Altman uses the term *noetic mentation* to refer to concept formation, generation of ideas, and to some extent symbolic manipulation, whether for thought or for communication.)

FIGURE 9-3
Primary speech-language areas of the brain, as adduced by brain-damage and by cortical stimulation experiments. B = Broca's area; W = Wernicke's area; S = supplementary motor area.

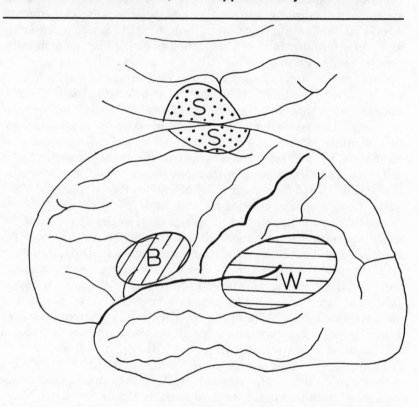

In recognition of this evolutionary triumph, Altman terms the dominant hemisphere of man the *anthropocephalon*.

Cortical Mechanisms of Language, Speech, and Emotion

Left (Dominant) Hemisphere

Whereas monkey vocalizations appear to have their brain loci in the limbic system, which is also an important emotional center of the monkey brain, the control of human vocalizations is associated with various regions of the cerebral cortex and a number of subcortical structures. Several focal areas of the human cortex have been identified with primary functions of speech production, speech understanding and language usage. Some of the more well-known areas are shown in Figure 9-3.

Broca's area (B in the figure) has to do generally with planning and execution. Damage to this area results in marked deficits in spoken language, that is, Broca's or nonfluent aphasia. In general, Broca's aphasia is characterized by lack of fluency of spontaneous speech, disturbances of syntactic structure, limited repetition and naming ability, failure to produce complete sentences, and a laborious articulation. Comprehension is generally intact. There is also evidence that Broca's area may be part of a central processor for hierarchically-structured material. Grossman (1980) reported that when Broca's aphasics were asked to construct nonlinguistic, hierarchical tree structures, they seemed to have forgotten the hierarchical organization of the visuo-spatial material and relied instead on a chain-like strategy. An important implication of this result is that the Broca's aphasics may have a cognitive deficit that is not restricted to linguistic material.

Although Broca's area is somewhat differently defined by different authors, a conservative definition is to locate it as the pars opercularis of the third frontal convolution (Bailey & von Bonin, 1951). Thus, Broca's area often is identified as Brodmann area 44. However, some authors include more extensive cortical territory. Monakow (1914) described Broca's area as including F3, the anterior insula, the connecting gyrus between F3 and the precentral convolution, and the Rolandic operculum. Refinements in neuroradiology should permit a clearer picture of the anatomic-functional relationships in this area of the cortex. For example, Tonkonogy and Goodglass (1981) reported on two patients with expressive speech disorders. One patient with transient word-finding problems had the lesion shown by the numeral "1" in Figure 9-4, that is, a softening of the cortex in the foot of the third frontal gyrus. The other patient, who had an infarction depicted by the second area in this illustration had primarily dysprosody and articulatory disturbances. The authors concluded that overlapping lesions in the two areas shown may determine different deficits in speech and language, with "word-finding difficulties being associated with lesions of posterior F3 and articulatory disorders with lesions of the Rolandic operculum." (p. 486)

Broca's area is controversial with respect to its functions in speech and language. Although aphasia has been linked with this cortical area since Broca (1861), several reports have indicated preservation of language despite substantial damage to this area (see reviews by Brown, 1979a; Mohr, 1976; Pribram, 1971). Among the most striking reports that serve to question the language functions of Broca's area are those that indicate little or no

FIGURE 9-4
Cortical lesions for a patient with transient word-finding problems
(area 1) and for a patient with dysprosody and articulatory disturbances
(area 2).

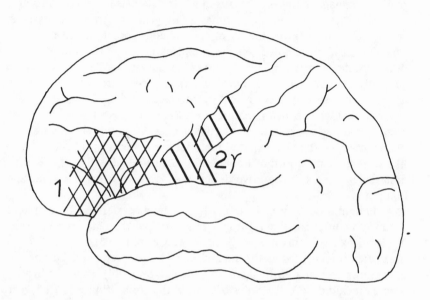

Adapted with permission from J. Tonkonogy & H. Goodglass, *Archives of Neurology*, 1981, *38*, Fig. 1, p. 486-490, copyright 1981, American Medical Association)

speech/language disturbance after bilateral topectomy of all or part of Broca's area in schizophrenic patients. However, recent neuroradiologic evidence (to be discussed) points to the functional significance of Broca's area and surrounding cortical regions in speech and language.

Wernicke's area, W in Figure 9-3, is located at the junction of the parietal and temporal lobes (Bogen & Bogen, 1976; Witelson, 1977a). It includes a region in the left superior temporal gyrus and an adjacent area of the middle temporal gyrus. Wernicke's area usually is associated primarily with Brodmann area 22, but is not limited to it. Damage to Wernicke's area often results in failure to comprehend or understand the spoken word. Wernicke's or fluent aphasia is characterized by fluent speech, often virtually free of articulatory (motor) disorders, yet the speech is highly abnormal because of neologisms, anomias, phonemic and verbal paraphasia, and phonemic or verbal jargon.

Interestingly, the anterior speech region, or Broca's area, may show a right-left size asymmetry similar to that now well-documented for Wernicke's area. Falzi, Perrone, and Vignolo (1982) reported that when both the extrasulcal and intrasulcal portions of the cortex were considered, the anterior speech region of the left hemisphere was larger than the homologous area of the right hemisphere. Thus, both anterior and posterior speech regions seem to be associated with a hemispheric size asymmetry, opposite in direction to that for the hemispheres as a whole (Kolb et al., 1982).

The supplementary motor area, S in Figure 9-3, is a controversial region as far as speech and language function are concerned. This area, located on the medial and superior surfaces of the frontal lobe in the parasagittal region just anterior to the motor strip, was identified by Penfield and Roberts (1959) as causing a variety of speech disturbances when it was electrically stimulated. Vocalization in response to electrical stimulation of the supplementary motor area has been reported by Brickner (1940), Penfield and Welch (1951), and Erickson and Woolsey (1951). Kirzinger and Jürgens (1982) note that speech produced during recovery from damage to the supplementary motor area is monotonous and difficult but is neither dysarthric nor dysphasic. Damasio and Van Hoesen (1980) reported that four patients with circumscribed lesions of the supplementary motor area initially presented with global akinesia and neglect. They described speech and gesture as similarly affected, but noted the absence of true aphasia or apraxia. A recent report by Jonas (1981) documents a variety of speech disturbances that result from damage to the supplementary motor area. He concluded that this area is involved in certain "language" aspects of speech, such as word finding and the facilitation of propositional over "automatic" speech. This region also appears to play a role in "motor" aspects of speech, including the control of rhythm and the control of phonation and articulation. Jonas concluded that the supplementary motor region plays several roles including: (1) facilitation of the initiation of propositional speech, (2) suppression of nonpropositional "automatic" speech, (3) pacing of propositional and nonpropositional speech, (4) control of some aspects of articulation, and (5) control of phonation. Interestingly, Jonas (1982) includes all but one of these functions in his discussion of the role of the normal dominant hemisphere of the thalamus in language processing. Jonas notes that this similarity in functions might be explained by Penfield and Robert's (1959) suggestion that the supplementary motor region and the thalamus interact via the pedunculus thalami superior.

Kornhuber (1980), who believed that both Broca's area and the supplementary motor area are involved in transducing motivations and plans

FIGURE 9-5
Composite drawings of lesions determined by CT scans for patients with three types of aphasia. The common area of brain damage is blackened to show the anatomic focus of the lesion across patients.

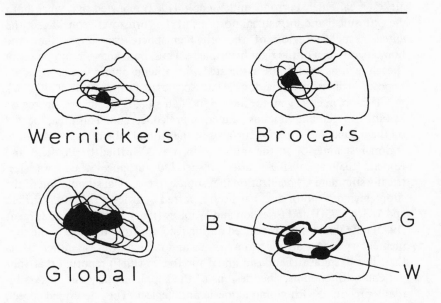

Wernicke's   Broca's

Global   B — G
          W

(Adapted with permission from Mazzocchi & Vignolo, *Cortex*, 1979, *15*, 627-654)

into speech motor behavior, thought it possible that these two areas can substitute for one another. A report by Roland, Larsen, Lassen, and Skinho, (1980) supports the role of the supplementary motor area in movement planning. They showed that local cerebral blood flow increased in the supplementary motor area not only during the actual performance of finger movements but also during the *imagined* performance of such movements. In addition, the increases in blood flow occurred for complex motor sequences, but not for a simple tapping task. In view of these results, Kirzinger and Jürgens (1982) concluded that the supplementary motor area is involved in the planning of volitional motor sequences, and not with their sensorimotor integration (cf. Eccles, 1982). Thus, both Broca's area and the supplementary motor area are implicated in the planning of sequences or in the recognition of hierarchical structure. Damasio and Van Hoesen (1980) considered the supplementary motor area to be an "energizer" unit for willed movement. This idea accords with Kornhuber's (1980) idea that this region transduces motivation into behavior.

A recent attempt at localizing lesions in different types of aphasia was conducted by Mazzocchi and Vignolo (1979), who used the method of Computerized Axial Tomography (CT scan). Figure 9-5 shows a depiction of their results for each type of aphasia. Composite drawings of the lesions are shown, and the blackened area represents the area of lesion common to the patients with a given type of aphasia. Thus, even though the individual lesions vary in extent and shape, the blackened area might be taken to be an anatomic focus of the injury. Notice that for Wernicke's aphasia, the lesion is in the expected area—near the junction of the temporal and parietal lobes. The lesion for Broca's aphasia is in the inferior frontal lobe, at or near Broca's area. Global aphasia is associated with damage to a relatively large area, usually invading both Broca's and Wernicke's areas. Global aphasia is characterized by both comprehension and formulation disturbances, generally so severe that the person's language is nonfunctional. Automatisms may be preserved in some patients but even these may not be used appropriately. The illustration at the bottom shows how the lesions for Broca's and Wernicke's aphasias are contained by the common lesion for global aphasia.

Other recent neuroradiologic studies also confirm, at least in the majority of cases, posterior lesions for Wernicke's (fluent) aphasic patients and anterior lesions for Broca's (nonfluent) aphasic patients (Basso, Salvolini, & Vignolo, 1979; Blunk, DeBleser, Willmes, & Zeumer, 1981; Noel, Bain, Collard, & Huvelle, 1980). However, one difference between the classical and modern views of the correlation between brain morphology and language disturbance is that the more recent studies often implicate damage to the insular cortex in association with Broca's aphasia. Although it may not be possible to show that there is any one area of the cortex for which damage always results in language impairment, it does seem reasonable to make probabilistic statements, e.g., damage to Wernicke's area and (to a lesser degree) Broca's area is associated with a relatively high probability of language impairment whereas damage to other cortical areas is associated with a relatively low probability of language impairment (c.f. Altman, 1978). Nonetheless, the door must be kept open to the possibility that cortical regions other than Wernicke's and Broca's areas may be strongly associated with language functions. For example, the work by Ojemann and Mateer (1979b) indicates that language tasks such as naming can be impaired by stimulation at various cortical sites in the temporal, parietal and occipital lobes.

Figure 9-6 combines the data for two studies, one based on electrical stimulation studies of the exposed human cortex, and one based on CT

FIGURE 9-6
Cortical areas serving functions of nonverbal facial movement, phoneme identification, and phonemic expression, as adduced from studies of cortical stimulation and from studies of errors in aphasic subjects.

Top sketch shows stimulation mapping results of Ojemann and Mateer (1979); FMP = final motor pathway, for which stimulation impaired all facial movements and arrested all speech; SM-PI = area in which stimulation impaired nonverbal facial movements and phoneme identification. (Adapted with permission from G.A. Ojemann & C. Mateer, *Science, 205,* pp. 1401-1403; Figure 1, 28 September 1979; copyright 1979 by the American Association for the Advancement of Science).

Center sketch shows lesions for patients with two types of fluent aphasia; P, a fluent aphasia with predominantly phonemic errors, and L, a fluent aphasia with predominantly lexical errors. (Adapted with permission from Cappa, Cavalotti, and Vignolo, *Neuropsychologia,* 1981, *19,* 174-175, Figures 1 & 3).

Bottom sketch shows how Ojemann and Mateer's SM-PI area compares with the general lesion area reported by Cappa et al. for fluent aphasia subjects having predominantly phonemic errors.

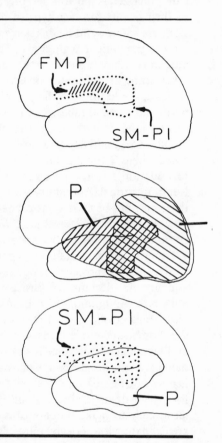

scans of patients with two types of fluent aphasis (Wernicke's aphasia). The sketch at the top shows the results of Ojemann and Mateer (1979b) for stimulation mapping during craniotomies under local anesthesia. The area identified as FMP is the final motor pathway, an area for which stimulation evoked impairment of all facial movements and arrest of essentially all speech. The region labeled SM-PI is an area in which stimulation impaired nonverbal facial movement *and* phoneme identification. This area assumes tremendous theoretical significance in that the authors considered it to be the neuroanatomic basis for the motor theory of speech perception which implies that a listener understands speech in terms of its movements. (I have suggested an alternative explanation for these results; Kent, in press).

The sketches in the middle illustration present the lesion results for two types of fluent aphasia (Cappa, Cavalotti, & Vignolo, 1981). Type P was a fluent aphasia with predominantly phonemic errors and Type L was a fluent aphasia with predominantly lexical errors. These results confirm the hypothesis that within the posterior language area, those regions nearer the lateral fissure (the perisylvian areas) are more critical to the use of phonemes than are the regions more remote from the lateral fissure (the marginal areas). The marginal areas appear to be more critical to the use of words as meaningful units.

The relationship between the P area for fluent aphasics with predominantly phonemic errors and the FM-PI area for nonverbal facial movement and phoneme identification is shown at the bottom of Figure 9-6. The two areas appear to overlap to a considerable extent, but comparison is admittedly crude and no strict interpretation should be made of the areas shown. Nonetheless, it is interesting that the results of both the lesion study and the stimulation study indicate a phonetic function in the general region of overlap.

Crucial cortical areas for the execution of simple oral gestures on imitation were described by Tognola and Vignolo (1980). Their CT scan results for patients with oral apraxia indicated damage to the frontal and central opercula, the anterior insula, and a small region of the first temporal convolution of the left hemisphere. Areas of common damage are shown in Figure 9-7 for patients with large superficial and deep lesions, medium-sized superficial and deep lesions, and small superficial and deep lesions. In each of these three groups, all patients suffered damage to the *insula*. The authors offered two explanations for this result: (1) the cortical region for controlling nonverbal oral movements includes the insula as well as the premotor and or precentral opercula, or (2) insular destruction also damaged the temporo- and occipito-frontal fasciculi, thereby interfering with the relay of visual information needed for imitation to the frontal operculum and the precentral motor face areas. In support of the first explanation, Tognola and Vignolo noted that the anterior insular cortex is continuous with the overlying opercula and has a similar cytoarchitectonic structure.

From these observations, a picture of general cortical function can be sketched (Figure 9-8). Certain areas appear to be involved more with the language functions of syntax, semantics, and word-finding, whereas other areas appear to be involved more with the speech functions of phonetic selection and articulation (including its motor aspects). Figure 9-8 shows the language areas as regions containing diagonal lines and the speech areas

FIGURE 9-7
Lesion sites for patients with oral apraxia. Areas of common damage
are shown for patients with large superficial and deep lesions (area
marked by horizontal lines), medium-sized superficial and deep
lesions (area marked by diagonal lines), and small superficial and
deep lesions (crosshatched area). All patients also had damage to
the insula.

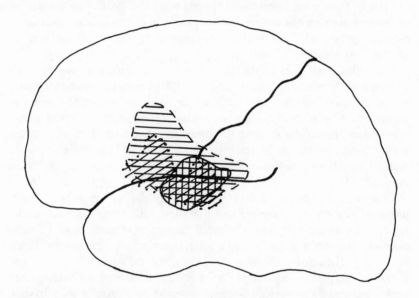

(Adapted with permission from G. R. Tognola & L. A. Vignolo, *Neuro-*
psychologia, 18, 1980, pp. 257-272, Figures 1, 2, & 3)

as the dotted regions. The supplementary motor area is shown with both
diagonal lines and dots because of its apparent association with both
language and speech functions (Jonas, 1981). The perisylvian area
represented by dots is a primary phonetic-articulatory area of the cortex,
containing the final motor pathway. It is bounded anteriorly and posteriorly
by cortical regions identified with such language functions as syntax, morphology and word finding. It is not known how these various cortical areas
communicate with one another, but the arcuate fasciculus, occipto-frontal
fasciculus, and cortico-thalamo-cortical loops are likely pathways (Kornhuber, 1977; Luria, 1980). Whitaker (1975) has proposed a similar anatomic
scheme in which a phonological component consists of Broca's and Wernicke's

FIGURE 9-8
Conceptualization of some cortical regions serving primarily language functions (areas of diagonal lines) and articulatory functions (dotted areas). These regions are not meant to be exhaustive but only to show a summary conception of results illustrated in Figures 4, 5, 6, & 7. Both language and articulatory functions are shown for the supplementary motor area.

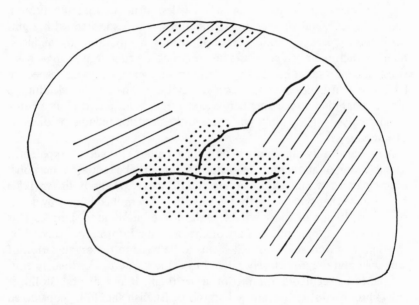

areas, and a central language system consists of the auditory association areas, the supramarginal gyrus, and the angular gyrus.

Right (Nondominant) Hemisphere

There is growing evidence to indicate that the right hemisphere is dominant for certain functions in speech perception and speech production. In its perceptual role, the right hemisphere has been said to process the intonational component of speech (Blumstein & Cooper, 1974; Goodglass & Calderon, 1977). Further, Goodglass and Calderon concluded from a study of trained musicians participating in a dichotic listening task, that "independent parallel processing takes place in the two hemispheres for their preferred (verbal vs. tonal) components of a complex stimulus" (p. 403). Ley and Bryden (1982) described a dissociation of emotional tone and verbal context according to ear advantage (a left-ear advantage applying to the emotional tone). Evidence for parallel independent and differentiated processing of the two hemispheres has been reported for commissurotomized subjects by Franco (1977).

Van Lancker (1980) proposed that vocal pitch contrasts of a highly structured nature, such as phonological tone and lexical type, are associated with left-hemisphere processing, whereas less structured pitch contrasts, such as attitudinal or emotional functions, are associated with right-hemisphere processing. Falling between the most highly structured and least highly structured pitch contrasts are intermediate functions such as word stress and phrasal contour; these tend to be ambiguous with respect to laterality. Van Lancker's analyses show that it can be quite misleading to assign vocal pitch processing per se to the right hemisphere. Only a functional analysis of the pitch patterns can be used for reliable predictions of laterality.

A similar duality may apply to durational patterns in speech. Apparently, a simple kind of alternating long-short rhythm may be central to the global timing pattern of English. Liberman and Prince (1977) and Bolinger (1981) have argued that syllable rhythm in English is determined largely by a succession of long and short syllables within the intonational phrase. This kind of rhythm may not be part of the prosodic information carried by the right hemisphere, because it seems to be basic to the organization of language and may be closely related to some properties ordinarily considered to be segmental (phonetic) rather than suprasegmental. Bolinger (1981) proposed that the reduced vowels of English should be considered as a separate subclass, with the processes of vowel reduction being assigned to a "preprosodic level" of morphology.

Studies of musical processing in brain-damaged populations show that patients with right-hemisphere damage, especially in the anterior zone, perform poorly on tasks of pitch, rhythm, and phrasing (Shapiro, Grossman, & Gardner, 1981). It was concluded from these results that the right hemisphere maintains an internal auditory representation of musical patterns. Seldon's (1981a, 1981b) work raises the possibility of a cytoarchetectonic biasing of the auditory cortex in the right hemisphere to analyze the more slowly varying parts of acoustic stimuli. The auditory cortex on the left seems to be biased in complementary fashion to process the more rapidly changing parts of auditory stimuli. This reasoning implies that lateralized forebrain function is a consequence of lateralized perceptual processing, especially during development. A similar conclusion has been expressed for the avian brain, in which lateralized visual and auditory input seems to govern the direction of lateralization in the forebrain (Rogers & Anson, (1979). Furthermore, lateralization for attack and copulation does not develop at the population level in chicks that were hatched from eggs incubated in darkness (Rogers, 1981).

Heilman, Scholes, and Watson (1975), Tucker, Watson, and Heilman (1977), Ross and Mesulam (1979), and Weintraub, Mesulam, and Kramer (1981) all provided evidence that patients with right temporoparietal disease have a defect in the comprehension and or expression of affective and intoned speech. Ross and Mesulam proposed that the affective components of language, including prosody and emotional gesturing, are a dominant linguistic feature of the right hemisphere. They went on to argue that the functional and anatomic organization of the affective components mirrors the organization of propositional language in the left hemisphere. It has been suggested that the initial left lateral eye movements that often follow emotional and stressful questions are an indication of initial right-hemisphere activation (Schwartz, Davidson, & Maer, 1975; Tucker et al., 1977). Hemispheric differences may extend even to the explanation of some psychotic conditions. Epileptic foci to the right hemisphere have been associated with mood-affective psychosis, whereas left-hemisphere foci have been associated with cognitive-paranoid psychosis (Flor-Henry, 1969; 1978) (For a review of cerebral laterality in relation to psychiatric illness, see Wexler, 1980).

There is evidence (reviewed by Brown, 1979a) that cortico-cortical fibers often connect homologous levels within and between the hemispheres. Brown suggested that the role of these various intra- and interhemispheric connections are not to transfer contents from one area to another, but rather to provide a temporal linkage, that is, to "maintain *in-phase* homologous levels of activity in different brain regions" (p. 145, emphasis in original). Similarly, Denenberg (1981) concluded that, "in order to comprehend and respond to a sentence containing information and affect, it is necessary for two sets of homologous brain regions connected via the corpus callosum to be activated." (p. 21)

The possible role of the right hemisphere in processing the intonational components of speech may relate to the use of Melodic Intonation Therapy (MIT) to facilitate speech production in aphasic adults (Albert, Sparks, & Helm, 1973; Sparks, Helm, & Albert, 1974). This technique uses variations in intonation, rhythm, and stress and has been demonstrated to be successful with some patients. An hypothesized explanation for its success is that nonlinguistic processing by the right hemisphere may activate certain dormant language areas in that hemisphere (Albert et al., 1973)[2]. Helm-Estabrooks (in press) has reviewed evidence that Melodic Intonation

Therapy is effective in the management of aphasia because it may facilitate right-hemisphere language. One of the strongest lines of evidence is that patients with bilateral brain lesions are not good candidates for this form of therapy, presumably because the right hemisphere has a diminished capability to assume language functions. It is instructive to consider the structure of Melodic Intonation Therapy with respect to the foregoing review of the suspected role of the right hemisphere in communicative functions. The therapy is structured in three stages. The first two incorporate multisyllabic stimuli (words and high-probability phrases) which are musically intoned while the therapist or patient simultaneously taps a syllable by syllable beat. The tapping may provide an overall rhythmic pattern whereas the musical intonation may give a kind of prosodic coherence or unity to the stimuli to be produced. The third stage uses longer or more phonologically complex phrases. These materials are first intoned, then spoken with exaggerated prosody, and finally spoken in a normal fashion. This progression can be interpreted as one of decreasing melodic/prosodic structure until only the normal prosody of speech remains.

A role of the right hemisphere in organizing motor mechanisms of affective behavior would explain lateral asymmetry in the intensity of emotional expression (Borod, Caron, & Koff, 1981; Sackeim & Gur, 1978). In addition to the right hemisphere's involvement in affective and intonational components of communication, there appears to be a right-hemisphere dominance or advantage in the recognition of faces and voices (Carmon & Nachshon, 1973; Jones, 1979; Mann, Diamond, & Carey, 1979; Van Lancker & Canter, 1982).

Support for affective and prosodic processing in the right hemisphere comes from studies of regional cerebral blood flow by Larsen, Skinhy, and Lasen (1978). They discovered that during automatic speech, there were changes in blood flow that were homologous in distribution to those in the left hemisphere. That is, blood flow changes were observed for both hemispheres for regions that we might denote as the supplementary motor area, inferior sensorimotor strip, and posterosuperior temporal lobe.

This result has been replicated by others. For example, Shahknovick, Serbinenka, Razumousky, Rodionov, and Oskolok (1980) reported that changes in regional cerebral blood flow during speech were found not only on the dominant left side but also on the right. They concluded that the pronounced changes in regional cerebral blood flow in the right hemisphere may reflect the nondominant hemisphere's active participation in various higher functions but also could result from other causes, such as hemispheric interaction via the corpus callosum. Jonas (1981) commented that increased regional blood flow in the nondominant hemisphere during speech may reflect the neural control of left-sided muscles involved in speech production. By this interpretation, the left hemisphere is dominant for mechanisms of both language and speech motor control.

Cooper (1981) contrasted the speech of patients with left- versus right-hemisphere lesions with respect to temporal and frequency aspects of intonation. Patients with left-hemisphere damage were characterized as having a greater impairment of timing patterns than of the vocal fundamental frequency (pitch) contours of speech. For instance, although Broca's aphasics often demonstrate inappropriate durations of words and interword pauses, certain aspects of their fundamental frequency contours (such as declination and terminal fall) are essentially normal. The contrast in regulation of timing and fundamental frequency is not so great with Wernicke's aphasics, but even with this group abnormalities in timing were predominant over abnormalities in fundamental frequency. On the other hand, Cooper described right-hemisphere patients as having greater abnormalities of fundamental frequency contours than of timing. For example, monotony of voice seems to characterize many patients with right-hemisphere lesion.

Although Cooper's generalization is not without exceptions, he points to a possibly significant difference in the speech patterns associated with right- and left-hemisphere damage. Smith (1980) reported that cortical stimulation of the dominant (left) hemisphere, especially in the anterior zones, resulted in significant increases of the duration of fricative /s/. Tobey and Harris (1981) observed longer utterance durations in patients with left than with right-hemisphere damage. Finally, Kent and Rosenbek (1982; in press) found abnormally long segment, word, and pause durations in the speech of patients having apraxia of speech and left-hemisphere damage. Right-hemisphere damage, on the other hand, was associated with speech patterns of essentially normal temporal structure (at least in terms of word and phrase durations) but a monotone, and apparently nasalized, voice quality.

Ross (1981) recently reported that disorders of affective and prosodic language in patients with focal lesion in the right hemisphere can be classified in the same manner as the aphasias, that is, recognizing disturbance categories such as motor, sensory, global, transcortical sensory, etc. Ross reached this conclusion after examining 10 patients with focal lesion to the right hemisphere, as they engaged in tasks requiring spontaneous prosody, prosodic repetition, prosodic comprehension, and comprehension of emotional gesturing. Ross introduced the term *aprosodia* to refer to these affective disorders of language. The nomenclature for classification of these disorders is parallel to that for the aphasias. Some examples are shown in Figure 9-9 which shows for four types of aprosodia the associated infarctions. Note, for example, that the lesion associated with the three cases

FIGURE 9-9
Infarctions associated with four types of aprosodia, or affective disorders of language.

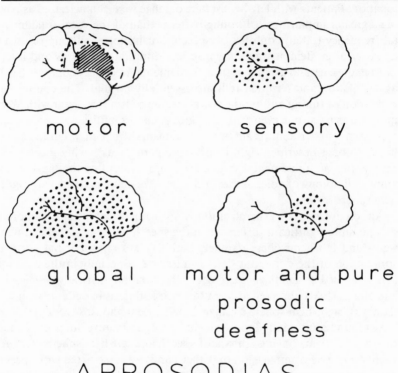

motor   sensory

global   motor and pure
               prosodic
               deafness

APROSODIAS

(Adapted with permission from E. D. Ross, *Archives of Neurology*, 1981, *38*, pp. 562-569, Figure 2; copyright 1981, American Medical Association)

of motor aprosodia is homologous to the lesion associated with Broca's (motor) aphasia, and that the lesion for the one case of sensory aprosodia is homologous to that for Wernicke's (sensory) aphasia.

Ross, Harney, deLacoste-Utamsing, and Purday (1981) offered hypotheses concerning the integration of propositional and affective language by callosal and subcortical pathways. They suggested that a "higher" order integration of propositional and affective components is accomplished through the corpus callosum. Essentially, this level of integration insures that propositional components are appropriately matched to affective-prosodic components of language. Ross et al. hypothesized that the subcortical *motor* integration of these language components takes place in the medial and lateral reticular formation and the motor nuclear groups in the brainstem. However, not all higher-order integration of propositional and affective components necessarily is accomplished by means of the corpus callosum. There are indications from split-brain patients that subtle affective information can be transferred subcallosally, although the paths of transfer are not known (Gazzaniga & LeDoux, 1978; LeDoux & Gazzaniga, 1977). Sperry (1977) observed that the effects of emotional stimuli presented to the right hemisphere of patients with transections of both callosal and anterior commissures are promptly bilateralized. He concluded that emotional tone is transferred from hemisphere to hemisphere via brainstem pathways.

But it is unwarranted to deny any role of the right hemisphere in the processing of linguistic material or propositional aspects of communication. Recent reports indicate the involvement of the right hemisphere in the processing of complex linguistic materials (Wapner, Hamby, & Gardner, 1981), contextual inferences (Dwyer & Rinn, 1981), and performance on anagram tests (Cavalli, DeRenzi, Faglioni, & Vitale, 1981). These studies demonstrate that the right hemisphere may serve both affective functions and some of the more global propositional functions of communication. Examples of the latter functions are situational inference, evaluation of the plausibility of elements embedded in a larger linguistic context, narrative integration, and thematic relevance. (From the point of view of linguistic analysis, theme-rheme distinctions are made prosodically as well as verbally and syntactically, which may also implicate the right hemisphere in integration of theme-rheme structure.) These global functions would seem to require complex integration over many communicative components and over relatively large periods of time and are therefore compatible with discrimination of emotional content, which also typically is based on a global analysis of contextually related factors.

Moreover, it is by no means clear that emotional content is restricted to the right hemisphere. Robinson and Szetela (1981) reported that the severity of depression following left-hemisphere brain injury is directly related to the proximity of the injury to the frontal pole, possibly implicating affective pathways that run through the frontal cortex. Some evidence points to a hemispheric segregation of emotion, with positive emotional states served more by the left and negative emotional states more by the right (Harman & Ray, 1977; Sackheim, Greenberg, Weiman, Gur, Hunger-buhler, & Geschwind, 1980; 1982). However, emotional reactions are not always easily interpreted with respect to hemispheric dominance. Geschwind (1981) stated that whereas an "appropriate retarded depressive response" is common to many patients with lesions of the left hemisphere, patients with severe Wernicke's aphasia sometimes show dramatic euphoric reactions. The person with Wernicke's aphasia may laugh at his communicative disorder or show a peculiar lack of concern over it, but is unlike the patients with right-hemisphere lesion who frequently show a more general form of neglect or lack of concern, such as a lack of modesty, incontinence or social inappropriateness. Likewise, Gainotti (1972) described the emotional reactions of patients with right-hemisphere injury to be facetious and inappropriately indifferent. (See Wexler, 1980, for additional discussion.)

Perhaps emotion and prosody are originally bilaterally represented, an idea in keeping with their presumably early development. The right hemisphere may come to control the negative emotions because these, especially fear and anger, may be associated with the defense of territory, which also presumably is represented in the right hemisphere because of its superiority in spatial matters. If emotions eventually are less potent in the left hemisphere, it may be because of ipsilateral inhibition that arises through the use of the propositional components of language.

Another complication in the attribution of affective dominance to the right hemisphere is that an asymmetry of emotional reactions may arise as the consequence of a right-left gradient of brain excitability, that is, attention, arousal or orienting response (Heilman & Van den Abell, 1979; Myslobodsky, 1981; Myslobodsky, Mintz, & Tomer, 1979). If the right hemisphere is dominant for functions of arousal and orienting, then emotional reactions evoked or influenced by such functions may appear asymmetric even if they are bilaterally represented. (Of course, it is also possible that *both* arousal and affective mechanisms have a laterality gradient favoring dominance of the right hemisphere.) Pathologic inattention or neglect is more likely to result from right than left hemisphere damage (Critchley, 1966; Heilman, 1979; Heilman & Valenstein, 1972; Watson, Heilman, & Cauthen, 1973). Heilman and Valenstein (1972) and Watson, Heilman and Cauthen (1973) proposed that neglect is a defect of the mechanisms of attention-arousal-intention resulting from damage to a cortico-limbic-reticular loop (cf. Sokolov, 1963).

Stuttering: A result of Anomalous Hemispheric Asymmetry?

Although the speech disorder of stuttering may seem somewhat out of place in this discussion, it is relevant from both a historical perspective (e.g., Travis' theory (1931) that stuttering results from failure to develop control of speech in the dominant hemisphere) and recent reports related to the neurology of stuttering. R. K. Jones (1966) described an interesting consequence of neurosurgery on four stutterers who were demonstrated by the Wada test to have bilateral representation of speech. Although the unilateral surgery was medically unrelated to stuttering, all four stutterers apparently were relieved of their stuttering and subsequently were shown to have unilateral control of speech in the unoperated hemisphere. Wood, Stump, McKeehan, Sheldon, and Proctor (1980), in a study of regional cerebral blood flow in two stutterers, observed greater simultaneous activity in Broca's area (or its homologue) in the right hemisphere and in Wernicke's area of the left hemisphere. Baratz and Mesulam (1981) reported in a case study of adult-onset stuttering that the neurological abnormalities included paroxysmal discharges in EEG for the left temporal region and sharp waves occurring independently in the posterior zone of the right hemisphere. These clinical observations, together with numerous experimental studies on motor laterality preference in stutterers (Moore & Lang, 1977; Sussman & MacNeilage, 1975a) are not conclusive but certainly raise a strong possibility of interhemispheric competition or dyscoordination as a factor in stuttering.

Differences between stutterers and nonstutterers have been reported for tests of central auditory function (Curry & Gregory, 1969; Hall & Jerger, 1978; Toscher & Rupp, 1978), and some authors therefore have suggested that a neurological central auditory dysfunction is an etiological factor in stuttering. However, Wynne and Boehmler (1982) obtained significant differences on a test of central auditory function between two groups of *nonstutterers*—a relatively fluent group and a relatively dysfluent group. This result may indicate that differences in central auditory function occur within the general population of speakers, and that stuttering may develop when central auditory dysfunction combines with other etiologic factors, perhaps largely environmental. These results also confirm the idea of a gradient of laterality (Lauter, 1982), perhaps at the individual level as well as at the population level.

Hemispheric Asymmetry: A Caution

A note of caution is appropriate concerning laterality effects and the assumption that we have two basically different brains locked in our heads. It appears that neither hemisphere is totally incapable of functions that normally seem to be accomplished by the other hemisphere. Furthermore, none of the dichotomies that have been proposed to distinguish right- versus left-hemisphere capabilities is without exception or controversy. Among the proposed dichotomies or functional contrasts are: verbal/nonverbal; analytic/holistic; serial/parallel; focal/diffuse; algebraic/geometric; propositional/oppositional; and propositional/affective-emotional. The only reliable dichotomy is that one hemisphere is on the left and the other is on the right. In short, we do not have a wedge driven between two anatomically and functionally separate hemispheres (Figure 9-10). The controversy over hemispheric specialization, dominance, or preference, is clear from recent articles in *The Behavioral and Brain Sciences* (Vol. 4, No. 1, 1981), the writings of Gazzaniga and colleagues (Gazzaniga, 1980; Gazzaniga & LeDoux, 1978; Gazzaniga, Volpe, Smylie, Wilson, & LeDoux, 1979), and a review by Walker (1980).

Cortical-Subcortical Loops and the Regulation of Language, Emotion, and Phonation

To explain asymmetries in various behaviors it may be necessary to consider excitatory and inhibitory balances between cortical and subcortical structures, as well as asymmetries in neurotransmitters. Levy (1981) mentioned this possibility in relation to Robinson's (1979) report that in the rat, norepinephrine levels in the ipsilateral locus coeruleus diminished after right-hemisphere infarction, but no significant changes were observed in either ipsilateral or contralateral locus coeruleus after left-hemisphere infarction. Glick, Jerussi, and Zimmerberg (1977) reported naturally occurring asymmetries in nigrostriatal dopamine levels in rats that apparently were related to behavioral asymmetries in T-maze tests. Of course, it is a large jump from rat to man, but it is noteworthy that histologic evidence points to an extensive cholinergic system in the cortex that is apparently continuous with, and similar to, the cholinergic system of the reticular formation in the brain stem (Krnjevic, 1964; Krnjevic & Silver, 1965). Krnjevic (1964) considered the cholinergic neuron connections to be afferent to the cortex. Evidence for lateral asymmetry of neurotransmitters also has been reported for the human brain (Glick, Ross, & Hough, 1982; Oke, Keller, Mefford, & Adams, 1978), but the behavioral implications of this asymmetry are essentially unknown.

It is becoming increasingly clear that it can be misleading to draw sharp lines of functional separation between cortical and subcortical structures. Whereas it was earlier believed by most authorities that language functions were vested in the cerebral cortex, it is now clear that language impairments can result from thalamic lesions (see, e.g., the special issue of *Brain and Language*, Vol. 2, No. 1, 1975; the review by Jonas, 1982; and the report of McFarling, Rothi, & Heilman, 1982). (However, Luria, 1980,

FIGURE 9-10
Illustration of hemispheric specializations or preferences related to communication functions: verbal (propositional) capabilities for left hemisphere and melodic (prosodic) and affective capabilities for right hemisphere.

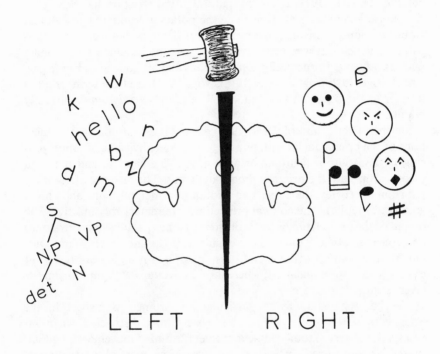

LEFT   RIGHT

considers the language impairment related to thalamic lesion to be a "quasi-aphasia" rather than a genuine aphasia.) Aphasia also has been reported in association with capsular/putaminal lesions (Naeser, 1982; Naeser, Alexander, Helm-Estabrooks, Levins, Laughlin, & Geschwind, 1982) and "circumscribed nonhemorrhagic infarctions of the anterior limb of the internal capsule and of the striatum, in the dominant hemisphere" (Damasio, Rizzo, Varney, & Gersch, 1981, p. 15). To understand the mechanisms of language, speech, and emotion, as well as their interactions, it is necessary to consider cortical-subcortical regulatory loops. Although it may still be correct to consider the cerebral cortex as the cognitive cap of the central nervous system, subcortical influences on cortical function are considerable and some subcortical structures appear to be capable of functions that have in the past been attributed solely to the cortex. The following section considers the basal ganglia, cerebellum, thalamus, limbic system, and reticular formation with respect to the theme of this chapter.

The basal ganglia are variously defined but will be taken here to include the main group of extrapyramidal nuclei: the caudate, putamen, and globus pallidus. Hassler (1979) notes that although the striatum has been considered for some 200 years to include the putamen, caudate nucleus, and globus pallidus, there are gross structural differences between the globus pallidus, which has a reticular structure, and the putamen and caudate nucleus, which are structurally homogeneous and are connected by the gray striae (Vogt, 1911; Vogt & Vogt, 1918). Vogt (1911) used the term *striatum* to refer to the putamen and caudate. The term *neostriatum* is currently popular.

McGeer, Eccles, and McGeer (1978) discuss the anatomic interconnections of the basal ganglia with respect to the three divisions of input, processing, and output neuronal arrangements. The caudate and putamen (neostriatum) are the primary processing areas. They receive afferent input from the cortex, thalamus, and midbrain (principally substantia nigra and rostral raphe). The cortical projections are remarkably massive. The output of the neostriatum is primarily to the globus pallidus (paleostriatum) and considerably less to the pars reticulata of the substantia nigra. Output from the globus pallidus and substantia nigra is highly divergent but chiefly involves the thalamus, where it often overlaps with input from the cerebellum.

The basal ganglia are of particular importance in respect to the extrapyramidal motor system. This system was discovered when investigators observed tonic-clonic movement, running movements, and impulses for generalized cortical seizures even after bilateral destruction of the motor cortex or pyramidal tracts (Hassler, 1979). As Kornhuber noted, damage to the basal ganglia results in profound speech disturbances. Whitaker (1976) concluded that chorea-like symptoms are associated with the caudate nucleus, athetoid symptoms with the putamen, and parkinsonian-like symptoms with the globus pallidus.

Kornhuber (1977) believed that speech is produced largely through the actions of the basal ganglia and the cerebellum. He argued that the role of the motor cortex has been overestimated, basing this assertion largely on reports that damage to subcortical structures such as the basal ganglia and cerebellum cause more profound impairments than does damage to the motor cortex. Kornhuber attributed to the basal ganglia the role of motor function generator or even motor program generator. Presumably, damage to these structures impairs a person's ability to generate motor programs, so that those residual motor programs spared by the lesion are repeated inflexibly and often under the disproportionate influence of external stimuli. The frequent repetition of residual actions (palipraxia) is a common characteristic of basal ganglia damage. In lower animals, bilateral destruction of the striatum results in an irresistible drive to run forward (Magendie, 1841; Nothnagel, 1873; Schiff, 1855). So far as speech is concerned, there is some evidence that in the dysarthria of athetoid cerebral palsy, individual articulators, such as the soft palate, undergo repetitive movements that are unrelated to, or inappropriate to, the intended phonetic sequence (Kent & Netsell, 1978).

The cerebellar hemispheres, which constitute nearly 90% of the human cerebellum, receive information from extensive areas of the cerebral cortex, including the motor association cortex and the motor cortex (via collaterals of the fibers of the pyramidal tract). Discharges from pyramidal tract cells of the association cortex are transmitted by the pontine nuclei and inferior olive to the contralateral cerebellar hemisphere. The cerebellum in turn sends signals through the ventrolateral thalamus to the motor cortex. This cerebrocerebellar circuit has been described as an open-loop system (McGeer et al., 1978).

The effects of cerebellar disease on speech production include errors in the timing, direction and range of movements and abnormalities in the prosodic structure of utterances (Brown, Darley, & Aronson, 1970; Kent & Netsell, 1975; Kent, Netsell, & Abbs, 1979). Generally, ataxic dysarthria (that is, the "ataxic" speech pattern associated with cerebellar damage) is slow in rate of utterance compared to normal speech and is deviant temporally in the relative durations of syllables and in the movements of individual articulators. Temporal errors seem to be most marked in the production of syllables that are normally short and unstressed. In severe ataxic dysarthria, these normally short syllables become about as long in duration as the longest syllables. In other words, normal differences in syllable duration are completely neutralized. Control of the f_0 contour can be irregular and variable (Kent & Netsell, 1975). Some of the speech disorders associated with cerebellar lesion are similar to disorders observed in apraxia of speech (Kent & Rosenbek, in press), perhaps indicating that the two disorders impair some similar functions of motor control for speech.

One difficulty in interpreting these results is that "the speech behavior of individuals with lesions of the nervous system has some characteristics that are directly related to the lesion's interference with motor control and other characteristics that are related to voluntary or involuntary compensations that may partially correct for the motor disturbance" (Kent et al., 1979, p. 645). Stimulation studies can be especially helpful in distinguishing compensation from genuine direct impairments of motor function. An example is Toth, Vajda, and Solyom's (1980) study of cerebellar function in patients with chronic implanted electrodes. They found that high-frequency stimulation impaired cerebellar function and resulted in simultaneous nystagmus, vertigo, hypotonia, dysmetria, and ataxia—the classic symptoms of cerebellar disease. Toth et al. concluded that their findings indicate that the cerebellar symptoms result directly from the cerebellar damage and not from the consequence of a two-step process of loss of function and subsequent compensation. It appears, then, that the cerebellar function in speech is to offer a fine regulation of muscle forces and the timing of movements. The speech disorder in response to cerebellar lesion is consistent with the idea that the motor instructions issued by the motor cortex are prefigurative and provisional and normally rely on cerebellar loops for updating and refinement (Eccles, 1969, 1973; Ito, 1970).

Perkins (William H. Perkins, personal communication, 1982) has observed equalized syllable durations in the speech of stutterers undergoing therapy with delayed auditory feedback. He reports that virtually all aspects of normal prosody disappears at a delay of 250 msec, and that equalized syllable durations tend to occur unless explicit instructions are given to shorten unstressed syllables. Perkins suggested that uniform syllable durations may be a consequence of the slowed speaking rates that dysarthric (and perhaps apraxic) speakers use in an effort to improve intelligibility.

The following general account of the involvement of the cerebral cortex, basal ganglia, and cerebellum in voluntary motor control is based on McGeer et al., (1978). The will to perform an action is indicated by patterns of excitation in the association cortex. This excitation is transmitted down to the basal ganglia and cerebellum, which participate in various open- and closed-loop dynamic sequences. The loops that play through the basal ganglia seem to be needed for the initiation of movement, and it is therefore understandable why Kornhuber (1977) would come to regard the basal ganglia as a motor program generator. McGeer et al. proposed a simultaneous activation of open loops of the basal ganglia and the cerebellum. These loops begin the initial programming of the movement and feed back to the motor cortex through the ventrolateral thalamus, but also project back to the association cortex, thus providing a complex neural circuitry for the programming of movement. A number of closed loops involving the cerebrum, cerebellum, basal ganglia, and spinal centers also contribute to the control of movement. One of these closed loops relies on the pars intermedia of the cerebellum to update the movement by determining the position and velocity of the relevant structures.

The complexity of the neural regulatory loops also offer the possibility of *afferent gating*, particularly for learned, skilled movements such as

FIGURE 9-11
Brain structures seen in coronal section: Am - amygdala, Ca - Cacaudate, Ci - cingulum, Cl - claustrum, EC - external capsule, Hy - hypothalamus, IC - internal capsule, In - insula, MB - mamillary bodies, Pa - pallidum, Pu - putamen, Th - thalamus. (Redrawn after Clara, 1953)

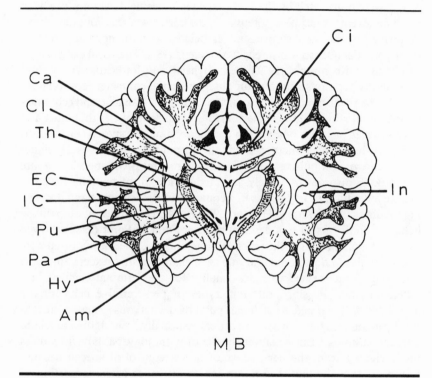

speech. Rushton, Rothwell, and Craggs (1981) identified a primary complex of evoked potentials that arise in the somatosensory area only 2 to 3 msec later than components that arise in the thalamocortical radiation. As an explanation of these results, Rushton et al. supposed that following initial processing in the cortex, motor impulses are transmitted elsewhere in the brain for other uses or for further processing, but return to the motor cortex, possibly in a form that can be suitably integrated into the continuing cortical motor output. They noted two prominent candidates for such a feedback loop: (1) cerebello-thalamo-cerebral, from sensorimotor cortex to area 4, and (2) cortico-striato-pallido-thalamo-cortical, which also feeds back to area 4.

The right hemisphere is not alone in its ability to yoke emotion and speech. The basal ganglia seem to be similarly endowed. Damage to these structures frequently results in impairment of speech and an apparent emotional disorder. For example, in diseases of the basal ganglia such as Gilles de la Tourette's disease, the patient may have tic and choreiform movements including vocal tics. The subcortical origin of the tics in Tourette's syndrome is demonstrated by the fact that such movements are not prefaced by a premovement negative potential at the cortex whereas voluntary jerks performed by the same subjects are associated with the normal premovement potential (Obeso, Rothwell, & Marsden, 1981). The vocal expressions, according to Kornhuber (1977) are "offensive and foul expressions" and "frequently acquire at puberty an obscene, sexual character (coprolalia)" (p. 32). The vocal expressions also include echolalia, palilalia, and echopraxia. Electrical stimulation of the ventro-oral nucleus of the thalamus and in Forel's area has been observed to produce compulsive speech (Kornhuber, 1977). Both of these structures are in the output path of the basal ganglia.

Palilalia, or compulsive and pathological reiteration of speech, is a rare but striking disorder. A widely accepted definition of palilalia is "compulsive reiteration of utterances in a context of increasing rate and decreasing loudness" (LaPointe & Horner, 1981, p. 34). However, not all palilalic behavior conforms to this description. Kent and LaPoint (1982) showed by acoustic methods that the reiterated utterances of one subject often were highly similar in durational and intensive characteristics, except for some differences that seemed to mark finality for the terminal element in a reiterated train. Possibly, different types of perseverative behavior are associated with damage to different parts of the nervous system. One major distinction might be between cortical (especially frontal lobe) and subcortical pathology. But whatever the site of pathology, palilalic utterances are intriguing from the perspective of motor control of speech because it appears that the motor program for an utterance or some portion of an utterance is replayed over and over, sometimes with remarkable similarity between items in a repetition train.

One interpretation of palilalic behavior is that the self-generated auditory stimulus, which is normally ineffective to release verbal behavior, bypasses the normal actuating mechanism and triggers a subprogram (Locke, 1978). If this speculation is correct, then it might be possible to influence palilalia by altering the patient's auditory feedback, for example, by the use of delayed auditory feedback. In fact, delayed auditory feedback has been used successfully in the treatment of "festinating" speech, in which words or syllables are repeated in an accelerando-decrescendo pattern (Downie, Low, & Lindsay, 1981; Hanson & Metter, 1980). Locke (1978) emphasized the role of reafferentation, both auditory and proprioceptive, in the regulation of speech and suggested that palilalic reiteration results from the incorrect use of the reafferent signal in an attempted correlation with a motor plan.

The nature of palilalia should become clearer as more information is reported on site of lesion, phonetic and linguistic properties of the reiterated utterances, and effective treatment methods. Data on site of lesion are needed to determine the number and location of neural structures associated with this disorder. Apparently palilalia can result from damage to different regions of the brain, but it is not known if the characteristics of palilalia vary with site of lesion, such that cortical and subcortical damage can be distinguished. A detailed examination of the reiterative utterances may help to explain the mechanism of palilalia. For example, the intervals between repeated utterances may help to characterize the feedback loops that could contribute to the disorder. For the patient studied by LaPointe and Horner (1981) and Kent and LaPointe (1982), the interval was constant between items within a reiterated train, but varied across different trains. One approach to treatment, then, could be to break the temporal pattern of the individual reiterative utterances, or to control the overall pattern of speech. Helm (1979) reported successful use of a pacing board in controlling palilalic speech in a man with slowly progressing Parkinson's syndrome. She attributed the success of this treatment to Luria's (1967) suggestion that automatic motor acts can be transferred to a cortical level of "reactive" control by replacing the patterned response cycle with a series of conscious motor impulses.

Evidence that the basal ganglia participate in psychomotor activation has been reviewed by Hassler (1980). The striatum (caudate nucleus and putamen) appears to control the pallidum and serves to bring into attentional focus a particular event by suppressing all competitive stimuli. The pallidum was considered to be "a psychomotor centre that generates the nonspecific impulses for attention and reaction to events in the contralateral sensory field" (p. 612). Evidence for these functions was mainly in the form of surgical relief for anankastic conditions, motor and psychomotor hyperkinesias, and tic syndromes. According to Hassler, initiative power resides both in the pallidum and in the frontal lobes, especially Brodmann areas 9, 10, 24, 32, 45a, and 46 (Figure 9-12). Damage to many of these cortical areas causes a loss of initiative power, or the will to action (see also Luria's, 1980, description of "frontal syndrome").

Luria (1980) noted that similar impairments arise from lesions to medial and orbital zones of the frontal cortex and to limbic structures of the cingulate gyrus, hypothalamus, amygdala, and hippocampus. He attributed to the mediobasal zones of the cortex the regulation of

FIGURE 9-12
Brodmann areas of the cortex.

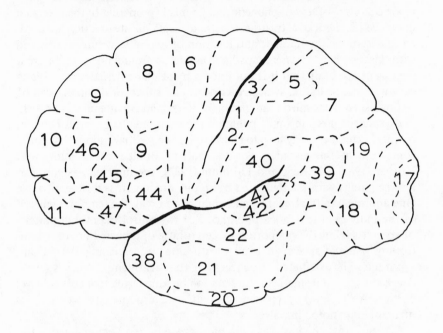

nonspecific activation processes. Some of the important neural structures and loops of the limbic system are illustrated in Figure 9-13. The limbic system has been described as a reverberatory system consisting of an inner ring and an outer ring. The inner ring is formed of part of the hippocampal formation, the archicortex and the olfactory structures. This ring projects by way of the fornix to the septal region, the hypothalamus, and the midbrain. The outer ring, composed of the cingulate gyrus, orbito-insulo-temporal cortex, and presubiculum, projects via the striatum to subcortical centers.

Information concerning internal states (hunger, thirst, sex, fear, pleasure, rage) is sent to the prefrontal lobes from the hypothalamus, septal nuclei, and limbic structures such as the hippocampus and amygdala (Nauta, 1971). These projections (Figure 9-13), which course chiefly through the dorsomedial thalamus can modify and emotionally color the perceptions based on sensory input (McGeer et al., 1978).

FIGURE 9-13
Structures and loops of the limbic system, arranged schematically
so that cortical structures surround a core of subcortical structures.
CG - cingulate gyrus, EC - entorhinal cortex, HG - hippocampal gyrus,
Hi - hippocampus, Hy - hypothalamus, OC - orbital surface of prefrontal
cortex, Se - septum, Th - thalamus, TP - temporal pole of cerebrum,
20 and 46 - Brodmann areas of cortex.

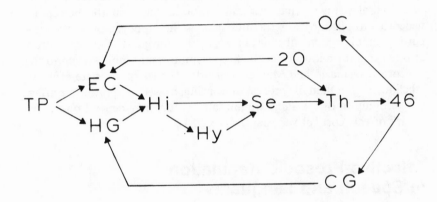

(Based on descriptions in McGeer, Eccles, and McGeer, 1978)

The primary sensory and related association areas of the parietal, occipital, and temporal lobes simultaneously project to the prefrontal lobes and the limbic system. In addition, the prefrontal cortex projects to the limbic system. From this complex circuitry "the prefrontal and limbic systems are in reciprocal relationship and have the potentiality for continuously looping interaction" (McGeer et al., 1978, p. 547). The dorsomedial thalamus is a critical way station that gives the prefrontal cortex a controlling influence over emotions arising from the limbic system.

Similar brain structures have been implicated in autism. Damasio and Maurer (1978) point out that the various disturbances in autism—disorders of motility, communication, attention and perception, as well as behavioral disturbances such as ritualistic and compulsive behaviors—are consistent with dysfunction in a complex of bilateral CNS structures including the medial and frontal lobes, basal ganglia (especially the neostriatum) and the dorsomedial and anterior nuclei of the thalami. The cortical areas are part of the phylogenetically older cortex and include the supplementary motor area, cingulate gyrus, entorhinal area, perirhinal area, parahippocampal gyrus, subicular and presubicular region. Damasio and Maurer remark that these areas are cytoarchitectonically distinctive, being a transitional type of cortex known as mesocortex or periallocortex. Furthermore, this ring of mesocortex together with the neostraitum is neurochemically distinctive in that this system is the complete terminating area of dopaminergic neurons arising in the midbrain. Damasio and Maurer note that the mesocortex is part of a neural pathway that transmits information from the perceptual neocortex to allocortical structures such as the hippocampus or to subcortical limbic system structures such as the amygdala. The mesocortex also relays information from the hippocampus and limbic system to the neocortex. Damasio and Maurer conclude, "Thus, appropriate affective labelling of stimuli in the process of learning, as well as appropriate affective recognition of the same stimuli later in life, may depend on the integrity of this cortical way station." (p. 783).

Affective-Prosodic Regulation in Speech and Language

Frequently, the segmental-suprasegmental (or segmental-prosodic) distinction is taken to apply without reservation to neurologically disordered speech in the same way that it does to normal speech. However, in many respects, segmental and prosodic aspects of speech production are woven together in the same fabric of motor expression, and are therefore not cleanly separable in either clinical or experimental analysis. For instance, the lengthening of segments, pauses, and articulatory transitions in apraxia of speech (Kent & Rosenbek, in press; Ryalls, 1981) is pertinent to both segmental and prosodic descriptions of the disorder. In addition, it has been argued that a feature such as nasalization, ordinarily considered to be a segmental feature of English, can exert wide-spread suprasegmental effects in the speech patterns associated with Parkinson's disease and perhaps right-hemisphere lesions as well (Kent & Rosenbek, 1982). Although such special effects might be called a voice quality deviance (hypernasality), this description does not convey the powerful shaping that nasalization can give to the syllable train, and hence the overall prosodic character of the speech pattern. In fact, precisely because nasalization has a potential realization over several syllables, it has been proposed as a suprasegmental or prosodic feature of some languages (Hyman, 1975; Leben, 1973a, 1973b). In short, there are situations in which the distinction between segmental and suprasegmental should be functionally defined for the speech pattern of an individual talker, and caution should be observed in clinical attempts to separate segmental and prosodic aspects, whether for diagnosis or treatment.

Acoustic properties of aprosodic and dysprosodic speech, as defined by Monrad-Krohn (1963), were described by Kent and Rosenbek (1982). Aprosodic speech characteristic of patients with Parkinson's disease and right-hemisphere lesion had a general pattern of reduced acoustic contrast, including limited f_0 variation, continuous voicing, weakly formed consonants, and extensive nasalization[3]. Dysprosodic speech, characteristic of cerebellar ataxia and verbal apraxia (apraxia of speech), had a slow rate with disproportionate lengthening of certain phonetic segments, and a tendency toward equal syllable durations. Major types of prosodic abnormality are illustrated in Figures 9-14 and 9-15.

Some of the major ipsilateral (thalamocortical) and contralateral (cerebello-cortical) connections important to the affective-prosodic regulation of speech are shown in Figure 9-16. Neural pathways and centers include: (1) the right cerebral hemisphere, which seems to be involved in the processing of prosodic and affective information; (2) contralateral cerebello-cerebral connections, which give cerebellar access to the prosodic line presumably maintained largely in the right cerebral hemisphere; (3) ipsilateral thalamocortical pathways, which are said to conduct essential affective and motivational information from the basal ganglia; (4) the thalamus, which seems to regulate information flow to the cortex and to give emotional coloring to the cortical input; and (5) the cerebellum, which participates in the coordination of movements and may be a system for the integration of prosodic and segmental-phonetic components of speech.

The thalamus appears to be a key structure in the behavioral integration of communication, emotion, and orientation to stimuli. W. M. R. Critchley (1981) notes that the ventrolateral nucleus of the left thalamus represents a convergence of certain speech functions, a specific alerting response, a connection with short-term memory, and respiratory changes suited to speech. The thalamus has long been implicated in functions of arousal and attention. Watson, Valenstein, and Heilman (1981) suggested that the medial thalamic nuclei participate in an arousal-activation process that allows the organism to be aroused by, and to respond to, novel or significant stimuli. Watson et al. also proposed that because these thalamic nuclei are closely associated with motor systems (e.g., basal ganglia, ventrolateral nucleus of the thalamus, and frontal cortex), they may have a critical function "in preparing a tonically aroused organism

FIGURE 9-14
Stylized representations of prosodic (intonation) patterns for a short sentence. Each pattern is shown as a graph of f_0 (vocal fundamental frequency) as a function of time.

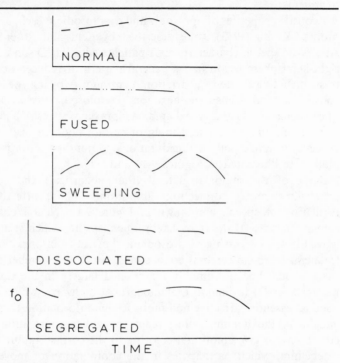

Compared to the normal pattern: the *fused* pattern is of normal or faster than normal rate, monotone, and tends toward continuous voicing (typical of accelerated speech or short rushes of speech in Parkinson's disease); *sweeping* pattern is slow rate, often with intersyllable pauses, and has large f_0 shifts (typical of some subjects with cerebellar disease), *dissociated* pattern has syllables of nearly equal duration, separated by intersyllable pauses of prolonged consonants, and frequently with a monotypic intonation pattern within syllables (i.e., no multisyllabic intonation contour); often observed in severe ataxic dysarthria or in apraxia of speech; *segregated* pattern has a slow rate but shows preservation of differences in relative syllable duration and preservation of sentence-like f_0 contour across the syllable train (characteristic of some subjects with ataxic dysarthria or apraxia of speech). (After Kent and Rosenbek, 1982)

FIGURE 9-15
Patterns of f_0 (vocal fundamental frequency) change for the phrase *please put the groceries* (derived from a larger sentence) produced by a normal talker (N), a talker with apraxia of speech and left-hemisphere damage (LH), and a talker with aprosody (reduced prosodic variation), and right-hemisphere damage (RH). Note fast speaking rate and monotone for RH and slow speaking rate and essentially normal f_0 variation for LH.

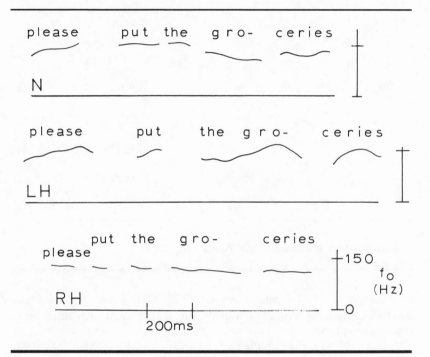

to respond to a meaningful behavioral event." (p. 505) Apparent language functions of the thalamus were mentioned earlier; speech functions are discussed by Guiot, Hertzog, Rondot, and Molimar, (1961), Bell (1968), Riklan and Cooper (1977), Mateer (1978a), and Ojemann and Mateer (1979). It is especially important to note that speech and language functions are asymmetrically organized at the thalamic level and that thalamocortical connections are essentially ipsilateral. Left thalamus and left cerebral cortex may be both supplementary and partially redundant in their regulation of speech and language functions (Kent & Rosenbek, 1982). Brown (1975) thought that the thalamus should not be regarded as an extrinsic control center that influences the neocortex but "as a participant

FIGURE 9-16
Pathways of subcortical input to the cerebral hemispheres. Callosal connections are represented by broken lines.

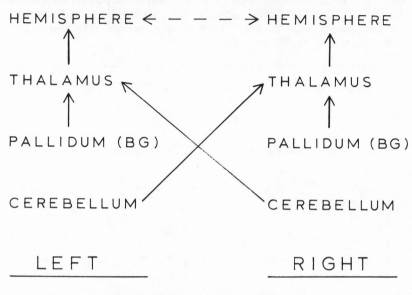

(Redrawn and adapted from Whitaker, 1975)

at each phase in the genetic sequence" (p. 28). Thus, thalamus and neocortex comprise a tightly coupled neurologic system with allied functional properties.

Brown (1979b) argued on the basis of anatomic evidence that the fluent-nonfluent distinction that usefully differentiates posterior and anterior aphasias resulting from cortical damage, also applies at the subcortical level. For example, he suggested that, "The aphasic jargon which is associated with a (?) pulvinar lesion, and the dysnomia which occurs on pulvinar stimulation, would correspond to the semantic jargon and verbal paraphasia, and anomia, which result from lesions of posterior...neocortex" (Brown, 1979a, p. 235). Support for this suggestion comes from Naeser's (1982) comparisons of language behavior in patients with cortical and subcortical lesions. She noted a similarity in language deficit (primarily reduced fluency with good comprehension) between patients with cortical Broca's aphasia and a patient with a subcortical anterior-superior capsular/putaminal lesion. Likewise, she reported fluent speech but poor language comprehension in patients with cortical Wernicke's aphasia and a patient with posterior capsular/putaminal damage.

Connections between cerebrum and cerebellum also seem to represent a strongly interactive neurologic subsystem. Lechtenberg and Gilman (1978) offered evidence that a speech disorder is more likely to result from lesion to the left, rather than right, cerebellar hemisphere. They noted that because cerebro-cerebellar connections are primarily contralateral, the left hemisphere interacts more with the right than the left cerebral cortex. Given that processing of melodies has been linked with the nondominant (usually right) hemisphere of the cerebrum, they suggested that the dysprosody of ataxic dysarthria results from a disturbance between the right cerebral hemisphere and the left cerebellar hemisphere. The predominant contralaterality of cerebello-cortical connections is confirmed by the work of Toth et al. (1980), who studied cerebellar function in patients with chronic implanted electrodes. During 1 Hz stimulation of the cerebellum, they recorded evoked potentials from the ventrolateral thalamus, pallidum, and the motor cortex on the opposite side. The responses were reliably contralateral.

It should also be noted with respect to Figure 9-16 that because some callosal neurons receive direct thalamic input, the callosal system may be a direct extension of the thalamocortical pathway to the contralateral hemisphere (Innocenti, 1981). Thus, in Figure 9-16 the broken lines connecting the hemispheres may be regarded as an extension of the thalamocortical pathway.

Figure 9-16 is a highly simplified representation of a very complex circuitry and shows only some of the most prominent subcortical inputs to the cerebral hemispheres. Connections like those shown in Figure 9-13 rapidly complicate the picture. The intent of this chapter is not to present the details of such connections, but only to summarize the potential importance of some of the major pathways to the organization of linguistic and affective behaviors.

Requin (1980) suggested a three-stage model of behavioral neurophysiology, with each stage having a structural and functional organization. The first stage, beginning in the association areas of the cortex and ending in the neocerebellum, has a functional responsibility for action "project definition" (response determination). The second stage, which begins in the neocerebellum and ends in the precentral motor cortex, selects and builds the motor program. The third stage, reaching from motor cortex to motoneuron activation, accounts for movement execution. Thus, stages are defined structurally by groups of structures, rather than by isolated neural centers. Each structure in the regulating pathway contributes to the characteristics of the evolving movement. As Thach (1975) succinctly summarized it: "A command for movement...occurs in cerebral association cortex and then sequentially feeds through pons, dentate, VA-VL thalamus, and motor cortex, gaining specifications at each stage." (p. 240)

The idea of stages or levels, as opposed to centers, also is at the heart of Brown's (1975, 1979a) model of cognitive and language processing in the brain. He rejects the "centers" of traditional neuropsychology in favor of levels by which cognitive processing is carried through different stages. In addition, he argues against the idea that pathways serve to associate ideas, or perceptions to movements, and proposes instead that pathways accomplish a temporal linkage of transformations that occur at different points in the "microgenetic sequence."

For example, Brown (1979a) considered the anterior aphasias (akinetic mutism, transcortical motor aphasia, agrammatism, and Broca's aphasia) as impairments affecting different phases of the nascent utterance. He supposed that the utterance proceeds in its formation from the "diffuse, labile affect of the limbic level" (p. 179), to a prefigurative motor envelope, to syntactic realization, and finally to phonological representation. Each of these stages can be related to one of the aphasias listed above.

One additional phase might be added to Brown's sequence of utterance evolution, viz., a phase of motor implementation, which could be used to describe errors in output motor programming. That is, phonological sequence is not necessarily the final output stage of utterance formation but must itself be followed by another stage concerned with the more fundamental aspects of motor programming, including selection of the muscles or muscle groups to be activated, determination of the function of effector units (e.g., agonistic-antagonistic or phasic-tonic), gauging the intensity and duration of activation, and specification of the temporal order and temporal structure by which the timing of the selected units is regulated (Semjen, 1977). Recent studies of aphasia and apraxia of speech distinguish phonetic from phonemic, or motoric from phonological, errors in the terminating stages of utterance formation (Blumstein, Cooper, Zurif, & Caramazza, 1977; Itoh, Sasanuma, Tasumi, & Kobayashi, 1979; Kent & Rosenbek, in press). The phonological representation is not yet a complete motoric prescription of the intended movement sequence, and thus needs to be followed by still another stage of utterance generation (see Roy, 1978, for similar arguments and a categorization of apraxia according to a model of motor skill performance).

One of the appealing aspects of Brown's model is that each level represents "components of perception, action and affectivity, as well as a specific consciousness-experience" (Brown, 1975, p. 28). Thus, affective and cognitive aspects of utterance formulation are quite widely distributed within the nervous system, and are not simply imposed or interpreted at some "center" of the brain. An evolving utterance takes cognitive and emotional form from a variety of stages of processing, so that the interaction of speech and language formulation with emotion is not monolithic but multilithic. Indeed, it appears that emotional functions, as well as speech-language functions, are controlled by integrated cortical and subcortical systems. Sackeim et al. (1982) wrote that "the evidence concerning location of lesions in cases of pathological laughing and crying suggests that emotional behavior is subserved by integrated networks comprising cortical and subcortical regions" (p. 217). Noting the growing evidence of lateralization of function at both cortical and subcortical levels, Sackeim et al. speculated that studies of neurotransmitter pathways may yield important clues to the identification of such integrated cortical-subcortical systems.

Milner (1976) suggested that at least three patterns of functional organization of the human nervous system need to be considered: (1) the hierarchical-reduplicative phylogenetic-legacy pattern, (2) the neuropsychological functional-subsystems pattern, and (3) the triple-system phylogenetic legacy pattern. The first of these refers to a complex lowest-center reduplicative pattern in which the highest centers are functionally dominant over lower centers. According to this view, lower levels are successively re-represented at ascending levels. The second pattern, that of neuropsychological functional-subsystems, holds that the nervous system is composed of numerous overlapping circuits, operating both within and across levels. Each of these circuits is supposed to act both as a function entity and in concert with the rest of the nervous system. Finally, Milner's suggested third pattern, triple-system phylogenetic legacy, recognizes three major neural-structure legacies: "a visceral, internally oriented subsystem; a sensorimotor subsystem interactive with the external environment; and a third system that coordinates the first two systems into a coherently functioning whole." (p. 65) Milner named these three subsystems the intra-organismic, the transactional, and the integrative.

Conclusion

This chapter represents an attempted synthesis of a large and diverse literature, and even at that, the review has been necessarily selective. The means to this synthesis admittedly has been speculation more often than the compulsion of data and logic. A recurrent theme has been that of interaction, e.g., interaction of factors in the determination of lateralized brain function; interaction of emotion with speech and language functions; interaction of cortical and subcortical structures for a variety of purposes, including some traditionally reserved for the cerebral cortex; and interaction of neural structures to form stages or levels of control and information processing. The interaction of variables related to a given function is often so complex that it is tempting to pose explanations based on conspiracies, or other interactive mechanisms, so as to recognize the multifaceted and sometimes subtle interactions among related variables.

In his review of Gallistel's (1980) book *The Organization of Action: A New Synthesis*, Hollerbach (1981) observed that whereas ten years ago thinkers in artificial intelligence were hotly debating the issue of hierarchical versus hetarchical control, the issue has now essentially disappeared because these concepts were too simple to offer the required explanatory power. Similarly, it may be fruitless to demand of a topic such as the brain mechanisms of human vocalization a model of any simple structure. Although a hierarchical model was favored in many of the papers reviewed in this chapter, it is doubtful that the requirements of hierarchical control are satisfied in any but the simplest of functions. Hollerbach notes that current work in artificial intelligence focuses on well-defined problems and allows the peculiarities of the individual problem to determine the nature of the control structure. The resulting control usually goes beyond simple notions like hierarchy or heterarchy. Nor do these simple structures seem to help much in organizing the conclusions (such as they are) of this chapter. The models fit too poorly even to the current data to hold any real promise of generating experimentally testable predictions.

Not surprisingly, then, it has been difficult to formulate simple deterministic mechanisms for such problems as the relationship of site of brain lesion to impairment of function, or the development of laterality preferences for individual behaviors, or for the interaction of emotional state with language expression. To propose a conspiratorial model or an interactive, multilithic model may not seem a satisfactory answer, but they are perhaps closer to the mark than any solution based on simple hierarchy or heterarchy. The evolutionary process generally does not simplify structure or function, nor can it always allow newly emerged capabilities to override more primitive ones, or vice versa. Consequently, the human nervous system must be viewed as an adaptive, highly complex structure composed of many interactive levels of organization. Milner's (1976) proposal (reviewed above) that three patterns of functional organization need to be considered is compatible with this perspective and offers a useful framework for the integration of a large and diverse experimental literature. The hierarchical-reduplicative phylogenetic-legacy pattern accounts for the redundancy of functional organization across levels. The neuropsychological functional subsystems pattern allows for overlapping circuits that transmit information within and across the levels of a structure that is either nonhierarchical or a lattice hierarchy[1]. Finally, the triple-system phylogenetic legacy pattern yields a tripartite division into a visceral system of internal orientation, a sensorimotor system that interacts with the external environment, and an integrative system that monitors and coordinates the first two. As these different patterns of functional organization are coalesced in behavior, one result would be that the highest level can coordinate the activities at lower levels but is in turn modulated by them. Such an interaction is not compatible with a strict hierarchical organization. Hierarchical models may preserve functional limitations that the brain has evolved to overcome.

Acknowledgments

This work was supported in part by NINCDS grant NS16763 from the U.S. Department of Health and Human Services. I am thankful to the following persons for comments on earlier drafts of the manuscript: Claudia Blair, Dwight Bolinger, William H. Perkins, Ronald Netsell, Diana Van Lancker, Charles S. Watson, and Gary Weismer. Carole Dugan expertly maintained the manuscript through seemingly endless changes and updating.

Notes

[1]In this review the word *hierarchy* is not necessarily given a simple unifying definition. Several writers represented in this review have argued for a hierarchical organization, and the word hierarchy and its derivatives are used to reflect such thinking. However, because the word hierarchy has come to mean quite different things to different thinkers, it really needs one or more modifiers to mark the semantic peculiarities that it invokes for an individual writer. For example, Gallistel (1980) distinguished a *partition* hierarchy from a *lattice* hierarchy. The former is the kind of hierarchical organization typically used in constructing tree diagrams in linguistics. In this structure, each node at any given level is partitioned into one or more branches that form a lower level, such that any one node is subordinate to one and only one node at the next higher level. In a lattice hierarchy, a multiple branching occurs between levels, such that any one node at any given level can be subordinate to one *or more* nodes at the next higher level. Hollerbach (1981) pointed out that in the limit the lattice hierarchy is a heterarchy, i.e., a structure in which composition by level vanishes and interactions among nodes or modules are unconstrained. Hierarchies also can be distinguished with respect to whether they are hierarchies of connection or hierarchies of classification (Dawkins, 1976). In the former, the control of superior over inferior elements is analogous to the issuing of orders from a captain to a lieutenant. In the latter, superior elements are actually composed of the inferior elements in much the same way as companies are formed from platoons. The meaning of the word hierarchy is further compromised (if not destroyed) when the structure it denotes permits bidirectional (ascending and descending) influences. In such a case, the concept of subordination loses its meaning.

²Other explanations can be posed. One is that the aphasic disturbance interrupts the normal integration of linguistic and prosodic material, which tend to be vested in different hemispheres. Any supporting use of cadence or melody reduces the burden on the presumably overtaxed residual function and thereby facilitates language expression. Another is that accentuation of prosody or melody results in a general activation of both hemispheres and also facilitates their interaction.

³The similarity in speech characteristics between some patients with Parkinson's disease and some patients with right-hemisphere lesion is not easily explained, but it is noteworthy that Bentin, Silverberg, and Gordon (1981) reported that patients with Parkinson's disease had a greater deterioration on functions normally associated with the right cerebral hemisphere than on functions associated with the left cerebral hemisphere.

References

Abbeduto, L., & Rosenberg, S. The communicative competence of mildly retarded adults. *Applied Psycholinguistics,* 1980, *4,* 405–426.

Aitken, P.G. Cortical control of conditioned and spontaneous vocal behavior in rhesus monkeys. *Brain and Language,* 1981, *13,* 171–184.

Albert, M., Sparks, R., & Helm, N. Melodic intonation therapy for aphasia. *Archives of Neurology,* 1973, *29,* 130–131.

Altman, J. Three levels of mentation and the hierarchic organization of the human brain. In G.A. Miller & H. Lenneberg (Eds.), *Psychology and biology of language and thought.* New York: Academic Press, 1978.

Anderson, R.C., Pichert, J.W., Goetz, E.T., Shallert, D.L., Stevens, K.V., & Trollip, S.R. Instantiation of general terms. *Journal of Verbal Learning and Verbal Behavior,* 1976, *15,* 667–680.

Anderson, S.R. *West Scandanavian vowel systems and the ordering of phonological rules.* (Doctoral dissertation, MIT, 1969).

Anderson, S.R. *The organization of phonology.* New York: Academic Press: 1974.

Anderson, S.R. On the subsequent development of the 'standard theory' in phonology. In D.A. Dinnsen (Ed.), *Current approaches to phonological theory.* Bloomington: Indiana University Press, 1979.

Anderson, S.R. Why phonology isn't "natural." *Linguistic Inquiry,* 1981, *12,* 493–539. Reprinted in *UCLA Working Papers In Linguistics, 51,* 36–93.

Angelini, L., Mazzucchi, A., Piccioto, F., Nardocci, N., & Broggi, G. Focal lesion of the right cingulum: A case report in a child. *Journal of Neurology, Neurosurgery and Psychiatry,* 1980, *43,* 355–357.

Angiolillo, C., & Goldin-Meadow, S. Experimental evidence for agent-patient categories in child language. *Journal of Child Language,* 1982, *9,* 627–643.

Anglin, J. *Word, object and conceptual development.* New York: Norton, 1977.

Anwar, M.S. Consonant devoicing at word boundary and assimilation. *Language Sciences,* October 1974, 6–12.

Aram, D., & Nation, J. Patterns of language behavior in children with developmental language disorders. *Journal of Speech and Hearing Research,* 1975, *18,* 229–241.

Arbib, M.A., & Caplan, D. Neurolinguistics must be computational. *The Behavioral and Brain Sciences,* 1979, *2,* 449–483.

Austin, J. *How to do things with words,* Oxford, NJ: Oxford University Press, 1962.

Bailey, P., & von Bonin, G. The isocortex of man. Urbana, IL: University of Illinois Press, 1951.

Baratz, R., & Mesulam, M.M. Adult-onset stuttering treated with anticonvulsants. *Archives of Neurology,* 1981, *38,* 132.

Barclay, J.R. The role of comprehension in remembering sentences. *Cognitive Psychology,* 1973, *4,* 229–254.

Barris, R.W., & Schuman, H.R. Bilateral anterior cingulate lesions. *Neurology,* (Minneapolis), 1953, *3,* 44–52.

Basso, A., Salvolini, U., & Vignolo, L.A. Localization of aphasic symptoms: Preliminary observations with C.T. scanner (Italian). *Rivista di Patologia Nervosa E Mentale,* 1979, *100,* 94–102.

Bates, E. Peer relations and the acquisition of language. In M. Lewis & L. Rosenblum (Eds.), *Friendship and peer relations: The origins of behavior.* New York: Wiley, 1975.

Bates, E. *Language and context: The acquisition of pragmatics.* New York: Academic Press, 1976. (a)

Bates, E. Pragmatics and sociolinguistics in child language. In D. Morehead & A. Morehead (Eds.), *Normal and deficient child language.* Baltimore, MD: University Park Press, 1976. (b)

Bates, E., Benigni, L., Bretherton, I., Camaioni, L., & Volterra, V. From gesture to the first word: On the nature of cognitive and social prerequisites. In M. Lewis & L. Rosenblum (Eds.), *Interaction, conversation, and the development of language.* New York: Wiley, 1977.

Bates, E., Benigni, L., Bretherton, I., Camaioni, L., & Volterra, V. *The emergence of symbols: Cognition and communication in infancy.* New York: Academic Press, 1979.

Bates, E., Bretherton, I., & Snyder, L. Predictors of language development: A longitudinal study. In preparation, 1983.

Bates, E., Bretherton, I., Snyder, L., Shore, C., & Volterra, V. Vocal and gestural symbols at 13 months. *Merrill-Palmer Quarterly,* 1980.

Bates, E., Camaioni, L., & Volterra, V. The acquisition of performatives prior to speech. *Merrill-Palmer Quarterly,* 1975, *21,* (3) 205–226.

Bates, E., & MacWhinney, B. A functionalist approach to the acquisition of grammar. In E. Ochs & B. Schieffelin (Eds.), *Developmental pragmatics.* New York: Academic Press, 1979.

Bates, E., & MacWhinney, B. Functionalist approaches to grammar. In L. Gleitman & E. Wanner (Eds.), *Language acquisition: The state of the art.* New York: Cambridge University Press, 1982.

Bates, E., MacWhinney, B., McNew, S., Devescovi, A., & Smith, S. Functional constraints on sentence processing: A cross-linguistic study. *Congition,* 1982, *11,* 245–299.

Bates, E., & Snyder, L. The cognitive hypothesis in language acquisition. In I. C. Uzgiris & J. M. Hunt (Eds.), *Research with scales of psychological development in infancy.* Champaign-Urbana: University of Illinois Press, in press.

Bateson, M.C. Mother-infant exchanges: The epigenesis of conversational interaction. In D. Aronson & R.W. Rieber (Eds.), *Annals of the New York Academy of Sciences* (Vol. 263): *Developmental psycholinguistic and communication disorders.* New York: New York Academy of Sciences, 1975.

Beatty, J., & Devitt, C.A. Call discrimination in chimpanzees. *Current Anthropology,* 1975, *16,* 668–669.

Bell, A. & Hooper, J. (Eds.). *Syllables and segments.* Amsterdam, Netherlands: North-Holland, 1978.

Bell, D.S. Speech functions of the thalamus inferred from the effects of thalamotomy. *Brain, 1968, 91,* 619–638.

Bellugi, U., & Klima, E.S. The acquisition of three morphological systems in American Sign Language. *Papers and Reports on Child Language Development,* 1982, *21,* 1–34.

Benedict, H. Early lexical development: Comprehension and production. *Journal of Child Language,* 1979, *6,* 183–200.

Benson, D. F. Neurologic correlates of anomia. In H. Whitaker & H.A. Whitaker (Eds.), *Studies in neurolinguistics* (Vol. 4). New York: Academic Press, 1979.

Bentin, S., Silverberg, R., & Gordon, H.W. Asymmetrical cognitive deterioration in demented and Parkinson patients. *Cortex,* 1981, *57,* 533–543.

Berko, J. The child's learning of English morphology. *Word,* 1958, *14,* 150–177.

Berko-Gleason, J. Talking to children: Some notes on feedback. In C.E. Snow & C.A. Ferguson (Eds.), *Talking to children.* London: Cambridge University Press, 1977.

Berko-Gleason, J., & Weintraub, S. The acquisition of routines in child language. *Papers and Reports on Child Language Development No. 10,* Stanford, CA: Stanford University, 1975.

Berko-Gleason, J., & Weintraub, S. Input language and the acquisition of communicative competence. In K. E. Nelson (Ed.), *Children's Language* (Vol. 1). New York: Gardner Press, 1978.

Bernard-Opitz, V. Pragmatic analysis of the communicative behavior of an autistic child. *Journal of Speech and Hearing Disorders,* 1982, *47,* 99–108.

Berwick, R.C., & Weinberg, A.S. Parsing efficiency, computational complexity, and the evaluation of grammatical theories. *Linguistic Inquiry,* 1982, *13,* 165–191.

Bever, T.G. The cognitive basis for linguistic structures. In J.R. Hayes (Ed.), *Cognition and the development of language.* New York: Wiley, 1970.

Bever, T.G. Cerebral asymmetries in humans are due to the differentiation of two incompatible processes: Holistic and analytic. In D. Aaronson & R.W. Reiber (Eds.), *Developmental psycholinguistics and communication disorders.* New York Academy of Sciences, (Vol. 263). New York: New York Academy of Sciences, 1975.

Bever, T.G. Broca and Lashley were right: Cerebral dominance is an accident of growth. In D. Caplan (Ed.), *Biological studies of mental processess.* Cambridge, MA: MIT Press, 1980.

Bever, T.G., Fodor, J., & Weksel, W. Theoretical notes on the acquisition of syntax: A critique of "contextual generalization." *Psychological Review,* 1965, *72,* 467–482.

Bever, T.G., Garrett, M.F., & Hurtig, R. The interaction of perceptual processes and ambiguous sentences. *Memory and cognition.* 1973, *1,* 277–286.

Bever, T.G., & Townsend, D.J. Perceptual mechanisms and formal properties of main and subordinate clauses. In W.E. Cooper & E.C.T. Walker (Eds.), *Sentence processing.* New York: Wiley, 1979.

Bhat, D.N.S. A general study of palatalization. In J.H. Greenberg (Ed.), *Universals of human language: Phonology* (Vol. 2). Stanford: Stanford University Press, 1978.

Black, J.B., & Bern, H. Causal coherence and memory for events in narrative. *Journal of Verbal Learning and Verbal Behavior,* 1981, *20,* 266–276.

Blank, M.A. *Dual-mode processing of phonemes in fluent speech.* Unpublished doctoral dissertation, University of Texas, Austin, 1979.

Blank, M., & Foss, D.J. Semantic facilitation and lexical access during sentence processing. *Memory and cognition,* 1978, *6,* 644–652.

Blank, M., & Franklin, E. Dialogue with preschoolers: A cognitively based system of assessment. *Applied Psycholinquistics,* 1980, *1,* 127–150.

Blank, M., Rose, S., & Berlin, L. *Preschool language assessment instrument.* New York: Grune & Stratton, 1978.

Bloom, L.M. *Language development: Form and function in emerging grammars.* Cambridge, MA: MIT Press, 1970.

Bloom, L.M. *One word at a time: The use of single word utterances before syntax.* The Hague: Mouton, 1973.

Bloom, L.M., Capatides, J., & Tackeff, J. Further remarks on interpretive analysis: In response to Christine Howe. *Journal of Child Language,* 1981, *8,* 403–412.

Bloom, L.M., Hood, L., & Lightbown, P. Imitation in language development: If, when and why. *Cognitive Psychology,* 1974, *6,* 380–420.

Bloom, L.M., & Lahey, M. *Language development and language disorders.* New York: Wiley, 1978.

Bloom, L.M., Lightbown, P., & Hood, L. Structure and variation in child language. *Society for Research in Child Development Monographs*, 1975, *40*, (Serial No. 160).

Bloom, L.M., Rocissano, L., & Hood, L. Adult-child discourse: Developmental interaction between information processing and linguistic knowledge. *Cognitive Psychology*, 1976, *8*, 521-552.

Blount, B.G. Aspects of Luo socialization. *Language in Society*, 1972, *1*, 235-248.

Blount, B.G. Studies in child language: An anthropological view. *American Anthropologist*, 1975, *77*, (3), 580-600.

Blount, B.G. Ethnography and caretaker-child interaction. In C.E. Snow & C.A. Ferguson (Eds.), *Talking to children*. Cambridge: Cambridge University Press, 1977.

Blount, B.G., & Kempton, W. Child language socialization: Parental speech and interactional strategies. *Sign Language Studies*, 1976, *12*, 251-277.

Blount, B.G., & Padgug, E.J. Prosodic, paralinguistic, and interactional features in parent-child speech: English and Spanish. *Journal of Child Language*, 1977, *4*, 67-86.

Blumstein, S.E., & Cooper, W.E. Hemispheric processing of intonation contours. *Cortex*, 1974, *10*, 146-158.

Blumstein, S.E., Cooper, W.E., Zurif, E.B., & Caramazza, A. The perception and production of voice-onset time in aphasia. *Neuropsychologia*, 1977, *15*, 371-383.

Blunk, R., DeBleser, R., Willmes, K., & Zeumer, H. A refined method to relate morphological and functional aspects of aphasia. *European Neurology*, 1981, *20*, 69-79.

Bogen J.E., & Bogen, C.M. Wernicke's region, where is it? In *Origins and Evolution of Language and Speech. Annals of the New York Academy of Sciences*, 1976, *280*, 834-843.

Bohannon, J.N., & Marquis, A.L. Children's control of adult speech. *Child Development*, 1977, *48*, 1002-1008.

Bolinger, D. *Two kinds of vowels, two kinds of rhythm*. Reproduced by Indiana University Linguistics Club: Bloomington, IN, 1981.

Boller, G., Cole, M., Vrtunski, P.B., Patterson, M., & Kim, Y. Paralinguistic aspects of auditory comprehension in aphasia. *Brain and Language*, 1979, *7*, 164-174.

Boomer, D.S., & Laver, J.D.M. Slips of the tongue. *British Journal of Disorders of Communication*, 1968, *3*, 2-12.

Borod, J.C., Caron, H.S., & Koff, E. Asymmetry of facial expression related to handedness, footedness, and eyedness: A quantitative study. *Cortex*, 1981, *17*, 381-390.

Bowerman, M. *Early syntactic development: A cross-linguistic study with special reference to Finnish*. Cambridge: Cambridge University Press, 1973.

Bowerman, M. Discussion summary-development of concepts underlying language. In R.L. Schiefelbusch & L.L. Lloyd (Eds.), *Language perspectives—Acquisition, retardation, and intervention*. Baltimore: University Park Press, 1974.

Bowerman, M. The acquisition of word meaning: An investigation into some current conflicts. In N. Waterson & C. Snow (Eds.), *The development of communication*. New York: John Wiley, 1978.

Bowerman, M. The structure and origin of semantic categories in the language learning child. In M. Foster & S. Brandes (Eds.), *Symbol as sense*. New York: Academic Press, 1980.

Bradshaw, J.L., & Nettleton, N.C. The nature of hemispheric specialization in man. *The Behavioral and Brain Sciences*, 1981, *4*, 51-91.

Braine, M. Children's first word combinations. *Monographs of the Society for Research in Child Development*, 1976, *41*, (1, Serial No. 164).

Braine, M., & Wells, R. Case-like categories in children: The actor and some related categories. *Cognitive Psychology*, 1978, *10*, 100-122.

Brannigan, G. If this kid is in the one-word period, so how come he's saying whole sentences? Paper presented at the meeting of the Second Annual Boston University Conference on Language Development, Boston, 1977.

Bransford, J.D., Barclay, J.R., & Franks, J.J. Sentence memory: A constructive versus interpretive approach. *Cognitive Psychology,* 1972, *3,* 193–209.

Bransford, J.D., & Franks, J.J. The abstraction of linguistic ideas. *Cognitive Psychology,* 1971, *2,* 331–350.

Bransford, J.D., & Franks, J.J. The abstraction of linguistic ideas: A review. *Cognition,* 1972, *1,* 211–249.

Bransford, J.D., & McCarrell, N.S. A sketch of a cognitive approach to comprehension: Some thoughts avout understanding what it means to comprehend. In W.B. Weiner & D.S. Palermo (Eds.), *Cognition and the symbolic processes,* New York: Wiley, 1974.

Bransford, J., & Nitsch, K. Coming to understand things we could not previously understand. In J. Kavanagh & W. Strange (Eds.), *Speech and language in the laboratory, school, and clinic.* Cambridge, MA: MIT Press, 1978.

Brazelton, T.B. Early parent-infant reciprocity. In V. Vaughn & T.B. Brazelton (Eds.), *The family—Can it be saved?* Chicago: Year Book Medical Publishers, 1976.

Brazelton, T.B., Tronick, E., Adamson, L., Als, H., & Wise, S. Early mother-infant reciprocity. In *Parent-infant interaction* (CIBA Foundation Symposium 33). Amsterdam, Netherlands: Elsevier, 1975.

Bresnan, J. A realistic transformational grammar. In M. Halle, J. Bresnan, & G. Miller (Eds.), *Linguistic theory and psychological reality.* Cambridge, MA: MIT Press, 1978.(c)

Bresnan, J. An approach to universal grammar and the mental representation of language. *Cognition,* 1981, *10,* 39–52.

Bresnan, J. Universal grammar and the mental representation of language. In J. Bresnan (Ed.), *The mental representation of grammatical relations.* Cambridge, MA: MIT Press, 1982.

Bretherton, I., McNew, S., & Beeghly-Smith, M. Early person-knowledge as expressed in gestural and verbal communication: When do infants acquire a "theory of mind"? In M. Lamb & L. Sherrod (Eds.), *Infant social cognition.* Hillsdale, NJ: Erlbaum, 1981.

Bretherton, I., McNew, S., Synder, L., & Bates, E. Individual differences at twenty months: Semantics and morphology. *Journal of Child Language,* in press.

Brewer, W.F. Memory for the pragmatic implications of sentences. *Memory and Cognition,* 1977, *5,* 673–678.

Brewer, W.F. Literary theory, rhetoric, and stylistics: Implications for psychology. In R. Spiro, B. Bruce, & W. Brewer (Eds.), *Theoretical issues in reading comprehension.* Hillsdale, NJ: Erlbaum, 1980.

Brickner, R.M. A human cortical area producing repetitive phenomena when stimulated. *Journal of Neurophysiology,* 1940, *3,* 128–130.

Bridges, A., Sinha, C., & Walkerdine, V. The development of comprehension. In G. Wells (Eds.), *Learning through intervention.* Cambridge: Cambridge University Press, 1981.

Brinton, B., & Fujiki, M. A comparison of request-response sequences in the discourse of normal and language-disordered children. *Journal of Speech and Hearing Disorders,* 1982, *47,* 57–62.

Broca, P. Remarques sur la siege de la faculte du langage articule suives d'une observation d'aphemie. *Bulletin de la Societe d' Anthropologie, Paris,* 1961, *2,* 235–257.

Broen, P. The verbal environment of the language-learning child. *Monograph of the American Speech and Hearing Association,* no. 17, 1972.

Brown, J., Darley, F., & Aronson, A. Ataxic dysarthria. *International Journal of Neurology,* 1970, *7,* 302–318.

Brown, J., Redman, A., Bass, K., Liebergott, J., & Swope, S. *Symbolic play in normal and language-impaired children.* Paper persented at the 50th Conference of the American Speech and Hearing Association, Washington, DC, 1975.

Brown, J.W. On the neural organization of language: Thalamic and cortical relationships. *Brain and Language,* 1975, *2,* 18–30.

Brown, J.W. Lateralization: A brain model. *Brain and language,* 1978, *5,* 258–261.

Brown, J.W. Language representation in the brain. In H.D. Steklis & M.J. Raleigh (Eds.), *Neurobiology of social communication in primates: An evolutionary perspective.* New York: Academic Press, 1979.(a)

Brown, J.W. Thalamic mechanisms in language. In M.S. Gazzaniga (Ed.), *Handbook of behavioral neurobiology: Neuropsychology,* (Vol. 2). New York: Plenum Press, 1979.(b)

Brown, J.W. (Ed.). *Jargonaphasia.* New York: Academic Press, 1981.

Brown, J.W., & Jaffe, J. Hypothesis on cerebral dominance. *Neuropsychologia,* 1975, *13,* 107–110.

Brown, K. *An analysis of enviromental and genetic influence on individual differences in the communicative development of fifty adopted one-year-old children.* Unpublished doctoral dissertation, Unversity of Colorado, 1980.

Brown, R. *A first language: The early stages.* Cambridge, MA: Harvard University Press, 1973.

Brown, R. Introduction. In C.E. Snow & C.A. Ferguson (Eds.), *Talking to children.* Cambridge: Cambridge University Press, 1977.

Brown, R., Cazden, C., & Bellugi, U. The child's grammar from 1 to 3. In J.P. Hill (Ed.), *The second annual Minnesota Symposium on Child Psychology.* Minneapolis: University of Minnesota Press, 1969.

Brukman, J. Language and socialization: Child culture and the ethnographer's task. In S.T. Kimbal & J.H. Burnett (Eds.), *Learning and culture: Proceedings of the American Ethnological Society.* Seattle: University of Washington Press, 1973.

Bruner, J.S. From communication to language: A psychological perspective. *Cognition,* 1974-75, *3,* 255–287.

Bruner, J.S. The ontogenesis of speech acts. *Journal of Child language,* 1975, *2,* 1–19.

Bruner, J.S. Learning how to do things with words. In J.S. Bruner & A. Garton (Eds.), *Human growth and development.* Oxford, Eng.: Oxford University Press, 1978.

Bryan, T., Donahue, M., Pearl, R., & Sturm, C. Learning disabled children's conversational skills: The TV talk show. *Learning Disability Quarterly,* 1981, *4,* 250–259.

Bryant, P., & Trabasso, T. Transitive inferences and memory in young children. *Nature,* 1971, *232,* 456–458.

Buckingham, H.W. Explanations for the concept of apraxia of speech. In M.T. Sarno (Ed.), *Acquired aphasia.* New York: Academic Press, 1981.

Buckingham, H.W. Apraxia of language vs. apraxia of speech. In R. Magill (Ed.), *Memory and control in motor behavior.* New York: North-Holland, 1983.

Buge, A., Escourolle, R., Rancurel, G., & Poisson, M. Mutisme akinetique et ramollissement bicingulaire: 3 observations anatomo-cliniques. *Revue Neurologie,* 1975, *141,* 121–137.

Buium, N. Interrogative types in parental speech to language-learning children: A linguistic universal? *Journal of Psycholinguistic Research* 1976, *5,* 135–142.

Buium, N., Rynders, J., & Turnure, J. Early maternal linguistic environment of normal and Down's syndrome language-learning children. *American Journal of Mental Deficiency,* 1974, *79,* 52–58.

Burr, C.W. Loss of sign language in a deaf mute from cerebral tumor and softening. *New York Medical Journal,* 1905, *81,* 1106–1108.

Byers, P. Biological rhythms as information channels in interpersonal communication behavior. In G. Bateson & M. Klopfey (Eds.), *Perspectives in Ethnology,* (Vol. 2). New York: Plenum, 1976.

Bynon, J. Berber nursery language. *Transactions of the Philological Society,* 1968, 107–161.

Bynon, J. Derivational processes in Berber nursery words. In C. Snow & C. Ferguson (Eds.), *Talking to children.* London: Cambridge University Press, 1977.

Cairns, C.E., & Feinstein, M.H. Markedness and the theory of syllable structure. *Linguistic Inquiry,* 1982, *13,* 193–226.

Cairns, H.S. *On the differential processing of lexical and underlying ambiguities.* Unpublished manuscript, 1971.

Cairns, H.S. Effects of bias on the processing and reprocessing of lexically ambiguous sentences. *Journal of Experimental Psychology,* 1973, *97,* 335–343.

Cairns, H.S., & Berkovits, R. *Effects of ambiguity and context on the speed of clausal processing.* Unpublished manuscript, 1975.

Cairns, H.S., & Blank, M. Word recognition latency and the duration of clausal processing. *Working Papers in Speech and Hearing Sciences* (Vol. 2). Graduate School and University Center of the City University of New York, 1976.

Cairns, H.S., & Cairns, C.E. *Psycholinguistics: A cognitive view of language.* New York: Holt, Rinehart & Winston, 1976.

Cairns, H.S., Cowart, W., & Jablon, A.D. Effects of prior context upon the integration of lexical information during sentence processing. *Journal of Verbal Learning and Verbal Behavior,* 1981, *20,* 445–453.

Cairns, H.S., & Jablon, A.D. The loss of syntactic information across a sentence boundary during language comprehension. *Working Papers in Linguistics.* Graduate School and University Center of the City University of New York, 1976.

Cairns, H.S., & Hsu, J.R. Effects of prior context upon lexical access during sentence comprehension: A replication and reinterpretation. *Journal of Psycholinguistic Research,* 1980, *9,* 1–8.

Cairns, H.S., & Kamerman, J.D. Lexical information processing during sentence comprehension. *Journal of Verbal Learning and Verbal Behavior,* 1975, *14,* 170–179.

Calvin, W.H., & Ojemann, G.A. *Inside the brain: Mapping the cortex, exploring the neuron.* New York: New American Library, 1980.

Camaioni, L. Child-adult and child-child conversations: An interactional approach. In E. Ochs & B. Schieffelin (Eds.), *Developmental pragmatics.* New York: Academic Press, 1979.

Caplan, D. Clause boundaries and recognition latencies for words in sentences. *Perception and Psychophysics,* 1972, *12,* 73–76.

Caplan, D. On the cerebral localization of linguistic functions: Logical and empirical issues surrounding deficit analysis and functional localization. *Brain and Language,* 1981, *14,* 120–137.

Caplan, D., & Chomsky, N. Linguistic perspectives on language development. In D. Caplan (Ed.), *Biological studies of mental processes,* Cambridge, MIT Press, 1980.

Cappa, S., Cavalotti, G., & Vignolo, L.A. Phonemic and lexical errors in fluent aphasia: Correlation with lesion site. *Neuropsychologia,* 1981, *19,* 171–177.

Caramazza, A., Berndt, R.S., & Brownell, H.H. The semantic deficit hypothesis: Perceptual parsing and object classification by aphasic patients. *Brain and Language,* 1982, *15,* 161–189.

Carmon, A., & Nachshon, J. Ear asymmetry in perception of emotional nonverbal stimuli. *Acta Psychologica,* 1973, *37,* 351–357.

Carpenter, E. Image making in arctic art. In G. Kepes (Ed.), *Sign, image, and symbol.* London: Studio Vista, 1966.

Carpenter, P.A., & Just, M.A. Intergrative processes in comprehension. In D. LaBerge & S.J. Samuels (Eds.), *Basic processes in reading: Perception and comprehension.* Hillsdale, NJ: Erlbaum, 1977.

Carroll, J.M. Process and content in psycholinguistics. In R. Patton (Ed.), *Current trends in the description and analysis of behavior.* Pittsburgh: University of Pittsburgh Press, 1958.

Carroll, J.M., Tanenhaus, M.K., & Bever, T.G. The perception of relations: The interaction of structural, functional, and contextual factors in the segmentation of sentences. In W.J.M. Levelt & G.B. Flores d'Arcais (Eds.), *Studies in the perception of language.* New York: Wiley, 1978.

Carrow-Woolfolk, E., & Lynch, J. *An integrative approach to language disorders in children.* New York: Grune & Stratton, 1982.

Carter, A. The transformation of sensorimotor morphemes into words: A case study of the development of "more" and "mine." *Journal of Child Language,* 1975, *2,* 233-250.

Carter, A. Prespeech meaning relations: An outline of one infant's sensorimotor morphene development. In Fletcher, P. & Garman, M. *Language acquisition.* London: Cambridge University Press, 1979, 71-92.(a)

Carter, A. The disappearance schema: Case study of a second-year communicative behavior. In E. Ochs & B. Schieffelin (Eds.), *Developmental pragmatics.* New York: Academic Press, 1979.(b)

Casagrande, J.B. Comanche baby language. *International Journal of American Linguistics,* 1948, *14,* 11-14.

Cassirer, E. *An essay on man: An introduction to a philosophy of human culture.* New Haven, CT: Yale University Press, 1944.

Cavalli, M., DeRenzi, E., Faglioni, P., & Vitale, A. Impairment of right brain-damaged patients on a linguistic cognitive task. *Cortex,* 1981, *57,* 545-556.

Cazden, C. *Environmental assistance to the child's acquisition of grammar.* Unpublished doctoral dissertation, Harvard University, 1965.

Cazden, C. The acquisition of noun and verb inflections. *Child Development,* 1968, *39,* 433-438.

Cazden, C. Peekaboo as an instructional model: Discourse development at home and at school. *Papers and reports in child language development,* 1979, *17,* 1-29.

Chapman, K., & Leonard, L. *Inappropriate word extensions in the speech of young language disordered children.* Paper presented at the meeting of the Symposium on Research in Child Language Disorders, Madison, WI, 1981.

Chapman, R. Comprehension strategies in children. In J. Kavanaugh & W. Strange (Eds.), *Speech and language in the laboratory, school, and clinic.* Cambridge, MA: MIT Press, 1978.

Chapman, R. Exploring children's communicative intents. In J. Miller (Ed.) *Assessing language production in children.* Baltimore, MD: University Park Press, 1981.(a)

Chapman, R. Mother-child interaction in the second year of life: Its role in language development. In R.L. Schiefelbusch & D.D. Bricker (Eds.), *Early language: Acquisition and intervention.* Baltimore: University Park Press, 1981.(b)

Chapman, R. Issues in child language acquisition. In N. Lass, J. Northern, D. Yoder, & L. McReynolds (Eds.), *Speech, Language and Hearing.* Philadelphia: W.B. Saunders, 1982.

Chapman, R., & Miller, J. Word order in early two and three word utterances: Does comprehension precede production? *Journal of Speech Hearing Research,* 1975, *18,* 355-371.

Chapman, R., & Thomson, J. What is the source of overextension errors in two-year olds? A response to Fremgen and Fay. *Journal of Child Language,* 1980, *7,* 575-578.

Chi, J.G., Dooling, E.C., & Gilles, F.H. Left-right asymmetries of the temporal speech areas of the human fetus. *Archives of Neurology,* 1977, *34,* 346-348.

Chiarello, C., Knight, R., & Mandel, M. Aphasia in a prelingually deaf woman. *Brain,* 1982, *105,* 29-51.

Chomsky, N.A. *Syntactic structures.* The Hague: Mouton, 1957.

Chomsky, N.A. *Aspects of the theory of syntax.* Cambridge, MA: MIT Press, 1965.

Chomsky, N.A. The formal nature of language. In E. Lenneberg (Ed.), *Biological foundations of language.* New York: Wiley, 1967.

Chomsky, N.A., & Halle, M. *Sound patterns of English.* New York: Harper & Row, 1968.

Chomsky, N.A. Conditions on tranformations. In S.R. Anderson & P. Kiparsky (Eds.), *A festschrift for Morris Halle.* New York: Holt, 1973.

Chomsky, N.A. Reflections on language. New York: Pantheon Books, 1975.

Chomsky, N.A. On cognitive structures and their development: A reply to Piaget. In M. Piattelli-Palmarini, (Ed.), *Language and learning: The debate between Jean Piaget and Noam Chomsky.* Cambridge, MA: Harvard University Press, 1980.(a)

Chomsky, N.A. Rules and representations. *The Behavioral and Brain Sciences,* 1980, *3,* 1–61.(b)

Chomsky, N.A. *Lectures on government and binding.* The Pisa Lectures. Dordrecht: Foris, 1981.

Cicourel, A.V., Jennings, K.H., Jennings, S.H.M., Leiter, K.C.W., McKay, R., Mehan, H., & Roth, D.R. (Eds.). *Language use and school performance.* New York: Academic Press, 1974.

Cirilo, R.K. Referential coherence and text structure in story comprehension. *Journal of Verbal Learning and Verbal Behavior,* 1981, 358–367.

Cirilo, R.K., & Foss, D.J. Text structure and reading time for sentences. *Journal of Verbal Learning and Verbal Behavior,* 1980, *19,* 96–109.

Clara, M. Das nervensystem des menschen: Ein lehrbüch für studirende und arzte (2 berb. Ausl.). Leipzig: Barth, 1953.

Clark, E. What's in a word? On the child's acquisition of semantics in his first language. In T. Moore (Ed.), *Cognitive development and the acquisition of language.* New York: Academic Press, 1973.

Clark, E. Some aspects of the conceptual basis for first language acquisition. In R. Schiefelbush & L. Lloyd (Eds.), *Language perspectives: Acquisition, retardation and intervention.* Baltimore: University Park Press, 1974.

Clark, E. Knowledge, context and strategy in the acquisition of meaning. In D. Dato (Ed.), *Proceedings of the 26th annual Georgetown University Round Table: Developmental psycholinguistics: Theory and applications.* Washington, DC: Georgetown University Press, 1975.

Clark, E. Strategies for communicating. *Child Development,* 1978, *49,* 953–959.

Clark, E., & O'Malley, C.D. *The human brain and spinal cord: A historical study.* Berkeley, CA: University of California Press, 1968.

Clark, H.H. Inferences in comprehension. In D. LaBerge & S.J. Samuels (Eds.), *Basic processes in reading: Perception and comprehension.* Hillsdale, NJ: Erlbaum, 1977.

Clark, H.H. Inferring what is meant. In W.M. Levelt & G.B. Flores d'Arcais (Eds.), *Studies in the perception of language.* New York: Wiley, 1978.

Clark, H.H., & Begun, J. The semantics of sentence subjects. *Language and Speech,* 1971, *14,* 34–46.

Clark, H.H., & Clark, E. *Psychology and language.* New York: Harcourt Brace Jovanovich, 1977.

Clark, H.H., & Sengul, C.J. In search of referents for nouns and pronouns. *Memory and Cognition,* 1979, *7,* 35–41.

Clark, R. Performing without competence. *Journal of Child Language,* 1974, *1,* 1–10.

Clark, R. What's the use of imitation? *Journal of Child Language,* 1976, *4,* 341–358.

Clements, G.N. Akan vowel harmony: A non-linear analysis. In G.N. Clements (Ed.), *Harvard Studies in Phonology,* (Vol. 2). Bloomington: Indiana University Linguistics Club, 1981.

Clifton, C., & Frazier, L. Comprehending sentences with multiple filler-gap dependencies. Unpublished manuscript, 1982.

Coggins, T., & Carpenter, R. The communicative intention inventory: A system for observing and coding children's early intentional communication. *Applied Psycholinguistics,* 1981, *2,* 235–252.

Cohen, L., & Strauss, M. Concept acquisition in the human infant. *Child Development,* 1979, *50,* 419–423.

Cole, R.A. Listening for mispronunciations: A measure of what we hear during speech. *Perception and Psychophysics.* 1973, *11,* 153–156.

Cole, R.A., & Perfetti, C.A. Listening for mispronunciations in a children's story: The use of context by children and adults. *Journal of Verbal Learning and Verbal Behavior,* 1980, *19,* 279–315.

Collis, G. Visual co-orientation and maternal speech. In H. Schaffer (Ed.), *Studies in mother-infant interaction.* London: Academic Press, 1977.

Collis, G., & Schaffer, H. Synchronization of visual attention in mother-infant pairs. *Journal of Child Psychology and Psychiatry,* 1975, *16,* 315–320.

Comrie, B. Ergativity. In W. Lehmann (Ed.), *Syntactic typology.* Austin: University of Texas Press, 1978.

Condon, W.S., & Sander, L.W. Neonate movement is synchronized with adult speech: Interactional participation and language acquisition. *Science,* 1974, *183,* 99–101.

Conel, J.L. *The postnatal development of the cerebral cortex* (Vols. 1-3). Cambridge, MA: Harvard Universtiy Press, 1939, 1941, 1947.

Connell, P.J. & Parks-Reinick, L.P. Discrimination of antineutralization devices by misarticulating children. Paper presented to the American Speech-Language-Hearing Association, Toronto, 1982.

Conrad, C. Context effects in sentence comprehension: A study of the subjective lexicon. *Memory and Cognition,* 1974, *2,* 130–138.

Cooper, W.E. The analytic/holistic disinction applied to the speech of patients with hemispheric brain damage (Commentary on J.L. Bradshaw & N.C. Nettleton's " The nature of hemispheric specialization in man"). *The Behavioral and Brain Sciences,* 1981, *4,* 68–69.

Corballis, M.C. On the evolution and growth of lateralization [Commentary on Denenberg's "Hemispheric laterality in animals and the effects of early experience"]. *The Behavioral and Brain Sciences,* 1981, *4,* 24–25.

Corballis, M.C., & Beale, I.L. *The psychology of left and right.* Hillsdale, NJ: Erlbaum, 1976.

Corballis, M.C., & Morgan, M.J. On the biological basis of human laterality: I. Evidence for a maturational left-right gradient. *The Behavioral and Brain Sciences,* 1978, *2,* 261–269.

Corbett, A.T., & Dosher, B.A. Instrument inferences in sentence encoding. *Journal of Verbal Learning and Verbal Behavior,* 1978, *17,* 479–491.

Corrigan, R. Language development as related to stage 6 object permanence development. *Journal of Child Language,* 1978, *5,* 173–189.

Corrigan, R. Cognitive correlates of language: differential criteria yield differential results. *Child Development,* 1979, *50,* 617–631.

Corsaro, W. The clarification request as a feature of adult interactive styles with young children. *Language in Society,* 1977, *6,* 183–207.

Corsaro, W. Sociolinguistic patterns in adult-child interaction. In E. Ochs & B.B. Schieffelin (Eds.), *Developmental pragmatics.* New York: Academic Press, 1979.

Corsaro, W. The development of social cognition in preschool children: Implications for language learning. *Topics in Language Disorders,* 1981, *2,* 77–95.

Coulthard, M. *An introduction to discourse analysis.* London, England: Longman, 1977.

Cowart, R.W. *Production, comprehension, and theories of the mental lexicon.* Paper presented at the Linguistic Society of America, Boston, December, 1978. (Reprinted in *City University of New York Forum: Papers in Linguistics,* 1978-1979, *5-6,* (ERIC Document Reproduction Service No. ED 182 985).

Craig, H., & Gallagher, T. Gaze and proximity as turn regulators within three-party and two-party child conversations. *Journal of Speech and Hearing Research,* 1982, *25,* 65–75.

Cramblit, N., & Siegel, G. The verbal environment of a language-impaired child. *Journal of Speech and Hearing Disorders,* 1978, *42,* 474–482.

Crichton-Browne, J. On the weight of the brain and its component parts in the insane. *Brain,* 1880, *2,* 42–67.

Critchley, M. The parietal lobes. New York: Hafner Press, 1966.

Critchley, W.M.R. Speech disorders of Parkinsonism: A review. *Journal of Neurology, Neurosurgery and Psychiatry,* 1981, *44,* 751–758.

Cromer, R.F. The development of language and cognition: The cognition hypothesis. In B. Foss (Ed.), *New perspectives in child development.* Hammondsworth, Middlesex: Penguin, 1974.

Cromer, R.F. The cognitive hypothesis of language acquisition and its implications for child language deficiency. In D. Morehead & A. Morehead (Eds.), *Normal and deficient child language,* Baltimore: University Park Press, 1976.

Cromer, R.F. Reconceptualizing language acquisition and cognitive development. In R.L. Schiefelbusch & D. Bricker (Eds.), *Early language: Acquisition and intervention.* Baltimore: University Park Press, 1981.

Cross, T.G. Some relations between motherese and linguistic level in accelerated children. *Papers and Reports on Child Language Development,* 1975, *No. 10,* Stanford, CA: Stanford University, 1975.

Cross, T.G. Mother's speech adjustments: The contributions of selected child listener variables. In C. Snow & C. Ferguson (Eds.), *Talking to children.* London: Cambridge University Press, 1977.

Cross, T.G. Mother's speech and its association with rate of linguistic development in young children. In C. Snow & N. Waterson (Eds.), *The development of communication.* Chichester, England: Wiley, 1978.

Curcio, F., & Paccia, J. Strategies in evaluating autistic children's communication. *Topics in Language Disorders,* 1982, *3,* 43-49.

Curry, F.K.W., & Gregory, H.H. The performance of stutterers on dichotic listening tasks thought to reflect cerebral dominance. *Journal of Speech and Language Research,* 1969, *12,* 73-82.

Curtiss, S., Prutting, C., & Lowell, E. Pragmatic and sematic development in young children with impaired hearing. *Journal of Speech and Hearing Research,* 1979, *22,* 534-552.

Dalby, J.T., & Gibson, D. Functional cerebral lateralization in subtypes of disabled readers. *Brain and Language,* 1981, *14,* 34-48.

Damasio, A.R. The frontal lobes. In K.M. Heilman & E. Valenstein (Eds.), *Clinical neuropsychology.* New York: Oxford University Press, 1979.

Damasio, A.R., Damasio, H., Rizzo, M., Varney, N., & Gersh, F. Aphasia with nonhemorrhagic lesions in the basal ganglia and internal capsule. *Archives of Neurology,* 1981, *39,* 15-20.

Damasio, A.R., & Maurer, R.G. A neurological model for childhood autism. *Archives of Neurology,* 1978, *35,* 777-786.

Damasio, A.R., & Van Hoesen, G.W. Structure and function of the supplementary motor area. *Neurology* (Minneapolis), 1980, *30,* 359.

Dawkins, R. Hierarchical organization: A candidate principle for ethology. In P.P.G. Bateson & R.A. Hinde (Eds.), *Growing points in ethology.* Cambridge: Cambridge University Press, 1976.

Denenberg, V.H. Hemispheric laterality in animals and the effects of early experience. *The Behavioral and Brain Sciences,* 1981, *4,* 1-21.

Dennett, D. *Brainstorms.* Montgomery, VM: Bradford Books, 1978.

Dennis, M. Capacity and strategy for syntactic comprehension after left or right hemidecortication. *Brain and Language,* 1980, *10,* 287-317.

Dennis, M., & Whitaker, H.A. Language acquisition following hemidecortication: Linguistic superiority of the left over the right hemisphere. *Brain and Language,* 1976, *3,* 404-433.

Dennis, M., & Whitaker, H.A. Hemispheric equipotentiality and language acquisition. In S.J. Segalowitz & F.A. Gruber (Eds.), *Language development and neurological theory.* New York: Academic Press, 1977.

de Villiers, J. The process of rule learning in child speech: A new look. In K.E. Nelson (Ed.), *Children's language* (Vol. 2). Gardner Press, 1978.

de Villiers, J., & de Villiers, P. Competence and performance in child language: Are children really competent to judge? *Journal of Child Language,* 1974, *1,* 11–22.

Dewart, M. *Children's preferences for animate and inanimate actor and object nouns.* Unpublished manuscript, Medical Research Council, London, England, 1976.

Dewart, M. Language comprehension processes of mentally retarded children. *American Journal of Mental Deficiency,* 1979, *84,* 177–183.

Dihoff, R., & Chapman, R. First words: Their origin in action. *Papers and reports in child language development,* 1977, *13,* 1–7.

Dinnsen, D.A. Atomic phonology. In D.A. Dinnsen (Ed.), *Current approaches to phonological theory.* Bloomington: Indiana University Press, 1979.(a)

Dinnsen, D.A. (Ed.). Current approaches to phonological theory. Bloomington: Indiana University Press, 1979.(b)

Dinnsen, D.A. Phonological rules and phonetic explanation. *Journal of Linguistics,* 1980, *16,* 171–338.

Dinnsen, D.A. *On the phonetics of phonological neutralization.* Paper presented to the Working Group on Language/Speech Behavior, 13th International Congress of Linguists, Tokyo, 1982.

Dinnsen, D.A. Methods and empirical issues in analyzing functional misarticulation. In M. Elbert, D.A. Dinnsen, & G. Weismer (Eds.), *Phonological theory and the misarticulating child.* ASHA Monographs, 1982, in press.

Dinnsen, D.A., & Eckman, F.R. Some substantive universals in atomic phonology. *Lingua,* 1978, *45,* 1–14.

Dinnsen, D.A., & Elbert, M. On the relationship between phonology and learning. In M. Elbert, D.A. Dinnsen, & G. Weismer (Eds.), *Phonological theory and the misarticulating child.* ASHA Monographs, 1982, in press.

Dinnsen, D.A., Elbert, M., & Weismer, G. *On the characterization of functional misarticulations.* Presented at the annual meeting of the American Speech-Language-Hearing Association, Atlanta, 1979.

Dinnsen, D.A., Elbert, M., & Weismer, G. *Some typological properties of functional misarticulation systems.* Presented at the fourth International Phonology Meeting, Vienna, Austria, 1980. Reprinted in W.U. Dressler (Ed.), *Phonologica 1980,* 83–88.

Dixon, R. Ergativity. *Language,* 1979, *55,* 59–138.

Donahue, M. Requesting strategics of learning disabled children. *Applied Psycholinquistics,* 1981, *2,* 213–234.

Donahue, M., Pearl, R., & Bryan, T. Learning disabled children's conversational competence: Responses to inadequate messages. *Applied Psycholinquisties* 1980, *1,* 387–403.

Donaldson, H.H. Anatomical observations on the brain and several sense organs of the blind deaf mute, Laura Dewey Bridgeman. *American Journal of Psychology,* 1981, *3,* 293–342; 1892, *4,* 248–294.

Donegan, P.J., & Stampe, D. The study of natural phonology. In D.A. Dinnsen (Ed.), *Current approaches to phonological theory.* Bloomington: Indiana University Press, 1979.

Dore, J. A pragmatic description of early language development. *Journal of Psycholinguistic Research,* 1974, *3,* 343–350.

Dore, J. Holophrases, speech acts, and language universals. *Journal of Child Language,* 1975, *2,* 21–40.

Dore, J. Conversation and preschool language development. In P. Fletcher & M. Garman (Eds.), *Language acquisition.* Cambridge, Eng.: Cambridge University Press, 1979.

Dore, J., Franklin, M., Miller, R., & Ramer, A. Transitional phenomena in early language acquisition. *Journal of Child Language,* 1976, *3,* 13–28.

Downie, A.W., Low, J.M., & Lindsay, D.D. Speech disorder in Parkinsonism: Use of delayed auditory feedback in selected cases. *Journal of Neurology, Neurosurgery and Psychiatry,* 1981, *44,* 852–853.

Drach, K. The language of the parent: A pilot study. *Working paper 14,* Language-Behavior Research Laboratory, University of California, Berkeley, 1969.

Duchan, J. The effect of cognitive bias on children's early interpretations of locative commands. *Language Sciences,* 1980, *2,* 246–259.

Duchan, J. Foreward to communication problems of autistic children: The role of context, *Topics in Language Disorders,* 1982, *3,* ix–xiv. (a)

Duchan, J. Temporal aspects of self-stimulatory behavior in abnormal speakers. In M. Davis (Ed.), *Interaction rhythms: Periodicity in communication behavior.* New York: Human Sciences Press, 1982.(b)

Duchan, J. Autistic children are non-interactive, or so we say. *Seminars in Speech, Hearing and Language,* 1983.(a)

Duchan, J. Language processing and geodesic domes. In T. Gallagher & C. Prutting (Eds.), *Pragmatic assessment and intervention issues in language.* San Diego, CA: College-Hill Press, 1983.(b)

Duchan, J., & Baskervill, D. Responses of black and white children to the Grammatic Closure Subtest of the ITPA. *Language, Speech and Hearing Services in the Schools,* 1977, *8,* 126–132.

Duchan, J., & Erickson, J. Normal and retarded children's understanding of semantic relations in different verbal contexts. *Journal of Speech and Hearing Research,* 1976, *19,* 767–776.

Duchan, J., & Lund, N. Why not semantic relations? *Journal of Child Language,* 1979, *6,* 243–252.

Duchan, J., & Oliva, J. Temporal aspects of the verbal and gestural production of an autistic child. In D. Ingram, F. Perg, & P. Dale (Eds.), *Proceedings of the first International Congress for the Study of Child Language.* Lanham, MD: University Press of America, 1980.

Duchan, J., & Siegul, L. Incorrect responses to locative commands: A case study. *Language Speech and Hearing Services in the Schools,* 1979, *10,* 99-103.

Duncan, S. Interaction units during speaking turns in dyadic, face to face conversation. In A. Kendon, R. Harris, & M. Key (Eds.), *Organization of behavior in face to face interaction.* The Hague: Mouton, 1975.

Duncan, S., & Niederche, G. On signalling that it's your turn to speak. *Journal of Experimental Social Psychology,* 1974, *10,* 234–247.

Dwyer, J.H., & Rinn, W.E. The role of the right hemisphere in contextual inference. *Neuropsychologia,* 1981, *19,* 479–482.

Eccles, J.C. The dynamic loop hypothesis of movement control. In K.N. Leibovic (Ed.), *Information processing in the nervous system.* New York: Springer-Verlag, 1969.

Eccles, J.C. A re-evaluation of cerebellar function in man. In J. Desmedt (Ed.), *New developments in electromyography and clinical neurophysiology* (Vol. 3). Basel: Karger, 1973.

Eccles, J.C. The initiation of voluntary movements by the supplementary motor area. *Archives of Psychiatry and Neurological Sciences,* 1982, *231,* 423–411.

Eckman, F.R. Markedness and the contrastive analysis hypothesis. *Language Learning,* 1977, *27,* 315–330.

Eckman, F.R. On the naturalness of inter-language phonological rules. *Language Learning,* 1981, *31,* 195–216.

Edwards, M.L., & Shriberg, L.D. *Phonology: Applications in Communicative Disorders.* San Diego: College-Hill Press, 1983.

Ellis Weismer, S. Constructive comprehension processes exhibited by language-impaired children. Unpublished doctoral dissertation, Indiana University, 1981.

Erickson, T.C., & Woolsey, C.N. Observations on the supplementary motor area of man. *Transactions of the American Neurological Association,* 1951, *76,* 50–56.

Ervin-Tripp, S. Wait for me roller skate. In S. Ervin-Tripp & C. Mitchell-Kernan (Eds.), *Child discourse*. New York: Academic Press, 1977.

Ervin-Tripp, S. Children's verbal turn-taking. In E. Ochs & B.B. Schieffelin (Eds.), *Developmental pragmatics*. New York: Academic Press, 1979.

Falzi, G., Perrone, P., & Vignolo, L.A. Right-left asymmetry in anterior speech region. *Archives of Neurology,* 1982, *39,* 239–241.

Fava, E., & Tirondola, G. *Syntactic and pragmatic regularities in Italian child discourse: Grammatical relations and word order.* Unpublished manuscript, Institute di Glottologia, Italy, 1977.

Fein, G. *Imagination and play: Some relationships in early development.* Paper presented at the meeting of the American Psychological Association, Toronto, August, 1978.

Fenson, L., & Ramsay, D. Decentration and integration of child play in the second year. *Child Development,* 1980, *51,* 171–178.

Ferguson, C.A. Baby talk in six languages. *American Anthropologist,* 1964, *66,* 103–114.

Ferguson, C.A. Baby talk as a simplified register. In C.E. Snow & C.A. Ferguson (Eds.), *Talking to children.* London: Cambridge University Press, 1977.

Ferguson, C.A. Learning to pronounce: The earliest stages of phonological development. In F. Minifie & L. Lloyd (Eds.), *Communicative and cognitive abilities: Early behavioral assessment.* Baltimore: University Park Press, 1978.(a)

Ferguson, C.A. Phonological processes. In J.H. Greenberg (Ed.), *Universals of human language: phonology,* (Vol. 2). Stanford: Stanford University Press, 1978.(b)

Ferguson, C.A., & Snow, C.(Eds.). *Talking to children.* London: Cambridge University Press, 1977.

Fey, M.E., & Leonard, L.B. Pragmatic skills of children with specific language impairment. In T. Gallagher & C. Prutting (Eds.), *Pragmatic assessment and intervention issues in language.* San Diego: College-Hill Press, 1983.

Fillmore, C. The case for case. In E. Bach & R. Harms (Eds.), *Universals in linguistic theory.* New York: Holt, Rinehart, & Winston, 1968.

Fillmore, C. *Deixis.* Unpublished lectures delivered at the University of California, Santa Cruz, 1973.

Fine, J. Conversation, cohesive and thematic patterning in children's dialogues. *Discourse Processes,* 1978, *1,* 247–266.

Fischer, J.S. Linguistic Socialization: Japan and the United States. In R. Hill & R. Konig (Eds.), *Families in East and West.* The Hague: Mouton, 1970.

Flechsig, P. Developmental (myelogenetic) localization of the cortex in human subjects. *Lancet,* October 19, 1901, 1027–1029.

Fletcher, C.R. Short-term memory processes in text comprehension. *Journal of Verbal Learning and Verbal Behavior,* 1981, *20,* 564–574.

Fletcher, R. Markedness and topic continuity in discourse processing. *Journal of Verbal Learning and Verbal Behavior,* in press.

Flores d'Arcais, G. Some perceptual determinants of sentence construction. In G. Flores d'Arcais (Ed.), *Studies in perception.* Milan: Martello-Guinti, 1975.

Flor-Henry, P. Schizophrenic-like reactions and affective psychoses associated with temporal lobe epilepsy: Etiological factors. *American Journal of Psychiatry,* 1969, *126,* 400–403.

Flor-Henry, P. Gender, hemispheric specialization and psychopathology. *Social Science and Medicine,* 1978, *12B,* 155–162.

Foerster, O. Motorische Felder und Bahnen. In O. Bumke & O. Forester (Eds.), *Handbuch der neurologie, Bd. VI.* Berlin: Springer, 1936, 1–448.

Fodor, J. *The language of thought.* New York: Thomas Y. Crowell, 1975.

Fodor, J. Discussion of Piaget's "Schemes of action and language learning." In M. Piatelli-Palmarini (Ed.), *Language and learning: The debate between Jean Piaget and Noam Chomsky.* Cambridge, MA: Harvard University Press, 1980.

Fodor, J.A., & Bever, T.G. The psychological reality of linguistic segments. *Journal of Verbal Learning and Verbal Behavior,* 1965, *4,* 414–420.

Fodor, J.D. Superstrategy. In W.E. Cooper & E.C.T. Walker (Eds.), *Sentence processing.* New York: Wiley, 1979.

Fodor, J.D., & Frazier, L. Is the human sentence parsing mechanism an ATN? *Cognition,* 1980, *8,* 418–459.

Folger, M.K., & Leonard, L.B. Language and sensorimotor development during the early period of referential speech. *Journal of Speech and Hearing Research,* 1978, *21,* 519–527.

Ford, J.M., Bresnan, J. & Kaplan, R. *A competence-based theory of syntactic closure: Occasional Paper #14.* The Center for Cognitive Science, MIT, 1981. (Reprinted in J. Bresnan (Ed.), *The mental representation of grammatical relations.* Cambridge, MA: MIT Press, 1982.)

Forster, K.I. Accessing the mental lexicon. In R.J. Wales & E.T. Walker (Eds.), *New approaches to language mechanisms.* Amsterdam, Netherlands: North-Holland, 1976.

Forster, K.I. Accessing the mental lexicon. In E. Walker (Ed.), *Explorations in the biology of language.* Montgomery, VT: Bradford Books, 1978.

Forster, K.I. Levels of processing and the structure of the language processor. In W.E. Cooper & E.C.T. Walker (Eds.), *Sentence processing.* New York: Wiley, 1979.

Forster, K.I., & Olbrei, I. Semantic heuristics and syntactic analysis. *Cognition,* 1973, *2,* 319–347.

Foss, D.J. Some effects of ambiguity upon sentence comprehension. *Journal of Verbal Learning and Verbal Behavior,* 1970, *9,* 457–462.

Foss, D.J., Cirilo, R.K., & Blank, M.A. Semantic facilitation and lexical access during sentence processing: An investigation of individual differences. *Memory and Cognition,* 1979, *7,* 346–353.

Foss, D.J., & Hakes, D.T. Psycholinguistics. Englewood Cliffs, NJ: Prentice-Hall, 1978.

Foss, D.J., & Jenkins, C.J. Some effects of context on the comprehension of ambiguous sentences. *Journal of Verbal Learning and Verbal Behavior,* 1973, *12,* 577–589.

Fraiberg, S. *Insights from the blind.* New York: Basic Books, 1977.

Francis, H. What does the child mean? A critique of the 'functional' approach to language acquisition. *Journal of Child Language,* 1979, *6,* 201–210.

Franco, L. Hemispheric interaction in the processing of concurrent tasks in commisurotomy subjects. *Neuropsychologia,* 1977, *15,* 707–710.

Frankel, R. Autism for all practical purposes: A micro-interactional view. *Topics in Language Disorders,* 1982, *3,* 33–42.

Fraser, C., Bellugi, U., & Brown, R. Control of grammar in imitation, comprehension and production. *Journal of Verbal Learning and Verbal Behavior,* 1963, *2,* 121-135.

Frazier, L. On comprehending sentences: syntactic parsing strategies. Unpublished doctoral dissertation, University of Connecticut, 1978.

Frazier, L., Clifton, C., & Raldall, J. Filling gaps: Decision principles and structure in sentence comprehension. *Cognition,* in press.

Frazier, L., & Fodor, J.D. The sausage machine: A new two-stage parsing model. *Cognition,* 1978, *6,* 291–325.

Frazier, L., & Rayner, K. Making and correcting errors during sentence comprehension: Eye movements in the analysis of structurally ambiguous sentences. *Cognitive Psychology,* 1982, *14,* (1), 178–210.

Freedman, D.G. *Human sociobiology: A holistic approach.* New York: Free Press, 1979.

Freedman, D.G. The social and the biological: A necessary unity. *Zygon,* 1980, *15,* 117-131.

Freedman, P. & Carpenter, R. Semantic relations used by normal and language-impaired children at stage I. *Journal of Speech and Hearing Research,* 1976, *19,* 784–795.

Fremgen, A., & Fay, D. Overextensions in production and comprehension: A methodological clarification. *Journal of Child Language,* 1980, *7,* 205-212.

French, P. & MacLure, M. Adult-child conversation. New York: St. Martin's Press, 1981.

French, P., & Woll, B. Context, meaning and strategy in parent-child conversation. In G. Wells (Ed.), *Learning through interaction.* Cambridge, Eng.: Cambridge University Press, 1981.

Fried, I., Ojemann, G.A., & Fetz, E.E. Language-related potentials specific to human language cortex. *Science,* 1981, *212,* 353–356.

Fromkin, V.A. The non-anomalous nature of anomalous utterances. *Language,* 1971, *47,* 27–52.

Fryer, D.M., & Marshall, J.C. The motives of Jacques de Vaucanson. *Technology and Culture,* 1979, *20,* 257–269.

Furrow, D. *The benefits of motherese.* Paper presented at the Society for Research of the Child Development Biennial Meeting, San Francisco, 1979.

Furrow, D., Nelson, K., & Benedict, H. Mother's speech to children and syntactic development: Some simple relationships. *Journal of Child Language,* 1979, *6,* 423–442.

Gainotti, G. Emotional behavior and hemispheric side of the lesion. *Cortex,* 1972, *8,* 41–55.

Galaburda, A.M. Histology, architectonics, and asymmetry of language areas. In M. Arbib, D. Caplan, & J. Marshall (Eds.), *Neural models of language processes.* New York: Academic Press, 1982.

Galaburda, A.M., LeMay, M., Kemper, T.L., & Geschwind, N. Right-left asymmetries in the brain: Structural differences between the hemispheres may underlie cerebral dominance. *Science,* 1978, *199,* 852–856.

Galaburda, A.M., Sanides, F., & Geschwind, N. Human brain: Cytoarchitectonic left-right asymmetries in the temporal speech region. *Archives of Neurology,* 1978, *35,* 812–817.

Gallagher, T. Contingent query sequences with adult-child discourse. *Journal of Child Language,* 1981, *8,* 51–62.

Gallagher, T., & Darntan, B. Conversational aspects of the speech of language disordered children: Revision behaviors. *Journal of Speech and Hearing Research,* 1978, *21,* 118–136.

Gallistel, C.R. *The organization of action: a new synthesis.* Hillsdale, NJ: Lawrence Erlbaum Associates, 1980.

Gardner, H., & Denes, G. Connotative judgments by aphasic patients on a pictoral adaptation of the semantic differential. *Cortex,* 1973, *9,* 183–196.

Gardner, H., Ling, K., Flamm, L., & Silverman, J. Comprehension and appreciation of humor in brain-damaged patients. *Brain,* 1975, *98,* 399–412.

Gardner, H., Silverman, J., Wapner, W., & Zurif, E.B. The appreciation of antonymic contrasts in aphasia. *Brain and Language,* 1978, *6,* 301–307.

Gardner, H., & Winner, E. The development of metaphoric competence: Implications for humanistic disciplines. In S. Sacks (Ed.), *On metaphor.* Chicago, IL: University of Chicago Press, 1979.

Garfinkel, H. The origins of the term ethnomethodology. In R. Turner (Ed.), *Ethnomethodology: Selected Readings.* Baltimore, MD: Penguin, 1974.

Garnica, O. *Some characteristics of prosodic input to young children.* Unpublished doctoral dissertation, Stanford University, 1974.

Garnica, O.K. Some prosodic and paralinguistic features of speech to young children. In C.A. Snow & C.A. Ferguson (Eds.), *Talking to children.* London: Cambridge University Press, 1977.

Garrett, M.F. Syntactic process in sentence production. In R.J. Wales & E. Walker (Eds.), *New approaches to language mechanisms.* New York & Amsterdam, Netherlands: North-Holland, 1976.

Garrett, M.F. Objects of psycholinguistic inquiry. *Cognition,* 1981, *10,* 97–102.

Garrett, M.F., Bever, T.G., & Fodor, J.A. The active use of grammar in speech perception. *Perception and Psychophysics,* 1966, *1,* 30–32.

Garvey, C. Contingent queries and their relations in discourse. In E. Ochs & B. Schieffelin (Eds.), *Developmental Pragmatics*. New York: Academic Press, 1979.

Garvey, C., & Berninger, G. Timing and turn-taking in children's conversations. *Discourse Processes*, 1981, *4*, 27–57.

Gatz, A.J. *Manter's essentials of clinical neuroanatomy and neurophysiology*. Philadelphia, PA: Davis, 1970.

Gazzaniga, M.S. The role of language for conscious experience: Observations from split-brain man. In H.H. Kornhuber & L. Deecke (Eds.), *Motivation, motor and sensory processes of the Brain: Electrical potentials, behavior and clinical use. Progress in brain research* (Vol. 54). Amsterdam: North Holland/Elsevier, 1980.

Gazzaniga, M.S., & LeDoux, J.E. *The Integrated Mind*. New York: Plenum Press, 1978.

Gazzaniga, M.S., Volpe, B.T., Smylie, C.S., Wilson, D.H., & LeDoux, J.E. Plasticity in speech following commisurotomy. *Brain*, 1979, *102*, 805–815.

Geertz, C. *The interpretation of cultures*. New York: Basic Books, 1973.

Geller, E., & Wollner, S. *Assessing pragmatic skills*. Paper presented at the International Symposiun on Autism, The Nassan Center, New York, February, 1982.

Gelman, R., Bullock, M. & Meck, F. Preschoolers' understanding of simple object tranformations. *Child Development*, 1980, *51*, 691–699.

Gentner, D. On relational meaning: The acquisition of verb meaning. *Child Development*, 1978, *49*, 988–998.

Geschwind, N. Disconnexion syndromes in animals and man. *Brain*, 1965, *88*, 237–294; 585–644.

Geschwind,. N. The significance of lateralization in nonhuman species [Commentary on Denenberg's "Hemispheric laterality in animals and the effects of early experience"]. *The Behavioral and Brain Sciences*, 1981, *4*, 26–27.

Geschwind, N., & Levitsky, W. Human brain: Left-right asymmetries in temporal speech region. *Science*, 1968, *161*, 186–187.

Gilbert, C. Non-verbal perceptual abilities in relation to left-handedness and cerebral lateralization. *Neuropsychologia*, 1977, *15*, 779–792.

Giurgea, C.E. How and why two brains? [Commentary on Denenberg's "Hemispheric laterality in animals and the effects of experience"]. *The Behavioral and Brain Sciences*, 1981, *4*, 27–28.

Givon, T. Topic, pronoun, and grammatical agreement. In C. Li (Ed.), *Subject and topic*. New York: Academic Press, 1976.

Givon, T. Deductive vs. pragmatic processing in natural language. In W. Kintsch, J. Miller, & P. Polson (Eds.), *Methodological issues in cognitive science*, in press.

Givon, T. *Topic continuity discourse: A quantitative cross-linguistic study*. Amsterdam: J. Benjamin, in press.

Gleason, J.B., & Weintraub, S. The acquisition of routines in child language. *Papers and Reports on Child Language Development No. 10*, Stanford University, 1975.

Gleitman, L., & Gleitman, H. *Phrase and paraphrase*. New York: Norton, 1970.

Gleitman, L., Gleitman, H., & Shipley, E. The emergence of the child as grammarian. *Cognition*, 1972, *1*, 137–164.

Glick, S.D., Jerussi, R.P., and Zimmerberg, B. Behavioral and neuropharmacological correlates of nigrostriatal asymmetry in rats. In S. Harnad, R.W. Doty, L. Goldstein, J. Jaynes & G. Krauthamer (Eds.), *Lateralization in the nervous system*. New York: Academic Press, 1977.

Glick, S.D., Ross, D.A., & Hough, L.B. Lateral asymmetry of neurotransmitters in human brain. *Brain Research*, 1982, *234*, 53–64.

Goetz, E.T., Anderson, R.C., & Shallert, D.L. The representation of sentences in memory. *Journal of Verbal Learning and Verbal Behavior*, 1981, *20*, 369–385.

Goffman, E. *Strategic interaction*. Philadelphia: University of Pennsylvania Press, 1969.

Goldberg, E., & Costa, L.D. Hemisphere differences in the acquisition and use of descriptive systems. *Brain and Language*, 1981, *14*, 144–173.

Goldfarb, R., & Bader, E. Espousing melodic intonation therapy in aphasia rehabilitation: A case study. *International Journal of Rehabilitation Research*, 1979, *2*, 333–342.

Goldin-Meadow, S., Seligman, M., & Gelman, R. Language in the two-year- old. *Cognition*, 1976, *4*, 189–202.

Goldsmith, J. *Autosegmental phonology*. Bloomington: Indiana University Linguistics Club, 1976.

Goldsmith, J. The aims of autosegmental phonology. In D.A. Dinnsen (Ed.), *Current approaches to phonological theory*. Bloomington: Indiana University Press, 1979.

Goldsmith, J. Subsegmentals in Spanish phonology: An autosegmental account. In W. Cressey & D.J. Napoli (Eds.), *Linguistic symposium on romance languages: 9*. Washington, DC: Georgetown University Press, 1981.

Golinkiff, R. The case for semantic relations: Evidence from the verbal and nonverbal domains. *Journal of Child Language*, 1981, *8*, 413–438.

Golinkoff, R., & Markessini, J. 'Mommy sock': The child's understanding of possession as expressed in two-noun phrases. *Journal of Child Language*, 1980, *7*, 119–136.

Goodglass, H., & Calderon, M. Parallel processing of verbal and musical stimuli in right and left hemispheres. *Neuropsychologia*, 1977, *15*, 397–407.

Goodglass, H., & Kaplan, E. *The assessment of aphasia*. Philadelphia: Lea & Febiger, 1972.

Goodglass, H., Klein, B., Carey, P., & Jones, K. Specific semantic word categories in aphasia. *Cortex*, 1966, *2*, 74–89.

Gordon, D., & Lakoff, G. Conversational postulates. In *Proceeding from the seventh Regional Meeting of the Chicago Linguistic Society*. Chicago: University of Chicago, 1971.

Goss, R.N. Language used by mothers of deaf children and mothers of hearing children. *American Annuals of the Deaf*, 1970, *115*, 93–96.

Gough, P.B. Grammatical transformations and speed of understanding. *Journal of Verbal Learning and Verbal Behavior*, 1965, *4*, 107–111.

Gough, P.B. The verification of sentences: The effects of delay of evidence and sentence length. *Journal of Verbal Learning and Verbal Behavior*, 1966, *5*, 492–496.

Gove, W. The labelling of deviance. New York: Wiley, 1975.

Graybeal, C. Memory for stories in language impaired children. *Applied Psycholinguistics*, 1981, *2*, 269–283.

Green, D., & Swets, J. *Signal detection theory and psychophysics*. Huntington, NY: Krieger, 1966.

Greenberg, J.H. (Ed.). *Universals of human language: Phonology*, (Vol. 2). Stanford: Stanford University Press, 1978.

Greenberg, M. Social interaction between deaf preschoolers and their mothers: The effects of communication method and communication competence. *Developmental Psychology*, 1980, *16*, 465–474.

Greenfield, P. Informativeness, presupposition and semantic choice in single-word utterances. In E. Ochs & B. Schieffelin *Developmental Pragmatics*. New York: Academic Press, 1979.

Greenfield, P., & Smith, J. *The structure of communication in early language development*. New York: Academic Press, 1976.

Greenfield, P., & Zukow, P. Why do children say what they say when they say it?: An experimental approach to the psychogenesis of presupposition. In K. Nelson (Ed.), *Children's Language* (Vol. 1). New York: Gardner Press, 1978.

Greenwald, C., & Leonard, L. Communicative and sensorimotor development in Down's syndrome children, *American Journal of Mental Deficiency*, 1979, *84*, 296–303.

Grice, H. Logic and conversation. In I. Davidson & G. Harmon (Eds.), *The logic of grammar.* Encino, CA: Dickenson Press, 1975.

Grossman, M. A central processor for hierarchically-structured material: Evidence from Broca's aphasia. *Neuropsychologia,* 1980, *18,* 299–308.

Grossman, M., Shapiro, B.E., & Gardner, H. Dissociable musical processing strategies after localized brain damage. *Neuropsychologia,* 1981, *19,* 425–433.

Gruber, J. Topicalization in child language. *Foundations of Language,* 1967, *3,* 37–65.

Gruendel, J. Referential extension in early language development. *Child Development,* 1977, *48,* 1567–1576.

Guiot, G., Hertzog, E., Rondot, P., & Molinar, P. Arrest or acceleration of speech evoked by thalamic stimulation in the course of stereotaxic procedures for Parkinsonism. *Brain,* 1961, *84,* 363–379.

Gumperz, J.J., & Hymes, D. (Eds.). The ethnography of communication. *American Anthropologist, 66,* (6, Part 2), 1964.

Gumperz, J.J., & Hymes, D. (Eds). *Directions in sociolinguistics: The ethnography of communication.* New York: Holt, Rinehart & Winston, 1972.

Hailman, P. Ontogeny of a instinct. *Behavior Supplement,* 1967, *15,* 1–159.

Hakes, D.T. Effects of reducing complement constructions on sentence comprehension. *Journal of Verbal Learning and Verbal Behavior,* 1972, *11,* 278–286.

Hakes, D.T., & Cairns, H.S. Sentence comprehension and relative pronouns. *Perception and Psychophysics,* 1970, *8,* 5–8.

Hall, J.W., & Jerger, J. Central auditory function in stutterers. *Journal of Speech and Hearing Research,* 1978, *21,* 324–337.

Halle, M., & Vergnaud, J.R. Three dimensional phonology. *Journal of Linguistics Research,* 1980, *1(1),* 83–105.

Halliday, M. *Learning how to mean: Explorations in the development of language.* London: Edward Arnold, 1975.

Halliday, M., & Hasan, R. *Cohesion in English.* London: Longman, 1976.

Hamburger, H., & Wexler, K. A mathematical theory of learning transformational grammar. *Journal of Mathematical Psychology,* 1975, *12,* 137–177.

Hammond, G.R. Hemispheric differences in temporal resolution. *Brain and Cognition,* 1982, *1,* 95–118.

Hanson, W.R., & Metter, E.J. DAF as instrumental treatment for dysarthria in progressive supranuclear palsy: A case report. *Journal of Speech and Hearing Disorders,* 1980, *45,* 268–276.

Harding, C., & Golinkoff, R. The origins of intentional vocalizations in prelinguistic infants. *Child Development,* 1979, *49,* 33–40.

Hardyck, C. A model of individual differences in hemispheric functioning. In H. Whitaker & H.A. Whitaker (Eds.). *Studies in neurolinguistics* (Vol. 3). New York: Academic Press, 1977.

Hardyck, C., & Petrinovich, L.F. Left-handedness. *Psychological Bulletin,* 1977, *84,* 385–404.

Harkness, S. Aspects of social environment and first language acquisition in rural Africa. In C. Snow & C. Ferguson (Eds.), *Talking to children.* London: Cambridge University Press, 1977.

Harkness, S., & Super, C.M. Why African children are so hard to test. *Research Annals of the New York Academy of Science,* 1977, *285,* 326–331.

Harman, D.W., & Ray, W.J. Hemispheric activity during affective verbal stimuli: An EEG study. *Neuropsychologica,* 1977, *15,* 457–460.

Harms, R.T. *Some non-rules of English.* Bloomington: Indiana University Linguistics Club, 1973. (Reprinted in M. Jazayery, E.C. Polome, & W. Winter (Eds.), *Linguistic and literary studies in honor of A.A. Hill.* The Hague: Mouton, 1974.)

Harnad, S. Neoconstructivism: A unifying theme for the congitive sciences. In T.W. Simon & R.J. Scholes (Eds.) *Language, mind, and brain*. Hillsdale, NJ: Lawrence Erlbaum, 1982.

Harnad, S., Doty, R.W., Goldstein, L., Jaynes, J., & Krauthamer, G. (Eds.). *Lateralization in the nervous system*. New York: Academic Press, 1977.

Hassler, R. Basal ganglia: Historical perspective. *Applied neurophysiology*, 1979, *42*, 5–8.

Hassler, R. Brain mechanisms of intention and attention with introductory remarks on other volitional processes. In H.H. Kornhuber & L. Deecke (Eds.), *Motivation, motor and sensory processes of the brain: Electrical potentials, behaviour and clinical use. Progress in brain research*. (Vol. 54). Amsterdam: Elsevier/North Holland, 1980, 585–614.

Hast, M.H., & Milojevic, B. The responses of the vocal folds to electrical stimulation of the inferior frontal cortex of the squirrel monkey. *Acta Otolaryngologica*, 1966, *61*, 196–204.

Hastings, A.J. *Natural equational phonology*. Unpublished doctoral dissertation, Indiana University at Bloomington, 1981.

Hatch, E., Peck, S., & Wagner-Gough, J. A look at process on child second-language acquisition. In E. Ochs & B.B. Schieffelin (Eds.), *Developmental pragmatics*. New York: Academic Press, 1979.

Haviland, S.E., & Clark, H.H. What's new? Acquiring new information as a process in comprehension. *Journal of Verbal Learning and Verbal Behavior*, 1974, *13*, 515–521.

Hécaen, H., & Sauget, J. Cerebral dominance in left-handed subjects. *Cortex*, 1971, *7*, 19–48.

Heilman, K.M. Neglect and related disorders. In K.M. Heilman & E. Valenstein (Eds.), *Clinical neuropsychology*. New York: Oxford University Press, 1979, 268–307.

Heilman, K.M., Scholes, R., & Watson, R.T. Auditory affective agnosia: Disturbed comprehension of affective speech. *Journal of Neurology, Neurosurgery, and Psychiatry*, 1975, *38*, 69–72.

Heilman, K.M., & Valenstein, E. Frontal lobe neglect in man. *Neurology* (Minneapolis), 1972, *22*, 660–664.

Heilman, M.K., & Van den Abell, T. Right hemispheric dominance for mediating cerebral activation. *Neuropsychologia*, 1979, *15*, 315–321.

Helm, D. *Strategic contextualization: A sensemaking practice*. Paper presented at the International Sociological Association's World Congress of Sociology, Mexico City, August 16, 1982.

Helm, N.A. Management of palilalia with a pacing board. *Journal of Speech and Hearing Disorders*, 1979, *44*, 350–353.

Helm-Estabrooks, N. Exploiting the right hemisphere for language rehabilitation: Melodic intonation therapy. In E.C. Perecman (Ed.), *Cognitive processing in the right hemisphere*. New York: Academic Press, in press.

Herriot, P. The comprehension of active and passive sentences as a function of pragmatic expectations. *Journal of Verbal Learning and Verbal Behavior*, 1969, *8*, 166–169.

Higgenbotham, J., & Yoder, D. Nonverbal communication and the severely communicatively handicapped: Speech is not enough ASHA Convention Short Course, Los Angeles, 1981.

Hildyard, A., & Olson, D.R. Memory and inference in the comprehension of oral and written discourse. *Discourse Processes*, 1978, *1*, 91–117.

Hirsh-Pasek, K., & Treiman, R. Doggerel: Motherese in a new context. *Journal of Child Language*, 1982, *9*, 229–237.

Hixon, T. J. *The mechanical bases of so-called "reversed breathing" in cerebral palsy*. Progress Report of Public Health Service Research Grant NS-09656, 1976.

Hixon, T.J. *Speech breathing kinematics and mechanism inferences therefrom*. Paper presented at the Symposium on Speech Motor Control, Stockholm, Sweden, May 11–12, 1981.

Holden, C. Paul MacLean and the triune brain. *Science*, 1979, *204*, 1066–1068.

Hollerbach, J.M. Effective procedures versus elementary units of behavior. [Commentary on Gallistel's *The organization of action: A new synthesis*]. *The Behavioral and Brain Sciences*, 1981, *4*, 625–627.

Holmes, V.M., Arwas, R., & Garrett, M.F. Prior context and the perception of lexically ambiguous sentences. *Memory and Cognition,* 1977, *5,* 103–110.

Holzman, M. The use of interrogative forms in the verbal interaction of three mothers and their children. *Journal of Psycholinguistic Research,* 1972, *1,* 311–336.

Holzman, M. The verbal environment provided by mothers for their very young children. *Merrill-Palmer Quarterly,* 1974, *20,* 31–42.

Hood-Holzman, L. The politics of autism: A socio-historical view. *Topics in Language Disorders,* 1982, *3,* 64–71.

Hooper, J.B. *An introduction to natural generative phonology.* New York: Academic Press, 1976.

Hooper, J.B. Substantive principles in natural generative phonology. In D.A. Dinnsen (Ed.), *Current approaches to phonological theory.* Bloomington: Indiana University Press, 1979.

Hooper, J.B. The empirical determination of phonological representation. In T. Myers, J. Laver, & J. Anderson (Eds.), *The cognitive representation of speech.* New York: North-Holland, 347–358, 1981.

Horgan, D. How to answer questions when you've got nothing to say. *Journal of Child Language,* 1978, *5,* 159–165.

Hornby, P. Surface structure and the topic-comment distinction: A developmental study. *Child Development,* 1971, *42,* 1975–1988.

Hornby, P., & Hass, W. Use of contrastive stress by preschool children. *Journal of Speech and Hearing Research,* 1970, *13,* 395–399.

Howe, C. The meanings of two-word utterances in the speech of young children. *Journal of Child Language,* 1976, *3,* 29–47.

Howe, C. *Acquiring language in a conversational context.* London: Academic Press, 1981.(a)

Howe, C. Interpretive analysis and role semantics: A ten-year mésalliance? *Journal of Child Language,* 1981, *8,* 439–456.(b)

Houlihan, K. *Is intervocalic voicing a natural rule?* Presented at the annual meeting of the Linguistic Society of America, San Diego, 1982.

Houlihan, K., & Iverson, G. Functionally-constrained phonology. In D.A. Dinnsen (Ed.), *Current approaches to phonological theory.* Bloomington: Indiana University Press, 1979.

Hsu, J.R. *The development of structural principles related to complement subject interpretation.* Unpublished doctoral dissertation, City University of New York, 1981.

Hsu, J.R., Cairns, H.S., & Fiengo, R.W. *The development of grammars underlying children's interpretation of complex sentences.* Paper presented at the annual meeting of the American Speech and Hearing Association, Detroit, 1980.

Hupfer, K., Jürgens, U., & Ploog, D. The effect of superior temporal lesions on the recognition of species-specific calls in the squirrel monkey. *Experimental Brain Research,* 1977, *30,* 75–87.

Hurtig, R. Toward a functional theory of discourse. In R. Freedle (Ed.), *Discourse production and comprehension.* Norwood, NJ: Ablex, 1977.

Hurtig, R. The validity of clausal processing strategies at the discourse level. *Discourse Processes,* 1978, *1,* 195–202.

Hurtig, R., Ensrud, S., & Tomblin, B. The communicative function of question production in autistic children. *Journal of Autism and Developmental Disabilities,* 1982, *12,* 57–69.

Huttenlocher, J. The origins of language comprehension. In R. Solso (Ed.), *Theories in cognitive psychology.* Potomac, MD: Erlbaum, 1974.

Hyman, L. *Phonology: Theory and analysis.* New York: Holt, Rinehart & Winston, 1975.

Hymes, D. Linguistic aspects of cross-cultural personality study. In B. Kaplan (Ed.), *Studying personality cross-culturally.* New York: Harper & Row, 1961.

Hymes, D. On communicative competence. In J.B. Pride & J. Holmes (Eds.), *Sociolinguistics.* Harmondsworth, Middlesex: Penquin, 1972.

Ibbotson, N.R., & Morton, J. Rhythm and dominance. *Cognition,* 1981, 125–138.

Ingham, B. Comparison of the verbal system in child and adult speech in Persian. In N. Waterson & C. Snow (Eds.), *The development of communication*. Chichester: Wiley, 1978.

Ingram, D. *Phonological disability in children*. New York: Elsevier, 1976.

Ingram, D. Transitivity in child language. *Language*, 1971, *47*, 888–910.

Ingram, D. Sensorimotor intelligence and language development. In A. Lock (Ed.), *Action, gesture and symbol: The emergence of language*. London: Academic Press, 1978.

Ingram, D. *Procedures for the phonological analysis of children's language*. Baltimore: University Park Press, 1981.

Innocenti, G.M. The development of interhemispheric connections. *Trends in Neurosciences*, 1981, *4*.

Ito, M. Neurophysiological aspects of the cerebellar motor control system. *International Journal of Neurology*, 1970, *7*, 162–176.

Itoh, M., Sasanuma, S., Tatsumi, I., & Kobayashi, Y. *Voice onset time characteristics of apraxia of speech*. Annual Bulletin No. 13, 123–132, Research Institute of Logopedics and Phoniatrics, Univerisity of Tokyo, 1979.

Jackson, J.H. Clinical remarks on cases of defects of expression in disease of the nervous system. *Lancet*, 1864, *2*, 610.

Jackson, J.H. On affections of speech from disease of the brain. *Brain*, 1878, *1*, 304–330. Reprinted in J. Taylor (Ed.) *Selected writings of John Hughlings Jackson*. (Vol. 2). London: Hodder & Stoughton, 1931.(a)

Jackson, J.H. On the nature of the duality of the brain. *Medical Press and Circular*, 1874, *1*, pp. 19; 41; 63. Reprinted in *Brain*, 1915, *38*. Also reprinted in J. Taylor (Ed.) *Selected writings of John Hughlings Jackson*. (Vol. 2) London: Hodder & Stoughton, 1931.(b)

Jacoby, L.L., Craik, F.I.M., & Begg, I. Effects of decision difficulty on recognition and recall. *Journal of Verbal Learning and Verbal Behavior*, 1979, *18*, 585–600.

Jakobson, R. *Child language, aphasia and phonological universals*, (A. Keiler, Ed, and trans.). (Originally published, 1941.) The Hague: Mouton, 1968.

Jarvella, R.J. Syntactic processing of connected speech. *Journal of Verbal Learning and Verbal Behavior*, 1971, *10*, 409–416.

Jefferson, G. Side sequences. In D. Sudnow (Ed.), *Studies in social interaction* New York: Free Press, 1972.

Jefferson, G. Error correction as an interactional resource. *Language in society*, 1974, *2*, 181-199.

Jenkins, C.M. *Memory and linguistic information: A study of sentence memory, linguistic form, and inferred information*. Unpublished doctoral dissertation, The University of Texas at Austin, 1971.

Jenkins, J.J., & Strange, W. *Context conditions meaning*. Paper presented at the meeting of the Midwestern Psychological Association, Chicago, 1977.

Jocić, M. Adaptation in adult speech during communication with children. In N. Waterson & C. Snow (Eds.), *The development of communication*. Chichester, England: Wiley, 1978.

Johnson H., & Smith, L. Children's inferential abilities in the context of reading to understand. *Child Development*, 1981, *52*, 1216–1223.

Johnson, J., & Scholnick, E. Does cognitive development predict semantic intergration? *Child Development*, 1979, *50*, 73–78.

Johnson, M., Bransford, J., & Solomon, S. Memory for tacit implications of sentences. *Journal of Experimental Psychology*, 1973, *98*, 203–205.

Johnston, J. Narratives: A new look at communication problems in older language-disordered children. *Language, Speech, and Hearing Services in the Schools*, 1982, *13*, 144–155.

Johnston, J. Cognitive prerequisites: The evidence from children learning English. In D. Slobin (Ed.), *The Cross Linguistic Study of Child Language Acquisition*. Hillsdale, NJ: Erlbaum, in press.

Johnston, J., & Kamhi, A. *The same can be less: Syntactic and semantic aspects of the utterances of language-impaired children.* Paper presented at the Symposium on Research in Child Language Disorders, University of Wisconsin-Madison, 1980.

Jonas, S. The supplementary motor region and speech emission. *Journal of Communication Disorders,* 1981, *14,* 349–373.

Jonas, S. The thalamus and aphasia, including transcortical aphasia: A review. *Journal of Communication Disorders,* 1982, *15,* 31–41.

Jones, B. Lateral asymmetry in testing long-term memory for faces. *Cortex,* 1979, *15,* 183–186.

Jones, M., & Quigley, S. The acquisition of question formation in spoken English and American Sign Language by two hearing children of deaf parents. *Journal of Speech and Hearing Disorders,* 1979, *44,* 196–208.

Jones, R.K. Observations on stammering after localized cerebral injury. *Journal of Neurology, Neurosurgery, and Psychiatry,* 1966, *29,* 192–195.

Jürgens, U. Neural control of vocalization in nonhuman primates. In H.D. Steklis & M.J. Raleigh (Eds.), *Neurobiology of social communication in primates.* New York: Academic Press, 1979.

Jürgens, U., & Müller-Preuss, P. Convergent projections of different limbic vocalization areas in the squirrel monkey. *Experimental Brain Research,* 1977, *29,* 75–83.

Jürgens, U., & Ploog, D. On the neural control of mammalian vocalization. *Trends in Neurosciences,* 1981, *4,* 77–80.

Jürgens, U., & Von Cramon, D. On the role of the anterior cingulate cortex in phonation. A case report. *Brain and Language,* 1982, *15,* 234–248.

Just, M.A., & Carpenter, P.A. A theory of reading: From eye fixations to comprehension. *Psychological Review,* 1980, *87,* 329–354.

Kahn, D. *Syllable-based generalizations in English phonology.* Doctoral dissertation, MIT, 1976.

Kahn, J. Relationship of Piaget's sensorimotor period to language acquisition of profoundly retarded children. *American Journal of Mental Deficiency,* 1975, *79,* 640–643.

Kahn, J. *Cognitive and language training with profoundly retarded children.* Paper presented at the Sixth Biennial Meeting of the International Society for the Study of Behavioral Development, Toronto, 1981.

Kail, R., Chi, M., Ingram, A., & Danner, F. Constructive aspects of children's reading comprehension. *Child Development,* 1977, *48,* 684–688.

Kamhi, A. Overextensions and underextensions: How different are they? *Journal of Child Language,* 1982, *9,* 243–248.

Karmiloff-Smith, A. *A functional approach to child language: A study of determiners and reference.* New York: Cambridge University Press, 1979.(a)

Karmiloff-Smith, A. *Language as a formal problem-space for children.* Paper prepared for the Max-Planck-Gesellschaft/National Institute for the Advancement of Science Conference on "Beyond description in child language," Nijmegen, Holland, June 11-16, 1979.(b)

Kay, D., & Anglin, J. Overextension and underextension in the child's expressive and receptive speech. *Journal of Child Language,* 1982, *9,* 83–98.

Kaye, J.D. On the alleged correlation of markedness and rule function. In D.A. Dinnsen (Ed.), *Current approaches to phonological theory.* Bloomington: Indiana Press, 1979.

Kaye, J.D., & Lowenstamm, J. *Syllable structure and markedness theory.* Unpublished manuscript, Universite du Quebec, 1979.

Kaye, K. Infants' effects on their mothers' teaching strategies. In J. Glidewell (Ed.), *The social context of learning and development.* New York: Gardner Press, 1976.

Kaye, K. *The mental and social life of babies.* Chicago: University of Chicago Press, 1981.

Kearsley, R. The newborn's response to auditory stimulation: A demonstration of orienting and defense behavior. *Child Development,* 1973, *44,* 582–590.

Keenan, E. Towards a universal definition of "subject." In C. Li (Ed.), *Subject and topic.* New York: Academic Press, 1976.

Keenan, E. Making it last: Repetition in child discourse. In S. Ervin-Tripp & C. Mitchell Kernan (Eds.), *Child Discourse.* New York: Academic Press, 1977.(a)

Keenan, E. Why look at planned and unplanned discourse? In E. Keenan and T. Bennett (Eds.), *Discourse across time and space* (Southern California Occasional Papers in Linguistics, No. 5). Los Angeles: Department of Linguistics, University of Southern California, 1977, (p. 1–43).(b)

Keenan, J.M., & Kintsch, W. The identification of explicitly and implicitly presented information. In W. Kintsch (Ed.), *The representation of meaning in memory.* Hillsdale, NJ: Erlbaum, 1974.

Kendon, A. Movement coordination in social interaction. *Acta Psychologica,* 1970, *32,* 100–125.

Kendon, A. Selected references to coenetics: The study of behavioral organization of face-to-face interactions. *Sign Language Studies,* 1979, *22,* 7–22.

Kent, R.D. *Structure and function times three (Yes, Virginia, there is still another stage theory).* Keynote address presented at the Symposium on Research in Child Language Disorders, Madison, WI, 1982.

Kent, R.D. Windows to the brain: Functional impairment and the surgical field [Commentary]. *Brain and Behavioral Sciences,* in press.

Kent, R.D., & Bauer, H. *Infants' vocal behavior: Acoustic-phonetic-ethologic analyses.* Miniseminar presented to the American Speech-Language-Hearing Association, Toronto, 1982.(b)

Kent, R.D., & LaPointe, L.L. Acoustic properties of pathologic reiterative utterances: A case study of palilalia. *Journal of Speech and Research,* 1982, *25,* 95–99.

Kent, R.D., & Netsell, R. A case study of an ataxic dysarthric: Cineradiographic and spectographic observations. *Journal of Speech and Hearing Disorders,* 1975, *40,* 115–134.

Kent, R., & Netsell, R. Articulatory abnormalities in athetoid cerebral palsy. *Journal of Speech and Hearing Disorders,* 1978, *43,* 353–375.

Kent, R.D., Netsell, R., & Abbs, J.H. Acoustic characteristics of dysarthria associated with cerebellar disease. *Journal of Speech and Hearing Research,* 1979, *22,* 627–648.

Kent, R.D., & Rosenbek, J.C. Prosodic disturbance and neurologic lesion. *Brain and Language,* 1982, *15,* 259–291.

Kent, R.D., & Rosenbek, J.C. Acoustic patterns of apraxia of speech. *Journal of Speech and Hearing Research,* in press.

Kenstowicz, M., & Kisseberth, C. Rule ordering and the asymmetry hypothesis. *Papers from the sixth regional meeting of the Chicago Linguistic Society,* 1970, 504–519.

Kenstowicz, M., & Kisseberth, C. *Topics in phonological theory.* New York: Academic Press, 1977.

Kenstowicz, M., & Kisseberth, C. *Generative phonology.* New York: Academic Press, 1979.

Kertesz, A. *Aphasia and associated disorders: Taxonomy, localization, and recovery.* New York: Grune & Stratton, 1979.

Kertesz, A. Comments on C.C. Wood presentation. In M.A. Arbib (Ed.), *Neural models of language processes.* COINS Technical Report 80-09. Amherst, MA: Computer and Information Sciences Department, Center for Systems Neuroscience, University of Massachusetts, 1980.

Kertesz, A. Evolution of aphasic syndromes. *Topics in Language Disorders,* 1981, *1,* 15–27.

Killen, M., & Uzgiris, I. Imitation of actions with objects: The role of social meaning. *Journal of Genetic Psychology,* in press.

Kimball, J. Seven principles of surface structure parsing in natural language. *Cognition,* 1973, *2,* 15–47.

Kimura, D. The neural basis of language qua gesture. In H. Whitaker & H.A. Whitaker (Eds.), *Studies in neurolinguistics,* (Vol. 2). New York: Academic Press, 1976.

Kinsbourne, M. The minor cerebral hemisphere as a source of aphasic speech. *Archives of Neurology,* 1971, *25,* 302–306.

Kinsbourne, M. Minor hemisphere language and cerebral maturation. In E.H. Lenneberg & E. Lenneberg (Eds.), *Foundations of language development; A multidisciplinary approach, II.* New York: Academic Press, 1975.

Kinsbourne, M., & Hicks, R.E. Functional cerebral space: A model for overflow transfer and interference effects in human performance. In J. Requin (Ed.), *Attention and performance, VII.* Hillsdale, NJ: Erlbaum, 1978.

Kintsch, W. *The representation of meaning in memory.* Hillsdale, NJ: Erlbaum, 1974.

Kintsch, W. On comprehending stories. In M.A. Just & P. Carpenter (Eds.), *Cognitive processes in comprehension.* Hillsdale, NJ: Erlbaum, 1977.

Kintsch, W., & Keenan, J.M. Reading rate as a function of the number of propositions in the base structure of sentences. *Cognitive Psychology,* 1973, *5,* 257–274.

Kintsch, W., Kozminsky, E., Streby, W.J., McKoon, G., & Keenan, J.M. Comprehension and recall of text as a function of content variables. *Journal of Verbal Learning and Verbal Behavior,* 1975, *14,* 196–214.

Kintsch, W., & VanDijk, T. Toward a model of text comprehension and production. *Psychological Review,* 1978, *85,* 363–394.

Kiparsky, P. *How abstract is phonology?* Bloomington; Indiana University Linguistics Club, 1968.

Kiparsky, P. Abstractness, opacity, and global rules. In A. Koutsoudas (Ed.), *The application and ordering of grammatical rules.* The Hague: Mouton, 1976.

Kiparsky, P. Metrical structure assignment is cyclic. *Linguistic Inquiry, 10* (3), 1979, 421–442.

Kirk, S., McCarthy, J., & Kirk, W. *The Illinois Test of Psycholinguistic Abilities* (Rev. Ed.). Urbana: University of Illinois Press, 1968.

Kirzinger, A., & Jürgens, U. Cortical lesion effect and vocalization in the squirrel monkey. *Brain Research,* 1982, *233,* 299–315.

Kisseberth, C.W. On the functional unity of phonological rules. *Linguistic Inquiry,* 1970, *1,* 291–306.

Klein, R. Word order: Dutch children and their mothers. *Publication 9,* Institute for General Linguistics, University of Amsterdam, 1974.

Klima, E., & Bellugi, U. Syntactic regularities in the speech of children. In J. Lyons & R. Wales (Eds.), *Psycholiguinstic Papers.* Edinburgh: Edinburgh University Press, 1966.

Knopman, D.S., Rubens, A.B., Klassen, A.C., Meyer, M.W., & Niccum, N. Regional cerebral blood flow patterns during verbal and nonverbal auditory activation. *Brain and Language,* 1980, *9,* 93–112.

Kohn, B. Right-hemisphere speech representation and comprehension of syntax after left cerebral injury. *Brain and Language,* 1980, *9,* 350–361.

Kolb, B., Sutherland, R.J., Nonneman, A.J., & Wishaw, I.Q. Asymmetry in the cerebral hemispheres of the rat, mouse, rabbit, and cat: The right hemisphere is larger. *Experimental Neurology,* 1982, *78,* 348–359.

Kolb, B., & Taylor, L. Affective behavior in patients with localized cortical excisions. Role of lesion site and side. *Science,* 1981, *214,* 89–90.

Kornhuber, H.H. Cerebral cortex, cerebellum, and basal ganglia; An introduction to their motor functions. In F.O. Schmidt & F.G. Worden (Eds.), *The neurosciences, 3rd study program.* Cambridge, MA: MIT Press, 1974, 267–280.

Kornhuber, H.H. A reconsideration of the cortical and subcortical mechanisms involved in speech and aphasia. In J.E. Desmedt (Ed.), *Language and hemispheric specialization in man: Cerebral ERPs. Progress in clinical neurophysiology,* (Vol. 3). Basel: Karger, 1977.

Kornhuber, H.H. Introduction. In H.H. Kornhuber & L. Deecke (Eds.), *Motivation, motor and sensory processes of the brain: Electrical potentials, behaviour and clinical use. Progress in brain research,* (Vol. 54). Amsterdam: Elsevier/North Holland, 1980, ix–xii.

Koutsoudas, A. The question of rule ordering: Some common fallacies. *Journal of Linguistics,* 1980, *16,* 19–35.

Koutsoudas, A., Sanders, G., & Noll, C. On the application of phonological rules. *Language,* 1974, *50,* 1–28.

Kozhevnikov, V.A., & Chistovich, L.A. *Rech: Artikulyatsiya i Vosprujatiye [Speech: Articulation and Perception].* Moscow-Leningrad: Nauka, 1965. (Translation available from the Joint Publications Research Service, U.S. Department of Commerce, Washington, DC, No. 30,543.

Krauss, R., & Glucksberg, S. The development of communication: Competence as a function of age, *Child Development,* 1969, *40,* 255–266.

Krnjevic, K. Micro-iontophoretic studies on cortical neurons. International Reviews of Neurobiology. *Neurobiology,* 1964, *7,* 41–98.

Krnjevic, K., & Silver, A. A histochemical study of cholinergic fibres in the cerebral cortex. *Journal of Anatomy,* 1965, *99,* 711–759.

Kuczaj, S. *Young children's overextension of object words in comprehension and/or production: Support for a prototype theory of early object meaning.* Paper presented to the Society for Research in Child Development, San Francisco, 1979.

Kuhl, P.K. The perception of speech in early infancy. In N.J. Lass (Ed.), *Speech and language: Advances in basic research and practice.* (Vol. 1). New York: Academic Press, 1979, 1–47.

Kuhl, P.K. Perceptual constancy for speech-sound categories in early infancy. In G. Yeni-Komshian, J. Kavanaugh, & C. Ferguson (Eds.), *Child phonology: Perception* (Vol. 2). New York: Academic Press, 1980.

Kuno, S. Subject, theme, and the speaker's empathy -- a reexamination of relation phenomena. In C. Li (Ed.), *Subject and topic.* New York: Academic Press, 1976.

Labov, W. Resolving the Neogrammarian controversy. *Language,* 1981, *57,* 267–308.

Labov, W., Yaeger, M., & Steiner, R. *A quantitative study of sound change in progress.* Philadelphia; National Science Foundation Report, 1972.

Ladefoged, P., DeClerk, J., Lindau, M., & Papcun, G. An auditory-motor theory of speech production. *Working papers in phonetics,* #22. UCLA Phonetics Lab. UCLA, 1972.

Langendoen, D.T. Finite-state parsing of phrase-structure languages and the status of read-justment rules in grammar. *Linguistic Inquiry,* 1975, *6,* 533–554.

LaPointe, L.L., & Horner, J. Palilalia. A descriptive study of pathological reiterative utterances. *Journal of Speech and Hearing Disorders,* 1981, *46,* 34–38.

Larsen, B., Skinhøj, E., & Lassen, N.A. Variations in regional cortical blood flow in the right and left hemispheres during automatic speech. *Brain,* 1978, *101,* 193–209.

Lashley, K.S. The problem of serial order in behavior. In L.A. Jeffress (Ed.), *Cerebral mechanisms in behavior.* New York: Wiley, 1951, 112–136.

Lasky, E.Z., & Klopp, K. Parent-child interactions in normal and language disordered children. *Journal of Speech and Hearing Disorders,* 1982, *47,* 7–18.

Lass, R. *On explaining language change.* Cambridge: Cambridge University Press, 1980.

Lassen, N.A., Ingvar, D.H., & Skinhøj, E. Brain function and blood flow. *Scientific American,* 1978, *239* (October), 62–71.

Launer, P.B. "A plane" is not "to fly": Acquiring the distinction between related nouns and verbs in American Sign Language. Doctoral dissertation, City University of New York, 1982.(a)

Launer, P.B. Early signs of motherhood: Motherese in American Sign Language. Paper presented at the meeting of the American Speech and Hearing Association, Toronto, 1982.(b)

Lauter, J.L. Dichotic identification of complex sounds: Absolute and relative ear advantages. *Journal of the Acoustical Society of America,* 1982, *71,* 701–707.

Leben, W.R. The role of tone in segmental phonology. In L.M. Hyman (Ed.), *Consonant types and tone. Southern California occasional papers in linguistics. No. 1,* Department of Linguistics, University of Southern California, 1973.(a)

Leben, W.R. Suprasegmental phonology. Unpublished doctoral dissertation, Massachusetts Institute of Technology, 1973.(b)

Leben, W.R. The phonological component as a parsing device. In D.A. Dinnsen (Ed.), Current approaches to phonological theory. Bloomington: Indiana University Press, 1979.

Lechtenberg, R., & Gilman, S. Speech disorders in cerebellar disease. *Annals of Neurology,* 1978, *3,* 285-290.

LeDoux, J.E. Neuroevolutionary mechanisms of cerebral asymmetry in man. *Brain, Behavior and Evolution,* 1982, *20,* 196-212.

LeDoux, J.E., & Gazzaniga, M.S. Manipulo-spatial aspects of cerebral lateralization: Clues to the origin of lateralization. *Neuropsychologia,* 1977, *15,* 743-750.

Lee, L. Developmental sentence types: A method for comparing normal and deviant syntactic development. *Journal of Speech and Hearing Disorders,* 1966, *31,* 311-330.

Lee, L. *Developmental sentence analysis.* Evanston, IL: Northwestern University Press, 1974.

Lee, L., & Canter, S. Developmental sentence scoring: A clinical procedure for estimating syntactic development in children's spontaneous speech. *Journal of Speech and Hearing Disorders,* 1971, *36,* 315-340.

Lee, S.M. Styles of communication interaction used by mothers of deaf and hearing children and their relationship to linguistic competence in deaf children. Doctoral dissertation, University of California, Berkeley, 1978.

Leischner, A. Die 'Aphasie' der Taubstummen. *Archiv Für Psychiatrie und Nervenkrankheiten,* 1943, *115,* 469-548.

Lemert, E. *Human deviance, social problems, and social control.* Englewood Cliffs, NJ: Prentice-Hall, 1967.

Lempers, J. Young children's production and comprehension of nonverbal deictic behaviors. *The Journal of Genetic Psychology,* 1979, *135,* 93-102.

Lempers, J., Flavell, F., & Flavell, J. The development in very young children of tacit knowledge concerning visual perception. *Genetic Psychology Monographs,* 1977, *95,* 3-53.

Leonard, L. Language impairment in children. *Merrill-Palmer Quarterly,* 1979, *25,* 205-232.

Leonard, L. What is deviant language? *Journal of Speech and Hearing Disorders,* 1972, *37,* 427-446.

Leonard, L. The role of nonlinguistic stimuli and semantic relations in the children's acquisition of grammatical utterances. *Journal of Experimental Child Psychology,* 1975, *19,* 346-357.

Leonard, L. *Meaning in child language.* New York: Grune & Stratton, 1976.

Leonard, L., Bolders, G., & Miller, J. An examination of the semantic relations reflected in the language usage of normal and language-disordered children. *Journal of Speech and Hearing Research,* 1976, *19,* 371-392.

Leonard, L., Camarata, S., Rowan, L., & Chapman, K. The communicative functions of lexical usage by language-impaired children. *Applied Psycholinguistics,* 1982, *3,* 109-126.

Leonard, L., Cole, B., & Steckol, K. Lexical usage of retarded children: An examination of informativeness. *American Journal of Mental Deficiency,* 1979, *84,* 49-54.

Leonard, L., Newhoff, M., & Mesalam, L. Individual differences in early child phonology. *Applied Psycholinguistics,* 1980, *1,* 7-30.

Leonard, L., Schwartz, R., Chapman, K., Rowan, L., Prelock, P., Terrell, B., Weiss, A., & Messick, C. Early lexical acquisition in children with specific language impairment. *Journal of Speech and Hearing Research,* 1982, *25,* 554-564.

Leonard, L., Schwartz, R., Morris, B., & Chapman, K. Factors influencing early lexical acquisition: Lexical orientation and phonological composition. *Child Development,* 1981, *52,* 882-887.

Leopold, W. *Speech development of a bilingual child: A linguist's record* (Vol. 2). Chicago: Northwestern University Press, 1947.

Lesgold, A.M., Roth, S.F., & Curtis, M.E. Foregrounding effects in discourse comprehension. *Journal of Verbal Learning and Verbal Behavior,* 1979, *18,* 291-308.

Levy, J. Lateral specialization of the human brain: Behavioral manifestations and possible evolutionary basis. In J. Kiger (Ed.), *The biology of behavior.* Corvallis: Oregon State University Press, 1973.

Levy, J. The origins of lateral asymmetry. In S. Harnad, R.W. Doty, L. Goldstein, J. Jaynes, & G. Krauthamer (Eds.), *Lateralization in the nervous system.* New York: Academic Press, 1977.

Levy, J. Cerebral asymmetry and the psychology of man. In M.C. Whitrock (Ed.), *The brain and psychology.* New York: Academic Press, 1980, 259-321.

Levy, J. Cross-species invariances and within-species diversity in brain asymmetry and questions regarding inferences about lateralization [Commentary on Denenberg's "Hemispheric laterality in animals and the effects of early experience"]. *The Behavioral and Brain Sciences,* 1981, *4,* 28-30.

Lewis, M. *Infant speech: A Study of the beginnings of language.* London: Routledge and Kegan, 1936.

Lewis, M., & Freedle, R. Mother-infant dyad: The cradle of meaning. In P. Pliner, L. Krames & T. Alloway (Eds.), *Communication and affect, language and thought.* New York: Academic Press, 1973.

Ley, R.G., & Bryden, M.P. A dissociation of right and left hemispheric effects for recognizing emotional tone and verbal content. *Brain and Cognition,* 1982, *1,* 3-9.

Li, C., & Thompson, S. Subject and topic: A new typology of language. In C. Li (Ed.), *Subject and topic.* New York: Academic Press, 1976.

Liben, L., & Posnansky, C. Inferences on inference: The effects of age, transitive ability, memory load, and lexical factors. *Child Development,* 1977, *48,* 1490-1497.

Liberman, M. *The intonational system of English.* Doctoral dissertation, MIT, 1975.

Liberman, M., & Prince, A. On stress and linguistic rhythm. *Linguistic Inquiry,* 1977, *8,* 249-336.

Lieven, E.V.M. Conversations between mothers and young children: Individual differences and their possible implication for the study of language learning. In N. Waterson & C.E. Snow (Eds.), *The development of communication.* New York: Wiley, 1978.

Lightner, T.M. The role of derivational morphology in generative grammar. *Language,* 1975, *51,* 617-638.

Locke, J.L. The inference of speech perception in the phonologically disordered child. Part I: A rationale, some criteria, the conventional tests. *Journal of Speech and Hearing Disorders,* 1980, *45,* 431-444.(a)

Locke, J.L. The inference of speech perception in the phonologically disordered child. Part II: Some clinically novel procedures, their use, some findings. *Journal of Speech and Hearing Disorders,* 1980, *45,* 445-468.(b)

Locke, S. Motor programming and language behavior. In G.A. Miller & E. Lenneberg (Eds.), *Psychology and biology of language and thought.* New York: Academic Press, 1978.

Loftus, E.F. Leading questions and the eyewitness report. *Cognitive psychology,* 1975, *7,* 560-572.

Loftus, E.F. Shifting human color memory. *Memory and Cognition,* 1977, *5,* 696-699.

Long, J. Contextual assimilation and its effect on the division of attention between nonverbal signals. *Quarterly Journal of Experimental Psychology,* 1977, *29,* 397-414.

Lovell, K., Hoyle, H., & Siddall, M. A study of some aspects of the play and language of young children with delayed speech. *Journal of Child Psychology and Psychiatry,* 1968, *9,* 41-50.

Lowe, M., & Costello, A. *Manual for the symbolic play test* (Experimental Ed.). London: National Foundation for Educational Research, 1976.

Lubinski, R., Duchan, J., & Weitzner-Lin, B. Analysis of breakdowns and repairs in aphasic adult communication. *Proceedings of the Clinical Aphasiology Conference,* 1980.

Lund, N., & Duchan, J. Phonological analysis: A multifaceted approach. *British Journal of Disorders of Communications,* 1978, *13,* 119–126.

Lund, N., Duchan, J. *Assessing children's language in naturalistic contexts.* Englewood Cliffs, NJ: Prentice-Hall, 1983.

Luria, A.R. *Traumatic aphasia.* The Hague: Mouton, 1967.

Luria, A.R. *Higher cortical functions in man.* (2nd ed.), New York: Basic Books, 1980.

Macken, M.A., & Ferguson, C.A. Phonological universals in language acquisition. *Annals of the New York Academy of Sciences,* 1981, *379,* 110–129.

MacLean, P.D. Psychomatic disease and the "visceral brain." Recent developments bearing on the Papez theory of emotion. *Psychomatic Medicine,* 1949, *11,* 338–353.

MacLean, P.D. New findings relevant to the evolution of psychosexual functions of the brain. *Journal of Nervous and Mental Diseases,* 1962, *135,* 289–301.

MacLean, P.D. Man and his animal brains. *Modern Medicine,* 1964, *32,* 95–106.

MacLean, P.D. The triune brain, emotion, and scientific bias. In F.O. Schmidt (Ed.), *The neurosciences: Second study program.* New York: Rockefeller University Press, 1970.

MacLean, P.D. Evolution of the psychencephalon. *Zygon,* 1982, *17,* 187–211.

MacNamara, J. The cognitive basis of language learning in infants. *Psychological Review,* 1972, *79,* 1–13.

MacWhinney, B. Rules, rote and analogy in morphological formations in Hungarian children. *Journal of Child Language,* 1975, *2,* 65–77.

MacWhinney, B. The acquisition of morphophonology. *Monographs of the Society for Research in Child Development,* 1978, *43,* (1-2, Serial No. 174.)

MacWhinney, B. Basic syntactic processes. In S. Kuczaj (Ed.), *Language development: Syntax and semantics.* Hillsdale, NJ: Erlbaum, 1980.(a)

MacWhinney, B. Levels of syntactic acquisition. In S. Kuczaj (Ed.), *Language development: Syntax and semantics.* Hillsdale, NJ: Erlbaum, 1980.(b)

MacWhinney, B., & Bates, E. Sentential devices for conveying givenness and newness: A cross-cultural developmental study. *Journal of Verbal Learning and Verbal Behavior,* 1978, *17,* 539–558.

Maestas y Moores, J. Early linguistic environment: Interactions of deaf parents with their infants. *Sign Language Studies,* 1980, *26,* 1–13.

Magendie, F. *Lecons sur les fonctions et les maladies du systeme nerveux.* Paris: Meguignon-Marvis, 1841.

Mandler, J.M., & Johnson, N.S. Remembrance of things parsed: Story structure and recall. *Cognitive Psychology,* 1977, *9,* 111–151.

Manelis, L., & Yekovich, F.R. Repetitions of propositional arguments in sentences. *Journal of Verbal Learning and Verbal Behavior,* 1976, *15,* 301–312.

Mann, V.A., Diamond, R., & Carey, S. Development of voice recognition: Parallels with face recognition. *Journal of Experimental Child Psychology,* 1979, *27,* 153–165.

Mantyh, P.W. Forebrain projections to the periaqueductal gray in the monkey, with observations in the cat and rat. *Journal of Comparative Neurology,* 1982, *206,* 146–158.

Maratsos, M., & Chalkley, M. The internal language of children's syntax: The ontogenesis and representation of syntactic categories. In K. Nelson (Ed.), *Children's language* (Vol. 2). New York: Gardner Press, 1980.

Marcus, M. *A theory of syntactic recognition for natural language.* Cambridge, MA: MIT Press, 1980.

Marinkovich, G., Newhoff, M., & MacKenzie, J. "Why can't you talk?": Peer input to language disordered children. Paper presented at the meeting of the American Speech and Hearing Association, Detroit, 1980.

Marler, P., Zoloth, S., & Dooling, R. Comparative perspectives on the ethology of perceptual development. In E. Gollin (Ed.), *Developmental plasticity.* New York: Academic Press, 1981.

Marshall, J.C. Minds, machines and metaphors. *Social Studies of Science,* 1977, *7,* 475-488.

Marshall, J.C. Models of the mind in health and disease. In A.W. Ellis (Ed.), *Normality and pathology in cognitive functions.* New York: Academic Press, 1982.

Marshall, N., Hegrenes, J., & Goldstein, S. Verbal interactions: Mothers and their retarded children vs. mothers and their nonretarded children. *American Journal of Mental Deficiency,* 1973, *77,* 415-419.

Marslen-Wilson, W.D., & Tyler, L.K. The temporal structure of spoken language understanding. *Cognition,* 1980, *8,* 1-71.

Marslen-Wilson, W.D., Tyler, L.K., & Seidenberg, M. Sentence processing and the clause-boundary. In W.J.M. Levelt & G.B. Flores D'Arcais (Eds.), *Studies in sentence perception.* New York: Wiley, 1978.

Marslen-Wilson, W.D., & Welsh, A. Processing interactions and lexical access during word recognition in continuous speech. *Cognitive Psychology,* 1978, *10,* 29-63.

Martin, J.G. Rhythmic (hierarchical) versus serial structure in speech and other behavior. *Psychological Review,* 1972, *79,* 487-509.

Mateer, C. Asymmetric effects of thalamic stimulation on rate of speech. *Neuropsychologia,* 1978, *16,* 497-499.(a)

Mateer, C. Impairments of non-verbal oral movements after left hemisphere damage: A followup analysis of errors. *Brain and Language,* 1978, *6,* 334-341.(b)

Mateer, C., & Kimura, D. Impairment of nonverbal oral movements in aphasia. *Brain and Language,* 1977, *4,* 262-276.

Maxwell, E.M. Competing analyses of a deviant phonology. *Glossa,* 1979, *13*(2), 181-214.

Maxwell, E.M. *A study of misarticulation from a linguistic perspective.* Indiana University Doctoral Dissertation. Indiana University Linguistics Club, Bloomington, 1981.

Maxwell, E.M. On determining child underlying phonological representations: A critique of the current theories. In M. Elbert, D.A. Dinnsen & G. Weismer (Eds.), *Phonological theory and the misarticulating child.* ASHA Monographs, in press.

Mazzocchi, F., & Vignolo, L.A. Localisation of lesions in aphasia: Clinical CT scan correlations in stroke patients. *Cortex,* 1979, *15,* 627-654.

McCall, R., Parke, R., & Kavanaugh, R. Imitation of live and televised models by children 1 to 3 years of age. *Monographs of the Society for Research in Child Development,* 1977, *42,* (5, Serial No. 173).

McCall, R.B., Eichorn, D.H., & Hogarty, P. Transitions in early mental development. *Monographs of the Society for Research in Child Development,* 1977, (Serial No. 171).

McCarthy, J. On hierarchic structure within syllables. Unpublished manuscript, Department of Linguistics, MIT, 1976.

McCarthy, J. *Formal problems in semitic phonology and morphology.* MIT doctoral dissertation, Indiana University Linguistics Club, Bloomington, 1979.

McCune-Nicolich, L. Toward symbolic functioning: Structure of early pretend games and potential parallels with language. *Child Development,* 1981, *52,* 386-388.(a)

McCune-Nicolich, L. The cognitive bases of relational words in the single word period. *Journal of Child Language,* 1981, *8,* 15-34.(b)

McCune-Nicolich, L., & Bruskin, C. Combinatorial competency in symbolic play and language. In K. Rubin (Ed.), *The play of children:* Current theory and research. D.J. Pepler & K.M. Rubin (Eds.), Basel, Switzerland: S. Karger, AB, 1982.

McDonald, J., & Blott, J. Environmental language intervention: A rationale for diagnosis and training strategy through rules, context, and generalization. *Journal of Speech and Hearing Disorders,* 1974, *39,* 244–256.

McDonald. L., & Pien, D. Mother converational behaviour as a function of interactional intent. *Journal of Child Language,* 1982, *9,* 337–358.

McFarling, D., Rothi, L.J., & Heilman, K.M. Transcortical aphasia from ischaemic infarcts of the thalamus: A report of two cases. *Journal of Neurology, Neurosurgery, and Psychiatry,* 1982, *45,* 107–112.

McGeer, P.L., Eccles, J.C., & McGeer, E.G. *Molecular Neurobiology of the Mammalian Brain.* New York: Plenum Press, 1978.

McKeever, W.F., Gill, K.M., & VanDeventer, A.D. Letter versus dot stimuli as tools for "splitting the normal brain with reaction time." *Quarterly Journal of Experimental Psychology,* 1975, *27,* 363–373.

McKeever, W.F., Hoemann, H.W., Florian, V., & VanDeventer, A.D. Evidence of minimal cerebral asymmetries for the processing of English words and American Sign Language stimuli in the congenitally deaf. *Neuropsychologia,* 1976, *14,* 413–423.

McKoon, G., & Keenan, J. Response latencies to explicit and implicit statements. In W. Kintsch (Ed.), *The representation of meaning in memory.* Hillsdale, NJ: Erlbaum, 1974.

McKoon, G., & Ratcliff, R. Priming in item recognition: The organization of propositions in memory for text. *Journal of Verbal Learning and Verbal Behavior,* 1980, *19,* 369–386.

McKoon, G., & Ratcliff, R. The comprehension processes and memory structures involved in instrumental inference, *Journal of Verbal Learning and Verbal Behavior,* 1981, *20,* 671–682.

McLean, J., & Snyder-McLean, L. A transactional approach to early language training. Columbus, OH: Merrill, 1978.

McNeill, D. *The acquisition of language.* New York: Harper & Row, 1970.

McNew, S., & Bates, E. The pragmatic bases of syntax. In R.C. Naremore (Ed.), *Language science.* San Diego: College-Hill Press, 1983.

McShane, J. *Learning to talk.* Cambridge, England: Cambridge Universsity Press, 1980.

Meadow, K.P., Schlesinger, H.S., & Hostein, C.B. The developmental process in deaf preschool children: Communicative competence and socialization. In H.S. Schlesinger & K.P. Meadow (Eds.), *Sound and sign: Childhood deafness and mental health,* Berkeley: University of California Press, 1972.

Meckler, R.J., Mack, J.L., & Bennett, R. Sign Language aphasia in a non-deaf-mute. *Neurology, (Minneapolis),* 1979, *29,* 1037–1040.

Mehan, H., & Wood, H. *The reality of ethnomethodology.* New York: Wiley, 1975.

Mehrabian, A., & Williams, M. Piagetian measures of cognitive development for children up to age two. *Journal of Psycholinguistic Research,* 1974, *1,* 113–124.

Meier, R. *Icons, analogues and morphemes: The acquisition of verb agreement in American Sign Language.* Doctoral dissertation, University of California, San Diego, 1982.

Menn, L. *Pattern, control, and contrast in beginning speech: A case study in the development of word form and word function.* Unpublished doctoral dissertation, University of Illinois at Urbana-Champaign, 1976.

Menyuk, P. Comparison of grammar of children with functionally deviant and normal speech. *Journal of Speech and Hearing Research,* 1964, *7,* 109–121.

Menyuk, P., & Bernholtz, N. Prosodic features and children's language production. *Research Laboratory of Electronics Quarterly Progress Report,* 1969, *93,* 216–219.

Mercer, B., Wapner, W., Gardner, H., & Benson, D.F. A study of confabulation. *Archives of Neurology,* 1977, *34,* 346–348.

Mercer, J. Understanding career patterns of persons labelled as mentally retarded. *Social Problems,* 1965, *13,* 18–34.

Mercer, J. *Labelling the mentally retarded.* Berkeley: University of California Press, 1973.

Mervis, C. *Tigers and leopards are kitty-cats: Mother-child interaction and children's early categories.* Paper presented at the Interdisciplinary Conference, Park City, UT, 1981.

Mervis, C. *Mother-child interaction and early lexical development.* Paper presented at the annual meeting of the Midwestern Psychological Association, Minneapolis, 1982.

Mervis, C., & Canada, K. On the existence of competence errors in early comprehension: A reply to Fremgen & Fay and Thomson & Chapman. *Journal of Child Language,* in press.

Mervis, C., & Mervis, C. Leopards are kitty-cats: Object labelling by mothers for their 13 month olds. *Child Development,* 1982, *53,* 267–273.

Mervis, C., & Rosch, E. Categorization of natural objects. *Annual Review of Psychology,* 1981, *32,* 89–115.

Messer, D.J. The integration of mothers' referential speech with joint play. *Child Development,* 1978, *49,* 781–787.

Metter, E.J., Wasterlain, C.G., Kuhl, D.E., Hanson, W.R., & Phelps, M.E.[18] FDG positron emission computed tomography in a study of aphasia. *Annals of Neurology,* 1981, *10,* 173-183.

Mettler, F. *Selective partial ablation of the frontal cortex.* New York: Hoeber, 1949.

Miller, G.A., & Johnson-Laird, P.N. *Language and perception.* Cambridge: Belknap Press, Harvard, 1976.

Miller, J.,(Ed.). Assessing language production in children. Baltimore: University Park Press, 1981.

Miller, J., Chapman, R., & Bedrosian, J. *Defining developmentally disabled subjects for research: The relationships between etiology, cognitive development, language and communicative performance.* Paper presented at the Second Annual Boston University Conference on Language Development, Boston, 1977.

Miller, J., Chapman, R., Branston, M., & Reichle, J. Language comprehension in sensorimotor stages V and VI. *Journal of Speech and Hearing Research,* 1980, *23,* 284–311.

Miller, J.R., & Kintsch, W. Readability and recall of short prose passages: A theoretical analysis. *Journal of Experimental Psychology: Human Learning and Memory,* 1980, *6,* 335–354.

Miller, L. Pragmatics and early childhood language disorders: Communicative interaction in a half-hour sample. *Journal of Speech and Hearing Disorders,* 1978, *43,* 419–436.

Mills, L., & Rollman, G.B. Left hemisphere selectivity for processing duration in normal subjects. *Brain and Language,* 1979, *7,* 320–335.

Milner, E. CNS maturation and language acquisition. In H. Whitaker & H.A. Whitaker (Eds.), *Studies in neurolinguistics* (Vol. 1). New York: Academic Press, 1976.

Minsky, M. A framework for representing knowledge. In P.H. Winston (Ed.), *The psychology of computer vision.* New York: McGraw Hill, 1975.

Mischler, E. Studies in dialogue and discourse: An exponential law of successive questioning. *Language in Society,* 1975, *4,* 31–51.

Mischler, E. Meaning in context. Is there any other kind? *Harvard Educational Review,* 1979, *49,* 1–21.

Mlcoch, A.G., & Noll, J.D. Speech production models as related to the concept of apraxia of speech. In N.J. Lass (Ed.), *Speech and language: Advances in basic research and practice* (Vol. 4). New York: Academic Press, 1980, 201–238.

Moerk, E.L. Principles of interaction in language learning. *Merrill-Palmer Quarterly,* 1972, *18,* 229–257.

Moerk, E.L. A design for multivariate analysis of language behavior and development. *Language and Speech,* 1974, *17,* 240–254.

Moerk, E.L. Verbal interactions between children and their mothers during the preschool years. *Developmental Psychology,* 1975, *11,* 788–795.

Moerk, E.L. Relationships between parental input frequencies and children's language acquisition: A reanalysis of Brown's data. *Journal of Child Language,* 1980, *7,* 105-118.

Moerk, E.L. Processes of language teaching and training in the interactions of mother-child dyads. *Child Development,* 1978, *14,* 537-554.

Mohr, J.P. Broca's area and Broca's aphasia. In H. Whitaker & H.A. Whitaker (Eds.), *Studies in neurolinguistics,* (Vol. 1). New York: Academic Press, 1976.

Molfese, D.L. Infant cerebral asymmetry. In S.J. Segalowitz & F.A. Gruber (Eds.), *Language development and neurological theory.* New York: Academic Press, 1977.

Molfese, D.L. Hemispheric specialization for temporal information: Implications for the perception of voicing cues during speech perception. *Brain and Language,* 1980, *11,* 285-299.(a)

Molfese, D.L. (Ed.). Neuroelectric correlates of language processes: Evidence from scalp recorded evoked potential research. *Brain and Language,* 1980, *11,* 233-397.(b)

Monakow, C.von. *Die lokalisation im grosshirn.* Wiesbaden: Bergmann, 1914.

Monrad-Krohn, G.H. On the dissociation of voluntary and emotional innervations in facial paresis of central origin. *Brain,* 1942, *47,* 22-45.

Monrad-Krohn, G.H. The third element of speech: Prosody and its disorders. In L. Halpern (Ed.), *Problems in dynamic neurology.* Jerusalem: Hebrew University Press, 1963.

Moore, W.H., & Lang, M.K. Alpha asymmetry over the right and left hemispheres of stuttering and control subjects preceding massed oral readings: A preliminary investigation. *Perceptual and Motor Skills,* 1977, *44,* 223-230.

Morehead, D. Early grammatical and semantic relations: Some implications for a general representational deficit. *Papers and Reports in Child Language,* 1973, *4,* 1-12.

Morgan, J., & Sellner, M. Discourse and linguistic theory. In R. Spiro, B. Bruce, & W. Brewer (Eds.), *Theoretical issues in reading comprehension.* Hillsdale, NJ: Erlbaum, 1980.

Morgan, M.J., & Corballis, M.C. On the biological basis of human laterality: II. The mechanisms of inheritance. *The Brain and Behavioral Sciences,* 1978, *1,* 270-336.

Morris, C.D., & Bransford, J.D. Effective elaboration and inferential reasoning. *Memory and Cognition,* 1982, *10,* 188-193.

Morton, J. The interaction of information in word recognition. *Psychological Review,* 1969, *60,* 329-346.

Morton, J., & Long, J. Effect of word transitional probability on phoneme identification. *Journal of Verbal Learning and Verbal Behavior,* 1976, *15,* 43-51.

Moscovitch, M. On the representation of language in the right hemisphere of right-handed people. *Brain and Language,* 1976, *3,* 47-71.

Moscovitch, M. Right-hemisphere language. *Topics in Language Disorders,* 1981, *1,* 41-61.

Mountcastle, V.B. An organizing principle for cerebral function: The unit module and the distributed system. In G. Edelman & V.B. Mountcastle (Eds.), *The mindful brain: Cortical organization and the group-selective theory of higher brain function.* Cambridge, MA: MIT Press, 1978.

Müller-Preuss, P., & Jürgens, U. Projections from the "cingular" vocalization area in the squirrel monkey. *Brain Research,* 1976, *103,* 29-43.

Munsinger, H., & Douglass, A. The syntactic abilities of identical twins, fraternal twins, and their siblings. *Child Development,* 1976, *47,* 40-50.

Murphy, C., & Messer, D. Mothers, infants, and pointing: A study of a gesture. In H. Schaffer (Ed.), *Studies in mother-infant interaction.* London: Academic Press, 1977.

Myslobodsky, M.S. Animal brain laterality: Functional lateralization or a right-left excitability gradient? [Commentary on Denenberg's "Hemispheric laterality in animals and the effects of early experience"]. *The Behavioral and Brain Sciences,* 1981, *4,* 31-32.

Myslobodsky, M.S., Mintz, M., & Tomer, R. Asymmetric reactivity of the brain and components of hemispheric imbalance. In J. Gruzelier & P. Flor-Henry (Eds.), *Hemisphere asymmetries of function in psychopathology.* Amsterdam: Elsevier, 1979.

Naeser, M.A. Language behavior in stroke patients. *Trends in Neurosciences,* February 1982, 52–59.

Naeser, M.A., Alexander, M.P., Helm-Estabrooks, N., Levine, H.L., Laughlin, S.A., & Geschwind, N. Aphasia with predominantly subcortical lesion sites: Description of three capsular/putaminal aphasia syndromes. *Archives of Neurology,* 1982, *39,* 2–14.

Neaser, M.A., & Hayward, R.W. Lesion localization in aphasia with cranial computed tomography and the Bostom Diagnostic Aphasia Exam. *Neurology,* 1978, *28,* 545–551.

Naeser, M.A., Hayward, R.W., Laughlin, S.A., & Zatz, L.M. Quantitative CT scan studies in aphasia: I. Infarct size and CT numbers. *Brain and Language,* 1981, *12,* 140–164.(a)

Naeser, M.A., Hayward, R.W., Laughlin, S.A., Becker, J.M.T., Jernigan, T.L., & Zatz, L.M. Quantitative CT scan studies in aphasia: 2. Comparison of the right and left hemispheres. *Brain and Language,* 1981, *12,* 165–189.(b)

Nauta, W.J.H. The problem of the frontal lobe: A reinterpretation. *Journal of Psychiatric Research,* 1971, *8,* 167–187.

Navon, D., & Gopher, D. On the economy of the human processing system. *Psychological Review,* 1979, *86,* 214–255.

Nellum-Davis, P. *Deaf high school students' ability to adjust communicative behavior to accord with their perspective of the listener: A pragmatic study of total communication.* Unpublished doctoral dissertation, State University of New York at Buffalo, 1980.

Nelson, K. Structure and strategy in learning to talk. *Monographs of the Society for Research in Child Development,* 1973, *38,* (1-2, Serial No. 149).

Nelson, K. Concept, word and sentence: Interrelations in acquisition and development. *Psychological Review,* 1974, *81,* 267–285.

Nelson, K. Facilitating children's syntax acquisition. *Developmental Psychology,* 1977, *13,* 101–107.

Nelson, K. Individual differences in language development: Implications for development and language. *Developmental Psychology,* 1981, *17,* 170–187.(a)

Nelson, K. Toward a rare-event cognitive comparison theory of syntax acquisition. In P. Dale & D. Ingram (Eds.), *Children's language development: An international perspective.* Baltimore: University Park Press, 1981.(b)

Nelson, K., & Bonvillian, J. Concepts and words in the two-year-old: Acquisition of concept names under controlled conditions. *Cognition,* 1973, *2,* 435–450.

Nelson, K., & Bonvillian, J. Early language development: Conceptual growth and related processes between 2 and 4 1/2 years of age. In K.E. Nelson (Ed), *Children's Language* (Vol. 1). New York: Gardner Press, 1978.

Nelson, K., Carskaddon, G., & Bonvillian, J. Syntax acquisition: Impact of experimental variation in adult verbal interaction with the child. *Child Development,* 1973, *44,* 497-504.

Nelson, K., & Gruendel, J. At morning it's lunchtime: A scriptal view of children's dialogues. *Discourse Processes,* 1979, *2,* 73–94.

Nelson, K., Rescorla, L., Gruendel, J., & Benedict, H. Early lexicons: What do they mean? *Child Development,* 1978, *49,* 960–968.

Netsell, R. The acquisition of speech motor control: A perspective with directions for research. In R.E. Stark (Ed.), *Language behavior in infancy and early childhood.* New York: Elsevier/North Holland, 1981.

Newhoff, M., Silverman, L., & Millet, A. *Linguistic differences in parents' speech to normal and language disordered children.* Paper presented to the Symposium on Research in Child Language Disorders, University of Wisconsin, Madison, 1980.

Newport, E., Gleitman, H., & Gleitman, L. A study of mothers' speech and child language acquisition. *Papers and Reports on Child Language Development No. 8,* Stanford University, 1975.

Newport, E., Gleitman, H., & Gleitman, L.R. Mother, I'd rather do it myself: Some effects and non-effects of maternal speech style. In C. Snow & C. Ferguson (Eds.), *Talking to children.* London: Cambridge University Press, 1977.

Newson, J. An intersubjective approach to the systematic description of mother-infant interaction. In H.R. Schaffer (Ed.), *Studies in mother-infant interaction.* London: Academic Press, 1977.

Ninio, A., & Bruner, J.S. The achievement and antecedents of labelling. *Journal of Child Language,* 1978, *5,* 1-15.

Noel, G., Bain, H., Collard, M., & Huvelle, R. Clinico- pathological correlations in aphasiology by means of computerized axial tomography: Interest of using printout and prospective considerations. *Neuropsychobiology,* 1980, *6,* 190-200.

Norman, D. *Memory and attention* (2nd ed.). New York: Wiley, 1976.

(2nd ed.). New York: Wiley, 1976.

Norman, D., & Bobrow, D. On data-limited and resource-limited processes. *Cognitive Psychology,* 1975, *7,* 44-64.

Norris, D. Autonomous processes in comprehension: A reply to Marslen-Wilson and Tyler. *Cognition,* 1982, *11,* 97-102.

Nothnagel, H. Experimentelle untersuchungen uber die funktion des gehirns. *Virchows Archiv pathologische Anatomie und Physiologie,* 1873, *57,* 184-214.

Nottebohm, F. Ontogeny of bird song. *Science,* 1970, *167,* 950-956.

Nottebohm, F. Does hemispheric specialization of function reflect the needs of an executive side? [Commentary on J.L. Bradshaw & N.C. Nettleton's "The nature of hemispheric specialization in man"]. *The Behavioral and Brain Sciences,* 1981, *4,* 76-77.

Obeso, J.A., Rothwell, J.C., & Marsden, C.D. Simple tics in Gilles de la Tourette's syndrome are not prefaced by a normal premovement EEG potential. *Journal of Neurology, Neurosurgery and Psychiatry,* 1981, *44,* 735-738.

Olber, L.K., Albert, M.L., Goodglass, H., & Benson, D.F. Aphasia type and aging. *Brain and Language,* 1978, *6,* 318-322.

Obler, L.K., Zatorre, R.J., Galloway, L., & Vaid, J. Cerebral lateralization in bilinguals: Methodological issues. *Brain and Language,* 1982, *15,* 40-54.

Ochs, E. Introduction: What child language can contribute to pragmatics. In E. Ochs & B.B. Schieffelin (Eds.), *Developmental pragmatics.* New York: Academic Press, 1979.(a)

Ochs, E. Transcription as theory. In E. Ochs & B. Schieffelin (Eds.), *Developmental pragmatics,* New York: Academic Press, 1979.(b)

Ochs, E. Talking to children in Western Samoa. Unpublished manuscript, 1980.

O'Connell, B., McNew, S., Bates, E., & MacWhinney, B. Manuscript in preparation, University of California at San Diego, 1983.

Ohala, J.J. The role of physiological and acoustic models in explaining the direction of sound change. *Project on Linguistic Analysis Reports,* University of California at Berkeley, 1971, *15,* 25-40.

Ohala, J.J. How to represent natural sound patterns. *Project on Linguistics Analysis Reports,* University of California at Berkeley, 1972, *16,* 40-57.(a)

Ohala, J.J. Physical models in phonology. In A. Rigault & R. Charbonneau (Eds.), *Proceedings of the Seventh International Congress of Phonetic Sciences.* The Hague: Mouton, 1972.(b)

Ohala, J.J. Experimental historical phonology. In J.M. Anderson & C. Jones (Eds.), *Historical linguistics II. Theory and description in phonology.* Amsterdam, Netherlands: North Holland, 1974.

Ohala, J.J. A model of speech aerodynamics. *Reports of the Phonology Laboratory,* University of California at Berkeley, 1976, *1,* 93-107.

Ohala, J.J. The contribution of acoustics to phonology. In B. Lindblom & S. Ohman (Eds.), *Frontiers in Speech Communication Research.* New York: Academic Press, in press. (Originally published, 1978.)(a)

Ohala, J.J. Phonological notations as models. In W.U. Dressler & W. Meid (Eds.), *Proceedings of the 12th International Congress of Linguists, 1977.* Innsbruck, Germany: Innsbrucker Beitrage zur Sprachwissenschaft, 1978.(b)

Ohala, J.J. Southern Bantu vs. the world: The case of palatalization of labials. *Proceedings of the Annual Meeting, Berkeley Linguistics Society,* 1978, *4,* 370–386.(c)

Ohala, J.J. Articulatory constraints on the cognitive representation of speech. In T. Myers, J. Laver, & J. Anderson (Eds.), *The cognitive representation of speech.* New York: North-Holland, 1981.(a)

Ohala, J.J. Speech timing as a tool in phonology. *Phonetica,* 1981, *38,* 204–212.(b)

Ohala, J.J. *The evaluation of phonetic explanations in phonology.* Paper presented at the workshop on Speech Production and Phonology, Eighth International Congress of Linguists, Tokyo, 1982.(a)

Ohala, J.J. The origin of sound patterns in vocal tract constraints. In P.F. MacNeilage (Ed.), *The production of speech.* New York: Springer-Verlag, 1982.(b)

Ojemann, G.A. Subcortical language mechanisms. In H. Whitaker & H.A. Whitaker (Eds.), *Studies in neurolinguistics,* (Vol. 1). New York: Academic Press, 1976.

Ojemann, G.A. Organization of short-term verbal memory in language areas of human cortex: Evidence from electrical stimulation. *Brain and Language,* 1978, *5,* 331–340.

Ojemann, G.A., & Mateer, C. Cortical and subcortical organization of human communication: Evidence from stimulation studies. In H.D. Steklis & M.J. Raleigh (Eds.), *Neurobiology of social communication in primates.* New York: Academic Press, 1979.(a)

Ojemann, G., & Mateer, C. Human language cortex: Localization of memory, syntax, and sequential motor-phoneme identification systems. *Science,* 1979, *205,* 1401–1403.(b)

Ojemann, G.A., & Whitaker, H.A. Language localization and variability. *Brain and Language,* 1978, *6,* 239–260.(a)

Ojemann, G., & Whitaker, H.A. The bilingual brain. *Archives of Neurology,* 1978, *35,* 409–412.(b)

Oke, A., Keller, R., Mefford, I., & Adams, R.N. Lateralization of norepinephrine in human thalamus. *Science,* 1978, *200,* 1411–1433.

Olsen-Fulero, L. Style and stability in mother conversational behaviour: A study of individual differences. *Journal of Child Language,* 1982, *9,* 543–564.

Onifer, W., & Swinney, D.A. Accessing lexical ambiguities during sentence comprehension: Effects of freguency of meaning and contextual bias. *Memory and Cognition,* 1981, *9,* 225–236.

Osgood, C. Where do sentences come from? In D. Steinberg & L. Jakobovits (Eds.), *Semantics.* Cambridge: Cambridge University Press, 1971.

Osgood, C., Suci, G., & Tannenbaum, P. The measurement of meaning. Urbann: University of Illinois Press, 1957.

Oviatt, S. The emerging ability to comprehend language: An experimental approach. *Child Development,* 1980, *51,* 97–106.

Panagos, J. Persistence of the open syllable reinterpreted as a symptom of a language disorder. *Journal of Speech and Hearing Disorders,* 1974, *39,* 23–31.

Parker, F. Distinctive features in speech pathology: Phonology or phonemes. *Journal of Speech and Hearing Disorders,* 1976, *41,* 23–39.

Paris, S., & Carter, A. Semantic and constructive aspects of sentence memory in children. *Developmental Psychology,* 1973, *9,* 109–113.

Paris, S., & Upton, L. Children's memory for inferential relationships in prose. *Child Development,* 1976, *47,* 660–668.

Peele, T.L. *The neuroanatomic basis for clinical neurology.* New York: McGraw-Hill, 1961.

Penfield, W., & Roberts, L. *Speech and brain-mechanisms.* Princeton, NJ: Princeton University Press, 1959.

Penfield, W., & Welch, K. The supplementary motor area of the cerebral cortex. *Archives of Neurology and Psychiatry,* 1951, *66,* 289-317.

Pentz, T. *Facilitation of language acquisition: The role of the mother.* Unpublished doctoral disseration, Johns Hopkins University, 1975.

Perfetti, C. *Reading skill, comprehension and verbal efficiency.* Paper presented at the Conference on Language, Learning, and Reading Disabilities, City University of New York: May 1980.

Perkins, W.H. Personal communication, 1982.

Peters, A. Language learning strategies: Does the whole equal the sum of the parts? *Language,* 1977, *53,* 560-573.

Peters, A. The units of language acquisition. *Working papers in linguistics, 12.* University of Hawaii, Department of Linguistics, 1980.

Phillips, J. *Formal characteristics of speech which mothers address to their young children.* Unpublished doctoral disseration, Johns Hopkins University, 1970.

Phillips, J. Syntax and vocabulary of mothers' speech to young children: Age and sex comparisons. *Child Development,* 1973, *44,* 182-185.

Piaget, J. *The child's conception of the world.* London, England: Routledge & Kegan Paul, 1929.

Piaget, J. *The origins of intelligence in children.* New York: Norton, 1952.

Piaget, J. *The construction of reality in the child.* New York: Basic Books, 1954.

Piaget, J. *Play, dreams, and imitation in childhood.* New York: Norton, 1962.

Piaget, J. *Genetic episteimology.* New York: Norton, 1970.

Piatelli-Palmerini, M. (Ed.). *Learning and language.* Cambridge, MA: Harvard University Press, 1980.

Pike, K. *Language in relation to a unified theory of the structure of human behavior.* The Hague: Mouton, 1967.

Pinker, S. Formal models of language learning. *Cognition,* 1979, *7,* 217-283.

Pinsky, S.D., & McAdam, D.W. Electroencephalographic and dichotic indices of cerebral laterality in stutterers. *Brain and Language,* 1980, *11,* 374-397.

Plank, F. *Ergativity.* London: Academic Press, 1979.

Ploog, D. Phonation, emotion, cognition, with reference to the brain mechanisms involved. *Ciba Foundation Symposium, 69,* 79-98. Amsterdam: Elsevier, 1979.

Poizner, H, & Battison, R. Cerebral asymmetry for sign language: Clinical and experimental evidence. In H. Lane & F. Grosjean (Eds.), *Recent perspectives on American Sign Language.* Hillsdale, NJ: Erlbaum, 1980, 79-101.

Posner, M.I., & Snyder, C.R. Facilitation and inhibition in the processing of signals. In P.M.A. Rabbitt (Ed.), *Attention and Performance V.* London: Academic Press, 1975.(a)

Posner, M.I., & Snyder, C.R. Attention and cognitive control. In R.L. Solso (Ed.), *Information processing and cognition: The Loyola Symposium,* Hillsdale, NJ: Erlbaum, 1975.(b)

Potts, G. Information processing strategies used in the encoding of linear ordering. *Journal of Verbal Behavior,* 1972, *11,* 727-740.

Prawat, R., & Cancelli, A. Constructive memory in conserving and nonconserving first graders. *Developmental Psychology,* 1976, *12,* 47-50.

Pribram, K.H. *Languages of the brain.* Englewood Cliffs, NJ: Prentice-Hall, 1971.

Pribram, K.H. The brain, the telephone, the thermostat, the computer, and the hologram. *Cognition and Brain Theory,* 1981, *4,* 105-122.

Priestly, T. Homonymy in child phonology. *Journal of Child Language,* 1980, *7,* 413-427.

Prince, A. A metrical theory for Estonian quantity. *Linguistic Inquiry,* 1980, *11,* 511-562.

Prince, G. *A grammar of stories.* The Hague: Mouton, 1973.

Prinz, P. Requesting in normal and language-disordered children. In K. Nelson (Ed.), *Children's Language* (Vol. 3). New York: Gardner Press, in press.

Prizant, B., & Duchan, J. The functions of immediate echolalia in autistic children. *Journal of Speech and Hearing Disorders,* 1981, *46,* 241–249.

Prutting, C. Process /prǎ/,ses/n: The action of moving forward progressively from one point to another on the way to completion. *Journal of Speech and Hearing Disorders,* 1979, *44,* 3–30.

Prutting, C. Pragmatics as social competence. *Journal of Speech and Hearing Disorders,* 1982, *47,* 123–133.

Pylyshyn, Z. Computational models and empirical constraints. *The Behavioral and Brain Sciences,* 1978, *1,* 93–127.

Pylyshyn, Z. Computation and cognition: Issues in the foundation of cognitive science. *The Behavioral and Brain Sciences,* 1980, *3,* 111–169.

Ramer, A. Syntactic styles in emerging language. *Journal of Child Language,* 1976, *3,* 49–62.

Ramsay, D.S. *Object word spurt, handedness, and object permanences in the infant.* Unpublished doctoral dissertation, University of Denver, 1977.

Ramsay, D.S. *Unimanual handedness and duplicated syllable babbling in infants.* Paper presented at the International Conference on Infant Studies, Austin, March 1982.

Ratcliff, J. *An investigation of the plausibility effect.* Paper presented at the Fifth Australian Experimental Psychology Conference, La Trobe University, May 1978. (Cited and described in Forster, 1979.)

Ratner, N., & Bruner, J.S. Games, social exchange and the acquisition of language. *Journal of Child Language,* 1978, *5,* 391–401.

Rayner, K., Carlson, M., & Frazier, L. The interaction of syntax and semantics during sentence processing: Eye movements in the analysis of semantically biased sentences. *Journal of Verbal Learning and Verbal Behavior,* 1983, *22,* 358–374.

Rees, N. Pragmatics of language. In R. Schiefelbusch (Ed.), *Bases of language intervention.* Baltimore: University Park Press, 1978.

Reich, P. The early acquisition of word meaning. *Journal of Child Language,* 1976, *3,* 117–123.

Reinhart, T. *The syntactic domain of anaphora.* Unpublished doctoral dissertation, MIT, 1976.

Requin, J. Toward a psychobiology for action. In G.E. Stelmach & J. Requin (Eds.), *Tutorials in motor behavior.* Amsterdam: North Holland, 1980, 373–398.

Rescorla, L. *Concept formation in word learning.* Unpublished doctoral dissertation, Yale University, 1976.

Rescorla, L. Overextension in early language development. *Journal of Child Language,* 1980, *7,* 321–335.

Rescorla, L. Category development in early language. *Journal of Child Language,* 1981, *8,* 225–238.

Rice, M. *Cognition to language: Categories, word meanings and training.* Baltimore: University Park Press, 1980.

Rice, M.L. Child language: What children know and how. In T.M. Field, A. Huston, H.C. Quay, L. Troll, & G.E. Finley (Eds.), *Review of human development.* New York: Wiley, 1982.

Riesbeck, C.K., & Schank, R.C. Comprehension by computer: Expectation-based analysis of sentences in context. In W.J.M. Levelt & G.B. Flores d'Arcais (Eds.), *Studies in the perception of language.* New York: Wiley, 1978.

Riklan, M., & Cooper, I.S. Thalamic lateralisation of psycho-logical functions and psychometric studies. In S. Harnad, R.W. Doty, L. Goldstein, J. Jaynes & G. Krauthamer (Eds.), *Lateralisation in the nervous system.* New York: Academic Press, 1977.

Riley, C., & Trabasso, T. Comparatives, logical structures, and encoding in a transitive inference task. *Journal of Experimental Child Psychology,* 1974, *17,* 187–203.

Risberg, J. Regional cerebral blood flow measurements by [133] Xe-inhalation: Methodology and applications in neuropsychology and psychiatry. *Brain and Language,* 1980, *9,* 9–34.

Roca, I.M. Ordering evidence from counter-feeding. *Linguistic Inquiry,* 1977, *7,* 718–724.

Robinson, R.G. Differential behavioral and biochemical effects of right and left hemispheric cerebral infarction in the rat. *Science,* 1979, *205,* 707–710.

Robinson, R.G., & Szetela, B. Mood change following left hemisphere brain injury. *Annals of Neurology,* 1981, *9,* 447–453.

Rodgon, M. Knowing what to say and wanting to say it: Some communicative and structural aspects of single-word responses to questions. *Journal of Child Language,* 1979, *6,* 81–90.

Rodgon, M., Jankowski, W., & Alenskas, L. A multi-functional approach to single-word usage. *Journal of Child Language,* 1977, *4,* 23–44.

Rodgon, M., & Kauffman, A. *Mothers' gestures to children acquiring language.* Paper presented to the Child Development Biennial Meeting of the Society for Research, San Francisco, 1979.

Roeper, T., LaPointe, S., Bingi, Junior, & Tavakolian, S. A lexical approach to language acquisition. In S. Tavakolian (Ed.), *Language acquisition and linguistics theory.* Cambridge: MIT Press, 1981.

Rogers, L.J. Environmental influences on brain lateralization [Commentary on V.H. Denenberg's "Hemispheric laterality in animals and the effects of early experience"]. *The Behavioral and Brain Sciences,* 1981, *4,* 35–36.

Rogers, L.J., & Anson, J.M. Lateralisation of function in the chicken fore-brain. *Pharmacolology, Biochemistry and Behavior,* 1979, *10,* 679–686.

Roland, P.E., Larsen, B., Lassen, N.A., & Skinhoj, E. Supplementary motor area and other cortical areas in organization of voluntary movements in man. *Journal of Neurophysiology,* 1980, *43,* 118–130.

Rondal, J. Maternal speech to normal and Down's syndrome children matched for mean utterance length. In C.E. Meyers (Ed.), *Quality of life in severely and profoundly mentally retarded people: Research foundations for improvement.* Washington, DC: American Association on Mental Deficiency, 1978.

Rosch, E. Cognitive representations of semantic categories. *Journal of Experimental Psychology: General,* 1975, *104,* 192–233.

Rosch, E. Principles of categorization. In E. Rosch & B. Lloyd (Eds.), *Cognition and categorization.* Potomac, MD: Erlbaum, 1977.

Rosch, E., & Mervis, C. Family resemblances: Studies in the internal structure of categories. *Cognitive Psychology,* 1975, *7,* 573–605.

Rosch, E., Mervis, C., Gray, W., Johnson, D., & Boyes-Braem, P. Basic objects in natural categories. *Cognitive Psychology,* 1976, *8,* 382–349.

Rosenblatt, D. *Learning how to mean: The development of representation in play and language.* Paper presented at the Conference on the Biology of Play, Farnham, England, 1975.

Rosenfeld, H. Conversational control functions of nonverbal behavior: An evaluative review. In A. Siegman & S. Feldstein (Eds.), *Nonverbal behavior and communication.* Hillsdale, NJ: Erlbaum, 1978.

Rosenham, D. On being sane in insane places. *Science,* 1973, *179,* 250–258.

Rosenthal, R., & Jakobson, L. *Pygmalion in the Classroom,* New York: Holt, Rinehart, & Winston, 1968.

Ross, E.D. The aprosodias. *Archives of Neurology,* 1981, *38,* 561–569.

Ross, E.D. Functional-anatomic organization of the affective components of language in the right hemisphere. *Archives of Neurology,* 1981, *38,* 561–569.

Ross, E.D., Harney, J.H., deLacoste-Utamsing, C., & Purdy, P.D. How the brain integrates affective and propositional language into a unified behavioral function. *Archives of Neurology,* 1981, *38,* 745–748.

Ross, E.D., & Mesulam, M.M. Dominant language functions of the right hemisphere: Prosody and emotional gesturing. *Archives of Neurology,* 1979, *36,* 144–148.

Ross, G. Categorization in 1- to 2- year olds. *Developmental Psychology,* 1980, *16,* 391–396.

Rowan, L., Leonard, L., Chapman, & Weiss, A. Performative and presuppositional skills in language disordered and normal children. *Journal of Speech and Hearing Research,* in press, 1983.

Roy, E.A. Apraxia: A new look at an old syndrome. *Journal of Human Movement Studies,* 1978, *4,* 191–210.

Rubens, A.B. Aphasia with infarction in the territory of the anterior cerebral artery. *Cortex,* 1975, *11,* 239–250.

Rubens, A.B. Anatomical asymmetries of human cerebral cortex. In S. Harnad, R.W. Doty, L. Goldstein, J. Jaynes, & G. Krauthamer (Eds.), *Lateralization in the nervous system.* New York: Academic Press, 1977.

Rūke-Draviņa, V. Modifications of speech addressed to young children in Latvian. In C. Snow & C.A. Ferguson (Eds.), *Talking to children.* London: Cambridge University Press, 1977.

Rumelhart, D.E. Notes on a schema for stories. In D.G. Brown & A. Collins (Eds.), *Representation and understanding: Studies in cognitive science.* New York: Academic Press, 1975.

Rumelhart, D.E. Understanding and summarizing brief stories. In D. LaBerge & S.J. Samuels (Eds.), *Basic processes in reading: Preception and comprehension.* Hillsdale, NJ: Erlbaum, 1977.

Rumelhart, D.E. Schemata: The building blocks of cognition. In R. Spiro, B. Bruce & W. Brewer, (Eds.), *Theoretical issues in reading comprehension.* Hillsdale, NJ: Erlbaum, 1980, 33–58.

Rushton, D.N., Rothwell, J.C., & Craggs, M.D. Gating of somatosensory evoked potentials during different kinds of movement in man. *Brain,* 1981, *104,* 465–492.

Russo, J., & Owens, R. The development of an objective observation tool for parent-child interaction. *Journal of Speech and Hearing Disorders,* 1982, *47,* 165-173.

Russell, B. On denoting. *Mind,* 1905, *14,* 479–493.

Ryalls, J.H. Motor aphasia: Acoustic correlates of phonetic disintegration in vowels. *Neuropsychologia,* 1981, *19,* 365–374.

Sachs, J. Recognition memory for syntactic and semantic aspects of connected discourse. *Perception and Psychophysics,* 1967, *2,* 437–442.

Sachs, J. Talking about the there and then. *In Papers and Reports on Child Language Development,* Stanford University, 1977, *13,* 56–63.(a)

Sachs, J. The adaptive significance of linguistic input to prelinguistic infants. In C. Snow & C. Ferguson (Eds.), *Talking to children.* London: Cambridge University Press, 1977.(b)

Sachs, J. Topic selection in parent-child discourse. *Discourse Processes,* 1979, *2,* 145–153.

Sachs, J., Bard, B., & Johnson, M. Language learning with restricted input: Case studies of two hearing children of deaf parents. *Applied Psycholinguistics,* 1981, *2,* 33–54.

Sachs, J., Brown, R., & Salerno, R.A. Adults' speech to children. In W. von Raffler-Engel & Y. Lebrun (Eds.), *Baby talk and infant speech.* Lisse, Netherlands: Swets & Zeitlinger, 1976.

Sachs, J. & Devin, J. Young children's use of age-appropriate speech styles in social interaction and role-playing. *Journal of Child Language,* 1976, *3,* 81-98.

Sachs, J., & Johnson, M. Language development in a hearing child of deaf parents. In W. von Raffler Engel & Y. LeBrun (Eds.), *Baby talk and infant speech* (Neurolinguistics 5). Amsterdam: Swets & Zeitlinger, 1976.

Sachs, J., & Truswell, L. Comprehension of two-word instructions by children in the one-word stage. *Journal of Child Langugae,* 1978, *5,* 17–24.

Sackeim, H.A., Greenberg, M.S., Weiman, A.L., Gur, R.C., Hungerbuhler, J.P., & Geschwind, N. *Functional brain asymmetry in the expression of positive and negative emotions: Lateralization of insult in cases of uncontrollable emotional outbursts.* Paper presented at the International Neuropsychological Society, Chianciano, Italy, June 2-5, 1980.

Sackeim, H.A., Greenberg, M.S., Weiman, A.L., Gur, R.C., Hungerbuhler, J.P., & Geschwind, N. Hemispheric asymmetry in the expression of positive and negative emotions. *Archives of Neurology,* 1982, *39* , 210–218.

Sackeim, H.A., & Gur, R.C. Lateral asymmetry in intensity of emotional expression. *Neuropsychologia,* 1978, *16,* 473–481.

Sacks, H. An initial investigation of the usability of conversational data for doing sociology. In D. Sudnow (Ed.), *Studies in social interaction.* New York: Free Press, 1972.

Sacks, H. On the analysability of stories by children. In R. Turner (Ed.), *Ethnomethodology.* Harmondsworth, Middlesex: Penguin, 1974.

Sacks, H., Schegloff, E., & Jefferson, G. The simplest systematics for the organization of turn-taking for conversation. *Language,* 1974, *50,* 696–735.

Safer, M., & Leventhal, H. Ear differences in evaluating emotional tones of voice and verbal content. *Journal of Experimental Psychology: Human Perception and Performance,* 1977, *3,* 75–82.

Sanders, G.A. Equational rules and rule functions in phonology. In D.A. Dinnsen (Ed.) *Current approaches to phonological theory.* Bloomington: Indiana University Press, 1979.

Sanides, R. Comparative neurology of the temporal lobe in primates including man with reference to speech. *Brain and Language,* 1975, *2,* 396–419.

Sapir, E. Nootka baby words. *International Journal of American Linguistics,* 1929, *6,* 32–47.

Savić, S. Strategies children use to answer questions posed by adults. In N. Waterson & C. Snow (Eds.), *The development of communication.* Chichester: Wiley, 1978.

Scaife, M., & Bruner, J. The capacity for joint visual attention in the infant. *Nature,* 1975, *253,* 265–266.

Schaffer, H.R.(Ed.). *Studies in mother-infant interaction.* London: Academic Press, 1977.

Schaffer, H.R., & Crook, C. Maternal control techniques in a directed play situation. *Child Development,* 1980, *16,* 54–61.

Schegloff, E., & Sacks, H. Opening up closings, In R. Turner (Ed.), *Ethnomethodology.* Baltimore: Penguin, 1974.

Schieffelin, B.B. Getting in together: An ethnographic approach to the study of the development of communicative competence. In E. Ochs & B.B. Schieffelin (Eds.), *Developmental pragmatics.* New York: Academic Press, 1979.

Schieffelin, B.B., & Eisenberg, A.R. Cultural variation in children's conversations. In R.L. Schiefelbusch (Ed.), *Communicative competence: Acquisition and intervention.* Baltimore: University Park Press, in press.

Schiff, J.M. *Untersuchungen sur physiologie des nervensystems. I.* Frankfort am Main, 1855.

Schiff, N. The influence of deviant maternal input on the development of language during the preschool years. *Journal of Speech and Hearing Research,* 1979, *22,* 581–603.

Schlesinger, I.M. Production of utterances and language acquisition. In D. Slobin (Ed.), *The ontogenesis of language.* New York: Academic Press, 1971.

Schlesinger, I.M. The role of cognitive development and linguistic input in language acquisition. *Journal of Child Language,* 1977, *4,* 153–169.

Schneider, W., & Shiffrin, R. Controlled and automatic human information processing: I Detection, search and attention. *Psychological Review,* 1977, *84,* 1–66.

Schuberth, R.F., & Eimas, P. Effects of context on the classification of words and nonwords. *Journal of Experimental Psychology: Human Perception and Performance,* 1977, *33,* 27–36.

Schvaneveldt, R.W., Meyer, D.E., & Becker, C.A. Lexical ambiguity, semantic context, and visual word recognition. *Journal of Experimental Psychology: Human Perception and Performance,* 1976, *2,* 243–256.

Schwab, R.S. Akinesia paradoxica. In J.P. Cordeau & P. Cleor (Eds.), *Recent contributions to neurophysiology.* Amsterdam: Elsevier, 1972.

Schwartz, G.E., Davidson, R.J., & Maer, F. Right hemisphere lateralization for emotion in the human brain: Interactions with cognition. *Science,* 1975, *190,* 286–288.

Schwartz, R. *The role of action in early lexical acquisition.* Paper presented to the American Speech-Language-Hearing Association, Detroit, 1980.

Schwartz, R., & Leonard, L. *Words, objects and actions in early lexical acquisition.* Paper presented to the Child Language Research Forum, Standford, CA, 1980.

Schwartz, R., & Leonard, L. Do children pick and choose? An examination of phonological selection and avoidance in early lexical acquisition. *Journal of Child Language,* 1982, *9,* 319–336.

Schwartz, R., & Leonard, L. *The acquisition of lexical categories of objects and actions in normal and language-impaired children,* in press.

Schwartz, R., & Terrell, B. The role of input frequency in lexical acquisition. *Journal of Child Language,* 1983, *10,* 57–64.

Scollon, R. A real early stage: An unzippered condensation of a dissertation on child language. In E. Ochs & B.B. Schieffelin (Eds.), *Development pragmatics.* New York: Academic Press, 1979.

Searle, J.R. *Speech acts: An essay in the philosophy of language.* London: Cambridge University Press, 1969.

Searle, J.R. Minds, brains, and programs. *The Behavioral Brain Sciences,* 1980, *1,* 215–226.

Segalowitz, S.J. (Ed.), *Language function and brain organization.* New York: Academic Press, 1983.

Segalowitz, S.J. & Gruber, F.A. (Eds.). *Language development and neurological theory.* New York: Academic Press, 1977.

Seldon, H.L. Structure of human auditory cortex. I. Cytoarchitectonics and dendritic distributions. *Brain Research,* 1981, *229,* 277–294.(a)

Seldon, H.L. Structure of human auditory cortex. II. Axon distributions and morphological correlates of speech perception. *Brain Research,* 1981, *229,* 295–310.(b)

Selkirk, E. The prosodic structure of French. Paper presented at the Ninth Annual Linguistic Symposium on Romance Languages, Georgetown University, Georgetown, VA, 1979.

Selkirk, E. The role of prosodic categories in English word stress. *Linguistic Inquiry,* 1980, *11,* 563–605.

Selkirk, E. On the nature of phonological representation. In T. Myers, J. Laver, & J. Anderson (Eds.), *The cognitive representation of speech.* New York: North-Holland, 1981.

Semjen, A. From motor learning to sensorimotor skill acquisition. *Journal of Human Movement Studies,* 1977, *3,* 182–191.

Semmes, J. Hemispheric specialization: A possible clue to mechanism. *Neuropsychologia,* 1968, *6,* 11–26.

Shakhnovich, A.R., Serbinenko, F.A., Razumovsky, A. Ye., Rodionov, I.M., & Oskolok, L.N. The dependence of cerebral blood flow on mental activity and on emotional state in man. *Neuropsychologia,* 1980, *18,* 465–476.

Schane, S.A. Nonsegmental phonology. In D.A. Dinnsen (Ed.), *Current approaches to phonological theory.* Bloomington: Indiana University Press, 1979.(a)

Schane, S.A. Rhythm, accent and stress in English words. *Linguistic Inquiry,* 1979, *10* (3), 483–502.(b)

Schane, S.A. The rhythmic nature of English word accentuation. *Language,* 1979, *55* (3), 559–602.(c)

Shank, R.C., & Abelson, R.P. Scripts, plans and knowledge. *Advance Papers of the Fourth International Joint Conference on Artificial Intelligence,* 1975, 151–157, (Tbilisi, Georgia, USSR).

Shank, R.C., & Abelson, R.P. Scripts, plans, goals, and understanding. Hillsdale, NJ: Erlbaum, 1977.

Shapiro, B.E., Grossman, M., & Gardner, H. Selective musical processing deficits in brain damaged populations. *Neuropsychologia,* 1981, *19,* 161-169.

Shattuck-Hufnagel, S., & Klatt, D.H. The limited use of distinctive features and markedness in speech production: Evidence from speech error data. *Journal of Verbal Learning and Verbal Behavior,* 1979, *18,* 41-55.

Shatz, M. How young children respond to language: Procedures for answering. *Papers and Reports on Child Language Development (No. 10).* Stanford, CA: Stanford University, 1975.

Shatz, M. Children's comprehension of their mothers' question-directives. *Journal of Child Language,* 1976, *5,* 39-46.

Shatz, M. On mechanisms of language acquisition: Can features of the communicative environment account for development? In E. Wanner & L. Gleitman (Eds.), *Language acquisition: The state of the art.* New York: Cambridge University Press, 1982.

Shatz, M., Bernstein, D., & Shulman, M. The responses of language-disordered children to indirect directions in varying contexts. *Applied Psycholinguistics,* 1980, *1,* 295-306.

Shatz, M., & Gelman, R. The development of communication skills: Modifications in the speech of young children as a function of listener. *Monographs of the Society for Research in Child Development,* 1973, *38,* (5, Serial No. 152).

Sheldon, A., & Strange, W. The relationship between perception and production in the acquisition of *r* and *l* by Japanese learners of English. *Applied Psycholinguistics,* in press.(Originally published, 1980.)

Shiffrin, R., & Schneider, W. Controlled and automatic human information process: II Perceptual learning, automatic attending, and general theory. *Psychological Review,* 1977, *84,* 127-190.

Shore, C., O'Connell, B., & Bates, E. *First sentence in language and symbolic play.* Paper presented to the Society for Research in Child Development on Infant Cognition, Austin, TX, 1982.

Shriberg, L., & Kwiatkowski, J. *Natural process analysis (NPA): A procedure for phonological analysis of continuous speech samples.* New York: Wiley, 1980.

Sidtis, J.J., Vople, B.T., Holtzman, J.D., Wilson, D.H., & Gazzaniga, M.S. Cognitive interaction after staged callosal section: evidence for transfer of semantic activation. *Science,* 1981, *212,* 344-346.

Siegel, L., Cunningham, C., & van der Spruy, H. *Interaction of language delayed and normal preschool children with their mothers.* Paper presented at the meeting of the Society for Research in Child Development, 1979.

Sinclair, H. Sensorimotor action patterns as a condition for the acquisition of syntax. In R. Huxley & D. Ingram (Eds.), *Language acquisition: Models and methods.* New York: Academic Press, 1971.

Sinnott, J.M., Beecher, M.D., & Stebbins, W.C. Speech sound discrimination by monkeys and humans. *Journal of the Acoustical Society of America,* 1976, *60,* 687-695.

Skarakis, E., & Prutting, C. Early communication: Semantic functions and communicative intentions in the communication of preschool children with impaired hearing. *American Annals of the Deaf,* 1977, *122,* 382-391.

Slobin, D.I. Grammatical transformations and sentence comprehension in childhood and adulthood. *Journal of Verbal Learning and Verbal Behavior,* 1966, *5,* 219-227.

Slobin, D.I. Cognitive prerequisites for the development of grammar. In C. Ferguson & D. Slobin (Eds.), *Studies of child language development.* New York: Holt, Rinehart, & Winston, 1973.(a)

Slobin, D.I. *Psycholinguistics.* Clearview, IL: Scott Foresman, 1973.(b)

Slobin, D.I. *Psycholinguistics* (2nd ed.). Glencoe, IL: Scott, Foresman, 1979.

Slobin, D.I., Ervin-Tripp, S., & Gumperz, J.J. *Field manual for the cross-cultural study of the acquisition of communicative competence.* Berkeley: Language Behavior Research Lab, 1967.

Smith, B.L. Cortical stimulation and speech timing: A preliminary observation. *Brain and Language*, 1980, *10*, 89–97.

Smith, N. *The acquisition of phonology: A case study.* Cambridge: University Press, 1973.

Smolak, L. Cognitive precursors of receptive vs. expressive language. *Journal of Child Language*, 1982, *9*, 13–22.

Snow, C. Mothers' speech to children learning language. *Child Development*, 1972, *43*, 549–565.

Snow, C. Mothers' speech research: From input to interaction. In C. Snow & C. Ferguson (Eds.), *Talking to children*. London: Cambridge University Press. 1977.

Snow, C. Conversation with children. In P. Fletcher & M. Garman (Eds.), *Language Acquisition*. London: Cambridge University Press, 1979.

Snow, C. Parent-child interaction and the development of communicative ability. In R. Schiefelbusch and D. Bricker (Eds.), *Communicative Competence: Acquisition and Retardation*. Baltimore: University Park Press, 1981.

Snow, C.E., & Ferguson, C.A. (Eds.) *Talking to children*. Cambridge, England: Cambridge University Press, 1977.

Synder, L. The early presuppositions and performatives of normal and language disabled children. *Papers and Reports on Child Language Development*, 1976, *12*, 221–229.

Snyder, L. Communicative and cognitive abilities and disabilities in the sensorimotor period. *Merrill-Palmer Quarterly*, 1978, *24*, 161–180.

Snyder, L. Defining language disordered children: Language disordered or just "low verbal" normal? *Proceedings of the Symposium for Research in Child Language Disorders*, 1982, *3*, in press.

Snyder, L., Bates, E., & Bretherton, I. Content and context in early lexical development. *Journal of Child Language*, 1981, *8*, 565–582.

Snyder, L., Downey, D., & Kintsch, E. *The discourse narratives of normal and reading disabled children.* Article in preparation.

Snyder, L., Haas, C., & Becker, L.B. *Discourse processing in normal and learning disabled children.* Article in preparation.

Soh, K., Larsen, B., Sinhøj, E., & Lassen, N.A. Regional cerebral blood flow in aphasia. *Archives of Neurology* 1978, *35*, 625–632.

Sokolov, Y.N. *Perception and the conditioned reflex.* Oxford: Pergamon Press, 1963.

Sparks, R., Helm, N., & Albert, M. Aphasia rehabilitation resulting from melodic intonation therapy. *Cortex*, 1974, *10*, 303–316.

Sperry, R.W. Forebrain commissurotomy and conscious awareness. *Journal of Medicine and Philosophy*, 1977, *2*, 101–126.

Spiro, R., Bruce, B., & Brewer, W. *Theoretical issues in reading comprehension.* Hillsdale, NJ: Erlbaum, 1980.

Steckol, K., & Leonard, L. Sensorimotor development and prelinguistic communication. *Journal of Speech and Hearing Research*, 1981, *24*, 262–268.

Stein, N., & Glenn, C. An analysis of story comprehension in elementary school children. In R. Freedle (Ed.), *New directions in discourse processing*, (Vol. 2). Norwood, NJ: Ablex, 1979.

Stern, D.N. Mother and infant at play: The dyadic interaction involving facial, vocal, and gaze behaviors. In M. Lewis & L.A. Rosenblum (Eds.), *The origins of behavior* (Vol. 1): *The effect of the infant on its caregiver.* New York: Wiley, 1974.

Stern, D.N. Handedness and the lateral distribution of conversion reactions. *Journal of Nervous and Mental Diseases*, 1977, *164*, 122–128.

Stern, D.N., Jaffe, J., Beebe, B., & Bennett, S.L. Vocalizing in unison and in alternation: Two modes of communication within the mother-infant dyad. In D. Aaronson & R.W. Rieber (Eds.), *Annals of the New York Academy of Sciences* (Vol. 263): *Developmental psycholinguistics and communication disorders.* New York: New York Academy of Sciences, 1975.

Stevenson, A. The speech of children. *Science*, 1893, *21*, 118-120.

Strohner, H., & Nelson, K. The young child's development of sentence comprehension: Influence of event probability, nonverbal context, syntactic form, and strategies. *Child Development*, 1974, *45*, 567-576.

Studdert-Kennedy, M. Cerebral hemispheres: Specialized for the analysis of what? *The Behavioral and Brain Sciences*, 1981, *4*, 76-77.

Sugarman, S. *A description of communicative development in the prelanguage child.* In I. Markova (Ed.), *The social context of language*. London: Wiley, 1978. (Revised edition of honors' thesis, Hampshire College, 1973.)

Sugarman, S. *Cognitive change in the early symbolic period: The development of classification in young children's block play.* Unpublished doctoral dissertation, University of California at Berkeley, 1979. (Rev. ed.) Cambridge University Press, in press.

Sussman, H.M., Franklin, P., & Simon, T. Bilingual speech: Bilateral control. *Brain and Language*, 1982, *15*, 125-142.

Sussman, H.M., & MacNeilage, P.F. Hemisphere specialization for speech production and perception in stutterers. *Neuropsychologia*, 1975, *13*, 19-26.(a)

Sussman, H.M., & MacNeilage, P.F. Studies of hemispheric specialization for speech production. *Brain and Language*, 1975, *2*, 131-151.(b)

Sussman, H.M., & Westbury, J.R. A laterality effect in isometric and isotonic labial tracking. *Journal of Speech and Hearing Research*, 1978, *21*, 563-579.

Sutton, D. Mechanisms underlying vocal control on nonhuman primates. In H.D. Steklis & M.J. Raleigh (Eds.), *Neurobiology of Social Communication in Primates*. New York: Academic Press, 1979, 45-67.

Swinney, D.A. Lexical access during sentence comprehension: (Re) Consideration of context effects. *Journal of Verbal Learning and Verbal Behavior*, 1979, *18*, 645-660.

Swinney, D.A., & Hakes, D.T. Effects of prior context upon lexical access during sentence comprehension. *Journal of Verbal Learning and Verbal Behavior*, 1976, *15*, 681-689.

Swinney, D.A., Onifer, W., Prather, P., & Hirshkowitz, M. Semantic facilitation across sensory modalities in the processing of individual words and sentences. *Memory and Cognition*, 1979, *7*, 159-165.

Tanenhaus, M.K., Leiman, J.M., & Seidenberg, M.S. Evidence for multiple stages in the processing of ambiguous words in syntactic contexts. *Journal of Verbal Learning and Verbal Behavior*, 1979, *18*, 427-440.

Tannenbaum, P., & Williams, F. Generation of active and passive sentences as a function of subject or object focus. *Journal of Verbal Learning and Verbal Behavior*, 1968, *7*, 246-250.

Tanz, C. *Studies in the Acquisition of Deictic Terms*. Cambridge, England: Cambridge University Press, 1980.

Taylor, J. (Ed.). Selected writings of John Hughlings Jackson. (Vol. 2). London: Hodder & Stoughton, 1931.

Thach, W.T. Timing of activity in cerebellar dentate nucleus and cerebral motor cortex during prompt volitional movement. *Brain Research*, 1975, *88*, 233-241.

Thatcher, R.W. Evoked-potential correlates of hemispheric lateralization during semantic information-processing. In S. Harnad, R.W. Doty, L. Goldstein, J. Jaynes, & G. Krauthamer (Eds.), *Lateralization in the nervous system*. New York: Academic Press, 1977.

Thoman, E.B. Affective communication as the prelude and context for language learning. In R.L. Schiefelbusch & D.D. Bricker (Eds.), *Early language: Acquisition and intervention*. Baltimore: University Park Press, 1981.

Thomas, D., Campos, J., Shucard, D., Ramsay, D., & Shucard, J. Semantic comprehension in infancy: A signal detection analysis. *Child Development*, 1981, *52*, 798-803.

Thomas, E. *It's all routine: A redefinition of routines as a central factor in language acquisition.* Paper presented at the meeting of the Society for Research in Child Development Biennial, San Francisco, 1979.

Thomson, J., & Chapman, R. Who is 'daddy' revisited: The status of two-year-olds' over-extended words in use and comprehension. *Journal of Child Language,* 1977, *4,* 359–375.

Thorndyke, P.W. Cognitive structures in comprehension and memory of narrative discourse. *Cognitive Psychology,* 1977, *9,* 77–110.

Tiffany, W.R. The effect of syllable structure on diadochokinetic and reading rates. *Journal of Speech and Hearing Research,* 1980, *23,* 894–908.

Tobey, E.A., & Harris, K.S. Adaptation to restricted-jaw conditions by cortically injured speakers. *Journal of the Acoustical Society of America,* 1981, *70,* Suppl. 1, S12–S13.

Tognola, G.R., & Vignolo, L.A. Brain lesions associated with oral apraxia in stroke patients: A clinic-neuro-radiological investigation with the CT scan. *Neuopsychologia,* 1980, *18,* 257–272.

Tonkonogy, J., & Goodglass, H. Language function, foot of the third frontal gyrus, and Rolandic operculum. *Archives of Neurology,* 1981, *38,* 486–490.

Toscher, M.M., & Rupp, R.R. A study of the central auditory processes in stutterers using the Synthetic Sentence Identification (SSI) test battery. *Journal of Speech and Hearing Research,* 1978, *21,* 779–792.

Toch, S., & Vajda, J. Multitarget technique in Parkinson surgery. *Applied Neurophysiology,* 1980, *43,* 109–113.

Toth, S., Vajda, J., & Solyom, A. The function of the human cerebellum studied by evoked potentials and motor reactions. *Applied Neurophysiology,* 1980, *43,* 48–58.

Tough, J. *The development of meaning.* New York: Halsted Press, 1977.

Tow, P.M., & Whitty, C.W.M. Personality changes after operations on the cingulate gyrus in man. *Journal of Neurology, Neurosurgery and Psychiatry,* 1953, *16,* 186–193.

Townsend, D.J., & Bever, T.G. Interclause relations and clausal processing. *Journal of Verbal Learning and Verbal Behavior,* 1978, *17,* 509–522.

Trabasso, T. Representation, memory and reasoning: How do we make transitive inferences? In A. Peck (Ed.), *Minnesota symposium on child psychology* (Vol. 9). Minneapolis: University of Minnesota Press, 1975.

Trachy, R.E., Sutton, D., & Lindeman, R.C. Primate phonation: Anterior cingulate lesion effects on response rate and acoustic structure. *American Journal of Primatology,* 1981, *1,* 43–55.

Travis, L.E. *Speech Pathology.* New York: Appleton, 1931.

Trevarthen, C. Conversations with a two-month-old. *New Scientist,* 1974, *2,* 230.

Tucker, D.M., Roth, R.S., Arneson, B.A., & Buchingham, V. Right-hemisphere activation during stress. *Neuropsychologia,* 1977, *15,* 697–700.

Tucker, D.M., Watson, R.T., & Heilman, K.M. Discrimination and evocation of affectively intoned speech in patients with right parietal disease. *Neurology,* 1977, *27,* 947–950.

Tureen, L.L., Smolik, E.A., & Tritt, J.H. Aphasia in a deaf mute. *Neurology, (Minneapolis),* 1951, *1,* 237–249.

Turner, R. (Ed.), *Ethnomethodology.* Baltimore: Penguin, 1974.

Tyler, L.K., & Marslen-Wilson, W.M. The temporal structure of spoken language understanding. *Cognition,* 1980, *8,* 1–71.

Underwood, J.K., & Paulson, C.J. Aphasia and congenital deafness: A case study. *Brain and Language,* 1981, *12,* 285–291.

Uzgiris, I., & Hunt, J. *Assessment in infancy: Ordinal scales of psychological development.* Urbana: University of Illinois Press, 1975.

Valian, V. The wherefores and therefores of the competence—performance distinction. In W. Cooper & E. Walker (Eds.) *Sentence processing: Psycholinguistic studies presented to Merrill Garrett.* Hillsdale, NJ: Erlbaum, 1979.

Valian, V., & Caplan, J. What children say when asked "What?": A study in the use of syntactic knowledge. *Journal of Experimental Child Psychology,* 1979, *28,* 424–444.

Valian, V., Winzemer, J., & Erreich, A. A "little linguist" model of syntax learning. In S. Tavakolian (Ed.), *Language acquisition and linguistic theory,* Cambridge: MIT Press, 1981.

Vande Kopple, W. The given-new strategy of comprehension and some natural expository paragraphs. *Journal of Psycholinguistic Research,* 1982, *11,* 501–520.

van Dijk, T. *Text and context: Explorations in the semantics and pragmatics of discourse.* London: Longman, 1977.

van Dijk, T., & Kintsch, W. *Strategies of discourse comprehension.* New York: Academic Press, in press.

Van Kleek, A., & Frankel, T. Discourse devices used by language-disordered children. *Journal of Speech and Hearing Disorders,* 1981, *46,* 250–257.

Van Lancker, D.R. Cerebral lateralization of pitch cues in the linguistic signal. *Papers in Linguistics: International Journal of Human Communication,* 1980, *13,* 201–277.

Van Lancker, D.R., & Canter, G.J. Impairment of voice and face recognition in patients with hemispheric damage. *Brain and Cognition,* 1982, *1,* 185–195.

Veneziano, E. Early language and nonverbal representation: A reassessment. *Journal of Child Language,* 1981, *8,* 541–564.

Vihman, M.M. Consonant harmony: Its scope and function in child language. In J.H. Greenberg (Ed.), *Universals of human language: Phonology* (Vol. 2). Stanford: Stanford University Press, 1978.

Vipond, D. Micro- and macroprocesses in text comprehension. *Journal of Verbal Learning and Verbal Behavior,* 1980, *19,* 263–275.

Vlugt, H. van der. Aspects of normal and abnormal neuropsychological development. In M.S. Gazzaniga (Ed.), *Handbook of behavioral neurobiology, neuropsychology,* (Vol. 2). New York: Plenum Press, 1979.

Vogt, C. Quelques considerations generales a propos du syndrome du corps strie. *Journal fur Psychologie und Neurologie* (Leipzig), 1911, *18,* 479–488.

Vogt, C., & Vogt, O. Erster versuch einer pathologisch-anatomischen einteilung stiärer motilitätssttörungen. *Journal Psychologie und Neurologie* (Leipzig), 1918, *24,* 1–19.

Volterra, V., Bates, E., Benigni, L., Bretherton, I., & Camaioni, L. First words in language and action: A qualitative look. In E. Bates, L. Benigni, I. Bretherton, L. Camanioni, & V. Volterra, (Eds.), *The emergence of symbols,* New York: Academic Press, 1979.

von Eckardt Klein, B. Inferring functional localization from neurological evidence. In E. Walker (Ed.), *Explorations in the biology of language.* Montgomery, VT: Bradford Books, 1978.

von Miller, J., & Yallop, C. Natural phonology-A brief survey. *Speech and Language Research Centre Working Papers,* 1981, *3*(1), 43–62.

Vygotsky, L. *Thought and language.* Cambridge: MIT Press, 1962.

Walker, C.H., & Meyer, B.J.F. Integrating different types of information in text. *Journal of Verbal Learning and Verbal Behavior,* 1980, *19,* 263–275.

Walker, S.F. Lateralization of functions in the vertebrate brain: A review. *British Journal of Psychology,* 1980, *71,* 329–367.

Walsh, T.J. *A critical review of 'Ordering evidence from counter-feeding.'* Unpublished manuscript, Indiana University, 1977.(a)

Walsh, T.J. *On the necessity of rule ordering in natural generative phonology.* Paper presented at the Seventh Linguistic Symposium on Romance Languages, Cornell University, 1977.(b)

Wanner, E. The ATN and the sausage machine: Which one is baloney? *Cognition,* 1980, *8,* 209–225.

Wapner, W., Hamby, S., & Gardner, H. The role of the right hemisphere in the apprehension of complex linguistic materials. *Brain and Language,* 1981, *14,* 15–33.

Ward, M.C. *Them children: A study in language learning.* New York: Holt, Rinehart & Winston, 1971.

Waszink, P.M. Paradigmatic and syntagmatic axes: Some evidence from aphasia. *International Journal of Linguistics,* 1978, *5,* 55–72.

Waters, H.S. Superordinate-subordinate structure in semantic memory: The roles of comprehension and retrieval processes. *Journal of Verbal Learning Behavior,* 1978, *17,* 587–598.

Waterson, N. Growth of complexity in phonological development. In N. Waterson and C. Snow (Eds.), *The development of communication.* New York: Wiley, 1978.

Watson, L. Conversational participation by language-deficient and normal children. Paper presented at the annual meeting of the American Speech and Hearing Association, Chicago, 1977.

Watson, L., & Lord, C. Developing a social communication curriculum for autistic students. *Topics in Language Disorders,* 1982, *3,* in press.

Watson, R.T., Heilman, K.M., Cauthen, J.C., & King, F.A. Neglect after cingulectomy. *Neurology* (Minneapolis), 1973, *23,* 1003–1007.

Watson, R.T., Valenstein, E., & Heilman, K.M. Thalamic neglect. *Archives of Neurology,* 1981, *38,* 501–506.

Watzlawick, P., Beavin, J., Helmick, A., & Jackson, D. *Pragmatics of human communication: A study of interactional patterns, pathologies and paradoxes.* New York: Norton, 1967.

Weiner, F. *Phonological process analysis.* Baltimore: University Park Press, 1979.

Weiner, S., & Goodenough, D. A move toward a psychology of conversation. In R. Freedle (Ed.), *Discourse production and comprehension.* Norwood, NJ: Ablex, 1977.

Weintraub, S., Mesulam, M.M., & Kramer, L. Disturbances in prosody. *Archives of Neurology,* 1981, *38,* 742–744.

Weismer, G., Dinnsen, D., & Elbert, M. A study of the voicing distinction associated with omitted, word-final stops. *Journal of Speech and Hearing Disorders,* 1981, *40,* 320–328.

Weiss, A., Leonard, L., Rowan, L., & Chapman, K. Linguistic and non-linguistic features of style in normal and language-impaired children. *Journal of Speech and Hearing Disorders,* in press.

Weiss, A., Leonard, L., Schwartz, R., Chapman, K., Rowan, L., Messick, C., Prelock, P., & Terrell, B. Lexical style in normal and language-impaired children. Unpublished paper, 1982.

Weitzner-Lin, B. *Interactive request analysis.* Doctoral dissertation, State University of New York at Buffalo, 1981.

Weitzner-Lin, B., & Duchan, J. Using movement to differentiate patterns of interaction and situational understanding in the verbal productions of a two and a half year old child. *Sign Language Studies,* 1980, *27,* 113–122.

Wells, C.G. Learning and using the auxiliary verb in English. In V. Lee (Ed.), *Language development.* London: Croom Helm, 1979.

Wells, C.G. Becoming a communicator. In G. Wells (Ed.), *Learning through interaction.* London: Cambridge University Press, 1981.

Wells, C.G., & Woll, B. The development of meaning relations in children's speech. Paper presented at the Child Language Seminar, Reading, PA, April 1979.

Wells, G. Review of *Learning to talk* by J. McShane. *Journal of Child Language,* 1982, *9,* 264–267.

Werner, H., & Kaplan, E. Development of word meaning through verbal context: An experimental study. *Journal of Psychology,* 1950, *29,* 251–257.

Werner, H., & Kaplan, B. *Symbol formation.* New York: Wiley, 1963.

Wexler, B.E. Cerebral laterality and psychiatry: A review of the literature. *American Journal of Psychiatry,* 1980, *137,* 279–291.

Wexler, K., & Culicover, P. *Formal principles of language acquisition.* Cambridge: MIT Press, 1980.

Wexler, K., Culicover, C., & Hamburger, H. Learning-theoretic foundations of linguistic universals. *Theoretical Linguistics*, 1975, *2*, 215–253.

Whitaker, H.A. *Levels of impairment in disorders of speech.* Paper presented at the Eighth International Congress of Phonetic Sciences, Leeds, England, 1975.

Whitaker, H.A. Disorders of speech production mechanisms. In E.C. Cartertte and M. Friedman (Eds.), *Handbook of perception. Language and Speech* (Vol. 7). New York: Academic Press, 1976.

Whitaker, H.A., Bub, D., & Leventer, S. Neurolinguistic aspects of language acquisition and bilingualism. In H. Winitz (Ed.), *Native language and foreign language acquisition. Annals of the New York Academy of Sciences,* (Vol. 379). New York: New York Academy of Sciences, 1981.

Whitaker, H.A. & Ojemann, G.A. Graded localization of naming from electrical stimulation mapping of left cerebral cortex. *Nature,* 1977, *270,* 50–51.

Whitty, C.W.M., & Lewin, M. Korsakoff syndrome in the post-cingulectomy confusional states. *Brain,* 1960, *83,* 648–653.

Wieman, L. Stress patterns of early child language. *Journal of Child Language,* 1976, *3,* 283–286.

Wilcox, M., & House, P. Children's use of gestural and verbal behavior in communicative misunderstanding. *Applied Psycholinguistics,* 1982, *3,* 15–27.

Williams, F. (Ed.), *Language and poverty: Perspectives on a theme.* Chicago: Markham, 1970.

Wills, D. Participant deixis in English and baby talk. In C. Snow & C. Ferguson (Eds.), *Talking to children.* London: Cambridge University Press, 1977.

Winer, G.A. Class inclusion reasoning in children: A review of the empirical literature. *Child Development,* 1980, *51,* 309–328.

Winner, E. New names for old things: The emergence of metaphoric language. *Journal of Child Language,* 1979, *6,* 469–492.

Winner, E., & Gardner, H. Comprehension of metaphor in brain-damaged patients, *Brain,* 1977, *100,* 719–727.

Witelson, S.F. Anatomic asymmetry in the temporal lobes: Its documentation, phylogenesis, and relationship to functional asymmetry. In S.J. Dimond & D.A. Blizard (Eds.), *Evolution and lateralization of the brain. Annals of the New York Academy of Sciences,* 1977, *299,* 328–354.(a)

Witelson, S.F. Developmental dyslexia: Two right hemispheres and none left. *Science,* 1977, *195,* 309–311.(b)

Witelson, S.F. Early hemispheric specialization and interhemispheric plasticity: An empirical and theoretical review. In S.J. Segalowitz & F.A. Gruber (Eds.), *Language development and neurological theory.* New York: Academic Press, 1977.(c)

Wittgenstein, L. *Philosophical investigations.* New York: Wiley, 1953.

Wolchik, S., & Harris, S. Language environments of autistic and normal children matched for language age: A preliminary investigation. *Journal of Autism and Developmental Disabilites,* 1982, *12,* 43–55.

Wolf, D., & Gardner, H. Style and sequence in symbolic play. In M. Franklin & N. Smith (Eds.), *Early symbolization.* Hillsdale, NJ: Erlbaum, 1979.

Wolf, D., & Gardner, H. On the structure of early symbolization. In R. Schiefelbusch, & D. Bricker (Eds.), *Early language intervention.* Baltimore: University Park Press, in press, 1983.

Wolff, P.H., Hurwitz, I., & Moss, H. Serial organization of motor skills in left- and right-handed adults. *Neuropsychologia,* 1977, *15,* 539–546.

Wood, F. Theoretical, methodological, and statistical implications of the inhalation rCBF technique for the study of brain-behavior relationships. *Brain and Language,* 1980, *9,* 1–8.

Wood, F., Stump, D., McKeehan, A., Sheldon, S., & Proctor, J. Patterns of regional cerebral blood flow during attempted reading aloud by stutterers both on and off haloperidol medication: Evidence for inadequate left frontal activation during stuttering. *Brain and Language,* 1980, *9,* 141-144.

Wood, F., Taylor, B., Penny, R., & Stump, D. Regional cerebral blood flow response to recognition memory versus semantic classification tasks. *Brain and Language,* 1980, *9,* 113-122.

Wooton, A.J. Talk in the homes of young children. *Sociology,* 1974, *8,* 277-295.

Wooton, A.J. Conversation Analysis. In P. French & M. MacLure (Eds.), *Adult-child conversation.* New York: St. Martin, 1981.

Wulbert, M., Inglis, S., Kriegsmann, E., & Mills, B. Language delay and associated mother-child interactions. *Developmental Psychology,* 1975, *11,* 61-70.

Wynne, M.K., & Boehmler, R.M. Central auditory function in fluent and disfluent normal speakers. *Journal of Speech and Hearing Research,* 1982, *25,* 54-57.

Yakovlev, P. Morphological criteria of growth and maturation of the nervous system. *Research Publications of the Association for Research on Nervous and Mental Diseases,* 1962, *39,* 3-46.

Yakovlev, P., & Lecours, A. The myelogenetic cycles of regional maturation of the brain. In A. Minkowski (Ed.), *Regional Devlopment of the Brain in Early Life.* Oxford, England: Blackwell, 1967.

Yates, J. Priming dominant and unusual senses of ambiguous words. *Memory and Cognition,* 1978, *6,* 636-643.

Yekovich, F.R., & Thorndyke, P.W. An evaluation of alternative functional models of narrative schemata. *Journal of Verbal Learning and Verbal Behavior,* 1981, *20,* 454-469.

Yngve, V. On getting a word in edgewise. *Papers from the Sixth Regional Meeting of the Chicago Linguistic Society,* 1970.

Young, R.M. *Mind, brain and adaptation in the nineteenth century.* Oxford: Oxford University Press, 1970.

Young, R.R. The differential diagnosis of Parkinson's disease. *International Journal of Neurology,* 1977, *12,* 210-235.

Zachry, W. Ordinality and interdependence of representation and language development in infancy. *Child Development,* 1978, *49,* 681-687.

Zaidel, E. Auditory language comprehension in the right hemisphere following cerebral commissurotomy and hemispherectomy: A comparison with child language and aphasia. In A. Caramazza & E.B. Zurif (Eds.), *Language acquisition and language breakdown: Parallels and divergencies.* Baltimore: The Johns Hopkins University Press, 1978.

Zaidel, E., & Peters, A.M. Phonological encoding and ideographic reading by the disconnected right hemisphere: Two case studies. *Brain and Language,* 1981, *14,* 205-234.

Zubin, D. Discourse function of morphology. In T. Givon (Ed.), *Syntax and semantics* (Vol. 121). New York: Academic Press, 1979.

Zukow, P., Reilly, J., & Greenfield, P. Making the absent present: Facilitating the transition from sensorimotor to linguistic communication. In K. Nelson (Ed.), *Children's language,* (Vol. 3). New York: Gardner Press, in press.

AUTHOR INDEX

SUBJECT INDEX

A

Agent concept
  & givenness, 76
  lack in here and now communication, 80
  in marking stress, 83
  in sensorimotor period, 79 (*see also* Sensorimotor developmental period)
  in single word speech, 80
  & subject hierarchy, 75-77
Akinesia, 282-283
American Sign Language (ASL), as native language, 55-57
Aprosodia, 309-310, 325-329 (*see also* Prosody)
Articulatory control, 248-249, 269
Autism, 323
Basal ganglia, 316-321
  & Gilles de la Tourette's disease, 320
  in learned, skilled movements, 318-319
  in linking emotion, speech, 320
  & palilalia, 320-321
  & psychomotor activation, 321
  & voluntary motor control, 318

B

Biological preparedness
  & competence of child, 93-95
  & language specific rule-learning theory, 38, 74, 108-111
  & orientation of 5-day-olds to speech sounds, 98
  & simultaneous access model, 70-74
Blind children, & caretaker interaction, 49-50

Broca's area, 296-301
  controversy regarding speech, language functions, 297
  damage to insular cortex, 301
  location of, 296-297, 300
  possible substitution by supplementary motor area, 299
Brodmann's cortical areas, 321-322

C

Categorizing linguistic behaviors, 3-5
Central nervous system, maturation
  & concept formation, unique to man, 295
  & hierarchy of development, 288, 290
  increased cortical mass in man, 295
  multidimensional vs. monolitic, 285
  & myelination, 286
  opposing views of, 286
  progression related to vocal control, 284-290
Cerebral dominance, laterality (*see also* Left hemisphere dominance, Right hemisphere function)
  articulatory control & handedness, 248-249
  & callosal inhibition, 252
  & callosal interaction, 254-255, 308-311
  degree of laterality & familial handedness, 245-246, 252
  evolutionary views, 293, 295
  increase of mass in cortex of man, 295
  & lexical retrieval, 250
  & linguistic processing, 247-248
  & motor speech control, 247
  neurobehavioral view, 293
  ontogenetic model, 292

Interpretative processing
  "bridging" to referents, 236–237
  clausal unit processing, 235
  cohesiveness of text, 236–238
  conceptual representation, 239–241
  high-level vs. lower-level propositions,
    238, 241
  & inferences from sentential context,
    240
  integration, linguistic, 234
  micro- vs. macroprocesses, 238–239
  organization framework, of text, 237
  plausibility of sentences, 234
  real world knowledge, 233
  short-term memory, 236, 238
Interpretive analysis, 34–36

L

Labeling theory, 159–160
*Language Development and Language
  Disorders*, 149–150
Language learning styles, children's, 50, 64
Left-hemisphere dominance (*see also*
  Cerebral dominance, laterality, Right
  hemisphere function)
    & Broca's area, 296–301
    in deaf population, 294
    final motor pathway for speech,
      301–302, 304–305
    in manual control, precise timing, 293
    & specific language vs. articulatory
      areas, 303–305
    & supplementary motor area, 299,
      304–305
    & Sylvian fissure, primary language
      zone, 269–270, 274–275, 301–302,
      304–305
    & Wernicke's area, 296–301
Lesion localization
  in fluent aphasia, 302–303
  in left hemisphere, 298–305
  in oral apraxia, 303–304
  electrophysiology, 263–270
Lexical processing
  ambiguous items, 216–218
  biasing context, 218
  cohort theory, 220–222
  context, effects of, 218–219, 223–224

integration theory, 224
priming theory, 217–220
search theories, 222–223
two-factor attentional theory, 217
unambiguous items, 218–219
Lexical retrieval & cerebral dominance, 250
Lexicons, early
  alternative paradigms, 27–30
  composition of, 12–20
  comprehension vs. production, 28–30
  & dynamic, functional & relational
    theory, 21
  infants' speech perception, 27–28
  & levels of shared features, 22
  metaphorical word usage, 23–24
  & nonlinguistic behaviors, 18, 126
  nonsense word paradigm, 14–17, 19
  object vs. action words, 13–15
  & overextension, underextensions,
    23–27
  relational vs. substantive words, 17–18
  & semantic feature theory, 20–21
  & symbolic play, 126–127

M

Markedness, feature
  in intervention, 205
  in second language learning, 202–203
  in substantive phonology, 200
Mean length of utterance (MLU)
  & correlation with child's output,
    89–91, 93
  in maternal speech, 40
Memory, short-term, 236, 238, 269
Motherese (*see also* Input/interaction)
  & beliefs about language, 61–63
  & children's differing styles, 50, 64
  & correlations with child's output,
    87–95
  in cross cultural studies, 54–63
  in ethnographic studies, 57–59
  & expansions, 42, 95–98
  & frequency, 41–42, 95, 98
  & gestural patterns, 100–104
  & grammatical acquisition, 91–93,
    99–100
  limited semantic base, early, 100

cooperative principle, 158
category taxonomy, in assessment,
178–180
& cohesion devices, 151–152
deixis, 166–167
deficit view vs. difference view, 174–175
disorder as context bound, 177
functionalism, 179
historical review, 147–160, *168–169*
inferences, 30–36
ingenuity of tester as factor in
assessment, 176
interactional management, 179–180
interaction with language-disordered,
160–161
& labeling theory, 159
linguistic rules, status of, 180
& maternal speech, 67–68
methodology, 179
nonverbal communication, 165–166
normative focus problem, 175–177
nurturant vs. teaching mode of
interaction, 159
& perspective taking, 157, 170
& phonological analysis, emphasis
period, 150
& prespeech communication, 156–157
presupposition, 164
recent research, summary, 169–173
in right hemisphere patients, 256
& schema theory, 154–155
semantic relations, emphasis period,
149–150
sensemaking, 179
& social context, 155–161
& speech acts, 153
& syntax, emphasis period, 148–149
text analysis, 151
turntaking, 162
as viewed from different emphases,
177–178
view of language within interaction,
178
Prelexical forms, 6–12
Prespeech communication, 156–157
Presupposition, 164
Prosody
acoustic properties in dysfunction, 325
dysfunction, 309–310

dysfunction vs. apraxia, left- and
right-hemisphere damage, 325, 327
neural pathways for regulation, 325
patterns, normal vs. various impaired,
325–326
right cerebral hemisphere & left
cerebellar hemisphere, in ataxic
dysarthria, 329
thalamic nuclei involvement, 325,
327–328

R

Referents, 236–237
Regional cerebral blood flow (rCBF)
studies, 261–263, 299, 308–309
Right hemisphere function (*see also*
Cerebral dominance, laterality, Left
hemisphere dominance)
& affect, 256–257, 307–309, 311–312
aprosodia, 309–310
& callosal inhibition, 252
cortical asymmetry, 270–275
degree of laterality & recovery, 252
& durational patterns, 306, 309
involvement during language
acquisition, 252
& interhemispheric interaction,
308–311
& intonation, 305–307, 309
& left-right asymmetries, 263
& linguistic processing, 311
& melody, 306–307
Melodic Intonation Therapy, 307–308
object identity vs. label, 254–255
in perception of meaningful words vs.
phonemes, 253
& pitch, 306
& pragmatics, 256–257
& regional cerebral blood flow studies,
308
& semantic activation, 254–255
in synthesis vs. analysis, 253–254
& temporal detection in voice onset
time, 263
in visual vs. linguistic processing,
252–253
Routinized forms, in motherese, 45–46, 100

WOMAN'S UNIVERSITY LIBRARY